CITY OF GODS

CITY OF GODS

RELIGIOUS FREEDOM, IMMIGRATION, AND PLURALISM IN FLUSHING, QUEENS

R. SCOTT HANSON

Empire State Editions
An imprint of Fordham University Press
New York   2016

 Funding for this book was provided by
Furthermore: a program of the J. M. Kaplan Fund.

Visit us online at:
www.fordhampress.com
www.empirestateeditions.com

Library of Congress Cataloging-in-Publication Data
available online at catalog.loc.gov.

Printed in the United States of America

18 17 16   5 4 3 2 1

First edition

For my parents, Dick and Kathie
my sons, Raj and Ravi
and the people of Flushing

Contents

Appendixes

Foreword

The novelist Henry James once spoke of the "solidity of specification." He would have found solidity *and* specificity in R. Scott Hanson's *City of Gods*. Not all readers would expect to find them in a book of this sort. Its title refers to a specific place, but one whose very name will be obscure or confusing to those who have not been there, or who have not known they've been there: "Flushing." It helps to know, as we soon learn, that it was settled and named by Dutch immigrants, in whose tongue it was "Vlissingen," but knowledge of that will not bring it much closer to home for many readers.

Perhaps, one may think, further exploration of the subtitle might help bring solidity to the subject. We learn that these chapters are about religious freedom, immigration, and pluralism, three hot topics in our present. But there are good reasons to be suspicious about many potential treatments of such subjects. "Religious freedom" can easily fall into the morass of legal arguments or rise to partisan conflict from which one may wish to turn before he or she is turned off by the unpleasantness. "Immigration" is another topic that connotes dust-dry debates over policy and the statistics of newcomers. Next comes "pluralism." Attach an "-ism" to a word like "plural" and you may be left marooned in abstractions, because philosophers, theologians, and their kin are so often called upon to debate it. The first impulse among many respondents may be to yawn.

Hanson will not settle for yawns, because this book is a story, a set of often exciting narratives, enhanced in contexts of philosophy and theology, to be sure, but, to be more sure, it is the story of people to whom he will help us get close and sometimes get to know. A few lines in one chapter make that prospect clear. We learn that historian Hanson has been at the scene off and on, and very often it is "on," for twenty years. I have long been familiar with his research and findings but was still dazzled by his reference to having been in "every part of every street at every hour of day and night." That claim, or admission, may be hard to believe, but the reader's trust will grow during the reading of the narratives about what has happened in such places at such hours for so long. The author is specific about all of this, and the potentially abstract becomes substantially concrete in his telling.

That element in the venture sets this book apart from so many near-kin works. Hanson's story is so solid and specific not because he is un-schooled in the languages of generalization or unaware of sophisticated methodological issues. Just the opposite: He is at home with them and cites and draws on them, to our benefit. Anyone who has read how leading theorists have dealt with these themes—sociologists like Will Herberg or theologians like John Courtney Murray—will see their theories and proposals examined, tested, and often approved and employed.

If, or because, so many citizens and their leaders now care about religious freedom, immigration, and pluralism, it is natural to ask: Why explore the three themes in Flushing, Queens, New York? Millions of citizens have been at events there, or passed through there, without realizing the history and outstanding character of the community and its environs. They may have seen its name on traffic signs as they attended a World's Fair there, just as their parents had done at another Fair, decades before. Why stop and explore the streets and the ways of citizens as Hanson did and does?

As for religious freedom, Hanson makes the claim, with good historical backing, that Flushing was the home of the first notable document supporting religious freedom in the colonies which became the United States. It is well remembered as "The Flushing Remonstrance." We will let Hanson take off from there as he explores the fates of "religious freedom" advocates as well as of those who suffered for, and some who triumphed in, causes raised there.

As for immigration: It is almost dizzying to picture all the people and peoples who chose to land and settle there, from places all over the world. In every part of Flushing, along every street at every hour of day and night, newcomers arrived as strangers and had to suffer and enjoy what all kinds of immigrants have experienced. These aliens-turned-citizens brought solidity in the midst of flux and change, and their heirs still do.

Then there is "pluralism." Hanson could have impressed with the simple observation of diversity in Flushing. "Diversity" indicates that there is a variety of different groups and people. But treating diversity as such is no doubt best done by alphabetizing and cataloging the names of such collectives. We need and here we get more than that. If I suspected that some readers would be dazzled by the mere "diversity" parts of this story, I would also expect that many might be dizzied by the accounts of the religious dimensions of the varied lives of newcomers and citizens, who built temples, churches, synagogues, mosques, and other gathering places next door to one another. In some cases, one has to conceive of some places in Flushing as palimpsests, for example when the author shows how one set of newcomers built atop the experiences of departing old-comers. We hear of a building that has had three different incarnations at the hands of three different sets of worshippers, who picture "God" and what a "City of Gods" ought to look like in their hands and their generation. The old have moved on, so what happens to our story? They don't always demolish their sanctuary; they see it refashioned for a different faith-community.

If anyone believes that it is easy to accomplish all this building and remodeling without pain, this book will suggest how difficult it is. And yet, "on every street," especially on Bowne Street, Hanson's favorite locale, images of the acts of generosity by some counter the examples of selfishness among other groups, while successes and failures, joys and sorrows, mix close at hand.

When space explorers came back from their lunar trip with moon rocks, these little pieces of remote subjects of curiosity were subjected to years upon years of analysis by scientists, whose telescopes henceforth find counterparts in their microscopes and what they learn from this close-up exploration. Hanson does not claim that Flushing is the only place where "pluralism" developed and has had to be experimented and lived with, while his story, because it intends to be a true story, cannot be one of simple triumphs. But through this narrative, the reader gets close to battlers for religious freedom, will see immigration not as an issue but in a story of people, and come to regard pluralism anew, not as a philosophical analysis of diversity but instead as the perplexing and yet promising story of how people of different faiths share some features of a common life, rich in solidity and specification, in places like Flushing, Queens, New York.

Martin E. Marty
Fairfax M. Cone Distinguished Service Professor Emeritus,
The University of Chicago

Figures

Acknowledgments

I started doing research for this book a long time ago, so there are many people to thank here who influenced or helped me along the way. The idea for the book began to evolve in the fall of 1993 when I was completing a master's degree in religion at Columbia University. I had begun studying American religious history with Randall Balmer, and I became especially interested in the intersection of religion and immigration in American history. I was puzzled by something: I had several close friends in college and graduate school who were Muslims, Sikhs, Hindus, and Buddhists—some were born in Pakistan, India, China, and Japan, others in the United States, but all had grown up in the United States and all were American citizens—yet I couldn't find hardly any mention of their communities or traditions in surveys of American history and religion. During the course of my graduate studies at Columbia I had the good fortune to meet John Stratton Hawley, a professor of religions and literature of India, who along with the sociologist of religion Courtney Bender teaches a class on Religious Worlds of New York. Hawley suggested I get involved with a new research project at Harvard University called the Pluralism Project, directed by comparative religion and Indian Studies professor Diana L. Eck, who was recruiting students for summer work. The Pluralism Project was an ambitious study funded by the Lilly Endowment to examine the new religious landscape of America since the Immigration Act of 1965. Students were sent out to cities across America to document the religions of these new immigrant communities by doing ethnographic fieldwork, and I was assigned to work in New York City because I had been living there. I was responsible for covering the Hindu, Sikh, Jain, and Tibetan, Sri Lankan, and Thai Buddhist communities, and some Muslim communities, in the city. The project was gigantic in scope, and after several years it resulted in the spectacular interactive multimedia CD-ROM *On Common Ground: World Religions in America,* which was published by Columbia University Press in 1997 (a second edition came out in 2001, along with Eck's book *A New Religious America: How a "Christian Country" Has Become the Most Religiously Diverse Nation*). My research took me all over the five boroughs of New York City and out to parts of Long Island, but I found I was spending the most time in Queens, and most often it was on the 7 train to Main St., Flushing. Walking around this vibrant urban neighborhood with so many different ethnic communities living closely together, I was struck by an incredible religious diversity unlike any place I had ever seen; I was also struck by a claim among residents that Flushing was "the birthplace of religious freedom." I wondered how such extreme religious diversity had developed and what issues that story might raise. What began as a small part of the Pluralism Project soon turned into a bigger project of my own when I discovered nothing substantial had been written about Flushing, and I realized I had stumbled onto a good topic to explore in further study. Diana Eck's encouragement and work was, and still is, a huge inspiration (she truly personifies Mahatma Gandhi's maxim "We must become the change we wish to see in the world"), and the Pluralism Project gave me a new sense of purpose.

In the early and mid-1990s, no one was really doing work on religion and immigration in American history since 1965, and I sought training that would give me the right background to study my particular project. In 1996, I began a Ph.D. in the interdisciplinary Committee on the History of Culture at the University of Chicago, where I built on my background in American religious history with Martin E. Marty and Catherine Brekus (now at Harvard) and where I also gained expertise in American immigration/ethnic and urban history with Kathleen Neils Conzen and Neil Harris. I am grateful for their instruction, guidance, and patience, as well as the rigorous level of scholarship they inspired and expected. I came to the University of Chicago to study with Marty (I was the last student he took on), and his influence runs throughout my work. I really cannot imagine how this book would have turned out without his input, and whatever new insights this study might add to our understanding of pluralism build on a theme that Marty has been thinking, teaching, and writing about for many years.

Other professors and colleagues at the University of Chicago also played an important role. Professor Robert S. Nelson (now at Yale) advised me as chair of the Committee on the History of Culture, and I thank him for years of counsel and encouraging me to cross interdisciplinary boundaries as needed. I am also indebted to the late Karl Joachim Weintraub, professor emeritus of history and former chair of the Committee on the History of Culture, for introducing me to the history of cultural history and Goethe's phrase *"in den Kleinen der Großen finden"* (to find the big in the small). I studied ethnography with John Comaroff and James W. Fernandez in anthropology, Gerald Suttles provided memorable background in urban sociology, and Marta Tienda (now at Princeton) introduced me to the sociological study of immigration. In the Divinity School, the philosopher of religion Paul Griffiths (now at UIC) and the sociologist of religion Martin Riesebrodt helped me to think more critically about religious pluralism and the nature of my project. I was also fortunate to study with a group of brilliant postcolonial and globalization theorists that included Homi Bhabha (now at Harvard), Arjun Appadurai, Carol Breckenridge, and Dipesh Chakrabarty. The many excellent workshops at the University of Chicago are a source of great help to many faculty and students, and I benefited from presenting early parts of my work in the Social History workshop, the Culture and Society workshop, and the South Asian Studies workshop. Colleagues in History of Culture, although many of us were involved in vastly different projects, were also a source of interdisciplinary inspiration and collegiality.

I came back to New York every summer to sublet an apartment and do more research; eventually, in 1999, I moved from Chicago to an apartment on Bowne Street in Flushing to gain a better sense of the daily rhythms so important for ethnographic fieldwork. I lived in Flushing from the summer of 1999 through the summer of 2001, and I continued to make periodic trips to Flushing even after later moving to Providence and then Philadelphia. I have also kept up with local news through the *Flushing Times* and numerous contacts there.

Because I have been a presence in Flushing off and on for over twenty years, I have come to know many people in the community whose help I would like to note. In the early days of my research, I was fortunate to meet Evangeline Egglezos, former executive director of the Bowne House Historical Society, who gave me office space in the Bowne House over a summer and opened many doors (literally and figuratively). I also had the pleasure of serving on the board of trustees at Bowne House for several years. Jim Driscoll shared his endless enthusiasm and native knowledge of Flushing while pointing me toward countless archival treasures in his twin roles as president of Queens Historical Society and as a librarian at the Long Island Division of the Queens Borough Public Library in Jamaica, Queens. Thanks also to Judith Box, John Hyslop, and the other fine staff members at the Long Island Division—I remember the "Eureka!" feeling the first time I visited the research collection there (it is such a wonderful gold mine of material, but I wonder if many scholars of New York even know about it since it is somewhat secretly tucked away on the second floor of the Jamaica branch). Richard Hourahan at the Queens Historical Society also assisted in tracking down dozens of early pictures and other assorted records of Flushing. The Queens historian Vincent F. Seyfried shared a lifetime of work and his unparalleled personal collection of photographs and maps. Ruth Hertzberg, a former director of the Queens Borough Public Library, Flushing Branch, made numerous local archival sources available, and I gained a better understanding of Flushing's early history through collaboration with the curators Lucy Davidson and Trudie Grace at Flushing Town Hall for an exhibit on the Bowne family. Countless residents of Flushing also gave of their time and shared the stories of their lives, personal experiences, and deepest thoughts in the oral history interviews I recorded and in many informal conversations over the years. I hope this book meets with their approval. Visiting all of the many different places of worship in Flushing, meeting and speaking with residents and various local leaders, attending festivals, parades, community meetings, eating my way around the world in all of the restaurants, and just walking around observing, taking pictures, and living there . . . it has been a remarkable journey for me that broadened my own beliefs and will be with me for the rest of my life.

As an Exchange Scholar at Columbia in 1999 and 2000, I had the opportunity to build on associations with faculty I met during my MA studies and gain background in new areas. I benefited tremendously from Kenneth T. Jackson's seminar in urban history and field trips to city archives, and I was honored to take him and students on a long tour of Flushing (and attend a triumphant Mets game against the Atlanta Braves) as part of his legendary course on the history of New York City. Ronald J. Grele offered instruction in oral history, and I became involved with the Oral History Research Center. A year-long seminar led by Nicholas Dirks and Partha Chatterjee in anthropology and history called "The Production of the Past" brought numerous luminaries to a series of excellent lectures. I would also like to express appreciation to the University Seminars at Columbia for their help in publication. Material in this work was presented to the University Seminar on Religion led by Randall Balmer. One other participant in the seminar, the American religious historian

Jesse Terry Todd (a fellow graduate student at Columbia who is now a professor at Drew University) was kind to share his research on religion at the 1939–1940 New York World's Fair. Kenneth R. Cobb, the director of New York City's Municipal Archives, helped open up the city's boundless resources during this time too, and Marybeth Cavanagh, Holly Hinsman, Eleanor Gillers, and Nicole Wells at the New-York Historical Society also provided exceptional assistance.

In the course of preparing the manuscript for publication, I gained valuable feedback from presenting my work at conferences, workshops, and public events. In addition to papers I presented at the American Historical Association, the American Academy of Religion, and the Conference on New York State History, I attended the first Global Conference on Critical Perspectives of Pluralism at Oxford University in September 2003, where I met a wonderful group of scholars from around the world who came at the topic from many different angles. During my time in the United Kingdom, I also visited the British equivalent of Flushing in Leicester, where I was taken on a tour of the city by Richard Bonney in the Department of History at the University of Leicester. Bonney's work studying religious pluralism in Leicester provided a great source for considering similar issues, and we coauthored an article comparing the two areas that I cite and discuss in the book. Initial funding for my project was made possible first from a tuition scholarship and stipend for graduate study from the University of Chicago. I was also awarded a fellowship (Grant No. 1999013) for 1999–2000 from the Louisville Institute for the Study of American Religion, a Lilly Endowment program based at Louisville Presbyterian Seminary. I cherished the supportive fellowship of colleagues there during the Winter Seminar in January 2000, where I first met its director James W. Lewis as well as the sociologists Nancy T. Ammerman and Omar M. McRoberts, among other scholars. McRoberts has been a close friend and respected colleague ever since, and our conversations about each other's work have been deep and numerous. I met a wonderful group of scholars for weekly symposia when I was a Regional Faculty Fellow for the 2003–2004 Penn Humanities Forum at the University of Pennsylvania, which focused that year on the theme of "Belief." I also later benefited from presenting in the Urban Ethnography Workshop at Penn hosted by the sociologist David Grazian. In addition, I refined more of my work when I participated in the 2005 NEH Summer Seminar on "Religious Diversity and the Common Good," directed by Alan Wolfe at the Boisi Center for the Study of Religion and American Public Life at Boston College. Finally, I had the opportunity to get feedback from many New Yorkers throughout 2007 when I gave several lectures about my work in the city for the 350th anniversary of the Flushing Remonstrance. All of these experiences were wonderfully stimulating intellectual opportunities to meet with a diverse group of people, and many may find references to our conversations in the pages that follow.

I would also like to thank the many other scholars who helped me along the way. The following read chapters or all of this book manuscript and shared comments: Martin E. Marty, Catherine Brekus, Kathleen Neils Conzen, Neil Harris, James W. Fernandez, Diana L. Eck, John Stratton Hawley, Randall Balmer, Lowell Livezey, Alan Wolfe, Omar McRoberts, Douglas Bradburn, David Grazian, Pyong Gap Min, Courtney Bender, Alyshia Galvez, Robert A. Orsi, Thomas A. Tweed, Gustav Niebuhr, Kenneth T. Jackson, Roy Rosenzweig, Richard Bonney, Meredith Baldwin Weddle, and James Wetzel. Madhulika Khandelwal was an early guide to the South Asian community in Queens—as was Alagappa Alagappan, the founder of the Hindu Temple Society of North America and a good friend for many years until he passed away in 2014. Raymond Brady Williams, a pioneer in the study of the religions of South Asian immigrants in America, shared his fieldnotes from research in New York during the 1980s.

As a postdoctoral research associate in the Center for the Study of Human Development at Brown University from 2001 to 2002, I joined a team of scholars for a project funded by the MacArthur Foundation. I was recruited to write a social-cultural history of the Portuguese, Dominican, and Cambodian immigrant communities in Providence that focused on education in middle childhood. Through my association with the project, John Modell and Cynthia García-Coll introduced me to work in sociology of education and developmental psychology, and this has influenced my discussion of children in Flushing.

I have had the pleasure of teaching at a number of different institutions while revising the manuscript, and my students at Philadelphia University, the State University of New York at Binghamton, Temple University, Delaware Valley College, and the University of Pennsylvania all have had to endure stories and occasional digressions about my work in Flushing. They also asked questions, and I am grateful for the stimulation they provided.

A big round of applause goes to the geographer/GIS guru Christopher Hermann, of GeoSpatial Innovations and an assistant professor in the Law and Police Science Department at CUNY John Jay College of Criminal

Justice, who worked with me to produce maps, tables, and charts for the book. I would also like to thank the excellent transcription team at TTC Tape Transcriptions for transcribing numerous oral history interviews. Finally, the demographer Ken Hodges, of Nielsen Claritas, was very kind to dig up work he did in 2001 on data from the 1990 and 2000 Census and then do similar work for me on the 2010 Census.

In the process of securing permissions/licenses for the use of archival images and other sources in the book, I was honored and grateful to be granted permission by Peter Rosen and David Beal at Bob Dylan Music Company to reprint the first stanza from "I Dreamed I Saw St. Augustine" as an epigraph in the Introduction to set the tone for the book. Thanks also to Wesley Stace (aka John Wesley Harding) and Jeroen Vandermeer.

Finally, I'd also like to thank the excellent editorial staff at Fordham University Press. Fredric Nachbaur, Will Cerbone, Eric Newman, Ann-Christine Racette, Robert Fellman, and Katie Sweeney were a pleasure to work with, and their input, guidance, and careful work, along with the comments and suggestions of various external reviewers over the years, helped turn a manuscript and collection of images into a book.

City of Gods took a long time to finish. I first visited Flushing for Pluralism Project research in 1994, I completed an initial draft in 2002, and it has taken many more years to revise that draft for publication. I needed time to refine everything, fill in gaps, and carefully, critically reflect on what I was writing, because even though Flushing is just a small neighborhood in New York City, it is a complex and densely populated, diverse place with a big story. I apologize to the people of Flushing if I got anything wrong or didn't go into as much depth as I could have on certain topics or groups, but there was a lot to cover! Various readers of the manuscript suggested different ideas for the structure of the book—some I incorporated; others I stubbornly resisted. I came back to the manuscript many times after presenting different parts of the project over the years, and I have tried to incorporate or address many of the comments and suggestions I received on different occasions. Of course, this is not to say that the book is now a perfect chronicle and the final word. Part of the problem with a project so long in gestation is that new material keeps coming out, but I have done my best to update it as needed (for instance, recent attention to transnationalism was just beginning as I was ending my study; there are references to it in the text, but it was simply not a major part of the original conceptual framework in the mid- and late 1990s).

The cultural historian Jacob Burckhardt modestly called his history of the Renaissance in Italy "an essay," knowing that his work was an attempt, *a* history, not *the* history. At some point, one has to end a research project and say, "Enough!" I hope other scholars will fill in the gaps, and I remain interested in Flushing's future—visiting when I can, maintaining ties, and keeping up with local news. I ended my research in 2001 in part because 9/11 turned out to be a logical event with which to end the story. Looking back, I also think ending then documented Flushing at a particular stage in the community's engagement with pluralism. Since then, Flushing seems to have begun moving in a new direction that I may document in a follow-up study someday, and I point to this in Chapter 5.

My parents were married the same year the Immigration Act of 1965 was signed into law, so I salute their fifty years together, and I owe them a world of thanks for their unending support, encouragement, and love during this journey.

There were times when it was hard to convince others (and occasionally myself) that I would ever be done with this, and over the course of revising the manuscript for publication, my two sons also were born. Finding the time and energy to write and revise became harder on top of teaching and parenting, but the final push to finish this came from Raj and Ravi, or maybe for them.

CITY OF GODS

Introduction

I dreamed I saw St. Augustine
Alive as you or me
Tearing through these quarters
In the utmost misery
With a blanket underneath his arm
And a coat of solid gold
Searching for the very souls
Whom already have been sold

—*Bob Dylan*

When the world was over fifteen hundred years younger, the out-
lines of all things seemed more clearly marked than they are to
us now.[1] As the great church father and theologian St. Augustine looked
back from his post as bishop of Hippo in North Africa to Rome just
after it was sacked by the Visigoths in 410 C.E., he reflected on his time
there as a teacher of rhetoric in Milan, the all-but-complete overthrow
of ancient Roman polytheism, and the gradual triumph of Christianity
in the Senate and throughout the empire. After several centuries of intolerance and persecution, it now was evident that, with the support of
Constantine, Christianity had risen as the dominant religion in the West,
even though many pagans remained. Over the course of fourteen years,
Augustine compiled a collection of theological and philosophical writings that would become a charter for a Christian future and a classic in
Western thought: *Concerning the City of God Against the Pagans,* or simply,
City of God.[2] Until fairly recently, *City of God* was understood to be part
of a tradition in the early church history of late antiquity from Origen to
Eusebius, who held that the Christianization of the Roman Empire was
evidence of God's divine providence to unite the nations under a single
polity to bring about universal salvation.[3] Yet *City of God* was not simply

1

an attack on the last vestiges of polytheism, a rejection of all "false gods," and a call to worship of "the one true God" so that, through belief in Christ, all of humanity could enter the heavenly City. Although Augustine initially was influenced by such ideas, scholars since the mid–twentieth century have argued that his own view actually evolved into a more complex acceptance of religious pluralism.[4] He foresaw the importance of a secular, theologically neutral political sphere in a religiously diverse city like Rome, and he explained that Christians would have to live alongside pagans: "both . . . alike enjoy the good things, or are afflicted with the adversities of this temporal state, but with a different faith, a different expectation, a different love, until they are separated by the final judgement, and each receives her own end."[5]

If Augustine were alive today, he might agree that New York City was the Rome of the twentieth century. One wonders what he would make of it. Imagine him on a visit to New York, standing in Times Square at the dawn of the new millennium, as he and millions of other spectators and television viewers gather to watch a large glimmering ball drop down a pole atop a building on Forty-Second Street—an odd pagan ceremony of sorts, but one that also marked two thousand years of Christianity. After the millennial hysteria fizzles, with no great conflagration, no sign of disturbance or Armageddon, not even a Y2K computer bug having occurred, Augustine walks among the crowd and happens to meet a Chinese American Catholic family that insists he stay with them. Heading down into the subway at Times Square, they take the 7 train, which emerges from under the city up onto scenic elevated tracks in Queens, rumbling out to the other end of the line at the Flushing–Main Street station. Over the weekend, Augustine is persuaded to tour the neighborhood. He attends Mass at St. Michael's, a Catholic church near the center of downtown that was built in the mid–nineteenth century, and notes that services are in English, Spanish, and Chinese, and he later sees four other Catholic churches with similar multiethnic congregations nearby, as well as a Korean Catholic church. He passes a wide variety of Protestant churches, too: a Quaker Meeting House dating back to the late seventeenth century—the oldest place of worship in continual use in New York City—as well as an Episcopal church from the eighteenth century and an African Methodist Episcopal church from the early nineteenth century—both now entirely surrounded by a variety of large retail stores, banks, little shops, Asian restaurants, parking lots, and a continuous, crowded stream of people from seemingly every place on earth coming and going on trains, buses, and cars. He sees Conservative, Reformed, and Orthodox Jewish synagogues that were established in the early and mid–twentieth century. He also walks by half a dozen Hindu temples among the houses and apartment buildings and commercial areas; two Sikh gurdwaras; several mosques; Japanese, Chinese, and Korean Buddhist temples; Taoist temples; countless Korean and Chinese churches; and several Latin American churches, as well as Falun Gong practitioners at a table outside the public library, Jehovah's Witnesses handing out copies of *The Watchtower* by the subway, and young Mormon missionaries out trying to win converts. In all, he counts over two hundred different places of worship densely concentrated in this vibrant residential neighborhood and bustling commercial district smaller than 2.5 square miles. For Augustine to experience everyday encounters with "the Other" and to see Christianity as just one among so many different and competing conceptions of God, or gods, would seem to challenge and complicate further any exclusive claims to absolute truth. He would no doubt be amazed by Flushing, yet it would probably confirm his belief that the earthly City was destined, as the historian Robert A. Markus has noted, to be forever "pluralistic in its nature, composed of diverse cultures, comprising groups . . . committed to different and conflicting value systems."[6]

From the "Birthplace of Religious Freedom" to a Microcosm of World Religions

Taking the 7 subway train from one end in midtown Manhattan out to the last stop in Queens is to take a trip between two very different places in New York City: One is urban, the other somewhat suburban; one is thought to be the core, the other the periphery—quite literally on the edge of the city. Even the journey on the train itself is an experience: The 7 became a new symbol of the diversity of New York in 1999 when it was recognized by the White House as one of sixteen National Millennium Trails for its role in immigration history.[7] Others have been less rhapsodic about the 7. A media frenzy catapulted the train into the national news when John Rocker, a pitcher for the Atlanta Braves baseball team, made offensive comments about the people he saw on the 7 while on his way to Shea Stadium for pregame practice. Asked if he would ever play for the Mets if traded, Rocker replied:

> I would retire first. It's the most hectic, nerve-racking [*sic*] city. Imagine having to take the 7 train to the ballpark, looking like you're [riding

7 train depot at former Shea Stadium–Willets Point station.

through] Beirut next to some kid with purple hair next to some
queer with AIDS right next to some dude who just got out of jail
for the fourth time right next to some 20-year-old mom with four
kids. It's depressing. The biggest thing I don't like about New York
are the foreigners. I'm not a very big fan of foreigners. You can walk
an entire block in Times Square and not hear anybody speaking English. Asians and Koreans and Vietnamese and Indians and Russians
and Spanish people and everything up there. How the hell did they
get in this country?[8]

Rocker was reprimanded by his team (including several teammates who
were themselves recent immigrants) and the media for his bigotry, but most
forgot all about it when the 2000 World Series raised the stature of the
old elevated tracks of the 7 even higher (at least in New York), when the
Yankees played the Mets in the first Subway Series since 1955.

Subway entrance to 7 train, at the junction of Main Street and Roosevelt Avenue.

When exiting the subway onto Main Street in downtown Flushing today, one is immediately struck by an atmosphere almost as crowded, busy, and noisy as Times Square. There is not nearly as much neon, nor are there any towering skyscrapers with gigantic underwear advertisements, but there are people—*all kinds* of people, as a walk around Flushing quickly reveals. Not far from the intersection of Main and Roosevelt, just under an overpass with a billboard that reads "Catch the New Spirit of Asia," is the sleek new Flushing public library, which opened in 1998—"the busiest branch in the nation's busiest library system . . . it shows clearly that the immigrant's path to the American dream includes frequent trips to the local library."[9] Nearby are major banks, hotels, familiar chain retail stores and fast-food restaurants, delis, pubs, even a Starbucks, but most striking are all the ethnic restaurants, cafes, grocery markets, jewelers, electronics shops, and dollar stores, with signs in Chinese, Korean, Hindi, Urdu, Spanish, and Russian—some with little or no English on the signs at all. The center of downtown Flushing is now well known as the city's second Chinatown, but it is also home to a Koreatown that is the largest on the East Coast as well as the oldest Little India in the United States. Although distinct ethnic enclaves are evident, they overlap and are so close together that the mishmash of so many different nationalities

The new Flushing branch of the New York public library system: the busiest branch in the nation's busiest library system.

(and the businesses that cater to them) challenges one to find the right label for the entire area. Main Street did resemble many other Main Streets across America until several decades ago, but it is now more likely that other Main Streets will come to resemble Flushing's Main Street in the future. Main Street, Flushing, is the new Main Street, America. Most outside visitors to Flushing see only this—they rarely venture farther than the restaurants near the subway exit, treating Flushing only as an exotic ethnic neighborhood in which to eat and shop (it is regularly featured in the *New York Times* as a dining destination for the adventurous). Yet to focus merely on the commercial and ethnic diversity of downtown Flushing is to miss a much deeper story about Flushing's history and real significance today.

Local residents of Flushing often proudly claim it is "the birthplace of religious freedom," which is a little misleading, but it did play a significant and often overlooked part in colonial America and in the evolution of this fundamental principle of American democracy. Flushing is actually the Anglicized form of the Dutch name Vlissingen (a town in Holland), and its town charter of 1645 was one of the first in colonial America to grant religious freedom, or "liberty of conscience" (as it was called then), which was important to many in town who became Quakers, or Friends. When this right was jeopardized by Governor Peter Stuyvesant, who was bent on persecuting anyone who was not a member of the Dutch Reformed Church, the people of Flushing came together to defend their town charter. In 1657, they drafted a document that has become known as the Flushing Remonstrance, which the American religious historian Martin E. Marty has described as a "pioneering plea for religious freedom [that] called diversity not a curse but a glory."[10] Stuyvesant was not moved, however, and it was not until 1663, when John Bowne was banished from Flushing for holding Quaker meetings in his house but then successfully appealed his case to the Dutch West India Company, that the town and the rest of the colony would more fully enjoy this liberty. Bowne House is the oldest house in Queens (built in 1661), and it has been operating as a historical society and museum since 1945, when it was declared "a national shrine to religious freedom." Today in Flushing there are now ten different places of worship just down the road from Bowne House on Bowne Street, with dozens more on nearby streets.[11] It is perhaps fitting that this "birthplace of religious freedom" is now home to all the religions of the world.

Flushing is perhaps the most compelling case of religious and ethnic pluralism in the world, and it is an ideal place to explore how America's long experiment with religious pluralism continues today. When Congress, during the Johnson administration, passed the Immigration (Hart–Celler) Act of 1965, it opened the door to people from parts of the world not represented before in large numbers in America. Just as other groups had done in previous centuries, the new immigrants brought with them new traditions and began to forge what the religion scholar Diana L. Eck has called "a new religious landscape" in America.[12] Not since waves of Irish Catholic immigrants began to arrive in the mid–nineteenth century, followed in the early twentieth century by even more Catholics from Italy and Poland as well as Eastern European Jews, did the country undergo such a shift in its religious makeup. The sociologist Will Herberg was able to speak of a Protestant-Catholic-Jewish America in the 1950s, but this label would have to be expanded significantly to include all of the world religions in the United States today.[13] Since 1965, Protestants, Catholics, and Jews have been joined by a substantial number of

Hindus, Sikhs, Buddhists, Muslims, and other religious groups from Asia, the Middle East, Africa, the Caribbean, and Latin America. In the last quarter of the twentieth century, Queens became the most diverse large county in the country, according to 1990, 2000, and 2010 census data, and perhaps nowhere else are the changes as dramatic as in Flushing.[14] Like many other communities across America, Flushing was predominantly Christian and Jewish, white and black, up through the 1950s. But as new immigrants from Asia settled in Flushing after 1965 and began to establish their own places of worship, Flushing's religious landscape grew so diverse and densely concentrated that it became a microcosm of world religions by the end of the century. Yet such dramatic change had a variety of effects on the community and led to a range of different responses to religious diversity.

Religious pluralism is not unique to Flushing—mosques, temples, and gurdwaras have risen up in cities and communities all over America, increasing the challenge of remaining one nation made up of so many. Similar areas, such as New Hampshire Avenue in Silver Springs, Maryland; Sixteenth Street NW in Washington, D.C.; Deer Park Avenue in Dix Hills, New York; West Rogers Park in Chicago, Illinois; Fort Bend, Texas; and Fremont, California, are all signs of a trend toward greater religious and ethnic diversity developing around the country.[15] However, what makes Flushing unique is the density and extent of this diversity. Nowhere are so many different religious traditions concentrated in such a small geographic area. Even in notably diverse cities abroad, such as Leicester in Great Britain, there is not the same degree of diversity.[16]

During a time when many Americans equate Islam with terrorism after 9/11 and ISIS and as hysteria continues over how to secure U.S. borders from illegal immigration, it is important to remember that religious diversity has always been a major theme in the nation's history—and it has been contested at nearly every turn. While the rise of the Religious Right in America in the early 2000s might have led some to believe that America is dominated by conservative evangelical Protestants, the United States has in fact become the most religiously diverse nation on earth. As with every other period of massive new immigration in the nation's history, Americans are learning to live with new cultures and traditions from around the world. There has always been a sense among some alarmists that certain newcomers were and are "unmeltable"—that is, that they would not jump in the "Great American Melting Pot" and come out as mainstream White Anglo-Saxon Protestants, that they would still insist on preserving foreign traditions and languages and live together in ethnic enclaves, and that "they" were not like "us" and that this was not good for America. This kind of xenophobia or nativism resurfaces every time a very different immigrant group begins to grow in the United States, revealing an atavistic pattern in American history that appears, disappears, and reappears in different forms repeatedly.

News headlines continue to show that religion is a tremendously significant factor in a post–Cold War and post-9/11 world of continuing clashes and conflict based on religious and ethnic difference, territory, history, fundamentalism, and seemingly incompatible worldviews. Battles over religion have torn communities and the country apart at different moments and places in American history, and though the United States has not had to deal with the kind of large-scale religious wars that rage in other parts of the world, acts of terrorism; cases of religious discrimination, nativism, and violence; and battles over religion in school curricula and politics still make the news in a nation that is increasingly diverse yet largely ignorant about world religions.

Questioning Diversity

There is an innumerable multitude of sects in the United States. They are all different in the worship they offer to the Creator, but all agree concerning the duties of men to one another.

The religious atmosphere of the country was the first thing that struck me on arrival in the United States. The longer I stayed in the country, the more conscious I became of the important political consequences resulting from this novel situation. All thought that the main reason for the quiet sway of religion over their country was the complete separation of church and state.

Alexis de Tocqueville

It sometimes takes an outsider to see things that locals take for granted, and Alexis de Tocqueville was perhaps the most celebrated foreign visitor to comment on the workings of American government soon after its birth. Touring the young nation in the 1830s, he noted (among many other observations) that Catholicism and the variety of Protestant denominations did not die out because they lacked political support after disestablishment and the First Amendment; rather, as essentially voluntary organizations, all religious groups small and large were able to grow and thrive throughout the nineteenth century—and religious freedom and this voluntary principle still guide American religious life.[17]

I was also a kind of outsider when I visited Flushing for the first time in 1994. I had lived in New York City for two years already, but I lived in Manhattan and was unfamiliar with Queens until I started exploring all five boroughs for my research with the Pluralism Project. I was also someone who grew up mostly in the South (in Texas and Georgia), in predominantly white, upper-middle-class, suburban neighborhoods where almost everyone I knew was Christian or Jewish and had a similar background (I was baptized Missouri Synod Lutheran from German-Norwegian-English immigrant roots and later grew up United Methodist but now identify as Unitarian Universalist). Walking around Flushing, I was initially struck by its extreme religious diversity—I had never seen anything like it, even in my trips to other neighborhoods throughout the city. I also learned about its fascinating colonial history and found it odd that I could not recall ever reading about it in surveys of American history and religion.

As I spent more time in Flushing, I began to think more critically about diversity. I wanted to go beyond my initial amazement with Flushing's extreme diversity (which most journalists and those who visit for a day are content to marvel at and celebrate) and instead ask deeper questions, because mere diversity is not very interesting. I began to wonder how it had become so diverse, what factors contributed to the incredible density and variety of so many places of worship in this community, if everyone got along, and if there were limits to how much diversity a community could absorb. I also wondered about Flushing's celebrated heritage of religious freedom and tolerance: what did it really mean to locals (both longtime residents and new immigrants)?

Fifty years ago, one of America's greatest public intellectuals of the mid–twentieth century, the theologian John Courtney Murray SJ, had similar issues on his mind, though under very different circumstances. An ordained Catholic priest with a doctorate in sacred theology from Gregorian University in Rome, Murray taught theology at Woodstock College (a Jesuit seminary in Maryland that was the oldest in the United States) for many years, but he also became a keen and provocative observer and commentator on church/state relations, religious freedom, and American public life. His essays were controversial and initially drew the ire of the Vatican, but his writings also put him on the cover of *Time* in 1960 and ultimately led to a reversal from Rome and an invitation for Murray to participate in the Second Vatican Council in 1963. In 1965, Murray was the principal author of *Dignitatis humanae personae,* the decree affirming religious liberty that reconciled the church's position on religious freedom and pluralism. At the time, religious pluralism in America was the same Protestant–Catholic–Jewish mix that the sociologist Will Herberg wrote about in the 1950s, but in a collection of essays published before Vatican II, Murray went beyond Herberg's concept of a "triple melting pot" and stressed that dialogue and even disagreement were necessary for civil society. At the same time, in Murray's work there is not so much a celebration of pluralism and what Herberg called the "American Way of Life" as there is a kind of grudging acceptance of it. Murray, like Augustine, knew that religious pluralism would always be the norm and that differing views (antithetical though they may be to one's own beliefs) actually served a purpose in directing human affairs. Yet he also wondered about the limits of pluralism:

> How much pluralism and what kinds of pluralism can a pluralist society stand? And conversely, how much unity and what kind of unity does a pluralist society need in order to be a society at all?[18]

Murray wrote during a very different time, but it is striking how relevant his questions still are. They are timeless questions that go to the root of fundamental ideas about the American experiment, echoing concepts that James Madison and Thomas Jefferson explored earlier. Yet they are questions that seem even more urgent today in a much more religiously diverse society, and they are particularly relevant for Flushing as the most extreme example of religious diversity imaginable.

After Vatican II, Murray became director of the La Farge Institute in New York City, which hosted Catholic, Protestant, and Jewish scholars who met to discuss interreligious and interracial tensions.[19] He died suddenly of a heart attack in Queens in 1967 at the age of sixty-two, but had he lived longer he might have been interested to see just how much Queens would change over the next several decades since the Immigration Act of 1965. Indeed, like a modern-day Augustine, he might have been especially intrigued by Flushing.

In this book I use the story of Flushing as a case study to explore and answer these important questions about the possibilities and limits of pluralism. I argue that the absence of widespread religious violence in a neighborhood with densely concentrated extreme religious diversity suggests that there is no limit to how much pluralism a pluralist society can stand. This demonstrates the remarkable possibilities of pluralism for civil society—that a pluralist society committed to democracy and religious freedom can accommodate an enormous amount of pluralism without it resulting in conflict.[20] On the other hand, I also argue that there are in fact some real limits of pluralism when it comes to cooperation and community—spatial limits, social limits, structural limits, and theological limits—and these limits illustrate the challenge of trying to find unity in a pluralist society. Is Flushing so diverse now (that is, is there too much pluralism?) that it is impossible to have a shared sense of community and history, or are there still some common topics of mutual concern that can bring people together? The question for the twenty-first century is: Will Flushing come together in new and lasting ways to build bridges of dialogue, or will it further fragment into a Tower of Babel? These questions reach far beyond Flushing to all communities coming to terms with religious pluralism; indeed, they are questions that face the nation as a whole.

The study of religious pluralism and ethnic relations that I present here is grounded in a history and ethnography of a neighborhood and the people who live, work, and worship in it. By exploring pluralism from a historical and ethnographic context, I have sought to integrate and sustain a theoretical component in my narrative and avoid mere description. In this way, I hope to answer Jon Butler's call to historians of American religion to "assess cause and context" in their work and reimagine the relationship of religion to modernity.[21] In a sense, this book is like other community or case studies in ethnic history, urban history, and urban sociology.[22] Yet other works about religious pluralism tend to take a much wider, or "macro," view of the United States (with occasional quick looks at various sites to relate at least some detail) or are based more in philosophy of religion.[23] This book takes a micro approach to help bring our understanding of pluralism down from a sometimes abstract realm into the real world of everyday lives over time in which people and groups are not depicted as fixed or isolated but as dynamic and interacting agents in a complex and constantly changing world of local, national, and transnational dimensions. Thus, by concentrating on how pluralism "works" at the local level, I have tried to conceive of a more comprehensive explanatory model and theory. As the anthropologist Clifford Geertz remarked in his classic comparative study of Islam in Morocco and Indonesia: "We hope to find in the little what eludes us in the large, to stumble upon general truths while sorting through special cases."[24] Thus, on the surface, this book appears to be a focused and specific history and ethnographic case study of a neighborhood in New York City. Flushing is an extreme case with a unique history, but there is reason to believe that other communities can learn from it—certainly other dense urban areas with similar recent economic histories and growing new immigrant populations, but similar changes in the religious landscape are likely to develop in many other types of communities across the country, too (in fact, they already are). Indeed, we may be able to glimpse the future of religion and inter-group relations in America by studying Flushing not only because the striking exaggeration of its diversity makes the issues more sharply defined but because the story of the neighborhood and its pioneering colonial history mirrors that of the nation in microcosm.

The analytical framework and historical problem of the book is based on two interrelated questions that seek to gauge interaction and different responses to religious (and ethnic) diversity: (1) How have the different religious and ethnic groups in Flushing associated with others across boundaries over time? (2) Where and when has conflict or cooperation arisen?[25] While the book is primarily a history, there is also an ethno-graphic component that shares something in common with the work of the sociologists of religion Fred Kniss and Paul D. Numrich, who have fo-cused on *sectarianism*, which they define as "the degree of tension between the religious group and the social environment . . . that influences which others are friends and which are foes," and sectarianism's relation to *civic engagement*, which they define as "the public action of individuals and groups as they interact with and participate in the organizations, associa-tions, and institutions of society."[26] The narrative of the book flows from these questions to illustrate changing degrees or levels of community from the founding of Flushing in 1645 to the present, though the focus is mainly on the period from 1945 to 2001.

A series of related questions follow from this analytical framework. How do people make sense of the religious diversity around them? How does it affect their lives, attitudes, and beliefs, if at all? What do they *do* with it (and what does it *do* to them)? Such questions reflect my focus in this book on religion among groups (rather than religious beliefs and practices), as it is by studying the history and interaction of different reli-gious groups in one community that we can learn more about the nature of religious pluralism. My focus on religious groups is guided by a defi-nition of religion by the sociologist Émile Durkheim, who held that "re-ligion is something eminently social . . . [and] religious representations are collective representations which express collective realities."[27] By an-alyzing how individuals and groups in the area choose to associate, I also hope to shed more light on the linkage of religion and ethnicity and ad-dress the complexities of religious, ethnic, and racial identity.[28] Finally, the study also explores at the neighborhood level how immigrant identity is formed and influenced by local, national, and transnational forces linked to globalization.

A word about terminology. To revisit part of Murray's question, "what kinds of pluralism" are there? What *is* "pluralism," anyway? Readers may note that I occasionally switch between using "diversity" and "pluralism" or "religious diversity" and "religious pluralism." Pluralism is a defining characteristic of American society, but it is itself difficult to define because it has been used and debated in so many different contexts.[29] In a separate essay that I wrote on the history of pluralism (and cosmopolitanism) in American thought I go on at length about the changing meanings of these terms over time, and I revisit the topic in Chapter 4 in my discussion of "The Possibilities and Limits of Pluralism" and "How Pluralism 'Works'"—ending with a conceptual model of religious pluralism in Flushing.[30] When we use the words "diversity" or "diverse" to describe a place we are making a casual observation about the visible presence of a variety of ethnic, racial, or religious groups. By "pluralism" I mean the coexistence of diverse groups in a community and the range of responses to living in such a community. Some speak of cultural or ethnic pluralism to highlight a particular facet of pluralism, and I focus mainly on religious pluralism here. There is a wide range of different responses to the religious diversity in Flushing, with different levels of engagement and different gradations of each level all taking place simultaneously within a small area. Taken as a whole, then, religious pluralism is *the range of responses to living in a diverse religious community, or the state of living in such a community*.

Flushing, Queens, in the Popular and Academic Imagination

The task of isolating which area in Queens represents Flushing is a bit complex, as there are a few different factors to consider. Geographically, Flushing is, in fact, part of Long Island (as is the rest of Queens, and Brooklyn, too), and it has only been a part of New York City for a little over one hundred years. Historically, Flushing was a town from 1645 until the end of the nineteenth century (the central area of the town was incorporated as the village of Flushing in 1837). When the county of Queens was split in 1898 during the consolidation of the five boroughs into the city, the eastern townships Oyster Bay, Hempstead, and North Hempstead became Nassau County of Long Island, and the western townships Flushing, Newtown, Jamaica, Long Island City, and the Rockaways all became the borough of Queens and part of New York City.[31] The official and administrative changes associated with consolidation took a while to sink in: many Flushing residents did not associate their town with the city until well into the twentieth century, as one can see by looking at addressed envelopes and stationery of the past that still said "Flushing, Long Island" instead of the more recent "Flushing, New York." The U.S. Postal Service now officially identifies Flushing as a much larger area than what most locals would imagine: anything with a zip code that begins with 113—which includes "Flushing" as well as Bayside, Bay Terrace, College Point, Corona-Elmhurst, Douglaston, Forest Hills, Fresh Meadows, Fresh Pond, Glendale, Jackson Heights, Little Neck, Maspeth, Middle Village, Oakland Gardens, Parkside, Pomonok, Rego Park, Ridgewood, Trainsmeadow, Whitestone, Woodside, and even La Guardia Airport. Obviously, this is a huge region: about one-third of Queens, itself the largest borough in the city. But of the area within these thirty-five zip codes, only a small area of about 2.5 square miles within 11354, 11355, and part of 11358 would fit within the 1837 village boundaries—what most locals still would call downtown Flushing. This distinction is reinforced in the popular imagination by current maps of New York City and Queens (for example, Department of City Planning maps, U.S. Census tract and block maps, and standard road maps such as Hagstrom's). Community board districts are slightly more precise—Community Board 7 encompasses much of the same area (whereas Community Board 4 would be Corona-Elmhurst), but even here there is some overlap with other areas. Civic associations offer yet another way to isolate particular neighborhoods just within Flushing, and different residents of Flushing also conceive of their neighborhood's boundaries in different ways (I often asked those I interviewed to share their thoughts about it). In general, most, if not all, of these sources support my designation of Flushing as this smaller region of 2.5 square miles surrounding the central downtown area.

Surprisingly, not much has been written about Flushing, or even Queens, for that matter—its colonial history is not widely known, and there are very few studies of Queens or its neighborhoods.[32] More is known about Brooklyn, but not the other outer boroughs. When people think of or say New York City (or just "The City"), they usually mean Manhattan. What can we possibly learn from Flushing or Queens? The name "Flushing" itself inevitably elicits bathroom humor until one learns of its Dutch origins and subsequent Anglicization. And just as many Flushing residents took a while to associate the former Flushing, Long Island, with New York City after consolidation, most residents of Manhattan probably took a while to associate Flushing (or any part of Queens, for that matter) with the city—many still do not, and it is common to hear some New Yorkers use the pejorative phrase "bridge and tunnel" to refer to anyone commuting to Manhattan. It is a part of New York City that many tourists and New Yorkers do not know, rarely visit, and most often ridicule.[33] Some also jokingly refer to it now as "Flu-shing" to reflect the large number of people of Asian descent in the community. To many people, perhaps, Flushing, Queens, may seem an unlikely place to warrant much attention, but this is because of an outdated image of it in popular culture. There are some signs, however, that this may be slowly changing: the popular Lonely Planet tour guide company recently named Queens the top tourist destination in the United States for 2015.[34]

Flushing's remarkable diversity is matched by an incredibly interesting and important history that is virtually unknown. In colonial New Amsterdam, Vlissingen (as Flushing was originally known in the Dutch period) had one of the first town charters in 1645 to guarantee "liberty of conscience," though what that meant precisely was difficult to know and led to numerous incidents. In the late eighteenth and early nineteenth century, Flushing was a desirable place for the Manhattan elite to own summer homes, and its well-known commercial tree and plant nurseries drew visitors such as President George Washington and Vice President John Adams in 1789, when the nation's capital was still in New York City. When immigration in the mid– to late nineteenth century started to transform the American population from its colonial mix, Flushing was already seen by new immigrants as an alternative to overcrowded neighborhoods in Manhattan like the Five Points: It became home to sizable Irish, German, and later Italian communities. Jews also chose to settle in Flushing by the turn of the twentieth century, with many more arriving during and after World War II. The extension of the IRT subway in 1928 to Flushing made it even more of a sensible place to settle down. Queens then basked in the international spotlight as the site of two very popular World's Fairs (1939–1940 and 1964–1965) held in Flushing Meadows–Corona Park, and the area was the first home of the United Nations General Assembly, from 1946 to 1951. Many more became at least somewhat familiar with Queens via Shea Stadium, the U.S. Open, and La Guardia and John F. Kennedy (previously Idlewild) airports.

But for several decades now, Queens has evoked less flattering associations in the popular imagination: "to Hollywood, Queens is a place of big hair, nasal accents, and gum-snapping."[35] To millions of Americans watching television from the 1970s to the present, this representation of Queens would stay with them. While those old enough would have remembered Queens as the recent host of the World's Fair that ended in 1965 (some would also remember the earlier one), new national pop-culture fame came in 1971 with *All in the Family*—the popular television sitcom set on a quiet street of rowhouses in nearby Astoria (although the house shown at the end of the opening credits, implicitly the Bunkers', is actually in Rego Park). The show featured the loud-mouthed but lovable bigot Archie Bunker, whose traditional views of society were often challenged by his daughter, son-in-law, neighbors, and the turmoil of the late 1960s and 1970s.[36] Oddly, Queens still has a similar look even in very recent shows like *The Nanny* (starring Fran Drescher as "the flashy girl from Flushing") or *The King of Queens*. Such programs have not accurately represented Queens and how it began to change dramatically after the Immigration Act of 1965, so television viewers who have never visited (even those who have only passed through quickly on their way directly to the U.S. Open or a Mets game) typically know very little about Queens today and even less about the colonial history of Flushing. Occasional newspaper articles since the mid- to late 1970s began to document the changes in immigration and ethnic diversity in Queens, and by the new millennium reporters had begun referring to it as the most ethnically diverse county in the country. But Queens and the other "outer" boroughs remain in relative obscurity compared with Manhattan.

Scholarship on the history of Flushing is scanty at best, and there are no recent studies.[37] There are numerous local histories of Flushing and biographical sketches of its principal leaders from the colonial period through the nineteenth century as well as a few thorough and fairly reliable (but now outdated) histories of Flushing, of Queens, and of Long Island covering the same period.[38] The Flushing Remonstrance and John Bowne also appear in books on New York history and in a few general histories of America and American religion.[39] What is perhaps more interesting is when they do not, as some historians have either overlooked Flushing or felt it was irrelevant to New York and American history.[40] Flushing (and therefore New Amsterdam/New York) needs to be reconsidered as part of the history of religious freedom and toleration in America. While the First Amendment and Jefferson's Statute of Virginia for Religious Freedom are better known, Flushing's colonial history provides an important local context to examine the same principles on a much smaller level—in addition to a necessary revision of earlier surveys of American history and religion. Indeed, the history of Flushing challenges previous dominant narratives that stressed the primary importance and legacy of New England Puritanism and British colonial settlements along the North Atlantic coast in general, shifting attention to the Mid-Atlantic colony of Dutch New Netherland (New York after the British takeover in 1664) and its long experiment with pluralism that is still, perhaps more, relevant today.[41] Indeed, it is not just Flushing or Queens that are largely unknown to the rest of America: New York itself is only recently being given more credit as a fundamental American story despite its popular reputation as the cultural capital of the world.

Scholars also have only recently begun to document the histories and religions of "new" immigrant groups in America. Most historians of immigration and religion in America who attempt a survey of the country have struggled to tell a complete and inclusive story about ethnic and religious pluralism in America.[42] Such a depiction may be a perpetually elusive ideal, yet what has long passed for the truth has been very partial. For instance, the historian David G. Hackett observed in 1995 that "as recently as the 1970s what we knew about the American religious past came primarily from the study of formal theology and the histories of the established churches"—which meant a "church history" that largely privileged a white, Anglo-Saxon, Protestant (New England Puritan) narrative.[43] The exclusion of other Americans from such histories reveals this bias, and for many years there was only occasional, very brief mention of Asian religions in the United States in the major surveys of American religion. Why was scholarship in these subjects still so nascent, and what did it mean? Were the numbers of such groups too small to warrant attention, or have historians of American religion perhaps regarded them as irrelevant? If quantity was the issue, why, then, have similarly small denominations, sects, and cults always been included and seen as important—indeed, even when their numbers were smaller than the above groups and their existence sometimes ephemeral? We could argue that studying such groups as the Shakers reveals something distinctive about American religion, but could we not say the same about examining Chinese Buddhists in nineteenth-century America? In an article he wrote in 1986 entitled "The American Religious History Canon," Martin E. Marty noted that contemporary historians were paying less attention to mainline denominations and more to "Eastern, Occult, Esoteric and 'New' Religions . . . [and that] the canon was absorbing movements that had once seemed marginal."[44] He added, however, that such research had not yet had time to mature.

New work that addressed this gap did not start in earnest until the curriculum debates about multiculturalism in higher education in the 1980s and 1990s, and a considerable amount of work has been published since September 11, 2001.[45] And, since 1991, the *Journal of Religion and American Culture* also has become an alternative for those doing work on religion in American culture not exclusively about Christian church history.

In the twenty-first century, the period from 1965 to 2000 is likely to become the next "period" that immigration historians will refer to as they have with the three other major periods of immigration in U.S. history: Western European immigration in the 1790s in the Early National period, which was similar to colonial migration but which led to the Naturalization Act and the Alien and Sedition Acts after the perception that many were foreign radicals; massive Irish and German immigration in the 1830s through 1860s, which led to widespread anti-Catholicism; and, last, even greater numbers of southern and eastern European and Asian immigrants from the 1880s to 1920s, which led to the Chinese Exclusion Act of 1882 and wider anti-immigrant sentiment and severe immigration restriction by the 1920s.[46] The Immigration Act of 1965 and subsequent legislation opened the door to people from every part of the world, and the effects were felt in the 1980s and 1990s when a similar hysteria over undocumented or illegal immigration coincided with the highest numbers of newcomers ever in 1991.[47] But whereas religious and cultural difference concerned a more Protestant America when Irish, German, and Italian Catholics and Jews immigrated in the nineteenth and early twentieth centuries, the same issues stand out even more now with the most recent wave of immigrants because they involve world religions largely new to the United States. As the filmmaker Ric Burns noted in an interview about *New York: A Documentary Film*:

> I mean, in the last—the immigration in the last 30 years alone makes the immigration of the turn of the 20th century look like an Episcopalian picnic. I mean, it's so complex now, and so much more—so many more kinds of people, from around the world. I mean that is really—the future is out there in Queens with all those people, coming from literally every continent. That's the Lower East Side of the 21st century.[48]

Historians of immigration have long recognized the importance of religion in understanding and writing about the foundations of immigrant settlement, yet there have been few studies that highlight this aspect of immigration and deal with related issues of interaction and pluralism.[49]

Early immigration historians and sociologists such as George Stephenson, William I. Thomas, and Florian Znaniecki were the first real pioneers in the field, and scholars of American religion and the new social history in the 1960s and 1970s doing work on religion/ethnicity and community history during the "Ethnic Revival" sparked renewed interest, along with the creation of ethnic studies departments.[50] The debates about multiculturalism in the late 1980s seemed to revive interest in immigrant religion again, and the field took on even greater interest after September 11, 2001. A growing number of historians and sociologists of immigration and American religion have recently published several important new studies that highlight interaction, contact, and encounter, but more work remains to be done.[51]

A focus on immigrant religion in cities since 1965 also helps us understand why religion did not disappear in the face of modernity as secularization theorists once predicted it would. Indeed, theorists like Peter Berger now say "the world is as furiously religious as it ever was, and in some places more so than ever."[52] Communities like Flushing show how religion among new immigrants is always of primary importance, and continuous waves of newcomers keep revitalizing a religion—sometimes saving a dying congregation if it welcomes new immigrants and becoming a multiethnic congregation (I discuss this in Chapter 4). Because of the separation from their countries of origin, new immigrants are sometimes even more conscious of authenticity in replicating and transplanting their religious traditions than they were before they emigrated—though they also often find that they have to improvise in a new environment, resulting in a kind of syncretism of religious practices.[53] As Robert Orsi has written, immigrants and migrants often find creative and innovative ways to do this in a city, an environment that may not seem hospitable to religion:

> By turning apartments into abattoirs (as the practitioners of Santería do), the basements of housing projects into venues of the spirits, the streets into penitential pilgrimage routes, city water flows into receptacles for sins or the resting places of Hindu gods, and intersecting street corners into vectors of spiritual power, immigrants and migrants dramatically re-placed themselves on cityscapes that had been explicitly designed to exclude them or to render them invisible or docile. By acting upon the urban environment in these different ways, immigrants and migrants denied the arrangements of space, the understanding of poverty, the marginalization or ostracism

of the foreign, and the alienation of the streets built into the urban landscape by law, architecture, and religion. Into every space hollowed out by contempt for the city and its peoples . . . migrants and immigrants have inserted themselves, making themselves present, indeed at times overpresent, usually on their own terms. This is the persistent subversive impulse of popular urban religions in the United States, the counter-story to the narrative inscribed by architects, city planners, and reformers on the streets and in the skies of American cities.[54]

For scholars of urban history, the study of Flushing also highlights the importance of considering immigration since 1965 in connection with a recently perceived rebirth of the American city.[55] It is generally acknowledged that cities suffered dramatically during a period of urban decline in the mid-1960s and 1970s, and this started in the post–World War II era with deindustrialization and white flight to the suburbs, which, in part, was brought about earlier by the Great Migration of African Americans away from Jim Crow and the collapse of the agricultural economy in the rural South to factory jobs in northern cities.[56] With the large numbers of new immigrants settling into American cities after the Immigration Act of 1965, the loss of white urban residents was met with the beginning of a strong and continuous gain of newcomers. The availability of commercial space and affordable apartments or homes with a small yard outside of the overcrowded decaying inner city made outer-borough neighborhoods in Queens and Brooklyn attractive to several generations of new immigrants, who played an undeniable role in revitalizing neighborhoods that had fallen on hard times by the mid-1970s. From roughly the 1980s to the present, for the first time since the early twentieth century, American cities also began to attract more whites from suburban and rural areas, resulting in the revitalization and gentrification of many urban neighborhoods at the same time that they were becoming more diverse from immigration since 1965.

In the essay "Urbanism as a Way of Life," the sociologist Louis Wirth argued that city people are inherently cosmopolitan because they live in a heterogeneous population in a dense, large urban environment and regularly come into contact with many other people in public.[57] He added, however, that this kind of tolerance is really quite impersonal because of a desire to protect one's personal space, which city people have a lot less of than do rural or suburban folk. Jane Jacobs echoed this line of thinking in *The Death and Life of Great American Cities* when she stressed the importance of a clear demarcation between public and private space for successful city neighborhoods.[58] As I explain in a section of Chapter 4 on "Public/Private Urban Space and the Social Limits of Religious Pluralism," such ideas may help explain why, in the most densely populated and diverse urban neighborhoods, individuals and groups with different religious backgrounds may encounter one another daily but generally do not interact. The same forces are at work in suburban and rural regions, but they are spread over areas that are less dense and diverse. Indeed, for many Americans, religious diversity is not something that they encounter very often or think much about—it is not really even on the radar. You can drive across the country through vast stretches of rural areas where the local population has been fairly homogeneous for a very long time. Yet there are signs everywhere that new immigrant communities and their religious institutions are taking root where one would least expect to find change—in Lincoln, Nebraska, and Postville, Iowa, for instance.[59]

If the historian Arthur M. Schlesinger was right about the importance of the city in American history—that the experiences and problems of American society are those of an urban society—then we stand to learn a lot from Flushing.[60] As I discuss at the end of Chapter 5, New York City is different from many other areas in the United States, but there is a saying that whatever happens in New York happens everywhere else ten years later. Flushing is an extreme case, but other cities, towns, and neighborhoods all across the country are becoming more diverse too, and each will have to learn to live with pluralism. They may not look exactly like Flushing, but many of the same issues will arise over time. Finally, Flushing's story is also relevant to other democratic societies where a similar openness to religious freedom and immigration exists. Indeed, the great importance of Flushing may be its example to the rest of the country and the world—an update on how the "lively experiment" of religious freedom, immigration, and pluralism in America is going.[61]

Research Methodology

Although this is primarily a book that deals with twentieth-century American history (and especially the post–World War II period), the scope of the book encompasses the history of Flushing from the colonial period to the present. Such a wide span of time would be difficult to cover with a larger area, but Flushing is small enough to make a fairly comprehensive case study of the community possible. I also narrowed my field of vision by focusing mainly on the history of immigration, religion, and ethnic relations in Flushing.

For all of the history up until World War II, I relied on the numerous archives and libraries in the city that I mention in the Acknowledgments, but the more recent history could only be told by a combination of archival research, oral history, and ethnography. The historian Ronald J. Grele has said, "It's a very odd thing for an historian to be called upon to analyze and interpret sources they have created." As with other works on twentieth-century history that involve living people who can share their perspective on the past (especially when little or no other documentary source material exists, as is often the case with recent immigrants), my research for the portion of the book that deals with the last fifty years relied heavily on oral history interviews that I conducted in addition to various archival sources.[62] A synthesis of archival sources and material drawn from an inclusive and balanced set of oral history recordings also fits well with recent trends in the "new cultural history" and narrative theory that stresses replacing the omniscient narrator and a unified point of view with multiple voices and perspectives.[63] Such considerations serve as a reminder of how important it is to be mindful of power and representation when choosing informants because, as the anthropologist and historian Michel-Rolph Trouillot reminds us, "Something is always left out while something else is recorded."[64] Without attempting to do systematic survey work, I consciously tried to talk to a real cross section of everyone in the community to gather information (fieldnotes) and general impressions, and occasionally this led to asking someone if they would sit down for an oral history interview. Such persons were chosen for a mix of reasons (race/ethnicity, religion, class, gender, age) but mainly because they seemed to be an interesting or good spokesperson/representative for a group—not necessarily a leader (although some were), but someone whose story somehow represented elements of the larger group story. Historians who do oral history also have to be careful not to be deluded into thinking that a person's world can be made coherent when it is really more incoherent and fragmentary—what the sociologist Pierre Bourdieu called the "synoptic illusion."[65] Because of such potential dangers, and following the ethnographic style of some classic works in urban sociology that I admire, the largely historical narrative is interspersed with numerous block quotations in the text from both oral histories and much older historical documents that may not be familiar or readily accessible to most readers. Typically, such quotations are shortened and/or paraphrased by historians, but I wanted there to be a more complete record that captured people in their own words as a lasting document that could be reinterpreted if needed. The raw material of all ethnographies should be as accurately and fully presented as possible so that someone else can take it, study it, and even see something else in it that I did not. I did not do any formal survey work for this study (though I do refer to one in Chapter 3 that was conducted in Flushing in 1962), as I prefer to let people talk openly and at length to understand the complexity of their life and deep beliefs rather than try to measure them with a questionnaire.[66]

As it is a mix of religious history, immigration history, urban history, and social and cultural history, this book is similar to the kind of study Robert A. Orsi did in *The Madonna of 115th Street*, which was a history and ethnography of Italian Harlem that explored urban popular religion.[67] Orsi's work came out during a time when a number of other historians of religion, such as Rhys Isaac and Natalie Zemon Davis, began incorporating ideas from cultural anthropologists like Victor Turner and Clifford Geertz.[68] Orsi was influenced in particular by Emmanuel Le Roy Ladurie's *Montaillou*, a classic text of the French *Annales* school of cultural history that sought to uncover a history of *mentalités*, or the mental and moral world, of a small French village.[69] Borrowing Ladurie's focus on microhistory and his concept of the *domus,* a word used to describe the family and home and taken to be the "chief unit of social relationships and cultural transmission," Orsi applied the concept to the families and apartments of Italian Harlem to explore the annual religious street celebration, or *festa,* in honor of la Madonna del Carmine.[70] Like Orsi, I was interested in exploring popular religion and the mental and moral world of an urban neighborhood, and I sought to understand what Flushing's heritage of religious freedom and tolerance meant to different residents in the community. The only difference is that Orsi relied on a large number of transcribed interviews recorded in the late 1920s and 1930s "to ask the people themselves about their values and perceptions," whereas I have used recordings I made myself.[71] The time period is different, but the type of primary source material is the same. In my attempt to study this aspect of a community's mental and moral world, I found the sociologist David Hummon's idea of a "community ideology" helpful (see Chapter 2) as a way of tracing a local tradition: its origins, retelling(s), the invention and practice of its celebratory public rituals, and its reception among new immigrants in modern Flushing.[72] I was also interested in exploring how people interact in a diverse community, and in this way I share an interest with cultural historians like Roger Chartier, who stresses the analysis of cultural practices.[73]

Although I had spent five summers in Flushing since beginning work for the Pluralism Project, I moved to Flushing in 1999 and lived there full time for over two years.[74] My decision to live in Flushing not only made my local archival research and oral history interviews easier: it also allowed me to do ethnographic fieldwork and helped me gain a fuller sense and feel for the details, rhythms, and everyday life in the community. While I am primarily a historian, I wanted to use my training in ethnography to help with the more recent history of Flushing. I immersed myself in Flushing and eventually knew every part of every street at every time of day and night. I engaged in participant observation by visiting and attending worship services and other functions at nearly every place of worship in Flushing over a ten-year period starting in 1994.[75] I took fieldnotes and kept a field journal throughout the course of research. I also took hundreds of pictures (slides) and compiled a database of every place of worship in Flushing. My weekends were busy research times, starting on Friday around lunch with *Jumu'ah* services at local mosques, followed by *Shabbat* services in the evening and Saturday at local synagogues, and then continuing on Sunday with a variety of services at churches as well as Hindu and Buddhist temples and Sikh gurdwaras. I read all the local papers, dined in most of the many local restaurants, had coffee at bodegas or Korean cafes and "bubble tea" at Chinese teahouses more than I frequented the local Starbucks, went to the gym at the local YMCA, rode my bicycle all over town, and attended block parties, street festivals and parades, and local meetings of civic associations, Community Board 7, historical societies, interfaith coalitions, multicultural events, and library and town hall events.

Social scientists, especially those who do ethnographic research, also strive to be self-reflexive in the elusive quest for objectivity. As the sociologist Elijah Anderson has noted,

A further aim of the ethnographer's work is that it be as objective as possible. This is not easy or simple, since it requires researchers to try to set aside their own values and assumptions about what is and is not morally acceptable—in other words, to jettison the prism through which they typically view a given situation. By definition one's own assumptions are so basic to one's perceptions that seeing their influence may be difficult, if not impossible. Ethnographic researchers, however, have been trained to look for and to recognize underlying assumptions, their own and those of their subjects, and to try and override the former and uncover the latter.[76]

I suppose I did feel like an outsider at first, and I know others at times viewed me as the researcher studying them under a microscope and writing a book. Visiting a religious center outside of one's tradition during worship has the potential to be intrusive or disruptive, but I typically contacted each place of worship before I visited and was made to feel welcome. I also often reread texts about each religious tradition before going, so I could be aware and respectful of particular customs.[77] Finally, as I conducted my research and started writing, I tried to reflect on my own background and beliefs while also trying to remain a detached observer—a tricky task that Robert Orsi also has described:

> Our lives and our stories are not simply implicated in our work; they are among the media through which we scholars of religion encounter and engage the religious worlds of others. . . . The challenge is to balance carefully and self-reflectively on the border between familiarity and difference, strangeness and recognizability, whether in relation to people in the past or in another cultural world.[78]

In visiting over a hundred places of worship and meeting and recording interviews with such a wide range of people from different religious traditions, I was reminded constantly of the simple fact that people with beliefs very different from my own all naturally felt that their religion was true. Whether I was listening to someone talk about Ganesha, the Guru Granth Sahib, the Gospel of John, God or gods, each spoke matter of factly as I nodded and took notes.

The Structure of the Book

Part I traces the early history of Flushing from the colonial period to the mid–twentieth century and consists of two chapters. Chapter 1 begins in 1945 at Bowne House, for the 300th anniversary, or tercentenary, of the founding of Flushing, when Bowne House was dedicated as "A National Shrine to Religious Freedom" and the town's heritage of religious freedom and tolerance was resurrected amid celebration of the end of World War II. This moment is then used to flash back to 1645 and connect the tercentenary in 1945 to the colonial context and founding of Flushing, or Vlissingen, as it was known originally in Dutch New Netherland. I focus on two key events in Flushing's colonial history that were still recounted by early historians of New York, Long Island, and Flushing in the nineteenth century, events that would be resurrected again in 1945 and 1957, respectively: the Flushing Remonstrance of 1657 and John Bowne's arrest, exile, and defense in 1662 of the town charter of 1645. The rest of the chapter (and book) traces the history of religious, racial, and ethnic pluralism in Flushing and follows this to the end of the nineteenth century and the consolidation of Queens with New York City in 1898, setting moments of change and transition, growing diversity and contestation against the memory of Flushing's founding: from Baptist and Quaker rejection of the Dutch Reformed Church, from Dutch to English rule and Quaker opposition to the established Anglican Church, from colony to independence to African Methodist Episcopalians asserting themselves against mainstream white Anglo-Protestantism, from Catholic intrusion into a Protestant world to eventual Irish political dominance, from liberal Protestant support for the Union and the abolition of slavery in the Civil War to segregation. Chapter 2 explores the growth of Flushing in the early to mid–twentieth century, the development of a community ideology of religious freedom and toleration that was born in the years around World War II and matured during the Cold War and civil rights movement at the same time that it was being fed by an emerging Judeo-Christian national identity and ecumenical spirit between Protestants, Catholics, and Jews that was on display when Flushing hosted the World's Fairs of 1939–1940 and 1964–1965. Amid these celebratory moments, Chapter 2 also traces a story of great change, struggle, and fault lines that expose deeper and growing tensions of pluralism in the community: Flushing's connection in 1928 to the New York subway system and the consequent population and real estate growth that transformed the small town and village; Jewish intrusion and eventual inclusion into a Christian world; city planning, zoning, and racism in downtown Flushing; and issues of religious and racial exclusion at the two World's Fairs.

Part II focuses on the history of immigration, religion, and ethnic relations in Flushing from 1965 to 2000 and its transformation from a primarily white and black Judeo-Christian community into a multiracial microcosm of world religions. To set the scene for what will happen in Flushing over the next thirty-five years, Chapter 3 turns from the second World's Fair to the historical context of 1965's watershed immigration legislation, the early history of Flushing's new immigrant communities and religions, why they chose to settle in Flushing, the construction of places of worship and transnational ties to religion in the home country, as well as issues specific to each group. The major immigrant communities in Flushing are based on nationality and further broken up into the religion(s) represented by each group, and the story (which relies heavily on oral history) continues to the end of the twentieth century. Chapter 4 explores the particular issues raised in the community by a radically and rapidly changing religious, racial, and ethnic landscape during this period, focusing mostly on the 1980s and 1990s and what set of factors contributed to this transformation. It chronicles both a clash of cultures in the community as well as the coming together of various groups trying to work positively with diversity in different ways, and it reveals how the community ideology of religious freedom and toleration so celebrated in the 1940s and 1950s would be tested to the breaking point as places of worship proliferated into a dense microcosm of world religions by 2000. Focusing on the levels and contexts of interaction between groups in modern Flushing, the narrative shifts into a more ethnographic mode and a more theoretical analysis of pluralism in Flushing. Referring back to the examples of each group in the history of Flushing that make up the bulk of the preceding chapters, I chart the range of different responses to religious diversity in Flushing and explore the possibilities and limits of religious pluralism. Finally, in the last chapter, I discuss the period since September 11, 2001; the reverberations of that day in a community with the largest Afghan population in the city; the work of interfaith groups, local politics, and the rise of Asian Americans as the dominant group in Flushing since the U.S. Census of 2000; fragmentation and regeneration of community; the rebirth of Flushing's community ideology of religious freedom and toleration in a microcosm of world religions; and children and the future of Flushing. I also discuss Flushing and New York City's relationship to other American cities, and I pose further questions about what it means to live with pluralism in Flushing and America today.

Part I

1

Religion in Vlissingen (Flushing) from 1645 to 1945

Consecrating a "National Shrine to Religious Freedom": Bowne House and the Tercentenary of Flushing in 1945

It had been five months since Hitler committed suicide, Germany surrendered, and the horror of the Holocaust ended, and it had been only two months since "Little Boy" and "Fat Man" obliterated the cities of Hiroshima and Nagasaki in Japan and introduced the world to the devastating power of nuclear energy in the atomic bomb. As peace washed over a bloodstained earth and America and the other Allied Powers celebrated the end of World War II, it finally was time to go home and return to more local affairs and ordinary life.

In a small town in New York City, residents of Flushing, Queens, were already immersed in preparations for another occasion to celebrate. October 10, 1945, marked the tercentenary of the founding of Flushing in 1645 and, with that, the "birthplace of religious freedom in America," as many residents still like to claim. Months before the end of the war, members of the Tercentenary Planning Committee knew they might be able to tap into lingering patriotic sentiment and attract interest at many levels by highlighting religious freedom as a timely and important theme. Hon. Charles S. Colden, the chairman and former New York State Supreme Court justice, was a lifelong area resident with a famous last name and powerful connections in the city, and he made a strong case for the event: "The committee feels that Flushing has contributed something of particular significance to the national life, especially at this time when religious freedom is one of the main points of the Atlantic Charter."[1] Colden took it even further by stressing another celebrated theme in the town's history, that of tolerance: "Flushing, by official records, is the first spot in the world where men risked imprisonment and loss of official positions in an attempt to gain the right of religious freedom, not for themselves, but for others. In planning this celebration, we are following that idea of tolerance and seeking to have persons of all races, creeds, colors, social and economic backgrounds to take a part."[2] The committee also was able to tap into the popularity, recent euphoria, and optimism of the 1939–1940 World's Fair in nearby Flushing Meadows–Corona Park right before the war. Scholars of American and European religious history would quibble with Colden's claims and argue that Flushing was *one* of the first spots in colonial America where men took on this risk and that others did so earlier in sixteenth-century Europe, but the attempt to look for fundamental American principles in local and community history during and immediately after the Allies' struggle against Nazi Germany in World War II is not surprising—indeed, the celebration of this history would develop into a kind of community ideology by the 1950s (see Chapter 2) that is still invoked today.

The program of events for the Tercentenary Celebration spanned an entire week: October 7–14, 1945, at various locations throughout greater Flushing. The spotlight was on Bowne House, a Dutch-English salt-box house built by John Bowne in 1661, the oldest house in Queens. The festivities began on October 7, with a live radio broadcast on WNYC from the living room of the house by Mayor Fiorello H. La Guardia, who chose the occasion for his regular Sunday broadcast. Part history lesson, part ceremony, La Guardia's speech traced the colonial history of Flushing and set the tone for the festivities: "This is to be a shrine. It belongs to our city because it made so much history here of endurance and fortitude. It belongs to our country because it is typical of America and it belongs to the world because it is a symbol of what the world is looking for today."[3] Addressing religious persecution and the history of legislation involving religious freedom in the colony, he added: "We went through some bad times, and sometimes there have been recurrences of intolerance, but they are isolated."[4] And, lending the moment real significance, La Guardia announced that he had been conferring with Park Commissioner Robert Moses and Queens Borough President James A. Burke about a city plan to buy the house and adjoining property to be developed as a shrine and park. With live chamber music in the background, he recited an old Dutch hymn, "The Prayer of Thanksgiving," and later read passages from

Judge Charles S. Colden, Mayor Fiorello H. La Guardia, and Queens Borough President James A. Burke inside Bowne House for the mayor's regular Sunday broadcast on WNYC to open Tercentenary Week in Flushing, October 7, 1945. Collection of the Queens Historical Society.

"The United Nations Fight for the Four Freedoms" (published in 1942 by the Office of War Information), concluding his broadcast with two quotations from the Bible: "In my Father's house are many mansions" and "Love thy neighbor as thyself." More radio attention would follow, as two national radio networks, WOR and WJZ, carried the ceremonies across the airwaves of the country, and the Army News Service also incorporated events into its broadcast to servicemen and women overseas.[5]

While Protestant and Catholic churches and Jewish synagogues in greater Flushing all held special services throughout the week, and other highlights included a tour of historic spots, lectures, a "historical pageant" (a play), antique shows, and even a window display at Abramson's department store, the focal event took place on October 10, again at Bowne House. The *New York Times* reported that "under towering oaks and elms shading tranquil Bowne Street, a thousand residents of Flushing, Queens," gathered outside the festooned house "with leaders of every faith" for a two-hour ceremony. In New York circa 1945, "every faith" meant Christianity and Judaism, but a historic tree on Bowne Street was dedicated to each member of the United Nations for the occasion, and Bowne Street was temporarily called "Avenue of the Allies." Bowne House was then dedicated as a "national shrine to religious freedom" by Senator James M. Mead, who addressed the crowd and emphasized that "Charters of liberty alone cannot insure the freedoms so essential to man's well-being and happiness. There must be a militant John Bowne in each generation to be ever watchful that the written words of the charters be held sacred." Mead went on to state that "as the strongest nation on earth, we must use our strength to banish war and thus make possible international liberty of conscience."[6] And, in a fitting gesture, a scroll was presented to Dr. Jacobus G. deBeus, consul of the Netherlands' embassy, from the citizens of "Flushing, U.S.A.," to those of "Flushing in Zeeland." After nine generations of Bowne descendants had lived there, Colden (as president of Bowne House Historical Society) announced plans to open the house as a public museum.

Building on the progressive momentum of optimism, many attended a town meeting the next day on "Going Forward Against Race Prejudice Today" that grew out of discussions about the United Nations and a lasting peace and called for community and government participation in combating intolerance.[7] And on October 12, twenty-five thousand lined the streets of downtown Flushing to watch a parade of three thousand marchers, with a colorful array of every conceivable representative group from Flushing—the first postwar parade in the community.[8] Finally, the hot ticket in town at the end of the week was for the costume ball at the Flushing Armory. The pervasive communal sense of history and place at the time was obvious to all outside visitors, as the *New York Times* observed that "Flushing, which though legally assimilated as part of the Borough of Queens, City of New York, in 1898, has steadfastly maintained its identity."[9] In another story, the *Times* placed the tercentenary in historical context: "The John Bowne House in Flushing, built in 1661, dedicated this week as a historical museum, recalls a time when religious liberty was not taken for granted in the New World."[10]

At the end of World War II, the United States celebrated victory by touting American ideals of democracy, religious freedom, and tolerance that recalled the nation's founding principles and commitment to a pluralistic society. In Flushing, such soul searching prompted some to look back even further, since the end of the war happened to coincide with the founding of Flushing in 1645. Residents of Flushing had reason to remember and highlight their town's history, which started with the earliest defense of religious freedom and tolerance in colonial America. In the years following World War II, a variety of local civic, religious, and political leaders in New York City revived this story as a timely message to the world in the wake of Nazi anti-Semitism, but Flushing and its legacy of tolerance itself was tested in the centuries following its founding in 1645 as the small town grew increasingly more pluralistic with many new religious groups by the end of the nineteenth century.

"Liberty of Conscience"

Over 300 years before Flushing's tercentenary celebration, the words "New Amsterdam" were first enunciated in a charter drawn up by Dutch traders with Algonquin tribes on October 11, 1614. Shortly thereafter, *Sewanhacky*, or the "Land of Shells," became more widely known as *Lange Eylandt* (Long Island) on Adrian Block's map of 1616. And, on January 15, 1639, Director-General (Governor) of New Amsterdam Willem Kieft secured a title from the local native Americans to what is now Queens County. The land was sold "for, and in consideration of, a party of merchandise, which they acknowledge to have received into their hands and power, to their full satisfaction and content." The chief sachem reserved the right, "with his people and friends, to remain upon the aforesaid land, plant corn, fish, hunt, and make a living there as well as they can, while he himself and his people place themselves under the protection of the said Lords."[11] Ethnic relations deteriorated quickly, however, when war with the Indians on Manahatta (Manhattan) erupted in the early 1640s and soon spread to Long Island. Peace was restored in the spring of 1645, and a Day of Thanksgiving was proclaimed on September 6, again encouraging new settlements in the colony: Matinecoc Indians sold land to the Dutch West India Company (DWIC) at the rate of fifty acres an axe to create an attractive parcel of land for sale to prospective settlers. Early land surveyors noted the area's good location on the terminal moraine ridge that runs the length of Long Island, and they no doubt had visions of its development: it would later be the key node for roads, railroads, highways, and the county seat—making it a transportation and governmental nexus of Queens.[12]

When fifteen Englishmen applied to Governor Kieft for the privilege of settling in the Matinecoc's former land in 1645, the charter they were granted on October 10 to establish a town was one of the most liberal arrangements for any settlement in colonial America by or on behalf of

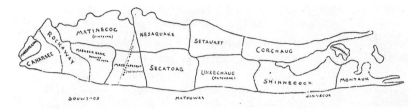

Map of Algonquin tribes on *Sewan-hacky* (Land of Shells), early seventeenth century, in Eugene L. Armbruster, *Long Island: Its Early Days and Development with Illustrations and Maps* (Brooklyn, 1914). Queens Borough Public Library, Flushing Branch.

any government. The patent granted seemed to offer almost complete religious freedom: "We do give and grant, unto the said Patentees . . . to have and Enjoy the Liberty of Conscience, according to the Custome and manner of Holland, without molestacon or disturbance, from any Magistrate or Magistrates, or any other Ecclesiasticall Minister, that may extend Jurisdicon over them."[13] The patentees were English planters who had migrated to Massachusetts and then back to Holland to escape persecution, and they named their new town Vlissingen after the Dutch town where they had found shelter.[14] One nineteenth-century chronicler described the first settlers as "freethinkers, who, being impatient of religious restraint in Massachusetts, sought a larger liberty under the Dutch."[15] The Dutch concept of "liberty of conscience" was familiar in the colonial world around this time and was used to entice prospective settlers seeking refuge from religious persecution at home, but its exact meaning was more ambiguous than is commonly supposed. The *Oxford English Dictionary* definitions for the mid–seventeenth century were "inward knowledge or consciousness; internal conviction," but these were obsolete by the end of the nineteenth century. As Evan Haefeli states in his book *New Netherland and the Dutch Origins of American Religious Liberty*, the Dutch words *gewetensvrijheid* or *geloofsvrijheid* meant liberty of conscience or freedom of belief, but what kind of tolerance this allowed and did not allow is complicated because of "Dutch unwillingness or inability to go into much detail about what liberty of conscience was and why they permitted it."[16] Holland's "Custome and manner" regarding religion was the most lenient attitude of all European nations then, but Flushing's charter did not extend to the rest of the colony, and residents of Flushing would learn that the liberty of conscience promised in their charter was a loosely defined concept and, according to the Dutch historian Maarten

Prak, "varied from place to place."[17] Haefeli adds: "In the eyes of Dutch authorities and Dutch law, there was a crucial and self-evident difference between an individual's liberty to believe and a group's freedom to worship."[18] The Dutch Reformed church was the official state religion, and the government had the power to forbid "assemblies or conventicles" of other faiths, which included, as the historian Jeremy Bangs explains,

> a series of restrictions on vital aspects of religious life: "no preaching, no prayer meetings, no group discussions of theology, no public marriage ceremonies (except civil marriages before magistrates in remote regions where no Reformed clergy could be found), no non-Reformed baptisms or burial ceremonies, no communion outside the Reformed Church." Inhabitants could "disagree with the Dutch Reformed, but only if they kept silence about it outside their own homes, and only if their beliefs led to no visible actions in society." Though non-Dutch Reformed people could live there, "the reality in New Netherland was scarcely freedom of religion."[19]

Governor Kieft, however, did little to enforce these limitations during his incumbency, and the presence of a diverse population speaking eighteen languages gave rise to a variety of religious groups. The laxity of the law illustrates what Haefeli refers to as

> the potent plasticity of Dutch tolerance, which lay precisely in the disagreement over what it was. The willingness of individuals to push at its borders . . . was as much a part of Dutch tolerance as any official interpretation of liberty of conscience. The enforcement of liberty of conscience varied across the Dutch world, both raising and crushing hopes of tolerance depending on the local circumstances.[20]

In 1647, when Petrus (Peter) Stuyvesant became director general, the liberty that had been enjoyed by many was jeopardized. Stuyvesant was a strict Calvinist and, in 1652, under pressure from churchmen in Holland and in the colony, he began persecuting certain groups who arrived in the colony, including Jews and Lutherans. The Dutch West India Company rebuked Stuyvesant for his treatment of the Lutherans and also wrote to him: "Jews and Portuguese people may exercise in all quietness their religion within their houses."[21] When several boisterous "Quakers" arrived by ship in August 1657, he thus quickly jailed them and issued a proclamation on placards throughout the colony banning all public worship except that of the Dutch Reformed.

The freethinking founding fathers of Flushing (and their families) were visited by several different denominational representatives before being won over by the "Friends of Truth" (later the Religious Society of Friends, and "Quakers" only in scorn). There was no settled pastor to the people of Flushing for two years, but in 1647 Stuyvesant sent Rev. Francis Doughty, a Presbyterian who had conformed to the Dutch Reformed Church, who had himself been expelled from the Massachusetts Bay Colony in 1642 for heretical doctrine (he later moved to Rhode Island and then Long Island).[22] Doughty lasted about a year before Capt. John Underhill, the town schout (sheriff), made him leave without pay, "on the ground that the governor had inveigled the town into calling a minister by taking the towns-people into a private room one after another, and threatening them with his resentment if they did not sign the articles for the maintenance of the minister."[23] Incidentally, Underhill had migrated to Massachusetts with John Winthrop in 1630 and became the captain and instructor of the military force of the colony. He was later banished for associating with the heretical Anne Hutchinson, was governor of Dover in New Hampshire, later moving to Stamford, Connecticut, and settling in Flushing by 1648.[24]

On their own again for the next ten years, their next visitor was a Baptist preacher from Providence, Rhode Island, named William Wickenden (alt. Wickendam), after whom a street is named in Providence, near Brown University, where he had a farm. A close friend of Roger Williams (the two had both fled from Massachusetts to found Providence), Wickenden was a signer of the Providence civil compact of 1637 and the Providence agreement for a government in 1640, and he was very active in the religious and political life of the city. Upon his visit to Flushing in 1656, Wickenden apparently made a better impression than Doughty had, and he drew a large crowd to Flushing Creek for baptism. His days were numbered also, however, as the Dutch ministers Rev. John Megapolensis and Rev. Samuel Drisius disapproved of him and filed this report:

> At Flushing, they have heretofore had a Presbyterian preacher who conformed to our church; but many people became endowed with divrs opinions, and it was with them *quot homines, tot sententioe* [every man had a creed of his own]. They absented themselves from preaching, nor would they pay the preacher his promised stipend. So he was obliged to leave and repair to the English Virginias. Now (Aug 5th 1657) they have been some years without a minister. Last year a fomenter of error came there. He was a cobbler from Rhode

Island, and stated that he was commissioned by Christ. He began
to preach at Flushing, and then went with the people into the river
and dipped them. This becoming known in New Amsterdam, the
public prosecutor proceded thither and brought him along. He was
banished from the Province.

Wickenden hereby was charged "for officiating as a gospel minister at
Flushing, w/o authority . . . fined 100 pounds, Flemish, and banished from
the Province, meanwhile to be imprisoned." Returning to Providence,
Wickenden later served as a minister at First Baptist Church. Flushing's
second town sheriff, William Hallett, was also removed from office and
fined fifty pounds "for daring to collect conventicles at his house and
permitting Wickenden to explain and comment on God's Holy Word,
and to administer sacraments."[25]

These were mild punishments compared to what the Quakers would
face after their arrival in 1657, when several first visited and held meetings on Long Island in Gravesend, Jamaica, and Hempstead. Disparagingly
called "Quakers" because the preachers were seen as boisterous and bold,
making their listeners "quake with the fear of God," the Friends had few
friends among the Dutch establishment. Stuyvesant issued an ordinance
forbidding the harboring of Quakers and arrested Robert Hodgson, who
was dragged to jail behind a cart and brutally tortured in a dungeon until
Stuyvesant's sister intervened.

Some in Flushing had attended the nearby Quaker meetings and had
already become converts by 1657, but they were now forced to meet
"secretly in the woods on the bounds of Jamaica, Newtown, and Flushing."[26] Their plight became a town cause. Two days after Christmas in
1657, thirty freeholders of different faiths who were gathered "from the
general votes of the inhabitants" banded together (including the town
clerk and sheriff) to sign what came to be known as the Flushing Remonstrance and to remind Stuyvesant of the conditions in their patent
and town charter.[27]

Remonstrance

OF THE INHABITANTS OF THE TOWNE OF FLUSHING
TO GOVERNOR PETER STUYVESANT

Right Honorable,
    You have been pleased to send up unto us a certain Prohibition
or Command, that wee shoulde not receive or entertaine any of

those people called Quakers, because they are supposed to bee by some seducers of the people; for our parte wee cannot condem them in this case, neither can wee stretch out our hands against them, to punish, bannish or persecute them, for out of Christ, God is a consuming fire, and it is a fearful thing to fall into the handes of the liveing God; we desire therefore in this case not to judge least wee be judged, neither to Condem least wee be Condemned, but rather let every man stand and fall to his own. Maister wee are bounde by the Law to doe good unto all men, especially to those of the Household of faith; and though for the present wee seeme to bee unsensible of the law and the Lawgiver; yet when death and the Law assault us: if we have not our advocate to seeke, who shall plead for us in this case of Conscience betwixt God and our own soules; the powers of this world can neither attack us neither excuse us, for if God justify who can Condemn, and if God Condem there is none can justifye; and for those Jealowsies and suspitions which some have of them that they are destructive unto Magistracy and Ministry that cannot bee; for the Magistrate hath the Sword in his hand and the Minster hath the sword in his hand as witnesse those two great examples which all Magistrates and Ministers are to follow Moses and Christ; whom God raised up Maintained and defended against all the Enemies both of flesh and spirit, and therefore that wich is of God will stand, and that which is of man will come to noething: and as the Lord hath taught Moses, or the Civill power, to give an outward libertie in the States by the law written in his heart designed for the good of all and can truly judge who is good and who is evill, who is true and who is false, and can pass definitive sentence of life or death against that man which rises up against the fundamental law of the States Generall, soe he hath made his Ministers a savor of life unto life, and a savor of death unto death.

The law of love, peace and libertie in the states [of Holland] extending to Jews, Turks, and Egyptians, as they are considered the sonnes of Adam, which is the glory of the outward state of Holland; soe love, peace and libertie, extending to all in Christ Jesus, Condems hatred, warre and bondage; and because our Savior saith it is impossible but that offence will come, but woe be unto him by whom they Commeth, our desire is not to offend one of his little ones, in whatsoever forme, name or title hee appears in, whether Presbyterian, Independent, Baptist or Quaker; but shall be glad to see anything of God in any of them; desireing to doe unto all men as wee desire all men should doe unto us, which is the true law both of Church and State; for our Saviour saith this is the Law and the Prophets; Therefore if any of these said persons come in love unto us, wee cannot in Conscience lay violent hands upon them, but give them free Egresse and Regresse into our Towne and howses as God shall perswade our Consciences; and in this we are true subjects both of Church and State; for wee are bounde by the law of God and man to doe good unto all men, and evill to noe man; and this is according to the Pattent and Charter of our Towne given unto us in the name of the States Generall which we are not willing to infringe and violate, but shall hold to our pattent and shall remaine your Humble Subjects the inhabitants of Vlishing; written the 27th of December in the Yeare 1657 by mee

Edward Hart, Clericus.

[signed by thirty freeholders]

What is most remarkable is that none of the signers were Quakers themselves, yet they clearly believed in the fundamental goodness of other religious people and in extending "the law of love, peace and libertie in the states [of Holland]" to the Quakers seeking refuge in Flushing—in addition to anyone else, including Presbyterians, Independents, and Baptists, as well as "Jews, Turks, and Egyptians." By appealing to the laws of Holland in the Remonstrance and in their town charter, the signers were referring to the Dutch policy of liberty of conscience in Article 13 of the 1579 Union of Utrecht, which specifically states, "each person shall remain free, especially in his religion, and that no one shall be persecuted or investigated because of their religion." The Dutch West India Company had been set up in 1621 with orders that the Reformed Church would be the only public church in the company's colonies, in the belief that religious conformity would help create cohesive communities, but in 1625 they were instructed to follow the laws of Holland and thus permit liberty of conscience (allowing people to practice their religion at home).[28] Stuyvesant chose, however, to follow and enforce a stricter interpretation of the law. The Flushing Remonstrance did not move him in the least, and he jailed, fined, and removed from office those signers whom he suspected as leaders.[29]

A few years later, in 1661, John Bowne began to welcome Friends to meet in his newly built house every Sunday, or "first day." Bowne was a merchant and farmer from Matlock, in Derbyshire, England, who had

View of Bowne House, 1825. Lithograph from the I. N. Phelps Stokes Collection, Miriam and Ira D. Wallach Division of Art, Prints and Photographs, The New York Public Library.

migrated first to Boston in 1651 with his father. Dissatisfied with the Puritans and the Massachusetts Bay Colony, he became a Friend in 1657 after moving to Flushing and marrying Hannah Feake, who had herself been converted during the Friends' recent wave of evangelism in New Amsterdam.[30]

Magistrates in Jamaica soon learned of the meetings, and a schout came on July 1 to arrest Bowne and take him to jail. When Stuyvesant was unable to get Bowne to pay a fine and agree to refrain from holding meetings, he banished him from the colony, sending the following letter to his superiors in Amsterdam:

> Honorable, right respectable Gentlemen,
>   We omitted in our general letter the troubles and difficulties which we and many of our good inhabitants have since sometimes met with and which daily are renewed by the sect called Quakers chiefly in the country and principally in the English villages, establishing forbidden conventicles and frequenting those against our published placards and disturbing in this manner the public peace,

in so far that several of our magistrates of our affectionate subjects remonstrated and complained to us from time to time of their insufferable obstinacy, unwilling to obey our orders on judgments—

Among others has one of their principal leaders, named John Bowne, who for his transgrefsions was in conformity to the placards condemned in an amount of 150 [guilders]—in who has now been under arrest for more than three months for his unwillingnefs to pay, obstinately persisting in his refusal, in which he still continues, so that we at last resolved, or were rather compelled, to transport him in this ship from this Province in the hope that others might by it be discouraged.

If henceforth by these means, no more salutary imprefsion is made upon others, we shall though against our inclinations be compelled to prosecute such persons in a more severe manner, on which we previously solicit to be favored with your Honor's wise Overseeing Judgment.

With which after our cordial salutations, we remain and your Honour's to God's protection and remain Honourable and right respectable Gentlemen.

Your Honour's faithful Servants
Fort Amsterdam in New Netherlands
9th January 1663[31]

This was not Stuyvesant's first complaint to the Dutch West India Company. Because New Amsterdam was surrounded by other colonies that had fought to maintain homogeneity (except Rhode Island, which he regarded with particular disgust), Stuyvesant did not grasp that the different direction his colony was headed would actually prove better. He wrote in 1661 that

the *English* and *French* colonies are continued and populated by their own nation and countrymen and consequently bound together more firmly and united, while your Honor's colonies in New-Netherland are only gradually and slowly peopled by the scrapings of all sorts of nationalities (few excepted), who consequently have the least interest in the welfare and maintenance of the commonwealth.

As the historian Michael Kammen has observed, "Stuyvesant did not simply fear pluralism per se; he feared the attendant instabilities and lack of cohesion that seemed socially impolitic as well as uncongenial to the creation of political society."[32] His plans, of course, backfired. Bowne made his way to

Amsterdam and eventually pleaded his own case to the Dutch West India
Company:

> I sead libertie was promised to us in a Patent given by virtew of a
> commission from the prince, the stats generall and the west indea
> companie: he sead who gave that patent? Governer Kieft—oh, sead
> he, that was before any or but few of your Judgment was harde of. I
> said we are known to be a peseable people. And will not be subject
> to the Laws and plakados [placards] which are published? we cannot
> sufer you in oure jurediction. I sead it is good first to consider
> whether that Law or plackerd, that was published, bee according to
> Justis and righteousnesse, or whether it bee not quite contrarie to it,
> and also to that libertie promised to us in oure Patent and I desier
> ye Company would red or heve it red. I have a copie of it by mee.[33]

Before he even arrived there, the Dutch West India Company had already
received Stuyvesant's letter and had grown concerned about his harsh
measures. As David Voorhees has noted, "in 1654 the States of Holland, the
supreme authority, also had rejected the appeals of the Dutch Reformed
Synod to impose doctrinal conformity as having 'very dangerous consequences.'"[34] They were persuaded by Bowne's appeal, let him return,
and also sent a letter to rebuke Stuyvesant for his intolerance of religious
dissent, effectively (albeit reluctantly) restoring liberty of conscience in
Flushing, if not the entire colony:

> Your last letter informed us that you had banished from the Province
> and sent hither a certain Quaker, John Bowne by name: although
> we heartily desire, that these and other sectarians remained away
> from there, yet as they do not, we doubt very much, whether we
> can proceed against them rigorously without diminishing the popu-
> lation and stopping immigration, which must be favored at a so
> tender stage of the country's existence. You may therefore shut your
> eyes, at least not force people's consciences, but allow every one to
> have his own belief, as long as he behaves quietly and legally, gives
> no offence to his neighbors and does not oppose the government.
> As the government of this city has always practised this maxim of
> moderation and consequently has often had a considerable influx
> of people, we do not doubt, that your Province too would be ben-
> efitted by it.[35]

Bowne left Holland on March 30, 1663—eventually making his way back
to his family on January 30, 1664.

John Bowne's journal and related papers, 1649–76, from Manuscript Coll.; neg #73123, New-York Historical Society.

Years before the religious controversies in Flushing, the Dutch West India Company had already learned that the town was an attractive, prosperous settlement worthy of support: one report to Amsterdam spoke of "Flushing, which is an handsome village, and tolerably stocked with cattle," and it was well known that the only tavern on Long Island was in Flushing (which was easily accessible through Flushing Bay and Flushing Creek).[36] The Dutch motto "difference makes for tolerance" derived from their understanding that growth and prosperity in a diverse area were best fostered by religious freedom, so they encouraged officials to employ *oogluiking* or *conniventie* (blinking and conniving) instead of imposing an established church order and crushing dissent.[37] As a result, "No other colony learned as rapidly as did New Amsterdam the lessons that circumstances imposed on their age."[38]

On August 27, 1664, the English wrested control of New Amsterdam from the Dutch and, as the colony's name changed to New York, Vlissingen Anglicized into Flushing.[39] In a letter to the new Governor Nichols, the Dutch strongly advised him not "to make any alteration in their Church Government or to introduce any other form of worshipp among them than what they have chosen."[40] As Evan Haefeli has stated:

> The result was a remarkable degree of continuity into a new colonial life no longer dominated by the Dutch, but still very influenced by what they had created. However, the English conquerors made one major change: they actively fostered the pluralism the Dutch regime had done all with its constitutional power to restrain by replacing the public church with an Erastian system in which the English governor mediated between *all* religious groups in the colony equally. No single group had privileged support as the Reformed had had under the West India Company rule.[41]

There were limits, however, for in 1665 Nichols called an assembly that created a new set of laws called the Duke's Laws, which "divided the English towns into parishes and allowed each to choose the sort of church it wanted by a majority vote of the householders" (as long as they were not Quakers, Baptists, or Catholics—the laws clearly favored Presbyterians, Lutherans, Dutch Reformed, Congregationalists, and Anglicans, and they also "discouraged proselytizing in the colony, a blow to the Quakers who were still spreading their faith").[42] Despite this, in 1666, Nichols confirmed the Flushing town patent, yet he grew frustrated when a number of men refused to serve in Flushing's militia because of the new Quaker "Peace Testimony" of pacifism, which was introduced in 1660 and had reached New York Quakers by 1667.[43]

In August 1672, George Fox (founder of the Friends in the 1640s and 1650s) rested at Bowne House after preaching outside under two oak trees to a crowd of several hundred.[44] Bowne and his wife joined Fox and William Penn on a preaching tour of Holland and Germany in 1676, and Bowne continued to welcome Friends to worship in his house for forty years. Elected as county treasurer in 1683 and in 1691 to the General Assembly, Bowne lived until he was sixty-eight. He died on October 20, 1695 (fifty years after the founding of Flushing), leaving a long line of descendants who would continue to be influential in Flushing and New York.

In October 1683, a representative assembly (with members from Flushing and other towns of the newly established Queens County) was established under the new governor Thomas Dongan, and the Charter of Liberties was drafted. One of its provisions stated that "no person or persons, which profess faith in God by Jesus Christ, shall at any time, be any ways molested . . . who do not actually disturb the civil peace of the province."[45] The Charter of Liberties effectively lasted until 1685, when King Charles II died and James II ascended the throne, revoking all charters of New York, New Jersey, and Massachusetts. Influenced by the philosopher John Locke and his "Letter Concerning Toleration," the pendulum swung back again when Parliament, under William III and Mary II, restored relative religious freedom with the Toleration Act of May 24, 1689—"An Act for Exempting their Majesties Protestant Subjects, Dissenting from the Church of England, from the Penalties of certain laws." The act permitted freedom of worship to Dissenters but excluded Roman Catholics (a policy that lasted until 1829 in England).

Nearly fifty years after Bowne's death, the implications of his defense of the town charter still seemed to reverberate in the colony: ministers of Anglican and Dutch churches in 1741 lamented the "spirit of confusion" resulting from New York's "perfect freedom of conscience."[46] The language of Flushing's town charter would also carry over into the state constitution. In postrevolutionary New York, representatives from the State of New York met on April 20, 1777, to ratify the new constitution, with Amendment XXXVIII reading:

> And whereas we are required, by the benevolent principles of rational liberty, not only to expel civil tyranny, but also to guard against that spiritual oppression and intolerance wherewith the bigotry and ambition of weak and wicked priests and princes have scourged mankind, this convention doth further, in the name and by the authority of the good people of this State, ordain, determine, and declare, that the free exercise and enjoyment of religious profession and worship, without discrimination or preference, shall forever hereafter be allowed, within this State, to all mankind: Provided, That the *liberty of conscience*, hereby granted, shall not be so construed as to excuse acts of licentiousness, or justify practices inconsistent with the peace or safety of this State.[47]

In 1791, the Congress of a new nation passed the First Amendment to the Constitution of the United States of America.

Residents of Flushing later would proudly claim it to be "the birthplace of religious freedom in America," and, to some extent, they would be right. In a very limited, local colonial context, Flushing does appear to be the first colonial town to have and defend liberty of conscience so explicitly and consistently—especially when the charter is taken together with the Flushing Remonstrance and Bowne's defense of both. There was, of course, no nation yet in Bowne's time, and the liberty of conscience in Flushing's charter did not extend to the rest of the colony, nor was it reinstated in Flushing until 1663, when Bowne was permitted to return. Despite this constellation of significance, Flushing is often clouded over in historical tugs of war over who was first and is thus largely overlooked in the history of religious freedom in America. In Rhode Island, for instance, similar claims are made on behalf of the Portsmouth Compact of March 7, 1638.[48] The town of Providence was founded by Roger Williams in the summer of 1636, and though a royal charter was obtained in 1644, "the lively experiment" and "full liberty in religious concernments" for which Rhode Island became so well known was not officially granted until a second revised Charter of Rhode Island and Providence Plantations was granted on July 15, 1663 (several months after Bowne's successful case to the Dutch West India Company that same year).[49] Maryland's charter of 1632, as well as "An Act Concerning Religion" in 1649 (better known as Maryland's Act of Toleration), favored Catholics. The Charter for the Province of Pennsylvania and William Penn's "holy experiment" also came later, in 1681. The Puritans in the Massachusetts Bay Colony (and Connecticut) lagged further behind: many "heretics" had already escaped to found or join other colonies (if they did not first suffer a fate similar to those in the Salem witch trials of the 1690s), and the colony did not grant full religious freedom until the state constitution of 1780. Thomas Jefferson, who apparently was moved by the persecution of the "poor Quakers" and had seen how the "sister states of Pennsylvania and New York . . . have long subsisted without any establishment at all," did not write his Statute of Virginia for Religious Freedom until 1777.[50] Although there is no evidence (to date) that the Flushing Remonstrance itself was later read by Jefferson or by James Madison (who is largely recognized as the principal author of the Constitution, First Amendment, and other amendments in the Bill of Rights), the evolution of liberty of conscience and sequence of events in New Amsterdam and New York does appear to have made an impression on the minds of the Founding Fathers.

Despite its significance, the Flushing Remonstrance, Bowne, and Flushing's history in general largely faded from memory (at least, outside of Flushing) until the nineteenth century, when some of the first comprehensive histories of New York were published (including some local histories of Flushing). Consequently, some church historians took note and began to include references to the Flushing Remonstrance and Bowne in their surveys of religion in America as early as 1898. Despite these occasional references, the dominant narratives of American history and religion at least until the late twentieth century stressed the primary importance and legacy of New England Puritanism and British colonial settlements along the North Atlantic coast in general. The history of Flushing shifts attention to the Middle Atlantic colony of Dutch New Netherland (New York after the British takeover in 1664) and its long experiment with pluralism that is still, perhaps more, relevant today—but this focus on the region's significance is recent.[51] The histories of New York and even the broader histories of religion in America did not reach a wide enough audience to make Flushing's history very well known. This would begin to change somewhat by the mid–twentieth century, however, when Flushing's sense of local history and civic pride would be at an all-time high.

The SPG Comes to Town: Quakers and Anglicans in Eighteenth-Century Flushing

A census compiled in 1698 by the town constable and clerk revealed that there were eighty families in Flushing (some households reported as many as twenty-one persons, including slaves): sixty-three English, twelve Dutch, five French (Huguenots), seventeen single freemen or white bachelors; there were in all 530 whites and 117 blacks. There were three hamlets of the town of Flushing then: Flushing (the hamlet and area that became the village of Flushing in 1837), Whitestone, and Bayside. Flushing was the largest settlement. Main Street was then known as Jamaica Road and was the chief land route to New York for persons unwilling to sail or row by boat through Hell Gate (taking the road was a day's journey of seventeen miles).[52]

At the end of his life, in 1694, Bowne and other Friends bought land to build a Meeting House on present-day Northern Boulevard. The first place of worship in Flushing, it is also the oldest place of worship in New York City in continual use. At the General Yearly meeting of Friends in Rhode Island in 1695, it was agreed that the new meeting house in Flushing would host the New York Yearly meeting—which it did until 1778, when the building was used as a hospital by British troops during the Revolutionary War.

Various records show that a guard house was used by numerous religious groups in Flushing well into the eighteenth century, but most residents in Flushing (excluding blacks, about whom little is known until later) were Quakers and came to the Meeting House. Church records and letters indicate its popularity (William Penn visited Flushing in 1700 and was the guest of John Bowne's son Samuel), and the congregation grew: in September 1703, an estimated two thousand attended the last day of Monthly Meeting (some also traveled to it from outside for Half-Yearly

Friends Meeting House (est. 1694), April 19, 1927. Queens Borough President print and photograph collection, Print Neg. No. 267-A, Courtesy New York City Municipal Archives.

Meeting, as Flushing's meeting house was for several years the only place of worship in Queens for miles). By 1719, the Meeting House had to build an addition.[53]

Although the colony enjoyed a greater liberty of conscience by the end of the seventeenth century, that did not mean there would not still be dissensus or conflict. Records document the "sufferings" of Friends under the Dutch but also, by 1700, under the Church of England's zealous missionary arm, the Society for the Propagation of the Gospel in Foreign Parts. St. George's Church of Royal Anglican Order was founded by the SPG as a mission of the Church of England in 1702, holding its first meetings in the guard house until a church was completed in 1746. The parish consisted of the three towns of Jamaica, Newtown, and Flushing and was one of the first missions of the Society. Perhaps the most divisive moment came in 1702, when Rev. George Keith returned to Flushing. Keith, a former Flushing resident and Scotch Presbyterian who had become a Friend around 1663, befriended William Penn and achieved great influence in the 1690s before growing disenchanted and critical (prompting the Keithian schism among the Quakers) and turning to the Church of England. He later became the first traveling missionary of the SPG in America—in Flushing.[54] Having just received orders in the Church of England, Rev. Keith returned to Flushing fired up with missionary zeal, but he ran into some trouble when he sought to gain converts in the middle of silent worship at the Meeting House (which he used to attend), igniting a small theological war:

> I went, Sept. 24th, to the Quaker's meeting, at Flushing, accompanied by Rev. Messrs. Talbot and Vesey, and divers other persons from Jamaica, well affected to the Church of England. After some time of silence I began to speak, standing up in the gallery where their speakers use to stand when they speak, but I was so much interrupted by the clamor and noise that several of the Quakers made, forbidding me to speak, that I could not proceed. After this one of their speakers began to speak and continued about an hour. The whole was a ramble of nonsense and perversion of Scripture with gross reflections on the Church and Government there. He said vice was set up (which was a reflection of on the Government there) because some were lately made justices of the peace on L.I. who were not greatly affected to Quakerism, &c, &c. After he had done, he went out of the meeting in all haste, fearing he should be questioned about what he had said. I stood up again to speak, but they made a new interruption and threatened me with being guilty of a breach of the Act of Toleration, and thereby put myself 20 pounds in the Queen's debt. I replied I was silent while their preacher was speaking but that they broke the Act by interrupting me. They said I had no right to speak in their meeting house, which they had paid for, and I had contributed nothing. One was so hot that he commanded me to go out of the house. I said that it was not his, and that all who have a mind to come in at meeting time may come, and ye are bound to keep your doors open, &c, &c. I again visited the Quaker meeting at Flushing (Dec. 3) having obtained a letter from my Lord Cornbury to two Justices of the peace to go along with me to see that the Quakers should not interrupt me; but they did, and took no notice of Lord Cornbury's letter, which was read to them by Mr. Talbot in their meeting house. I brought the printed Act of Toleration with me, and Talbot read some passages to show that

St. George's Episcopal Church (est. 1702). Queens Borough President print and photograph collection, Print Neg. No. 1731, Courtesy New York City Municipal Archives.

they had not qualified their meeting houses or their preachers as the Act requires. We staid and heard three speakers utter nonsense and perversions of Scriptures. The chief speaker, a most ignorant person, said "Balak (meaning Cornbury) had sent Balaam (Keith) to curse the people of God." After they had done and generally gone away (speakers and others) many who were not Quakers staid and heard me detect the perversions they made of the Scriptures, &c.[55]

It was tough love, as Rev. Keith no doubt merely sought to show his former Friends the errors of their ways, but his self-righteous airs were no match for the historic heart of the Society of Friends in New York. Many *would* convert in time as St. George's established itself, but the Meeting House remained Flushing's biggest draw through most of the eighteenth century.

Like numerous localities throughout the colonies, Flushing was also host to numerous itinerant revivalists. Jon Butler has noted that "between

1695 and 1740, Christian pluralism exploded in the middle colonies"—a period marked by such widespread religious renewal and revival that many historians referred to it as "the Great Awakening."[56] George Whitefield, "arguably the best-known Englishman of the mid–eighteenth century," was perhaps the most famous visitor to the area.[57] Besides drawing a number of Friends away from the Meeting House, he also annoyed and incurred the jealous wrath of the Anglican ministers who were trying to do the same thing: "Some itinerant enthusiastical teachers, have of late been preaching upon this Island the notorious Mr. Whitfield [sic] being at the head of them & among other pernicious tenets, have broached such false & erroneous opinions . . . as tend to the destruction of true religion & of a holy and virtuous life."[58] The spiritual battle for souls in Flushing would be joined by other voices in the next two centuries, but Quaker-Anglican tensions dominated the 1700s. A successor of Rev. Keith encountered similar difficulties even as St. George's first building was being completed in 1746:

> In my letter of the 26 March last I gave information to the Society of our being in a very likely way of having a Church erected in the town of Flushing a place generally inhabited by Quakers & by some who are of no religion at all which indeed has all along from the first settlement of the town been a great obstruction and discouragement to an undertaking of this kind but now by the kind providence of God . . . the work is actually begun so that I have hopes of performing divine Service in this new Church in about 3 months time and also that the Society will bestow upon it a Bible & Common Prayer Book according to their usual bounty for certainly there can be no set of People within this Province who are greater objects of the Society's pity & charity than those belonging to the town of Flushing.[59]

By 1759, Rev. Samuel Seabury was having an even harder time. Despite some success (he mentions baptizing "One White & One Negro Adult, fifteen White & three Negro infants"), he was exasperated and contemptuous:

> Flushing, in the last generation the ground seat of Quakerism, is in this the seat of Infidelity; a transition how natural. Bred up in an entire neglect of all religious principles, hatred to the Clergy & in contempt of the sacraments how hard is their conversion, especially as they disavow even the necessity of any redemption.[60]
>
> I heartily wish my success in this Mission was such as would justify my giving the honored Society an account thereof in some measure

equal to their expence and care of it. But such is the effect of the Deism & infidelity (for the spreading of which Quakerism has paved the way) which have here been propagated with the greatest zeal & the most astonishing success that a general indifference towards all religion has taken place & the too common opinion seems to be that they shall be saved without the mediation of Christ as well as with; and even among those who profess themselves as members of the Church of England a very great backwardness in attending her service prevails; and particularly with regard to the holy Sacrament of the Lord's Supper so great is their aversion to it or neglect of it that I fear the number of Communicants at present scarce exceeds twenty.[61]

Later that year, however, Seabury reported an apparent increase in conversions and attendance as well as the near completion of the church. He served as rector from 1757 to 1765 and later became the first bishop of the Episcopal Church in America. The new church attracted many, including Francis Lewis, a signer of the Declaration of Independence and warden at St. George's from 1765 to 1790. Meanwhile, the Meeting House was becoming less popular. In 1786, a certain Elisha Kirk wrote: "We rode to John Bowne's and attended meeting; but it is much decreased in numbers from what it formerly was."[62] Despite lower attendance (probably causing the Yearly Meeting to move to nearby Westbury in 1778), there were still notable moments: one Friend wrote in 1797 of a monthly meeting that lasted six hours, calling it "a glorious meeting. I thought I had never been a witness to such a solemnity at any meeting for so long a time together."[63]

By the end of the eighteenth century, Flushing had risen as one of the most desirable locales in New York, with many prominent families either visiting or moving there. Whitehead Hicks was serving his tenth year as mayor of New York when the American Revolution broke out. On Valentine's Day, 1776, he resigned from the mayoralty, saying he was tired and "desirous to retire from the Town." His place of retirement was Flushing, where he died in 1780. In 1775, Robert Bowne (great-grandson of John) established a stationer and printing press at South Street Seaport named Bowne & Co. Until 2010 (when it was acquired by RR Donnelly), it was the oldest business in New York operating under the same name since its incorporation.[64] The seeds of Flushing's international fame as a horticultural mecca were planted in 1725, when the first commercial nursery in America was established by William Prince, and in 1793, when his grandson, William Prince II, established the Linnaean Botanical Gardens. (The Bloodgood nursery would come later in 1798, and Samuel Parsons' nursery in 1837.) The widespread acclaim drew a number of high-profile visitors. On August 7, 1782, Prince William, later King William IV, came to Flushing to visit the Prince nurseries, and on October 10, 1789, President George Washington and Vice President John Adams also sailed into town for the same reason (they arrived again in 1790 on an inspection tour of Long Island while looking for possible sites for the new nation's capital). The horticultural heritage of Flushing would be highlighted again in the twentieth century when the 1939–1940 World's Fair featured Flushing in its "Gardens on Parade" pavilion, which later became the Queens Botanical Garden of today.

"Good Morning, Macedonia!"

In 1790, the new government of the United States instituted the first federal census. It had been nearly one hundred years since Flushing's first census in 1698, and the town had grown by one thousand, from 647 to 1,607. A constant one-sixth of the population was of African descent (117 slaves in 1698, three hundred slaves and free blacks by 1800). Available historical sources for blacks in colonial Flushing include slaveowners' account books and wills, runaway slave advertisements, manumission records, revivalist preaching, Quaker testimonies, and the few records of baptisms at St. George's by SPG missionaries. In 1789, however, a female slave named Nelly set fire to the office of her owner, the town clerk, destroying many town records.

The lack of historical sources for blacks began to change dramatically by 1811, when the African Methodist Society in Flushing bought land to build a church that would become the third place of worship in town.[65] An offshoot of Richard Allen and Absalom Jones' Free African Society in Philadelphia, the Flushing Society followed a similar path. Born into slavery in Philadelphia, Allen had been reborn when a Methodist circuit rider (an itinerant evangelist on horseback) visited the Delaware plantation to which he had been sold. Purchasing his freedom in 1782 for two thousand dollars, Allen became a lay preacher and attended St. George's Methodist Church in Philadelphia. When he and other black members of the congregation were evicted one Sunday for mistakenly sitting in seats reserved for whites, Allen left in 1793 to found Bethel African Church the following year. Ordained as the first black deacon in the Methodist Church by Bishop Asbury in 1795, Allen and others changed the name of his society to the African Methodist Episcopal Church in 1816 after several struggles with white clergy, with (Mother) Bethel AME in Phila-

Macedonia African Methodist Episcopal Church, est. 1811.

delphia being the first.[66] The Flushing church name had a slightly different origin. Church records and oral history relate the story of an eighteen-year-old white circuit rider named Benjamin Griffin, who rode into Quaker-Anglican Flushing in the early 1800s, when no one was interested in Methodism except those in the new African Methodist Society, which offered him food and shelter.[67] Griffin, it is said, likened his good hosts to the poor but generous people the apostle Paul encountered on his journey to Macedonia; thus the society changed its name to Macedonia AME church.[68] It would not be the only time Macedonia would help others in need. Throughout the nineteenth century, Macedonia was one stop among several in Flushing and throughout New York on the Underground Railroad.[69] Beneath the chapel, in the basement area (now the boiler room), fugitive slaves were offered shelter until they were ready to head off again through a side door to their next stop.

The Society of Friends became another ally in the struggle for abolition as early as the 1688 Germantown Quaker Petition Against Slavery, but slavery was still acceptable among most Quakers until an influential journal by the Quaker minister John Woolman began to circulate in 1749 entitled "Considerations of the Keeping of Negroes." The following year, the New York Friends Meeting voted that henceforth no Quaker could import slaves—a position that gained greater emphasis in the 1770s with the urging of another influential itinerant minister from Long Island named Elias Hicks. Publishing and disseminating "freedom narratives" based on oral stories of escaped slaves, Hicks's outspoken conviction awakened many to the cause. His views on salvation estranged some, however, and in 1827 the Flushing Society split into Hicksite and orthodox factions. The Meeting House in Flushing reflected this shift and became Hicksite; the orthodox built a new meeting house just east of the old one by 1854.[70] Many Quaker families on Long Island assisted blacks on the Underground Railroad, with perhaps the most notable being Samuel Bowne Parsons. The son of the nursery owner and abolitionist Quaker preacher (and a Bowne descendant through his mother), "It was his boast that he assisted more slaves to freedom than any other man in Queens County."[71] Quakers had taken the unpopular stance of abolition even as they lost outside respect for their pacifist exemption from fighting in the Revolutionary War, so it is no coincidence that the number of Friends at the Meeting House dwindled significantly by the mid–nineteenth century: by the end of the war, many had moved to Canada and the West Indies.[72] Others were perhaps also drawn to new denominations sprouting up everywhere around town.

"Our Village Is Becoming a Community of Churches"

During the colonial period, the town and hamlet of Flushing was under the jurisdiction of nearby Jamaica, Queens, and residents of Flushing had to travel there to petition for benefits and transact business; Flushing became an incorporated village on April 15, 1837, presumably to gain self-rule (that is, a board of trustees and municipal officers).[73] The boundaries of the new charter carved out a small area of modern Flushing and part of Whitestone: Twenty-First Avenue to the north, Sanford Avenue to the south, Bowne Avenue to the east, and Flushing Creek to the west. "Downtown" was located near the lower end of Northern Boulevard at the creek. Flushing then was primarily residential, with a population of about four thousand.[74] The *Gazeteer of the State of New York*, published in 1836, describes Flushing as a village of about 140 dwellings, "some of which are neat and several magnificent. The facility of conveyance, the attractiveness of the Linnaean Garden, the delightful voyage, whether by land or water, make this a favorite place of resort to citizens of New York."[75] The stature of Flushing also increased when Walter Bowne (another Bowne descendant) was mayor of the City of New York from 1829 to 1833 and hosted such visitors as Alexis de Tocqueville.[76] Two steamboats brought new

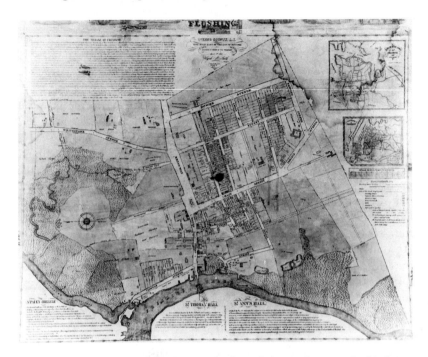

Map of Flushing, 1841, by Elijah A. Smith. Collection of Vincent Seyfried.

multitudes of passengers to and from the landing dock at Flushing Creek until 1854, when the new Flushing railroad station was completed on Main Street—moving the center of downtown to its present location and setting in motion an even larger number of commuters. Board of Trustee town records from the 1850s and 1860s also document a number of public works projects, including the paving of streets and sidewalks and a new ordinance that prohibited owners of livestock from letting their cows and goats graze freely around downtown.[77] Word was getting around, too, as the new local newspaper reported: "Flushing is looking its loveliest in this June and July and is attracting the tastes of a great many who are in search of rural quarters for the summer months. An infusion of more wealth and taste is an inevitable sequence of our fittings–up and surroundings."[78] Into this context came new migrants and new churches.

Unlike other parts of the country, Flushing did not seem as affected by the revolutionary and postrevolutionary revivals that led up to another period from 1805 to 1820 quickly labeled by some historians as the

Second Great Awakening, but it did reflect the overall national explosion of denominational growth between 1790 and 1860 resulting from the separation of church and state.[79] One reporter for the *Flushing Journal* observed in 1854, "Our village is becoming a community of churches."[80] A rapid-fire list gives a sense of the variety and reflects similar patterns across the country at this time. By 1822, Methodism had expanded into the white community, which built a new church just off of Main Street; in 1842, whites also followed Macedonia in establishing a First Methodist Episcopal church. In 1841, centuries after struggles with Quakers, a Dutch Reformed church finally was built on Bowne Street. And, from starting out in a schoolhouse, a First Congregational church went up across the street in 1851. On January 17, 1857, a Baptist church was organized in Flushing, and a small church was dedicated later in October.[81] St. John's Church, of the German Evangelical Lutheran Synod of Missouri, followed as the number of German immigrants rose. In all, the tally by 1857 included thirteen Protestant churches and one Catholic church in a town of approximately nine thousand people—a number of whom identified themselves as Deists and atheists.[82]

The denominational growth was also accompanied by the massive waves of Irish and German Catholic immigration of the mid–nineteenth century. In 1826, St. Michael's Roman Catholic parish was formed by the only twelve Catholics in Flushing. They first met for worship in a small house on Main Street, later purchased a larger house, expanded it twice, and then purchased four lots in 1841 to build a new church by 1854. The arrival of the Catholic Church and, in particular, the many Irish immigrants who attended it, set off the first major religious tension since the Dutch-Quaker and Quaker-Anglican skirmishes of previous centuries. The racial, ethnic, and religious composition of Flushing's population had virtually remained the same until the 1830s, when it hovered in the two thousand range, but the village had grown to over four thousand by 1840 and over ten thousand by 1860. Anti-Catholic nativism was rampant in much of the country at this time, and the rash of irrational fear reached Flushing too. It did not help that crime had also risen significantly. Some blamed bandits from the city, no doubt lured by news of well-stocked stores and well-heeled residents. Some blamed blacks, but most blamed the Irish, who were generally very poor workers living in a shantytown by the creek. Recognizing this in 1843, the village attempted to help and voted to establish "a poor house for 25 paupers"; its membership had swelled to 125 by 1857. But the problem was also religious. In 1854, the *Flushing Journal* ran an approving review of the "'Great Red Dragon,' or,

'The Mystery Key to Popery,'" whose Spanish author was reported to be an ex-priest bent on revealing "the Papal plot" against the school system and freedom of thought in America.[83] On March 31, 1855, the paper defended the infamous Order of the Star-Spangled Banner (also known as the Know-Nothing Party and, later, the American Party, a fraternal order of Protestant politicians bent on reducing the influence of immigrants and Catholics), and, in April 1855, the following headline read: "High Tide of No-Nothingism: supervisors of Flushing, Hempstead and North Hempstead all elected from the American or Know-Nothing ticket."[84]

The proliferation of new churches coincided with the growth and expansion of older churches as well. The Friends Meeting House had already split into Hicksite and orthodox factions. St. George's Episcopal Church built a second church in 1821 and a third (the present one) in 1854. Continuing its history of luminaries, the church thrived under a new rector named Rev. Dr. William August Mühlenberg (a great-grandson of the German American Lutheran patriarch Henry M. Mühlenberg), who was himself raised as an Anglican and came to exemplify "the most productive forces in his church during the pre–Civil War years, especially those factors and appeals which account for the remarkable expansion of Episcopalianism in America's urban centers." Mühlenberg was rector of St. George's from 1826 to 1829, when he founded the Flushing Institute, one of the earliest and most elite models of private preparatory schools in America.[85]

"The Great Question Which Now Agitates the Republic"

Despite a brief brush with division brought about by the nativism of the 1850s, the Civil War displayed a different side of Flushing—one that showed new unity and the village's clear alignment with the Union.[86] On March 20, 1862, the *Flushing Journal* ran a story on Rev. Henry Ward Beecher, the influential liberal preacher from Plymouth Congregational Church in nearby Brooklyn, who visited Flushing and delivered a lecture at the Congregational Church on Bowne Avenue:

> Our village was honored on Thurs. night by the presence of this distinguished individual who in the Congregational Church and before quite a large audience, delivered a most brilliant lecture which was very well received and by frequent bursts of applause. The subject was "The Results of the Past and our Policy for the Future." We have not the room to give even an abstract of the topics discussed.

The effect on the major part of the audience was definitely good. Many of those who supposed the lecturer to be a rank Abolitionist and were prepared, if not to confute, to deride his positions, came away impressed with the idea that Henry Ward Beecher is sound in regard to the great question which now agitates the Republic. The rebellion is to be crushed out once and forever. Upon that point all are agreed. But when it is put down, then comes the question what are to be the relations of the Govt. to slavery. It is not probable that the people of this country, after expending two thousands of millions of dollars and overwhelming themselves and their posterity with unprecedented taxation, will acquiesce in a settlement that will leave matters as the war found them. The system of slavery is bound to go to the wall in some shape before the majestic uprising of the people. Now is the time to canvass the matter and to enlighten the public mind respecting the most equitable and righteous method of adjustment and it is with satisfaction that we heard Mr. Beecher and witnessed the profound attention which our citizens of all shades of opinions gave to his eloquent denunciation of a system that in its consequences has involved our country in blood and carnage.[87]

Newspaper stories are, of course, not always accurate barometers for the population they represent on all issues, but they may be more representative in smaller towns—as Flushing still was at the time. The opposition to slavery and support of the Union seemed quite solid all the way through to the end of the war:

Not only is it a matter of economy but of national importance that volunteers should be hurried to the front as quickly as possible that the last finishing stroke may be put to the rebellion before the opening of spring. Never has the cause of the Union appeared more cheering and prosperous than at this moment. The rebellion is reeling under the well-directed blows of Grant, Sherman & Thomas and every man, now put in the field, is of more consequence than if put there a day or two hence. Let Flushing then fill up her quota at once.[88]

The Queens historian Vincent F. Seyfried notes that the onset of the war may have shaken up the social and economic life of Flushing, "but the local churches pursued the even tenor of their ways unaffected by the national crisis."[89] Growing sympathy with abolition had also led to a new interest in Flushing's historic black church. A report in the *Flushing Journal* on the dedication of a new church for Macedonia AME in January 1862 read:

The room was crowded with parents, children and members of the congregation who listened respectfully and attentively to addresses from the Revs. Mr. Myers and P. M. Bartlett. It was gratifying to observe the good order and quiet behavior of the children and the interest manifested in the remarks made to them. The Rev. John Washington, the preacher in charge, has succeeded in creating considerable interest among the adults in the study of the Holy Scriptures, quite a number meeting regularly with the children for religious instruction. The Sabbath school numbers about 50 and it is hoped the interest will increase until all the parents with their children will convene every Sabbath and diligently improve the opportunity afforded them.[90]

Segregation was still the norm, however, and after a division occurred among members of the First Baptist Church in 1861, Flushing's black Baptist population established its own Ebenezer Missionary Baptist Church in 1873.[91] Flushing also drew a number of successful free blacks who settled there during the nineteenth century to join the older black population—among them Lewis H. Latimer, who had supervised the installation of electric street lights in New York City, Philadelphia, Montreal, and London, and, as the only African American member of Thomas Edison's team of inventors, had improved on the light bulb by developing a carbon filament.

From Small Town to "Part of a Hurly-Burly City"

Flushing grew and became more ethnically diverse in the years before consolidation with the city, leading several historians to chronicle seemingly less complex early years when Flushing was still a discernible small town of white and black Protestants. Real estate activity was strong even during the Civil War, with development reaching further away from downtown. The Bowne and Parsons families also began to divide and sell parcels of land from their estates. In 1862, construction of Flushing Town Hall began with a ceremony and time capsule deposited in a cornerstone determined by local masons. And, in 1864, another major transportation development occurred: Queens Road (later Boulevard) opened, connecting Flushing directly with points east.

In a remarkable turnaround, Irish Americans essentially had taken over local politics, just as they had begun to do in the city by the mid–nineteenth century with the Democratic Party political machine of Tammany Hall. Membership on the village Board of Trustees was now a roster of Irish names.[92] A small Italian and Jewish population also grew, reflecting the second massive wave of new immigration from southern and eastern Europe that began in the 1880s. Where old-stock Protestants once had reigned for centuries, Catholics now had become a major force along with the aristocratic Anglicans around town—so much so that residents could state about the time that "St. Michael's and St. George's ran Flushing."[93]

It was churchmen who composed the most ambitious histories of Flushing through the nineteenth century, following the lead of Rev. G. Henry Mandeville of the Dutch Reformed Church in 1860.[94] Two other histories came from rectors at St. George's: a history of the parish by Rev. Dr. John Carpenter Smith (pastor from 1847 all the way to 1897) and a substantial history of Flushing by Rev. Henry D. Waller in 1899.[95] Waller notes the strong opposition Flushing had to the proposal for consolidation in 1896 and how the members of the Village Board, supported by their fellow townsmen, appeared before the Senate Committee to oppose the consolidation. Despite the protests of the people, Flushing was annexed by the city in 1896, and the act was signed by the governor, taking effect on January 1, 1898, as Flushing became a part of the City of New York and "one of the most beautiful towns in the United States . . . became a part of a hurly-burly city."[96]

2
Heralding the "World of Tomorrow"
Religion and Community in Flushing, 1898–1965

> Sound the brass, roll the drum:
> to the world of tomorrow we come.
> See the sun through the gray:
> it's the dawn of a new day.
> Here we come young and old,
> come to watch all the wonders unfold.
> And the tune that we play,
> it's the dawn of a new day.
> Tell the wolf at the door
> that we don't want him 'round anymore.
> Better times here to stay,
> as we live and laugh the American way.
> Listen one, listen all:
> there can be no resisting the call.
> Come, come hail the dawn of a new day!
>
> —"Dawn of a New Day" (song of the 1939–1940 New York
> World's Fair), composed by Ira Gershwin and George Gershwin

After incorporation into New York City in 1898, dramatic changes were underway that would quickly link Flushing to Manhattan in more ways, even as Flushing itself expanded. A small village with streetcars from 1899 to 1937 suddenly found itself caught up in a string of major transportation changes: in 1909, the Queensboro Bridge opened; in 1928, the IRT Queensboro Line (begun in 1915 and subsequently renamed the IRT Flushing Line) subway extended to Flushing, Main Street; in 1936, the Triborough Bridge opened; in 1939, La Guardia Airport opened in Flushing Bay (followed in 1948 by New York International, or Idlewild, Airport in nearby Jamaica Bay, later renamed John F. Kennedy

International Airport in 1963); and, in 1940, the Queens–Midtown Tunnel opened.[1]

As transportation changes made Flushing increasingly more connected to the city, real estate agents saw an opportunity to build properties and lure new residents. Once suburban (if not rural), Flushing was on its way to becoming an attractive urban outpost where people could live and own a house yet also work in the city. In 1910, the Business Men's Association of Flushing (BMAF) distributed a booklet entitled "Flushing: The Premier Suburban Colony of the City of New York." By 1916, no more private homes were being built, and the first three- and four-story apartment buildings went up. In 1917, BMAF published an even larger booklet with the following introduction:

> Flushing is villagy, and therein lies its old-fashioned charm. Its heritages of old houses and old trees, old friends and old ways possess a magic lure to all who once come under its spell. Flushing doesn't have to be apologized for or explained—it needs only to be introduced to weary, long-suffering, pent-up flat occupants to become the belle of New York's suburban beauties. Flushing is hospitable, Flushing people are hospitable, and a few more choice souls will be welcomed into its delightful community.[2]

Postcards of Main Street and other areas around Flushing from the early 1900s through the 1940s reflected the new push by various community leaders to put Flushing on the map and present an inviting and orderly commercial downtown surrounded by an attractive residential neighborhood. Such postcards were ubiquitous in many American cities during this period and illustrated a national trend. As the historian Alison Isenberg has noted, "the postcards and city plans of the early twentieth century articulated a new commercial vision—a dense streetscape of entrepreneurs presiding over a managed, simplified, and beautified retail corridor."[3] But perhaps the biggest force for growth was Halleran Agency Real Estate and Insurance. Established in the 1840s, Halleran Agency was led in the mid–twentieth century by John J. Halleran, whose "Ask Mr. Halleran" ads appeared everywhere in newspapers throughout Flushing in the 1930s and 1940s. Also president of the Flushing Chamber of Commerce, Halleran was Flushing's own "power broker"—wielding as much influence over the town as the legendary parks commissioner Robert Moses did over the city at large. In 1941, during a record-breaking year of new construction (also when Queens College held its first commencement), Halleran ran the following "Invitation to Flushing" to push his duplexes and two- and three-story "garden apartments" in the "New City of the North Shore":

> It's quite natural for us to think Flushing and the North Shore are just a bit better than any other community. But this isn't mere civic pride, or home-town boosting.
>
> Every year nearly three thousand new families are discovering that Flushing and the contiguous North Shore communities ... offer an ideal home environment.
>
> Whether your taste is for a cottage or a mansion, a modest flat or an ultra-modern duplex apartment; whether you prefer to live in a quiet country-like atmosphere, along the shore front or "in the midst of things"—you will find the kind of home you want right here.
>
> Yes, Flushing and the North Shore have just about everything: convenient and friendly neighborhood stores; one of the finest retail shopping centers in the metropolitan area; churches of every religious faith and denomination; public, parochial and private schools; nearly two thousand acres of parks and playgrounds; golf and yacht clubs; transportation by bus, subway, and railroad; highways that afford a quick and pleasant drive by auto to every part of New York City, to the beaches and famed resorts of Long Island—or wherever you want to go. Then, too, if you want to travel by plane, you will find the world's greatest air terminal at Flushing's front doorstep.
>
> At the same time, this thoroughly modern community still retains all the neighborliness of a suburban village, with many social and cultural activities. Flushing has organizations devoted to art, music, literature, gardening, and many other interests.
>
> Flushing's streets are lined with the most famous—and most beautiful—collection of trees in the country, many of them rare specimens planted more than a hundred years ago. Historic landmarks of three centuries lend further distinction and an undeniable charm.
>
> The North Shore also is not lacking in opportunities for business and industry. Residential development provides an extensive and ever-growing retail market, while facilities for new industry are available in established localities.
>
> All things considered, we think we have a mighty fine community.
>
> To anyone interested in a place to live—or a place for business ... we invite attention to the many advantages offered by the "New City of the North Shore."[4]

Main Street, Flushing, August 9, 1930. Collection of Vincent Seyfried.

That Flushing still identified with the North Shore of Long Island shows how slow residents were to let go of Flushing's former preconsolidation status—addresses on envelopes and stationery still read "Flushing, L.I." well into midcentury. For instance, Thomas Merton, who lived in Flushing with his family from 1916 to 1921 and occasionally attended the "ancient [Quaker] meeting house," mentions "Flushing, Long Island, which was then a country town" in his famous autobiography, *The Seven Storey Mountain.*[5] Yet as building development surged before the Great Depression (and again by the late 1930s), so did the numbers of new residents—including thousands of people escaping cramped conditions in Manhattan. Population figures speak for themselves: 20,000 in 1890; 35,000 in 1920; 45,000 in 1922; 55,000 in 1930; and 105,000 in 1941.

As Flushing grew from a suburban outpost on Long Island to an urban neighborhood of New York City after 1898, the old town became more diverse because of transportation changes, a real estate boom, an

Advertisement for new apartment building, c. 1930s. Collection of Vincent Seyfried.

influx of people after World War II, and its proximity to two World's Fairs—prompting advocates like Halleran to boast of "churches of every religious faith and denomination" in his "Invitation to Flushing" above. The increasing pluralism of early- to mid-twentieth-century Flushing did not lead, however, to fragmentation of community but to an increased sense of a shared community ideology that ultimately mirrored the emerging national Protestant-Catholic-Jewish consensus of the era combined with powerful commemorations of local history. The tercentenary in 1945 was only the first in a series of anniversaries that marked a post–World War II (and Cold War) revival of history and birth of a community ideology in Flushing that focused on its heritage of religious freedom and tolerance—at a time when America (and Flushing) was just coming to terms with a broader acceptance of Jews and the civil rights movement was gathering steam.

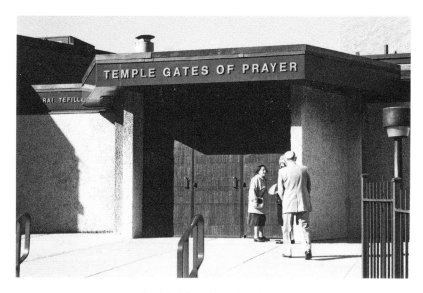

Rosh Hashanah services, 2000.

"Israel Was Born in Queens"

Although a large number of "white ethnics" (Polish, Italian, Greek, and Slavic immigrants) came to Flushing during this period, the majority of new residents in Flushing during the first half of the twentieth century were Jewish immigrants (Ashkenazic, versus the earlier Sephardic Jews who came in the seventeenth century). Part of a massive wave of migrants from southern and eastern Europe that came to Ellis Island from the 1880s through the early 1920s, many Jewish immigrants settled in tenements on the Lower East Side of Manhattan before moving to the outer boroughs and places like Flushing. Many more who escaped during the rise of the Third Reich or survived the Holocaust during World War II would come in the 1930s and after 1945. Those who stayed in self-sufficient ethnic enclaves like lower Manhattan and Williamsburg, Brooklyn, were largely able to live in reclusion from the rest of the city, but the pioneers who branched out to the outer boroughs often discovered that they had not yet totally escaped anti-Semitism. There had already been a small Jewish population in Flushing at least since the late nineteenth century, including the family of the urban historian Lewis Mumford, who was born in Flushing in 1895 and whose father was Jewish.[6] Reflecting the

Free Synagogue of Flushing, "Celebrating 83 years of Community Service," 2000.

anti-Semitism and general anti-immigrant sentiments of the early 1900s, Jews initially had trouble gaining acceptance in the neighborhood. In 1926, a group of men established the Jewish Men's Swim Club because they were not welcome at the YMCA, country clubs, and golf courses in the area. Despite such prejudice, a more affluent early Jewish community developed in Flushing and soon began to build its own places of worship.

Jewish synagogues were the first new religious institutions in Flushing since the proliferation of churches from various Protestant denominations in the mid–nineteenth century. Temple Gates of Prayer, a Conservative synagogue, came first and was established in 1900. Starting with fewer than thirty families, the temple's first permanent home was built in 1921; a school building and community house were added in 1931. As the oldest Jewish congregation in Queens, Temple Gates attracted Jews from all over the borough. Taking in many new members after the war, in 1960 the congregation moved to its current and larger location.[7] In 1917, the "Hebrew Ladies Aid Society" responded to the need for a liberal Reformed synagogue in Queens by founding the Free Synagogue of Flushing. Modeled after Rabbi Stephen S. Wise's Free Synagogue in Manhattan, Free Synagogue of Flushing is the oldest Reformed synagogue on

Long Island and the first in the United States to be founded by women. As the Jewish community in Flushing grew more diverse, there was also a need for an Orthodox synagogue, and in April 1958 the groundbreaking ceremony for Kissena Jewish Center on Bowne Street took place with a vow to provide "Traditional Judaism for Modern Americans."[8]

The World of Tomorrow in Flushing's Backyard

The tremendous housing and real estate boom in Flushing that had slumped during the Great Depression began to take off again in the mid-1930s as locals became excited about a huge event that was about to take place in their backyard of Flushing Meadows: the 1939–1940 New York World's Fair. As one person described Flushing's anticipation:

> The town is fully prepared to enjoy its period of fame. The local merchants are anticipating increased trade; the home-owners are waiting for an increase in land valuations; the younger elements of the town are thrilled with their proximity to such an exciting event; those who are proud of the town's venerable heritage are hopeful that the hurried visitors to the Fair will find time to admire their town's relics and beauties, and accord it the admiration its long and eventful history deserves.[9]

The World's Fair would put Flushing in the news and on the map like never before, and it would be one of the greatest feats of civil engineering, urban planning, and design in history.

Parks Commissioner Robert Moses stayed in power for decades, and he oversaw not just the 1939–1940 fair but the 1964–1965 fair as well. His dream as a child was to build "a great park, the greatest within the limits of any city in the world, the ultimate urban park."[10] Realizing that Flushing Meadows was the geographical and population center of New York City, Moses thought "a park there . . . would be a true 'Central Park' to the whole city."[11] Actually, it would be a string of three parks: Kissena, Cunningham, and Alley Pond—to serve not only the single-family homes of 1930s but also the high-rise apartments he foresaw. But this was no mere conversion of existing park space. The Flushing Meadow Improvement plan would turn the ugliest place in the city into its most beautiful. An immense and once beautiful tidal marsh half again as large as Manhattan's Central Park, Flushing Meadows had become one of the biggest eyesores in the city since 1914. Like Manhattan did with the Fresh Kills Landfill in Staten Island from 1948–2001, the Brooklyn Ash Removal

Company had begun dumping all of Brooklyn's trash in the marsh; by the 1920s, 110 railroad cars dumped loads of refuse daily. Flushing Creek, the waterway to Forest Hills, had become a sewer. So infamous was the dump that F. Scott Fitzgerald wrote about it in *The Great Gatsby:*

> This is a valley of ashes—a fantastic farm where ashes grow like wheat into ridges and hills and grotesque gardens, where ashes take the forms of houses and chimneys and rising smoke and finally, with a transcendent effort, of men who move dimly and already crumbling through the powdery air. Occasionally a line of grey cars crawls along an invisible track, gives out a ghastly creak and comes to rest, and immediately the ash-grey men swarm up with leaden spades and stir up an impenetrable cloud which screens their obscure operations from your sight.
>
> The valley of ashes is bounded on one side by a small foul river, and when the drawbridge is up to let the barges through, the passengers on waiting trains can stare at the dismal scene for as long as half an hour.[12]

One pile was so high that locals called it "Mount Corona." Moses too had noticed it. Coming across a passage in Isaiah 61:3—"Give unto them beauty for ashes," he had an idea. Beginning in 1936, he would have the marsh completely filled with dirt from subway excavations and create the park of his dreams by making the new New York World's Fair Corporation use and pay for the work. Governor of New York Al Smith would later comment: "Well, I can remember this part of New York when it was old, and it's hard to believe that in such a short period of time you could transform an ash dump into what can be seen here today."[13] It was not Moses's dream alone but also one of social planners and designers. A generation of such minds had read a book by the Englishman Ebenezer Howard entitled *Garden Cities of Tomorrow* (1902), who said, "Town and country must be married, and out of this union will spring a new hope, a new life, a new civilization." The planners of the World's Fair hoped to turn Flushing Meadows into such a garden city, a completely planned city, and thereby show the world that tomorrow could be achieved today.

Fairs had become a worldwide movement after the success of London's Crystal Palace Exhibition of 1851 and a pervasive influence in America by the turn of the century. From 1876 to 1916, Philadelphia, Chicago, New Orleans, Atlanta, Nashville, Omaha, Buffalo, St. Louis, Portland, Seattle, San Francisco, and San Diego all had hosted fairs. Firing the imagination and giving hope during times of economic hardship and class struggle, they displayed American accomplishments to foster confidence, yet "far from simply reflect-

A freight car drops a load at the infamous Corona ash dumps, c. 1930. Brooklyn Ash Removal Company photo, collection of Vincent Seyfried.

ing American culture, the expositions were intended to shape that culture."[14] As Robert W. Rydell has explained, fairs were "theaters of power"—they "reflected the efforts by America's intellectual, political, and business leaders to establish a consensus about their priorities and their vision of progress."[15]

More than any previous fair, the 1939–1940 New York World's Fair showcased the availability of new goods and services, combined with advances in technology and planned communities—all "streamlined" to be more efficient.[16] So that no one would miss their point, the designers of the fair structured the pathways to lead visitors to a central Theme Center inside a gigantic stark white Perisphere: "Democracity," the perfectly planned community of Henry Dreyfuss that represented the World Fair's central ideology of the future. The "corporatist nature" of the fair for America's future was also a major selling point to big business, and the popular Futurama exhibit by General Motors stressed the need for superhighways to increase automobile usage and sales.[17]

Yet the fair also displayed a kind of religious nature. Rydell has noted:

The term "fair" derives from the Latin *feria,* "holy day." More explicitly, the German *Messen* connotes both "mass" and "fair." America's world's fairs resembled religious celebrations in their emphasis on

The ash dump transformed into the "World of Tomorrow." Perisphere and Trylon, NY World's Fair 1939–40—McLaughlin Air Service—Aerial Views, Queens; Neg #60912-16971, New-York Historical Society.

symbols and ritualistic behavior. They provided visitors with a galaxy of symbols and [what the sociologists Peter L. Berger and Thomas Luckmann called] ritualistic "symbolic universes." These constellations, in turn, ritualistically affirmed fairgoers' faith in American institutions and social organization, evoked a community of shared experience, and formulated responses to questions about the ultimate destiny of mankind in general and of Americans in particular.[18]

More explicitly, fairs also incorporated religion itself. Chicago's Columbian Exposition of 1893 had featured the famous World Parliament of Religions where, for the first time, representatives of the world's major religions all gathered in America for a rare moment of interfaith dialogue. The 1933–1934 Chicago World's Fair included a Hall of Religion that featured various Christian denominations as well as Judaism and even the Bahá'í, but it and successive fairs never came close to repeating the historic occasion of 1893. The World of Tomorrow was no exception and, in fact, seemed stuck far back in yesterday.

J. Terry Todd has stated that no one even remembers religion having been represented at the 1939–1940 New York World's Fair, but it *was* there in the form of the Temple of Religion and a few other exhibits.[19] Surrounded by the Works Progress Administration pavilion, the Jewish Palestine Pavilion, the Young Men's Christian Association, and the Christian Science Pavilion close to the Theme Center stood one of the least popular pavilions of the fair. The motif on the upper façade of the Temple of Religion read: "For All Who Worship God and Prize Religious Freedom," yet non-Western religions and Islam were banned.[20] Devoted to "the three great Faiths," it was erected by Protestant, Catholic, and Jewish lay representatives as a "symbol of the individual's belief in God, irrespective of the form of that belief."[21] Neither the building nor the ground was consecrated, nor were formal religious services held, but religious pageants and dramas took place on an outside porch, and programs "designed to express the value of spiritual things" were presented in an auditorium that seated 1,200.[22] Not surprisingly, the most interested participants had been the Jewish representatives, as anti-Semitism was still widespread and even subtly present in the official guidebook of the fair. A passage about the Jewish Palestine Pavilion read: "Because of its significance as an answer to the charge of unproductiveness leveled against the Jew, the Palestine Exhibit has received the united support of the Jews of America, from whom funds for the project were raised by popular subscription."[23]

Yet despite the Temple of Religion's shortcomings, it is notable for helping shape a tri-faith Judeo-Christian model that became widespread by the 1950s.[24] Social historians in the 1960s would later look back derisively on American history written in the 1950s and earlier as "consensus" history because it tended to depict a relatively homogenous society and emphasize the stability and continuity of American experience over the centuries rather than deal truthfully with the nation's flaws.[25] Thus Will Herberg wrote about "the great faiths" and an "American Way of Life" in *Protestant-Catholic-Jew,* and immigration historians like Oscar Handlin still accepted rapid assimilation of immigrants as a given.[26] Similarly, President Dwight D. Eisenhower commented: "Our government makes no sense unless it is founded on a deeply felt religious faith—and I don't care what it is."[27] In the 1950s, record numbers of churchgoers led many to perceive a nationwide religious revival, but critical observers have noted it was "a shallow, customary style of participation rather than a deep or theologically grounded commitment."[28]

Flushing's own connections to the fair and to the Temple of Religion are virtually unknown. When plans for the fair were still being drawn up, a group of Manhattan real estate brokers toured the fairgrounds in 1937 with Laurence B. Halleran (also of the Halleran Real Estate Agency), who

The Temple of Religion, 1939–1940 World's Fair souvenir postcard. Author's collection.

discussed the historical background of the site.[29] Flushing's horticultural heritage would become part of a display at the Gardens on Parade pavilion (sandwiched between the Chile, Italy, and Great Britain pavilions), which later became the Queens Botanical Garden of today. But there also had been hopes that Flushing's history of religious freedom might somehow be included at the Temple of Religion. In a letter dated December 12, 1938, to the Patriotic and Historic Committee of the World's Fair, Inc., Alice Bowne (an Advisory Committee member of the Temple of Religion and Bowne descendant) wrote to William Osborn proposing that a replica of the Bowne House be erected on the grounds of the Temple of Religion. There was no record of response from Temple of Religion, Inc.[30] Others voiced their ideas in the *New York Times:*

> Not everyone believed the project was possible, or even desirable. Jonathan C. Pierce, a Quaker from White Plains, wondered why the old Flushing Friends Meeting House, site of the 1657 Flushing Remonstrance, could not serve as a "vital Hall of Religious Freedom." Why build something new, Pierce asked, with such a historic site so close to the fairgrounds? Besides, the old Meeting House was more impressive than any new structure could possibly be.[31]

Flushing's history of religious freedom may not have made it into the World's Fair, but it would be highlighted soon thereafter on an equally large scale in 1957.

The fair also had an even more objectionable side that is often glossed over in fond remembrances. In earlier expositions, there were often ethnological exhibits along the midways of nonwhite "primitive types" living in villages. These exhibits charted a course of racial progress toward an image of utopia reflected in the main exposition buildings—an interpenetration of Darwinian theories about racial development and utopian dreams about America's material and national progress.[32] It was, as the historian Neil Harris has noted, "a way of coping with an exoticism that didn't seem to fit into the Anglo-American tradition, and many displays had a patronizing, even contemptuous air to them."[33] The pseudoscientific sanction for the American view of the nonwhite world as barbaric and childlike not only lent such exposition planners a spurious scientific basis for building a white utopia; it was also used to validate imperial policies overseas.[34] Such sentiments were more pronounced at earlier expositions but would be blatant in the 1964–1965 fair. For the 1939–1940 fair, the Lama Temple, a replica of a Tibetan Buddhist Potala Monastery in Jehol, Manchuria (present-day Cheng-te in Hupei Province), was brought back by the explorer Vincent Bendix and reassembled in Flushing Meadows. Proceeds from admissions went to the Committee for Relief of Chinese War Orphans from the Sino-Japanese War, but Buddhism was kept out of the Temple of Religion. Similarly, the Japanese Pavilion had a Shinto shrine. The Turkish Pavilion displayed Islamic architecture but no Islam. Lebanon and Iraq also had exhibits in the Hall of Nations, as well as Siam (Thailand), and they also left religion out. The most telling moment, however, came in 1940, when the Amusement Zone was renamed "The Great White Way," in a reminiscent recall of the "White City" at the Chicago Columbian Exposition of 1893.

Toward the end of the 1940 season of the fair, Paramount Sound News ran a news short with the caption "New York Hidden by Smoke!"[35] Showing exclusive footage of an Army defense demonstration to bolster fair attendance and further highlight technological advances in the military during a growing sense of apprehension about the war in Europe, the clip said: "Lower Manhattan, with its towering skyscrapers, the heart of America's trade and commerce, needs the greatest protection our nation can provide. Every modern method of defense is being tested to give this vital spot the greatest protection possible." The footage showed a Lieut. Col. Longanecker at Mitchell Field on Long Island giving orders to four Army Air Corps pilots about how properly to lay a smoke screen above the south-

The General Assembly Building, Flushing Meadows, New York.

The New York City Building from the 1939–1940 World's Fair became the first home of the United Nations General Assembly in 1946 before moving to permanent headquarters in Manhattan in 1952. The NYC Building was reused for the 1964–1965 World's Fair (with the Unisphere constructed where the Trylon and Perisphere once stood) and later became the home of the Queens Museum of Art. Postcard from author's collection.

ern tip of Manhattan to conceal New York's skyline. Streaking down from the sky, the planes let out a blinding curtain, and the announcer boasted, "World's largest city almost totally obscured by man's newest marvel: the new nonpoisonous smoke screen that is being tested for New York's wartime defense." A year after the fair closed (and two years after "Japan Day" at the fair, where the mayor of Tokyo presented a torch to stress the cordial relations between the United States and Japan), Japan attacked Pearl Harbor on December 7, 1941, and America entered the war. Although the continental United States was untouched by enemies during World War II, New York would experience another day of infamy sixty years later, when no smoke screen was around to protect lower Manhattan.

After the war, the United Nations General Assembly was temporarily located in Flushing Meadows when it moved into the defunct New York City Building of the fair from 1946 to 1952. Albert Thaler, who would later become the rabbi at Temple Gates of Prayer in 1980, was a young man when an historic vote was held at the General Assembly on

November 29, 1947. Years later, Rabbi Thaler would be proud to say that "Israel was born in Queens."[36] Many foreign dignitaries chose to live in Flushing because of its proximity to the United Nations, and Flushing's prominence continued to rise.

Commemoration and Community Ideology

At the peak of such massive transportation developments, population growth, and international attention, one might expect Flushing to begin losing some of its old ways. Yet instead of disappearing or fading away, Flushing's sense of local history and civic pride was at an all-time high, and residents of Flushing marked several important anniversaries in the years before and after World War II:

> Flushing in 1945 was the last gasp of the WASPs, because everybody was so prideful. John J. Halleran built his real estate career on selling the history of Flushing. After he sold the history of Flushing, he *sold out* the history of Flushing, and all the work that he did up until 1945 was then destroyed from 1945–1970. Everything . . . the Aspinwall house, it was owned by his family: he sold it to build a bunch of *stores!* I mean, you're talking about someone . . . and people, you're talking about people who were Yankees—this was a Yankee town. This was old New England stock. These were people who were aristocrats, they were the new Victorians, they were the Gatsby-era people. These are people who, yes, they had civic pride—this town *loved* itself in 1945, it had a love affair with itself—and then it *all* changed within a very short period of time.[37]

There was a definite sense of neighborhood and community, if not outright "filiopietism," or excessive praise of one's ancestors and their contributions. The historian Henry Steele Commager often commented upon the fact that Americans, often more so than any other people, were engaged constantly in "the search for a usable past," a phrase that suggests the desire not merely to nourish one's roots but to appropriate and, in some cases, to invent those roots for usable purposes in the present.[38]

Flushing had real roots and occasions to celebrate, but the community was so engaged in such celebratory activities that one wonders why it was taken to such an extreme. The historian John Higham has used the term "Anglo-American localism" to describe the innumerable local historical societies that English-speaking Americans created to foster a historical identification with the founders and early leaders of a local community and to demonstrate a continuity of descent and civic leadership from the early settlers to the social elite of their own day.[39]

The tercentenary celebration in 1945 of Flushing's founding in 1645 was only one among several events in Flushing around the first half of the twentieth century that illustrate something about local tradition and memory. The sociologist David M. Hummon proposes that "conceptions of community life are fundamental elements of American culture, with a history and a life that transcends the experience of the individual."[40] He defines "community ideologies" as "systems of belief that define a unique perspective on the landscape of urban, suburban, and small-town life" and argues that "people, in adopting such ideologies, incorporate assumptions, beliefs, and values that enable them not only to understand this or that locale but also to *make sense* of reality and their place in the everyday world."[41] In this way, community ideologies are similar to the *mentalités,* or mental habits, that pervade people's thoughts in a particular place. And, in Flushing, the community ideology, local tradition, or *mentalité* has revolved around memory of the "liberty of conscience," or religious freedom, guaranteed in the town charter, upheld in the Flushing Remonstrance, and personified in the stance of John Bowne.

In 1937, Flushing celebrated the centennial anniversary of the incorporation of the village of Flushing in 1837 with a parade and "The Pageant of Flushing Town" at the State Armory before a crowd of 1,500. This was just a dress rehearsal compared to the bigger celebration of the tercentenary in 1945. The biggest celebration, however, came in 1957, with the tercentenary of the signing of the Flushing Remonstrance. Local leaders were able to line up the highest-profile event committee ever, and New York State officially lent its support with the Joint Legislative Committee for the Celebration of the 300th Anniversary of the Signing of the Flushing Remonstrance.[42] The festivities culminated in a celebration on October 10 at Bowne House, with an impressive guest list that included Mayor Robert F. Wagner, Governor W. Averell Harriman, Senator Jacob K. Javits, Parks Commissioner Robert Moses, and a host of other local, city, and state leaders. Even President Eisenhower sent a wire: "It is a privilege to join in the observance of the 300th anniversary of the signing of the Flushing Remonstrance. This historical document states a basic premise in the American way of life—our freedom of religion. The individual liberties of our people begin with the free conscience of each citizen."[43] Will Herberg, the prophet of consensus himself, could not have said it any better. Several weeks later, the Friends Meeting House sponsored a series of forums on "What Does Freedom of Religion Mean in

Original Flushing Remonstrance document, delivered to City Hall, in Manhattan, under special guard, 1957. Received by Mayor Robert Wagner, Judge Colden, and others. Collection of the Queens Historical Society, Flushing, N.Y.

1957?" Bowne House made the cover of the 1957 Queens telephone directory, and the Flushing Remonstrance was featured on a special commemorative three-cent stamp. The penultimate hurrah came in 1962, when Flushing Federal Bank opened the 1862 time capsule that had been deposited in Flushing Town Hall. Taken together as a measure of memory, the celebrations seem to show how conscious Flushing residents were of their local history by midcentury, and, whether or not it was a covert tactic by real estate agents to sell out Flushing history, it worked.

Another explanation for all of this pride of place and shared sense of history at the time might have come from the prevailing mood of the 1950s: the Cold War and climate of anticommunism led to an era of consensus and pressure to conform because of the fear of being labeled a communist. Since atheism was associated with communism, there was an increase in church and temple attendance during the decade, though not because a religious revival was sweeping the nation like the Great Awakening of the 1740s or early 1800s. As mentioned earlier, President

Final design for the stamp commemorating the Flushing Remonstrance. Collection of the author.

Eisenhower also had said: "Our government makes no sense unless it is founded on a deeply felt religious faith—and I don't care what it is"; Congress added "under God" to the Pledge of Allegiance in 1954 and "In God We Trust" to U.S. currency in 1955. Jews were more welcome in the United States by this time too, and it became increasingly common to hear the expression "Judeo-Christian America." But perhaps it was just easier for everyone to come together when religious pluralism circa 1955 meant you were either Protestant, Catholic, or Jewish (when the sociologist Will Herberg wrote a book with a similar title). The population of Flushing was also still relatively small compared to the densely populated area it is today (really only half of what it is now), so it was possible to know more of one's neighbors. In any case, it was a time of cohesion and a shared story, and there was a definite sense of neighborhood and community.

"Come Back to the Fair"

Flushing actually had one more occasion to celebrate in the 1960s, when the New York World's Fair returned to Flushing Meadows in 1964–1965, again focusing international attention on the area. Urging America to "Come Back to the Fair," the new international exhibition, with Parks Commissioner Robert Moses as president of the Fair Corporation, was supposed to enshrine his reputation; instead, it harmed it to some extent. With no central plan and no one in the upper echelons of administration with exposition experience, chroniclers of the time suggest Moses ran the fair like a megalomaniac—and his arrogance put off other countries.[44] Like the former fair, the new one had a lofty and admirable theme— "Peace Through Understanding"—which was most symbolic in the huge

Unisphere erected where the Trylon and Perisphere once stood. But if the 1939–1940 New York World's Fair achieved unsurpassed sophistication, the 1964–1965 Fair was a bit tacky —"Democracity" versus "Bel-Gem" waffles (Belgian waffles with strawberries and whipped cream were reportedly what most people remembered most about the 1964–1965 fair).[45] But the difference was also obvious in the new fair's treatment of religion.

Because the 1939–1940 fair had been criticized by some for a perceived lack of religion, Moses had offered land rent free to religious denominations that would build pavilions at the 1964–1965 fair.[46] Despite this, non-Western religions were relegated to minor displays in their national pavilions while Christian pavilions eclipsed even the Protestant-Catholic-Jewish flavor of the Temple of Religion in 1939–1940. The Billy Graham Pavilion featured a bizarre, space-age twenty-eight-minute film called "Man in the Fifth Dimension," and it was joined by the Protestant Center, a Christian Science Pavilion (again), the Church of Jesus Christ of Latter-Day Saints Pavilion, a Masonic Center, and a Russian Orthodox Church. Moses's cordial relations with the Catholic Archdiocese of New York had influenced Pope Paul VI to lend Michelangelo's statue of the *Pieta* for the Vatican Pavilion. Unfortunately, the designers of the exhibit were heavily criticized for making it resemble more of a sideshow than a sacred space.[47] As one observer put it: "All the cumulative pop novelties in the world became urbane by comparison. Accompanied by twinkling electric candles, moving sidewalks, a plastic screen, canned music, chicly costumed usherettes, and an overdose of cold light, the Michelangelo is lost to us forever."[48] But perhaps the most egregious display was the Two Thousand Tribes Pavilion sponsored by Wycliffe Bible Translators (WBT). With a souvenir brochure entitled "From Savage to Citizen," WBT seemed to suggest that WASP supremacy could and should conquer "savage tribes" by converting them into a more civilized Christianity. The brochure began by relating the story of an Amazon Indian chief:

> "I was an unhappy savage chief. I used to cut off the heads at the shoulders, then cut the back of the head for scalping. I loved to kill—I took many heads. We went on raids. We speared, we killed, we hated . . . We set fire to houses. . . ." Chief Tariri learned from his forefathers to hate, and kill, and shrink the heads of his enemies. He plundered and murdered in an isolated corner of the great Amazon River basin.[49]

The story ended with Chief Tariri's conversion and renunciation of his savage beliefs: "We fervently loved Satan—the boa is really Satan. Now that we love Jesus and have taken Him as the missionaries have taught us, we have done away with boa worship. We want no more of that."[50] The 1964–1965 World's Fair may have been devoted to "Peace Through Understanding," but evidence of this was hard to find. As one commentator summarized:

> What it all added up to was that despite its international theme, the Fair was in many ways a piece of white-bread America—religious, conservative, middle-class—plunked down in the heart of ethnic New York. To the dismay of civil rights leaders, there was not a single black or Puerto Rican on the Fair's administrative staff of two hundred, and few were employed, even in menial posts, around the building. The whole enterprise was a throwback to a more homogenous era in which blacks, like slums and other "social problems," were kept out of sight and out of mind. Any hint of inequality, conflict, or injustice was excluded from the social purview of the Fair.[51]

Right outside the gates of the fair, protests raged—even before opening day. The civil rights movement was just beginning to gain momentum, but tensions had begun in Flushing as early as 1951, when an entire black community around Macedonia AME church was displaced to build a new parking lot.[52]

The only African Americans accorded respect at the fairs were entertainers.[53] Bill "Bojangles" Robinson had performed in the "Hot Mikado" for the 1939–1940 fair, and in 1964, Ben Webster recorded "See You at the Fair." But ever since the 1920s, many key players in the history of jazz had lived in Queens. Louis Armstrong purchased a home in Corona in 1943 and lived there all his life. Billie Holiday moved to Queens at the end of the 1940s, living first in Addisleigh Park and, later, in a modest second-floor apartment in the new housing project of Parsons Gardens in Flushing. Dizzy Gillespie also lived in Parsons Gardens before saving enough money to buy a home in Corona, near Armstrong. Upon their deaths, "Satchmo" and "Diz" were buried (along with Johnny Hodges) in Flushing Cemetery. Years later, the Armstrong Archives at Queens College would become a major resource for jazz historians and, in 2000, Armstrong's house would open as a museum.[54]

Building on the attention of the 1964–1965 fair, New York acquired a new baseball stadium that would also draw more people to Flushing in the years to come. Dedicated on April 17, 1964, Shea Stadium (named after William A. Shea, an attorney who was instrumental in acquiring a new team for New York following the city's abandonment by the Giants and the Dodgers in the 1950s) became the home of the New York Mets. The noisiest outdoor ballpark in the majors (because it was in the flight path of La Guardia Airport), Shea Stadium was also the site of one of the very last public concerts by the Beatles on August 23, 1966 (who also performed there on August 15, 1965). The concert was surrounded by controversy, however, because the band was still tarnished by John Lennon's scandalous remarks on March 4 that "We're more popular than Jesus Christ now."

But the greatest pull exerted by the two New York World's Fairs would be symbolized in the iconic Unisphere built for the 1964–1965 fair: over the next thirty-five years, Queens would attract the most diverse population in the country of immigrants from around the world after the Immigration Act of 1965—and Flushing, thanks to its location near the two fairs and enjoying greater accessibility because of changes in transportation, truly would become the World of Tomorrow. At the same time, the community ideology of religious freedom and tolerance that peaked and was shared by the mainly Protestant-Catholic-Jewish residents of Flushing in the post–World War II era would be tested in the years to come by the introduction of the religions of new immigrant groups.

Part II

3

Beyond Protestant-Catholic-Jew
The Immigration Act of 1965 and the Religions of New Immigrants in Flushing

> Religion and race define the next stage in
> the evolution of the American peoples. But
> the American nationality is still forming: its
> processes are mysterious, and its final form,
> if there is ever to be a final form, is as
> yet unknown.
>
> —*Nathan Glazer and Daniel P. Moynihan,*
> Beyond the Melting Pot *(1963)*

Far away from the fairground in Flushing Meadows, the U.S. Congress during the Johnson administration had been busy pushing through new legislation advocated by the late John F. Kennedy that built on immigration policies born after World War II during the Truman and Eisenhower administrations.[1] As a senator, Kennedy, the first Catholic president and a descendant of Irish immigrants, had written *A Nation of Immigrants*—a book in which he denounced the restrictive national origins quota system that had been in place since the 1920s, when pervasive nativist sentiment led Congress to close the door on immigrants from Asia and southern and eastern Europe and set limits on those from western Europe. Efforts to monitor immigration more carefully had been around since the Alien and Sedition Acts of 1798 but were not enforced, and the entry of waves of Europeans continued virtually unrestricted for a century. The clamor to close the door had been building since the anti–Catholic nativism of the 1840s and 1850s and reached an alarming pitch when racist pseudoscience and notions of White Anglo-Saxon Protestant supremacy similarly influenced many to regard many immigrants from 1880 to 1920 as inassimilable—or unmeltable (to use the imagery from a popular play by Israel Zangwill in 1908 called *The Melting Pot*). After the homogenizing forces of the 1920s held sway for two decades, nativist sentiment began to ease as early as 1943, when the Citizens Committee to Repeal the Chinese Exclusion Acts persuaded Congress at least to give China an annual quota of 105; similar provisions for Indians and Filipinos were made in 1946. An apparent setback came in 1952 with the McCarran–Walter Immigration Act (which was supposed to keep the national origins quotas in effect), but special laws and presidential decisions had permitted hundreds of thousands of refugees to come under the Displaced Persons Acts of 1948 and 1950 (European refugees from war), the Refugee Relief Act of 1953 (European refugees from war and escapees from communist-dominated countries), and the Refugee-Escapee Act of 1957 (Europeans and Asians fleeing persecution and war in communist countries—Hungarians, Koreans, Yugoslavs, and Chinese). By the 1960s, a mixture of economic confidence, foreign policy, ethnic lobbying, and a new tolerance brought about by the civil rights movement helped galvanize support for greater changes in immigration policy. The Immigration (Hart–Celler) Act of 1965 threw open the door again—especially to people from parts of the world not represented before in large numbers in America, and another massive movement of people began.[2] Although it was primarily meant to aid family reunification, the new legislation also gave preference to migrants with special skills and to more refugees (Cubans and, later, Vietnamese, Laotians, and Cambodians displaced by the war in Southeast Asia).

The flow of newcomers increased when the Refugee Act of 1980 raised the annual limit of immigrants admitted to 320,000 (up from 290,000 in 1978). And, in 1986, the Simpson–Rodino Act, formally the Immigration Reform and Control Act (IRCA), attempted to restrict undocumented immigrants but actually ended up giving amnesty to almost three million illegal aliens. Four years later, the Immigration Act of 1990, like the 1965 act, favored immigrants with special skills—in this case, those in the rising high-tech and computer industry. This last major legislation of the twentieth century boosted immigration 35 percent, with 1991 reaching the largest figure in American history: 1.8 million persons.[3]

In the last quarter of the twentieth century, Queens became the most diverse large county in the country, according to studies of 1990, 2000, and 2010 U.S. Census data, with perhaps the most striking changes taking place in Flushing.[4] A town almost exclusively white and black would absorb several different waves of newcomers between 1965 and 2000: South

President Lyndon B. Johnson signs the Immigration Act as Vice President Hubert Humphrey, Lady Bird Johnson, Muriel Humphrey, Senator Edward (Ted) Kennedy, Senator Robert F. Kennedy, and others look on, at Liberty Island, New York, October 3, 1965. LBJ Library photo by Yoichi Okamoto.

Asians, Chinese, and Koreans were among the earliest and largest groups, and these were joined by smaller numbers of Eastern Europeans and various immigrant groups from Latin America, the Caribbean, and Africa (see Tables 1 and 2 in Appendix B). The older ethnic mix shifted: Asians outnumbered whites by 2000, and the former Protestant-Catholic-Jewish community gave way to a much more complex microcosm of world religions. At the same time, the dramatic and rapid demographic change tested Flushing's legacy of tolerance and the limits of pluralism. The earlier sense of community began to fracture during a period when the nation itself was already being torn by assassinations, urban blight, race riots, the Vietnam War, protest movements, and Watergate.[5]

Riots, Race, and Religion

By the 1960s and 1970s, Flushing's older ethnic mix began to diminish. Many moved out to the suburbs or passed away, and their children chose not to stay. Reflecting a post–World War II decline in cities across

America, the downtown central business district (which had been the principal commercial area for the North Shore of Long Island) began to suffer as more property went up for sale, with nearly every third storefront empty. Local business was also siphoned away with the opening of new shopping malls nearby.[6] New York City had plunged into a fiscal crisis by 1975, and those effects were felt everywhere. Compounding this were new welfare reform and housing policies in the 1970s that changed many areas in the city, including Flushing. Introduced in 1974, the housing choice voucher program, better known as the Section 8 Leased Housing Program, was (and still is) the federal government's major program under the U.S. Department of Housing and Urban Development (HUD) to assist low-income families, the elderly, and the disabled to afford decent, safe, and sanitary housing in the private market. Under the voucher program, tenants received a portable subsidy to allow them to afford to rent an apartment or single-family home. As the city branch of the government serving residents throughout the five boroughs, the New York City Housing Authority (NY-CHA) provided thousands of vouchers to people (mostly African Americans and Hispanic immigrants, but also low-income European Americans and other immigrants) who came to Flushing seeking apartments. At the same time, Flushing was also being transformed by a national trend among city planners of the 1950s and 1960s, who favored slum clearance policies of urban renewal.[7] The demolition of houses belonging to an old black neighborhood around Macedonia AME church to build a parking lot already had displaced an entire community and led to the construction of a monstrous city-owned housing project named Bland Houses. So called not for its depressing dullness, the project memorialized Flushing native James A. Bland (1854–1911), a composer and Howard University graduate who at twenty-four wrote "Carry Me Back to Old Virginny," which was adopted in 1940 as Virginia's state song. Another project opened in the early 1970s under Section 8, but the new black migrants were much poorer than the descendants of Flushing's colonial black population. Despite the efforts of a few progressive liberals, racial prejudice reigned, and the latter days of the civil rights movement reached Flushing too. In May 1968, just weeks after Rev. Dr. Martin Luther King Jr. was murdered in Memphis, many places of worship in Flushing participated in a "Week of Concern" in connection with "Riots, Race, and Religion," organized by Rev. Dr. Timothy P. Mitchell, the pastor at Ebenezer Baptist Missionary Church. Mitchell had marched with King in Alabama and welcomed his help later with housing protests in nearby Corona-Elmhurst, Queens, where most of Mitchell's congregation now came from because of segregated housing in Flushing.[8] With a kickoff meeting at First Unitarian Church, Mitchell protested the intolerable slum housing conditions and discrimination against African Americans and Puerto Rican immigrants who wanted to integrate white cooperative apartment houses. Referencing President Johnson's "Great Society" speech of 1964, Mitchell said, "We black people are proud of what we are, but we want to be able to live like anyone else and benefit from the fruits of this great society."[9] Subsequent meetings were held at the Free Synagogue, First Congregational Church, St. Michael's RCC, Ebenezer, and Flushing High School. Unfortunately, the housing problem would linger to the present, and, as crime rose and downtown was viewed as unsafe for the first time since the 1850s (a sentiment that did not wholly disappear until the 1990s), many whites blamed blacks and fled Flushing. Although a number of these whites were upwardly mobile and would have moved away anyway, most did so to escape a deepening sense of urban decay.

Years later, longtime residents would reflect upon the time and say that "the 1970s almost destroyed Flushing."[10] Similar sentiment about the local cityscape was expressed in a report by a graduate student of architecture named Robert Kalish, who had lived in Flushing since 1954 and had witnessed tremendous growth: "in the early 1960s, an unprecedented housing boom transformed the placid face of the area [and, since then,] houses and apartments have sprouted up like weeds, shooting up wherever they possibly can."[11] Bothered by abnormally high numbers of pedestrians competing for space in the downtown area, Kalish wanted something to be done to "the heart of Flushing" and felt that solving problems of public transportation would battle the declining quality of life.[12] His proposal was never implemented, but elements of it would be echoed later in the Flushing Public Transportation Plan of 1992 and the Downtown Flushing Plan by the New York City Department of City Planning in 1993.

While the period of Flushing's decline in the 1960s and 1970s was troubling to longtime residents unable to reverse the downward spiral on their own, it presented opportunities to new immigrants, who would help revitalize the community and also transform it in ways more familiar to them.

Queens: The Lower East Side of the Twenty-First Century

Between 1880 and 1930, over twenty-seven million people entered the United States—about twenty million through Ellis Island in the Port of New York. New York City was the gateway, and many settled in a ghetto of overcrowded tenements in the Lower East Side of Manhattan before moving on to other locales. Jewish enclaves, Little Italy, and China-town became discernible areas within this district, and a vibrant street life both appalled and attracted other city dwellers. Seeking more space and a slower pace, many also chose Queens, which began to transform into a great new suburban expansion borough as it became more accessible from Manhattan (and elsewhere) thanks to the construction of new roads, bridges, and tunnels, the extension of subway service, and the opening of the city's two airports.

After 1965, immigrants to New York rarely arrived by boat; most now flew into John F. Kennedy International Airport (formerly New York In-ternational Airport but frequently called Idlewild), and many began to settle in the borough where the airport is located; others arrived in Queens via domestic flights to La Guardia Airport. But whereas most immigrants to the Lower East Side started out poor, many of the first post-1965 wave of immigrants were educated and skilled professionals who sought and could afford a more middle-class area to live and raise a family.

Flushing and other neighborhoods in Queens had already become a destination for many Jews and other "white ethnics" after World War II looking to escape the Bronx and a crowded inner city, and it remained one of the top destinations for many upwardly mobile New Yorkers and new immigrants arriving after 1965 who were looking to escape over-crowding in Manhattan and have more space and perhaps a yard. The in-ternational attention from the two World's Fairs and temporary home of the United Nations General Assembly in nearby Flushing Meadows also began to attract many new residents. In addition, Flushing was (and still is) centrally located, with the largest intermodal transportation point in the city—bus and subway routes terminate in Flushing, La Guardia Air-port is five minutes away and JFK about fifteen to twenty minutes, and it is a major nexus of highways and roads. Desirable for its convenience as the transportation hub of Queens, Flushing was often the first and last stop for many new immigrants. Also, by the 1960s, many older upwardly mobile Jewish families began to move out, and many others left too as the community suffered with the city's fiscal crisis in the mid-1970s. This exodus left a lot of vacant property and commercial space. Finally, a very flexible zoning law from 1961 allowed many different immigrant groups to build so-called community facilities (which includes religious institu-tions) in residential neighborhoods as long as they met building and fire department codes.[13] The Department of City Planning could not have imagined then what the implications of this law would mean for a diverse

Flushing: the largest intermodal transportation point in New York.

and thriving immigrant neighborhood like Flushing several decades later, but it gradually led to a dramatically different architectural landscape by the end of the century.

The Origins of a Microcosm of World Religions in Flushing

It is difficult to reconstruct the history of some of Flushing's earliest new immigrants and their religious life in the 1960s, but archival sources and oral history help sketch part of the picture. The Bureau of the Census collected information in the Census of Religious Bodies from 1906 to 1936, but Public Law 94-521 has since prohibited the U.S. Census from asking a question on religious affiliation on a mandatory basis. Numerous studies conducted since then help fill this void, some national and some local.[14]

In the summer of 1962, Paul Van Elk, a college student and assistant minister at the Protestant Reformed Dutch Church, undertook his own religious census of Flushing in the neighborhood around the church (roughly, the old village of Flushing's boundaries) for outreach purposes.[15] An upsurge in the building of large apartment buildings since the early 1950s had led to a great influx of new residents, and the church wanted

The figures in this table reflect the picture of the religious affiliation of
1- The families contacted
2- The families not contacted
3- The families represented by the apartments under construction.

In column I is the percentage of the various categories and in column II this figure is translated into actual numbers, that is, the number of people that were contacted and gave the various replies. Column III represents the projected figures that cover the 1213 families in the apartment houses that were not contacted. Column IV represents the sum on columns II and III. In column V there are the projected figures for the 7 apart- ment houses in the area that are either under construction or not yet fully occupied. (These are the houses represented by the empty boxes on the map). Column VI represents the sum of columns IV and V. In attempting to evaluate these figures it must be remember- ed that only columns I and II are absolute figures. All the other columns include "projected" figures.

		CONTACTS	761			
		FAMILIES	1974			
		PER CENTAGE	38.6			

Category	I	II	III	IV	V	VI
Protestant	13.4	102	163	265	94	359
Catholic	34.7	264	421	685	243	928
Jewish	25.8	196	313	509	180	689
No Answer	17.9	136	216	352	125	477
No Affiliation	5.6	43	68	111	39	150
Hindu	.3	2	4	6	2	8
Greek Orthodox	.8	6	10	16	6	22
Russian Orthodox	.6	5	7	12	4	16
Moslem	.1	1	1	2	1	3
*Non-Christian	.3	2	4	6	2	8
Rosicrucian	.1	1	1	2	1	3
Bahaism	.3	2	4	6	2	8
Buddhist	.1	1	1	2	1	3
Total	100.0	761	1213	1974	700	2674

* Families would not give any further information

Table of 1962 Religious Census Report of Flushing by Paul Van Elk, a college stu- dent and assistant minister at the Protestant Reformed Dutch Church (later, Bowne Street Community Church) in the 1960s. Rev. Dr. Elton J. Bruins, Hope College Collection of the Joint Archives of Holland at Hope College, Holland, Michigan.

to spread the word about its new Daily Vacation Bible School. While Van Elk's report lacked the demographic detail of U.S. Census data and only covered a particular sample of Flushing, his work does offer a good snapshot of the emerging religious diversity. Working from June 5 to September 4, 1962, Van Elk went door to door in twenty-one buildings and visited (and often revisited) a total of 1,974 families, asking the fol- lowing questions: (1) Does the family have any religious affiliation, or do they have none? (2) If they do, what is their affiliation? (3) Do they attend a church or synagogue here in Flushing, travel outside of Flushing, or are they not attached to any particular one? The Protestant-Catholic-Jewish picture was about what one would expect for New York at this time, but a number of other world religions were represented too: Hindus, Muslims, Ba'hai, Buddhists, and Greek and Russian Orthodox Christians. And their numbers were probably higher. In his concluding comments, Van Elk at- tributed the large number of "No Answers" to the language difficulties he encountered with Spanish and "Oriental" families. In any case, Van Elk's religious census report of Flushing in 1962 showed that the times were changing—and the picture would change dramatically after 1965 (see Tables 3 and 4 in Appendix B).

Religions of Immigrants from South Asia

The largest and most visible new immigrant group in Flushing came from the Indian subcontinent. Preferences in the Immigration Act of 1965 for those with occupational skills needed in the United States had created what has been called a "brain drain" in India and Pakistan, bringing many South Asian doctors, lawyers, and engineers to America, as well as the first substantial wave of Hindus, Sikhs, and Muslims.[16]

Aside from what they learned from the nineteenth-century transcendentalist writings of Ralph Waldo Emerson and Henry David Thoreau and the Theosophical Society started by Helena Petrovna Blavatsky and Henry Steel Olcott in the 1870s, Americans (and Westerners in general) knew little of South Asian religious traditions until the Parliament of World Religions brought a host of Eastern emissaries to Chicago in 1893. Among those attending was Swami Vivekananda, the first modern teacher of *Vedanta* ("the final aim of the *Veda*"), to come to the West. Over the course of a year, a group of American students gathered about Vivekananda and, in 1894, the first Vedanta Society in the United States was established in a brownstone on the Upper West Side of Manhattan as an official branch of the Ramakrishna Order (the monastic organization established by Swami Vivekananda in India).[17]

In 1936, when a researcher for President Franklin Delano Roosevelt's WPA Federal Writers' Project took on the task of documenting "Hindus in New York," he concluded that:

> There is no Hindu quarter in New York. Still there are about 500 Hindus scattered throughout the boroughs of the city. Of these, constituting the earliest migration from India, businessmen are in the great majority. Next come students and missionaries. They all followed in the wake of the Swami Vivekananda. . . . The American Hindus observe none of the holidays that are kept in India, nor do they practice any of their religion outdoors. They have become thoroughly Americanized.[18]

While the reporter was correct to mention "missionaries" like Vivekananda and other gurus who followed such as Swami Paramahansa Yogananda (and, later, Maharishi Mahesh Yogi and A. C. Bhaktivedanta Swami Prabhupada), a closer glance at the rest of the researcher's work reveals a crude understanding of "Hindu," which could mean Hindu, Sikh, Muslim, or Zoroastrian, among others. Such usage of the word was common for the time, and the writer had few contacts outside of the Vedanta Society on which to base his study. It is also doubtful that all "American Hindus" in New York in the 1930s did not observe any Hindu holidays or that they had become "thoroughly Americanized"—even if the reporter did not observe any outdoor festivals, many Hindus have a *puja* (worship) area in their home, and these were especially important in the early immigrant community before obtaining a larger worship space or building a temple.

Despite this early effort to try to document "Hindus" in New York and what is more generally known about the several gurus who came from the 1890s to the 1960s, there is a growing body of literature on South Asian history in America. Karen Isaksen Leonard has written about Sikh immigrants in late-nineteenth-century California (where they met and often married Mexican women), and Vivek Bald has been able to uncover an early and more detailed history of South Asians in New York and around the country from the 1880s to 1960s.[19]

Of course, a larger and more diverse South Asian community developed in New York and the United States in the years after 1965.[20] Madhulika S. Khandelwal notes that when several Indian professionals settled in Flushing in the 1960s, "they became pioneers whose selection of Flushing attracted more newcomers from India to the neighborhood."[21] As this "chain migration" developed and the Indian community grew and began to take root in Flushing, the neighborhood became what Khandelwal has called a "core area of ethnic life," where places of worship draw South Asians from further away, "particularly on weekends [when] these spaces attract a large number of suburban Indians who travel to ethnic spaces from their mixed but essentially white neighborhoods."[22] This early community soon improvised ways to continue their religious traditions in America just as other immigrant groups had before them: humble beginnings in living rooms, basements, rented halls, storefronts, and converted buildings soon led to newly constructed temples, gurdwaras, and mosques.[23]

"Little Kashi": Hinduism in Flushing

There were thirty-two Indian families in our building of fifty apartments, so specialized as to language, religion, caste, and profession that we did not need to fraternize with anyone but other educated Punjabi-speaking Hindu Jats. There were six families more or less like [ours] (plus Punjabi-speaking Sikh families who seemed friendly in the elevator and politically tame, though we didn't mingle), and three of the families also had aged parents living in.[24]

Bharati Mukherjee, *Jasmine*

In *Jasmine*, Bharati Mukherjee's novel about a Punjabi Hindu woman's life as an Indian immigrant in late-twentieth-century America, the main character lives briefly in Flushing and encounters an already large and well-established South Asian community. Amazed by the variety of ethnic stores and services in the Indo-Pak-Bangla-Afghani shopping district on Main Street (perhaps the first Little India in America, though not the largest), Jasmine later reflects back on her time there: "Flushing was safe, a cocoon to hatch out of."[25] The community had become so settled that the degree of replicating an entire culture approached what sociologists would call "institutional completeness," with South Asian groceries; appliance, video, jewelry, and *sari* stores; beauty salons; newsstands; car services; restaurants; and sweet shops—as well as places of worship and other ethnic organizations. Like other upwardly mobile immigrants who eventually find the familiarity of the ethnic enclave stifling, Jasmine grows restless and soon takes "the #7 train out of the ghetto."[26] Many who come back still remember Flushing as a primarily South Asian community, and they are surprised to see how it has absorbed other new immigrant groups. Taiwanese and Korean immigrants eventually took over more area as their businesses and institutions grew in central downtown Flushing, but in the 1970s through the 1980s (*Jasmine* was published in 1989), South Asians were the most visible new immigrant group, and their presence was felt more.[27]

Similar and even larger South Asian commercial areas would form later in Jackson Heights, Richmond Hill, in two areas of Manhattan, and in nearby Edison, New Jersey, as enterprising pioneers from Flushing moved on, but it would remain the mother of the South Asian community in America. People stayed and returned to Flushing not so much for the shops but because it was also where most of the first temples, gurdwaras, and mosques were established.[28] It was a "Little India," but, more specifically, it also became, as a woman at one of the newer Hindu temples in Flushing put it, a "Little *Kashi*"—a reference to the city of Varanasi (or Benares or Banaras), India, to which Hindus make pilgrimages to visit ancient temples, bathe in the Ganges River for ritual purification, and where many hope to be taken when they die to have their cremated remains deposited in the water. Some South Asians in America still wish to make that final return to India, but, until then, Flushing would be the principal spiritual location for the greater tristate area (New York, New Jersey, and Connecticut) and beyond.

> This is the land of Vishnu, because Vishnu's mount is the eagle, and that is the national bird here.
> Alagappa Alagappan, interview with author, 1994

For several years, longtime residents of Bowne Street in Flushing probably had no idea that a small group of Hindus had purchased and converted the old Church of the Nazarene (by then a Russian Orthodox church) to worship according to their beliefs. They may have found it rather interesting and perhaps even appropriate considering the religious heritage of Flushing. But when in 1975 the church was replaced and construction began of an immense and elaborate edifice in the traditional architectural style of a South Indian Hindu temple, there simply had been no precedent.[29]

As the first Hindu temple in North America built according to the *Agama Sastras* (scriptures relating to temple building), composed largely of imported materials, and constructed by artisans from India, the Hindu Temple Society of North America was one of the most impressive and historically important Hindu temples in the West.[30] More commonly known as the Ganesha temple after the elephant-headed god of wisdom and remover of obstacles, the central deity in the worship area, the temple owes its success to the visionary who founded it, a record of sound leadership and organization, a central location in an area with the largest concentration of Indians in the United States, and, many would insist, divine grace. Finally, its strength and influence outside of New York is proven by the fact that the temple has served as a model for many other Hindu communities.

Flushing, Queens, was chosen as the location for the Ganesha temple based on three criteria: it was the gateway of the United States—all Indian immigrants came here, and there was a large concentration of Hindus in the tristate area; it was within walking distance for many and for others one bus or subway fare; and the possibility existed to purchase a suitable site.

That the temple's first building was a converted Russian Orthodox church with several other layers of history is illustrative of the kind of processes that can take place with congregations of any faith through time: as a congregation dwindles or grows, it may be necessary to close down,

Dr. Alagappa Alagappan in his living room, where the Hindu Temple Society of North America was established in 1970.

add on to the existing place of worship, or move to a larger space. And if a place of worship is sold, the next tenant is usually another, often quite different, congregation. When this happens a number of times, as it did with the site on Bowne Street, the structure becomes an ethnic palimpsest and demonstrates the phenomenon of adaptive reuse. In 1890, the First Baptist Church of Flushing built what it called a "park branch" on what was then called Bowne Avenue and Hitchcock Park—where it was described as "a neat chapel" and depicted as such in a 1904 atlas of Queens.[31] In 1919, the structure then became the site of the First Church of the Nazarene until the late 1950s, when it moved to another location nearby; the old building was sold to another group and became the Russian Orthodox Church of the Holy Annunciation.[32] The property went on the market for the last time in 1971, when a committee at the Russian Orthodox church found it too needed a larger space.

A year earlier, on January 26, 1970, the first meeting of a board of trustees to incorporate the Hindu Temple Society of North America took place in the living room of a modest two-story house in Jamaica Estates, Queens, where a South Indian gentleman named Dr. Alagappa Alagappan lived with his family. The group planned to obtain funds for a place of worship, and the project started with a check for fifty-one dollars. The search for a suitable building took Alagappan all over Queens, and he eventually learned of the Russian Orthodox Church when it was made available.

Alagappan emigrated in March 1961 from Chettinad, India—a prominent cluster of villages in Tamil Nadu, three hundred miles south of Madras, whose inhabitants, the Chettiars, are businesspeople with a long tradition of building temples. At that time there were no Hindu temples, and he and other Indians worshipped in houses, churches—anywhere. Alagappan attended London University and was called to the bar from Middle Temple, and he then joined the United Nations as a career civil servant, moving with his family to Parkway Village (where other UN employees from around the world lived) and then to the house in nearby Jamaica Estates. He said he later realized, however, that his mission was to be an instrument for temple building through the sage Lord Agasthya, or Gurumuni—the preeminent sage of all the Hindu gurus.

The board of trustees was the product of Alagappan and his colleague and friend at the United Nations, C. V. Narasimhan, the former under-secretary general and chef de cabinet.[33] Narasimhan's stature and their combined experience at the United Nations helped them establish a solid foundation. The remaining members of the board consisted of two Indians and four non-Indians—including the late scholar of Hinduism Barbara Stoler Miller and E. C. Grigg, a sociologist at the United Nations who was chairman of the board for the first seven years. Many Indians were not interested at first. There was a lot of criticism. Some felt the board should have chosen a site with more parking space out on Long Island; others felt the project would never get off the ground or, worse, that everyone would lose sight of the traditions and become too American. Alagappan has explained that this was perhaps to be expected—"they want you to prove yourself . . . they want to have success before they associate themselves, and people don't want to start with some crackpot project."[34] When the Russian Orthodox Church was bought, a small group of Hindus began to worship there for about two or three years, but temple attendance did not increase dramatically until 1977. By that time, Alagappan had secured the sponsorship of the Tirumala Tirupati Devasthanam (TTD) and the Endowments Department of the government of the state of Andhra Pradesh in India. A work camp of about 150 artisans was established near Hyderabad to prepare the architectural inputs, including the stone sanctum for the Ganesha temple at New York, and construction of the temple began in 1975 on the site where the old church used to stand.

Alagappan said he was particularly inspired to act on building a temple to Ganesha in New York through divine advice read out by trained mediums from *nadisastras*. Essentially, he explained, this involves a set of palmyra leaves, through which the sages speak—in this case, Lord Agasthya. The messages appear to have been written centuries ago, but actually the letters only appear at that point in time when they are read out—and then they disappear. Apparently, the messages were very specific in their instructions:

> What happens is (1) depending on the date of birth, your horoscope is cast, (2) then immediately the medium begins to read, and the letters begin to appear. Obviously, a superior spirit communicates—a deity or whatever you call it—but then those things impart more than an astrologer can say. So what happened was that when I had been in India in the summer of 1968 I was told that there was a message for me from Lord Agasthya. I went the next day to visit, and the medium read out the letters that appeared from Lord Agasthya, saying that Ganesha will take a small abode in a city the name of which begins with the letter *N*. The second day I went, and he said that this temple was to do something very important—to develop deep and abiding ties between India and this country. The third day I knew something was happening: he said, "You take on this project and get it done!" which meant that his blessings were there. He also, after a few years, gave the instruction that the stone from which Ganesha would be made should come from Tiruvannamalai, India—where Ganesha lives.[35]

Construction of the temple was completed in 1977. His Holiness Sri La Sri Pandrimalai Swamigal, a great *siddha* (an illumined sage) from Chennai (Madras), had prepared twenty-six *yantras* (small metallic plates in which the particular deity is inscribed; *puja*, or worship, is done to it) for the temple, and had done *pujas* for them for five years before installing them on July 4, 1977.

The Ganesha temple was not the only temple planned, but it was the first. Narasimhan (who would become the first president of the temple), Alagappan, and other members of the Hindu Temple Society of North America had formulated plans for establishing five temples in this continent back in January 1970:

> Everything in Hinduism starts with worship of Ganesha. We were thinking of five temples at that time, but Ganesha came first. Then we wanted Vishnu in Pittsburgh, then Shakti Meenakshi in Houston. But then people began to express differences over property. So

The present Ganesha temple, built and consecrated on July 4, 1977. The temple architecture is classical South Indian style, reflecting the majority of its members.

we decentralized ownership, and each temple became separate, with its own board of trustees and separate legal identity. Even though we call it the Hindu Temple Society of North America, each temple is run differently by the local lay trustees—we do not have any gurus. They are not all part of the Hindu Temple Society of North America; however, the temples are members of a loose organization called Council of Hindu Temples of North America. We didn't come to Rama and Krishna [the other two temples which were planned], but now there are seventy temples all over. There are seven Vishnu temples—this is the land of Vishnu, because Vishnu's mount is the eagle, and that is the national bird here.[36]

The Pittsburgh temple was consecrated around the same time, but the Ganesha temple would be the primary focus of the fledgling American Hindu community for religious reasons—and for the simple fact that it was established in an area with the first and largest concentration of South Asians in the country.

A few years after it opened, the temple organized a small street parade to celebrate Chaturthi, the birthday of Ganesha, which would later grow into an enormous public spectacle in downtown Flushing. Every year during the Chaturthi parade, the *ratha yatra* (chariot) carrying priests and the small *vigraha* (statue) of Ganesha would pass a number of other places of worship throughout downtown Flushing and on Bowne Street. As it neared the Swaminarayan Hindu temple (also known as Bochasanwasi Akshar Puroshottam Sanstha, or BAPS), the chariot was traditionally greeted by one of its older priests. After exchanging blessings, the parade continued—passing an Orthodox synagogue, a Sikh gurdwara, a Chinese evangelical church, and an Afghani Hindu temple. Later that day, five hundred devotees at the Swaminarayan temple would celebrate Ganesh Chaturthi separately on a cruise that sails around Manhattan. The fact that two different Hindu temples were just down the street from each other in the 1970s (with a third nearby and more to follow) was a sign that Flushing was becoming a microcosm of the variety in Indian religious life.

Described as the last of the medieval Hindu saints and the first of the neo-Hindu reformers, Swaminarayan rose to prominence around 1800 in the western Indian state of Gujarat. He stressed a disciplined, ascetic life and is best understood in the tradition of devotional Hinduism known as *bhakti*. Widely popular in among Gujaratis, it began to spread around the world as they became one of most numerically large Indian immigrant groups. Raymond Williams has noted, "Swaminarayan Hinduism is one of the fastest-growing, regional-linguistic based Hindu sects both in India and abroad [claiming] over one million followers."[37]

Originally, starting in 1970, members of the temple on Bowne Street met in the basement of Dr. K. C. Patel's house a block away. The present structure was inaugurated on August 28, 1977, by Pramukh Swami (literally, "president swami"), and it was the first Swaminarayan temple in North America; it is now the continental headquarters of BAPS, the major branch in the United States of the religion today. Curiously, however, some of the early members say they did not know at first that another temple had been active down the street in the Russian Orthodox church—apparently it was pure coincidence that Bowne Street, at least initially, became such a refuge for temples and other places of worship; only later did anyone learn of the history behind the street's name.

In the early years there were difficulties with some neighbors. The temple has been egged, electronic equipment has been stolen, windows have been broken, and cars have been vandalized. In addition to attacks on the facilities, there have been some physical confrontations. Upon leaving one Sunday evening in the early 1990s, the temple architect was beaten so severely by young hoodlums that he required plastic surgery.[38] At another point, when a woman who lived near the temple went over to complain about noise and parking problems to one of the priests, he recoiled at her approach because of a strict code segregating men and women at the temple. She later said: "I don't think they're used to women talking to them."[39] Like the Ganesha temple, the Swaminarayan temple also suffered from parking problems and complaints from neighbors—although it eventually acquired space for three modest parking lots, crowds are still overwhelming during important functions such as visits by the spiritual leader Pramukh Swami.

Yet despite this history of tense relations, the temple has been quite active in the community. Though more insular and exclusionary than the Ganesha temple, devotees believe you cannot separate your personal life from religion, and most generously give of themselves in the form of *swayam sevak* (volunteer force). Many of the men who are doctors run a free medical clinic that provides basic care (mainly to recent Indian immigrants) and also sponsors blood drives and antiaddiction campaigns. In addition, there is an annual Thanksgiving food drive and a winter coat distribution program.

Perhaps more than any other Hindu organization, the Swaminarayan temple has taken on a truly transnational dimension—signs of which are clearly evident at the temple on Bowne Street. Aside from being a major node in the global Swaminarayan network as a national headquarters for BAPS, the temple is attuned to the goings on of all the other temples worldwide, especially the whereabouts of Pramukh Swami and any news from Gujarat. Indeed, every major event at the temple is likely being carried out simultaneously in every other Swaminarayan temple. On another level, the ascetic impulse built into the tradition is also luring increasing numbers of Gujarati men who have achieved significant professional success abroad to "renounce the world" and become *sadhus* (saints). And for the majority who do not take that step, many still contribute significantly of their time and money to the temple and cause in India (as well as relief efforts for a recent earthquake), illustrating a kind of "transnational ethnicity" that describes those persons in the diaspora who have come to be known as Non-Resident Indians (NRIs).[40]

A third Hindu temple (again, catering mainly to a different regional-linguistic group) was constructed in the 1990s. Its largely North Indian membership reportedly began to meet as far back as 1966.[41] The Hindu Center is a temple but also, its members claim, a community center because of the services it provides to recent immigrants. Dozens of deities are installed in the three levels of the center, but the biggest event of the year has always been the parade through downtown Flushing during the

Pramukh Swami visits the BAPS Swaminarayan Mandir on Bowne Street for special devotional prayers at dawn.

celebration of *Janmashtami,* the birthday of Krishna. Overlapping with some of the same streets in its parade route but much less publicized than the huge Ganesh Chaturthi, the event still draws many people. More interesting perhaps, though, have been the center's festivals to honor the goddess Vaishno Devi—a deity popular not only among certain Hindus in North India but also with Sikhs and Muslims who come to the center on festival days. Asked about this, the president explained that many people at the center are from the Punjab, and they often have relatives who are Sikh because of a Punjabi tradition requiring the eldest son of a Hindu family to be a Sikh.

Finally, several more recent temples have added to the complex picture of Hinduism in Flushing. In May 1999, a group of immigrants from Afghanistan bought a townhouse diagonally across from the Ganesha temple, which they converted into the Asamai Hindu Temple—named after the mountain range around the old city of Kabul, which members say has an ancient Hindu temple built into a cave at the peak. A very small religious minority today, one that has had to remain secretive about their religion for centuries (and that largely fled during the Taliban regime), they are a merchant caste that claims descent from Aryan peoples

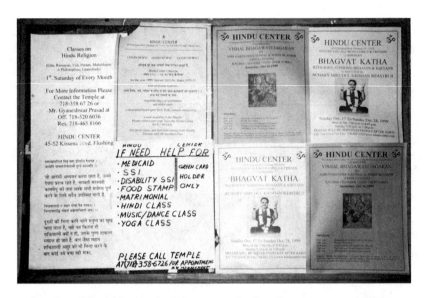

Bulletin board inside the Hindu Center. Note the flyer (bottom row, second from left) advertising services for new immigrants.

and the later Kushana clan. Before the house was acquired, most devotees went to the North Indian Geeta temple in nearby Corona, and the temple now coordinates some activities with the Hindu Center, although they also boast that theirs is a "purer" Hinduism and involves different rituals and practices. Already there is a schematic on the wall inside the temple that shows plans for a large new temple. Other newer temples include the Shirdi Sai temple, a townhouse converted into a shrine devoted to Sri Sai (1854–1918), a widely popular guru from Shirdi, Maharashtra, India; and Shiv Shakti Peeth (Temple), established by a swami from Kurukshetra, Uttar Pradesh, India, in converted retail space along the Indo-Pak-Bangla-Afghani commercial district on Main Street.

As newer Hindu temples came into the picture, earlier temples like the Ganesha temple grew and matured into established community centers of religion and culture. Formally renamed Sri Maha Vallabha Ganapati Devasthanam in the early 1990s (but often still referred to as the Hindu Temple Society of North America and more commonly as the Ganesha temple), the small group of Hindus who met in a living room, bought a converted church, and eventually built a two-story South Indian temple ultimately expanded to a mailing list of over fifteen thousand and acquired more than 64,000 square feet of the surrounding property for offices, priests' quarters, and a gigantic new combination auditorium, wedding hall, gift shop, and casual temple restaurant (the "canteen") with an industrial kitchen.[42] Great care was taken to make the temple as authentic as possible, thanks to a steady flow of donations from the smallest regular contributions of less-affluent members to huge sums from wealthy professionals. Dr. Uma Mysorekar, president of the temple since 1988, explained: "Back home, you take everything for granted. Here, you have the hunger for it. When we are missing something, we want to be sure everything is getting done exactly the way it is to be done."[43] The amount of money, effort, and time put into the detailed productions of festivals and their accompanying ceremonies is astounding—by the 1990s, turnout for Ganesh *Chaturthi* would approach staggering numbers and proclaim the strength and function of the temple in the community.

The temple has been and is still many things to many people. Although founded and attended mainly by South Indians for the fledgling Hindu community, Hindus from nearly every region of India and the diaspora have always come to the temple (for friends' weddings and cultural functions, if not for worship), and it is constantly changing better to represent all of its members. This evolution is evident when the board of trustees decides to install another deity to appeal to Hindus from a certain region. For instance, a figure of the goddess Durga was installed in the temple because a number of Bengalis (who hold the deity in particular esteem) had begun to come. Such a policy of open arms has far-reaching effects. Now there are children from the West Indies who have never been to India but are of Indian descent. The temple's inclusiveness is also reflected in the variety of groups who use it, such as the Gujarati *Samaj* (a society from the western Indian state of Gujarat) and followers of Satya Sai Baba (a popular contemporary charismatic Hindu saint). In addition to curious neighbors and visitors, non-Indians have also been attracted to the temple, and European Americans are a common minority. Members of the International Society for Krishna Consciousness (more commonly known as "Hare Krishnas") founded by A. C. Bhaktivedanta Swami Prabhupada in 1965 and aging hippies typically join the crowd for Chaturthi, and an elderly white woman led a group worshipping the gods Skanda and Jyothi for several years. Several interracial and interfaith couples also come regularly, and morning yoga classes are well attended by a diverse bunch.

The success, growth, and expansion of the temple have also been noted by the temple's neighbors, however, and relations have not always been good. Largely a residential neighborhood of single-family homes, older churches, and synagogues, many did not greet the new temple warmly. Some who had grown up going to the Church of the Nazarene were quite upset to see it knocked down and replaced with an immense Hindu temple. Neighbors also grew alarmed when crowds numbering in the thousands caused parking problems and sometimes left trash in their yards. Only a month after the temple was consecrated, newspapers reported instances of vandalism (graffiti, eggs, destruction of lights) and attacks on South Asians in the area by a mix of white, black, and Hispanic neighborhood teenagers. But often the main problem was just a parking issue. Although the temple eventually acquired nearby property to build a fifty-car parking lot, on weekends and major holidays it cannot accommodate the hundreds of families that gather for worship (not to mention thousands during festivals and important holidays). "When they have their services, there is really no place to park," said one temple neighbor. "They take up the whole street."[44] Yet another resident who has lived across the street for over fifty years said the increased activity from the worshippers going to and from the temple has made the neighborhood safer: "I feel safer, and I'm sure crime has gone down, because there are people all the time bustling around. Sometimes when someone's parked in my driveway, I'm ready to tear my hair out, but I remind myself of the good. You just have to be tolerant and it's really not so bad."[45] Neighborhood hostility largely subsided when the temple employed a security guard and installed a gated fence, yet relations would remain somewhat tense until about the mid-1980s, when the temple began to blend in more as Flushing became increasingly diverse. It was no doubt difficult for a Hindu temple to blend into a Judeo-Christian suburban neighborhood at first, as Hindus had to deal with being a very small minority while coming from a country where Hinduism is dominant and where temples, gurdwaras, and mosques are ubiquitous and familiar fixtures of everyday life. Over the years, however, the Ganesha temple became so representative of the larger Hindu community in America that it would often be the first place reporters call for news—Mysorekar was once asked to comment on a booklet by the Southern Baptist Convention that described Hinduism as dark and demonic.[46] Being the first very visible Hindu temple on the block (and in the country) naturally drew many curious outsiders over time, and some temple-goers have become accustomed to giving impromptu tours to visitors with lots of questions (who are always made to feel welcome). The leadership at the Ganesha temple also realized early on it was in the best interests of community to reach out to the neighborhood. They began to do little things like sending Christmas cards and Indian sweets to neighbors and local officials, as well as formal invitations and flyers to give advance notice of expected crowds—for Chaturthi, the temple sends a letter to the police precinct with dates, times, and the planned route, and a number of officers are then dispatched to the parade as a free service. A large circular gold plaque was also placed on the exterior of the temple depicting a light surrounded by inscribed symbols of the major world religions (it is based on a symbol used by the popular contemporary charismatic Hindu saint Satya Sai Baba). Mysorekar explained, "Our worship may be different from other faiths, but ultimately we aim at reaching the same God. We take different paths but ultimately we reach the same goal. As the Rig Veda said: 'The wise speak of what is One in many ways.'"[47] The temple has also been active on the leadership level in several interfaith organizations, and Mysorekar and other temple representatives attend various conferences and functions on occasion.

The Ganesha temple has been very effective in reaching out to South Asians in the local and tristate area, as well as the national and transnational community, through a number of different media. Businesses in the nearby Indo-Pak-Bangla-Afghani shopping district post flyers about temple events, and several tristate, national, and international South Asian newspapers feature ads and regular reports. A newsletter and calendar are distributed to all members in the temple's computer database and mailing list, reaching thousands. A one-hour television program called *Ganeshvani* is also broadcast every Saturday morning in the New York metropolitan area, featuring devotional *bhajans* (religious songs) and topics about Hindu religion and culture. Finally, like many other temples, the Ganesha temple maintains a website to reach the transnational diaspora of devotees around the globe.[48] Well known even in India, the temple regularly draws famous swamis, intellectuals, actors, and musicians from overseas for various functions. The temple's founder, Dr. Alagappa Alagappan, also assisted the development of the Sri Jyothi Trust in India (an organization devoted to the god Jyothi); he was active in promoting the Jyothi philosophy and in building the main temple and headquarters in Chennai, India. In addition, Alagappan was the chairman of Arupadai Veedu Trust in Chennai, which is setting up six stone temples for the god Skanda in Besant Nagar/Tiruvanmyur, Chennai. The Ganesha temple is not, however, a satellite of any organization in India; everything is separate and has its own dynamics and different leadership. But this transnational dimension is crucial to understanding the South Asian immigrant community and the globalization of Hinduism (as well as Buddhism, Sikhism, Islam, Jainism, and Zoroastrianism).

Temple politics also draws many to become and stay involved, but it can also spark intraethnic tensions. The assets of the Ganesha temple are vested in a board of trustees headed by a chairman and co-chairman. The implementation of the program and conduct of various activities is the responsibility of a president, aided by an executive and several standing and ad hoc committees. Alagappan offered these words regarding temple politics:

> You see, many Indians, the people who came here were very gifted. I'm sure many of them had ambitions of becoming high up in their own country in the political life. They came here, they didn't know where to—they couldn't get into the political life of this country. One of the places they get into is the temples. And then politics starts. It didn't happen in the New York temple [initially], because [of] our by-laws. But in many other temples, there are more proving grounds for democracy other than running the institution, and it has created a lot of problems—annual elections, who will win, who will lose, the situations, enmities.[49]

Such active participation has generally served the temple well (despite some recent disputes), and Alagappan shared his experience and some general guidelines for the management of temples with others through the Council of Hindu Temples.[50]

The challenge that remains will occur in the next century and new millennium. Although some children of the first post-1965 generation of immigrants now have families of their own, the temple will have to continue to adapt to new circumstances for later generations to maintain its relevance and vitality. Alagappan expressed his thoughts on the situation:

> Religion is a daily, living thing. If it can't help you, it isn't needed. Religion must be relevant to daily life. The temple is now a healthy, vital movement. It has served the first generation of Indians very well. The process has begun. It is not entirely satisfactory, but it has to move forward. For some Indian children born in America, the Ganesha temple is important because some of them only know this temple—they have not been to and they don't know the grandeur or the scale of India. As children become part of the mainstream here (which is bound to happen), we will have a mixed audience here. Several non-Indians come now, but that might increase—some Indians might drop off. It's a changing sociological process. The deities bring the devotees. You fall in love with a deity, you come.[51]

Ultimately, he continued, it will be a matter of faith and perhaps some greater reason that will keep the devotees coming to the Ganesha temple—and other Hindu temples in the West:

It has become a good focal point for the community—a neutral framework in which you can follow your worship, whichever you want: Shiva, Vishnu, Lakshmi, Saraswati—whatever you want, you can follow. And, while doing that, you are allowed to do what you like, go on your own, and there's no one twisting your hand, you know—you do what you like; no proselytization, no conversion, no pressure of any type. We are organized, and we see to it that it's available for all people—if you like, you can sit in the corner and meditate—no one will bother you. And so it catches on. It has its own momentum. The pujas are conducted carefully. It has, you see, *divine grace*—it is charged with an atmosphere, it has got the vibrations that people who are psychics can experience. If you have the perception, you can see much more than what meets the eye. So all that is happening.[52]

Alagappan died in 2014 at the age of eighty-eight, and a funeral service was held near the *puja* area in the living room of his home—the same place where the Hindu Temple Society of North America was incorporated in 1970. In an obituary, the *New York Times* referred to Alagappan as "the father of the temple-building movement in North America."[53]

With nearly forty years of history already behind it, the Ganesha temple offers the most complete glimpse into traditional Hinduism in America and illustrates some of the changes that accompany adaptation. As the religion scholar Raymond B. Williams has observed, current Hindu practices in the United States will result in "an American Hinduism that will have some continuity with religious traditions in India but that will be a new form of Hinduism."[54] Such a conclusion has been echoed by the historian Madhulika S. Khandelwal, who has stated that "it appears that the flexible, multi-layered religious system of Hinduism has adaptive features that are capable of expression in a new situation without altering, many Hindus believe, the basic tenets of a five thousand year-old tradition."[55]

Sikhism in Flushing

A popular dance club DJ named Rekha Malhotra who grew up in Flushing may have one of the more interesting stories about the history of Sikhism in the area (as well as South Asian youth culture in New York). Although Punjabi Hindu, Rekha's background and experiences illustrate the hybrid religious identity common to many persons from the northwestern region of India known as the Punjab (which a large number of Sikhs feel should become a separate country called Khalistan). Her parents are from New Delhi but were both born in modern-day Pakistan; they only settled in Delhi after the Partition of India in 1947. In 1970, they immigrated to England. Rekha was born in London in 1971 (west London/Middlesex near Southhall, which people equate to the "Little India" commercial areas of Jackson Heights in Queens; Oaktree Road in Edison, New Jersey; and Devon Street in Chicago), and her family lived there for six years. In 1976, the family moved to the United States. Eventually they settled in Flushing, where they moved to a house on the corner of Ash Avenue and Bowne Street, and Rekha and her sister attended PS 20 (the public John Bowne Elementary School). Rekha's mother worked as a nurse; her father owned a business and drove a taxi on the side. She remembers the construction of the Ganesha temple: "our bus used to go down Bowne Street, and I remember the temple being built—watching people make that temple. I distinctly remember, especially because it's a South Indian temple, and it's very ornate on the outside. And I remember seeing workers, and they were Indian, and they were building this temple."[56] She grew up with a sense that Flushing had a large Indian population, but one that was becoming as differentiated (and clannish) as India itself—with all the various regional-linguistic and religious groups:

> My parents only socialized with people that were Punjabi from west Delhi. Amongst my parents, there was absolutely no fluidity within their social circle. Now it's different. I think everyone pretty much stuck to their own group. The Ganesha temple was mostly South Indians, but there were a lot of Punjabis too. In terms of Punjabiness, it sort of translates to temple and gurdwara—again, I think gurdwara is very much a cultural station for them. They would go to the Geeta temple too. I mean, you know the whole concept of being Hindu is like you believe in every god—it's *all* good, you know? It's like, the more the merrier, bring it on—we'll go to church too! You know? It's like, talk about pluralism, you know? Yeah, they went to every-thing. . . . My mom personally was into both. I don't know, I wear a *kara* [steel bangle]—I always have since growing up.[57]

Region and dialect, then, might separate South Asians socially, but they also bring different religious groups together from the same background. The Sikh Cultural Society was founded in 1965. It held *kirtans* (devotional singing) in homes and then at St. Francis School in Flushing. In 1972, the group purchased a defunct nineteenth-century church in the nearby Richmond Hill area and converted it into a *gurdwara* (a Sikh temple, literally, "door to the guru"), keeping the church's stained-glass windows of Jesus and Mary intact. The Richmond Hill gurdwara was the first in the

The new Sikh Center of Flushing under construction in the 1990s.

northeastern United States, and it became a focal point for a growing Sikh and Punjabi Hindu community in the city.[58] Rekha's family often attended the gurdwara until a local Flushing group established the Sikh Center of New York in 1974. Starting out in a basement near Forty-First Street, the first Flushing gurdwara moved to "this cute little house" opposite the Temple Gates of Prayer (a Conservative synagogue) before being demolished to make way for a larger, three-story concrete structure. Rekha's family used to give *langars* (community meals), and she remembers handing out napkins after *prasad* (a sweet distributed after *kirtan*). And although the family sometimes went to the Geeta temple (a North Indian Hindu temple in nearby Corona-Elmhurst) and the Hindu Center in Flushing, it was the familiar Punjabi culture at the gurdwara that drew them back most often.

The founding gurus of Sikhism in the sixteenth century taught the rejection of the Hindu caste system to reaffirm the equality and oneness of all humankind, and caste seemed to lose even more power in the early South Asian community in Flushing. Rekha explained:

Punjabi classes at the Sikh Center.

I think caste does not play itself out in the same way. I think people are more conscious of differences on a regional or ethnic level—more parochially in terms of Gujarati, Punjabi, etc. I didn't even really know what the hell caste meant until I was a teenager. I also think that there was a translation of Hindu-Muslim tension, definitely. There was that kind of racism that was learned from previous generations, no question.[59]

Certain religious lines were/are not crossed, but it was mainly language and geographic origin that had replaced caste as boundaries of social interaction.

As the first newcomers who stood out in colorful *saris* and *kurtas* from other Flushing residents, South Asians in general also faced neighborhood hostilities from the beginning. Rekha recalls numerous young friends and relatives getting picked on coming home from school, and there was a basic fear of African American and Latino teenagers, as well as animosity between Jewish kids and everyone else:

A lot of the white kids on the block were really nasty, and I distinctly remember being scared or being hesitant or being worried about walking down the block when certain kids were playing on the street [yelling] "Hindus smell," "Hindoo-doo," and "potato head" [to young Sikh boys with their growing hair tucked in a small mound under turbans], this and that—a lot of those kinds of slurs coming from a mixed crowd (not just whites). But I mean, part of that is just kids bullying other kids. It's not necessarily attributed to race, but race becomes a factor when you're trying to identify why you're superior to somebody, and you grab whatever you can—if you're fat, they're going to call you fat; if you're black, they're going to . . . you know? So I think some of those things came into play as well.[60]

Gangs, "posses," and "crews" were also fairly prevalent in Flushing and, in time, as the South Asian community grew, Indian and Pakistani teenagers would form their own.[61] One group called the Main Street Posse (MSP) consisted of South Asian boys from John Bowne High School and, later, Queens College. That some South Asian youth would be caught up in an underworld of crime and mischief may come as a surprise to those who know only the enterprising, professional image of the early Indian community in the United States, but Rekha notes that it illustrates something about class that really has not been addressed:

There is this whole "model minority" myth—but if we examine different economic classes, we find that those things aren't necessarily the same or true—and I think that a lot of these kids were also struggling in the same ways as their counterparts within the same economic class of, like, struggling to finish high school and thinking about where they were going, and *not* necessarily having such a hopeful sense of future, and *not* always doing so good in school—and I think they represented some of that.[62]

Many poorer South Asian families lived (and still live) in Colden Towers, a huge high-rise apartment complex near the Indo-Pak-Bangla-Afghani shopping district on Main Street, a complex comparable to the same oppressive squalor as nearby housing projects.

But Rekha and her older sister Sunita found other diversions, especially music and movies. Her parents liked to entertain, and their house was always packed every year for a big New Year's party, where they would dance all night to Bollywood (Bombay's Hollywood) film soundtracks like *Qurbani* and *Hum Kisise Kum Naheen* on the family's eight-track player. The other major social activity was going to one of several Indian movie theaters nearby: Bombay Cinema Queens and Deluxe Cinema Woodside. Before the theaters opened, people also rented out the auditorium at PS 20 and played Hindi movies. For her seventh birthday, Rekha's mother

At the Unisphere, Flushing Meadows Park, 1977. From left: Rekha's mother, a family friend (Sonia Kalra, in hooded coat), her sister, and Rekha. Photo courtesy of Rekha Malhotra.

bought her the soundtrack to *Saturday Night Fever,* and after that she was rarely seen without her Sony Walkman and cassette tapes. She took guitar, piano and, later, *tabla* lessons at the gurdwara but became particularly entranced by *bhangra* as a teenager, when her mother brought back a record from a trip to England (an early album by Malkit Singh with the song "Tootak Tootak Tuthiyan," which Rekha describes as an old party favorite up there with the "chicken dance"). Bhangra can be traced back to traditional Punjabi folk music, but it really comes out of the United Kingdom—mostly in Birmingham and London, where a second- and third-generation community has given it a more popular modern sound. In England, bhangra was used during weddings and funerals and originally acted as a form of cultural preservation in the community. Rekha got involved with it (beyond just being a fan of the music) when two of her cousins put together a local bhangra dance, around the same time that she became the vice president and then president of the India Club at Queens College, where she was responsible for throwing parties. With the

DJ Rekha of Basement Bhangra. Photo by Nisha Sondhe, courtesy of Rekha Malhotra.

right gear and mixing techniques, it was not long before the dance party outgrew its Indian college crowd, crossed over into a wider New York audience ever hungry for new trends, and came to be known in the 1990s as Basement Bhangra. DJ Rekha was now at the helm of one of the most popular regular dance parties held in hip clubs around the city.[63]

Diagonally across from the Swaminarayan temple on Bowne Street, Gurdwara Singh Sabha of New York came into being because of a disagreement over how the nearby Sikh Center of New York was being run.[64] Komal Singh and Harinder Singh Kanwal had discussed the idea at a party, and a group first met in the house of Inderjit Singh Anand. In 1985 the group began looking for another building and temporarily rented a hall on Bowne Street before purchasing and converting an old storefront (a butcher shop) across the street, near the Kissena Jewish Center, an Orthodox synagogue. Such striking religious diversity was not new to them: the Sikh Center also sat across from a Conservative synagogue, the Temple Gates of Prayer. There are now about three hundred thousand Sikhs and twenty gurdwaras in the New York metropolitan area, but when the pioneering Richmond Hill gurdwara was founded in 1972, there were fewer than one hundred Sikh families in all of New York City.[65] Smaller in size and membership than the Sikh Center several blocks away, Gurdwara Singh Sabha's membership comprises mainly people within walking distance. By the late 1990s, membership size ranged from three hundred to four hundred on the weekends and up to five hundred on special occasions (for example, when a famous *ragi*, or religious singer, came to perform).

Like other gurdwaras and many other places of worship in the new immigrant community in America, Gurdwara Singh Sabha and the Sikh Center of Flushing have served not only as places of worship; they have also served as meeting places for Sikhs to get information about current events in India. Shockwaves were definitely felt in Flushing, and many Sikhs in America were terrified for their relatives in India after Operation Bluestar, when Indian army troops stormed the Darbar Sahib (popularly known as the Golden Temple) in Amritsar, a city established in the sixteenth century in the Punjab region of northwestern India that is the historical and spiritual center of the Sikh tradition. The military action unleashed Sikh rage, and Prime Minister Indira Gandhi was assassinated in 1984 by her Sikh bodyguards, which, in turn, led to anti–Sikh riots. The common bond with India often brought South Asians in Flushing to each others' places of worship prior to this chain of events, but those I spoke to said relations became more strained between Sikhs and Hindus for some time after these incidents. Such moments illustrate how transnational ethnicity among recent immigrants (and perhaps for the life of their generation at least) can affect relations within an immigrant community from an ethnically and religiously diverse region like South Asia.

Islam in Flushing

Shortly after the Sikh Center of New York was established, a number of Muslims who had been meeting in different homes for worship gathered together in May 1975 to establish a weekly Islamic School and a mosque for the growing Muslim community in the area (at the time, there were no mosques in Queens).[66] Largely Urdu-speaking Pakistani immigrants, the group also included a number of families from Saudi Arabia and Kuwait.[67] With a modest rented apartment on Forty-First Avenue, the Muslim Center of New York came into existence. In November 1979, a single-family house was purchased on Geranium Avenue for congregational *salat* (prayers) and day-to-day activities of the center at a cost of $79,000 and modified into a makeshift mosque. Like Bowne Street, Geranium was a quiet street of mostly single-family homes, and the mosque was right around the corner from the Hindu Center. An adjoining house was purchased a few years later, but the two houses combined could only accommodate two hundred, making it inadequate for larger gatherings. Starting out with ten to fifteen families, MCNY gradually evolved into a full-fledged community center and a democratically operated, nonprofit Islamic and educational institution with tax-exempt status, also becoming a member of the Council of Masajid and of the Majlis-Ash-Shura, New York.

Neighbors of the MCNY began to notice more and more Muslims coming and going particularly on Friday afternoon for *Jumu'ah* (the main weekly salat), and the numbers would swell to 1,500 by 1990, when construction of a new mosque had begun. On May 21, 1989, the group had broken ground for the current large mosque, with a ceremony presided over by Dr. Shaikh Saleh Abdullah Bin Hamid, an imam from Al Masjid Al Haram in Mecca, Saudi Arabia.[68] Mayor Edward I. Koch also attended, along with numerous city officials, and said, "In my twelve years as mayor of the city of New York, I have welcomed many important peoples from around the world, but I am most happy to welcome the imam."[69] Over the years, the predominantly Pakistani Muslims were joined by many Saudis and Kuwaitis, who were able to obtain financial support for the new mosque from King Fahad bin Abdul Aziz of Saudi Arabia and Kuwait's Ministry of Auqaf. The new three-story red and gray granite structure, with its minaret rising above oaks and maples (and a tiled dome proclaiming the basic Islamic creed "There is no Deity except Allah and Muhammad is the Messenger of Allah"), was inaugurated on September 21, 1996—again by Dr. Shaikh Saleh Abdullah Bin Hamid and a host of city and state officials, with a Democratic Party representative reading a message from President Bill Clinton. The total cost of project had reached $3.4 million but led to a major Islamic community center: not only was the mosque used for prayer; it had a full-time elementary school (prekindergarten to second grade), weekday Qur'an classes, Sunday Islamic school, a library, a community hall for wedding parties and social events, a kitchen, residential apartments for the imam and staff, an indoor parking lot for thirty cars, and counseling, matrimonial, and funeral services.[70] All of this activity, however, did not sit well with some of the neighborhood's earlier residents. Helun Dunn, a local civic association member who had lived on Geranium Avenue for thirty years, said, "We are concerned about the increase in traffic because these folks worship five times a day."[71] Fridays bring an especially large, yet temporary, crowd for *Jumu'ah*, with a sudden influx of people arriving during their lunch hour before 1:00 and then departing en masse by 2:30, leaving the street empty and quiet again. A Hispanic building superintendent who has worked directly across the

The Masjid Hazrat-I-Abubakr, an Afghani mosque.

street from the mosque for twenty years saw the mosque go up "piece by piece." He said he often watched the new neighbors, and, despite some double parking and congestion, he noticed that most people actually seemed to walk there and that "they come, pray, and go in fifteen, twenty minutes."[72] That many do walk to the mosque underscores the fact that the mosque, like many other new immigrant places of worship in Flushing, is a neighborhood institution, not a remote destination to which people commute. Efforts were also made to limit the building's impact on the surrounding neighborhood: there is no chanting from the minaret, and signs are posted about parking regulations. The mosque has also been led by Dr. Mohammad T. Sherwani, a devout Muslim who is quick to stress the merits of Islam to visitors and who also participates in local interfaith groups.

Another mosque was underway by the mid-1980s several blocks northeast of downtown Flushing when a growing number of Afghani Muslims established the Masjid Hazrat-I-Abubakr.[73] A dramatic increase in immigrants from Afghanistan coincided with the Soviet invasion of Afghanistan in 1979. Originally meeting in a house nearby for several years, the group moved to another house next door to the mosque's present location in 1986, raised money, and opened the new mosque after four years of construction. Assistant Imam Ahmad Wais Afzali was involved for much of mosque's history. Born in 1971 in Kabul, when he was seven his family migrated to America (settling in Flushing), before the Soviet invasion. Although a large number of Arab Muslims concentrated around Atlantic Avenue in Brooklyn, Flushing became the largest Afghani community in the city. The son of a successful businessman, Afzali decided to study and eventually become an imam when he was about eighteen. Growing up in Queens (and never once returning to Afghanistan) left its imprint on his accent and made him aware of the borough's religious and ethnic diversity, but Afzali nonetheless felt free to apply strict Islamic principles to his life. (In fact, because of his long beard and traditional Afghani attire, he said other Muslims he met on a visit to Saudi Arabia were surprised that he could dress in this fashion in America.) By the late 1990s, membership at the mosque grew to over four thousand, and, although the mosque's open-door policy brings some Pakistanis, Arab Muslims, Bosnians, African Americans, European Americans, and even Chinese Muslims, the majority (90 to 99 percent) are Afghani. Afzali (who speaks English for non-Afghanis) and the head imam both speak Eastern Farsi, or Persian; many from the south speak Pashto, and a few speak dialects from other parts of Afghanistan. Another smaller Afghani mosque in a nearby house, Sayyid Jamal al-Din Afghani, serves yet another group of Afghani Muslims.[74] With other Afghani voluntary associations such as the Afghan Immigrants Center in Flushing and Afghan Community in America, the community became established in the area and fairly self-sufficient. Language tends to be a factor in the larger Muslim community, too: Afzali said he sent his son to the school at the nearby Muslim Center of New York (predominantly Pakistani Urdu speakers) and that the two mosques are affiliated on certain occasions, "but pretty much they have their own system and we have our own system."[75] By the mid-1990s, Islam had little competition in Taliban-controlled Afghanistan (besides a small Hindu community, for instance), but the Afghan members of Masjid Hazrat-I-Abubakr found themselves surrounded by many other traditions in Flushing. In one of the more unusual juxtapositions, a Korean Presbyterian church was built right next door; a synagogue and other churches are nearby. Afzali said the mosque gets occasional curious visitors (who are welcomed), and he and the Koreans from the church next door often visit with each other for common neighborhood issues (the children also play volleyball together behind the mosque). In recent years, the mosque has also been contacted by reporters wanting to know more about the Taliban. Afzali acknowledged there are Afghan Muslims in Queens who sympathize with the Taliban, but they are just one faction:

> Oh yeah. In Queens, it's such a diverse community, we have people from so many different backgrounds. In Afghanistan we have different people from different places of Afghanistan—if you see the map, we have some twenty or thirty states. And somehow, when they come to America, they live in the same area in the same community but they all share one common ground—which is being from the same country. Being a Muslim first, of course being from the same country. Now, they might speak different language, different dialect. Some people who like Taliban they are pro-Taliban; some people they don't like Taliban, they have no problems expressing their views that they don't like Taliban. Some people who like other ethnic groups from the north—it makes no difference. If you like one politician or another politician—just like America. We have different parties and different people to support those parties. Nothing like that gets out of proportion, nothing like we have to sit here and talk about it. They're there, we're here. No one's going back, let's face it. Our kids (or at least my kids are) born here, we pay taxes, we own houses here, we own businesses. This is small talk, you know. Especially if you saw that thing on CNN—I don't know if you saw it or not. There was this young lady from England, her father was Afghani Muslim [Saira Shah's documentary "Behind the Veil"]. She went to Afghanistan with hidden cameras. So for the past few weeks, it was a very hot subject.[76]

In the mid-1990s, the Taliban sent a delegation to America, and they opened an office on Main Street in Flushing to provide services as an unofficial embassy to the Afghani community. Apparently, upward of 90 percent of families who fled Afghanistan after the Soviet invasion never had a chance to sell their property (including Afzali's father), and the Taliban office in Flushing was established mainly to return houses and land to their rightful owners as well as help with passports. Many Afghanis came (even those who were against the Taliban), but it was closed in 1998 after the bombing of two U.S. embassies in Tanzania and Kenya was tied to Osama bin Laden and Al Qaeda, who had training camps in Afghanistan.

After the Clinton administration authorized the use of force against targets in the Sudan and Afghanistan shortly after the bombings, the trouble temporarily seemed far away from Flushing:

> We've been here fourteen years, fifteen years, so we are pretty much established. As far as being a neighbor, we are surrounded by people from different faiths. So it's not a problem—we pretty much fit in with this area. This area is a quiet area. I don't see any problems. I don't see a problem at all. Thank God, that in the fifteen years that we've been here, by the mercy of God, I do not recall one incident that happened at a mosque. Only the first . . . two years ago at Halloween, we had a couple of kids throw a couple of eggs at the mosque. It's kids. But, as far as that goes, thank God, no other problems. I don't see that, especially in America, especially where the laws and regulations goes. . . . Most of the people that come to America, whether they are fanatics or extremists, it's only just an outside appearance. *You're not going to have some guy come here and do something . . . because of what happened back in his country . . . I doubt that's going to happen.*[77]

When asked why he thought there was little conflict in a diverse neighborhood like Flushing compared to other parts of the world torn apart by religious conflict, Imam Afzali said:

> I doubt that's going to happen here. Most of the people who came over here, even Hindus, Jews, or Muslim—whoever they are, whatever their religion—when they left their countries and their brothers, it's common sense why they came here: for economic reasons. They came here to have better lives. They came here to have a piece of the American Dream so called. To have the houses. The living example of that is that most of the Afghanis that came here, 80 percent of them, they're not here now. They build this mosque, they all live in Long Island now. They have their houses, they have successful businesses. You only have a few of them that just came recently who just come here. So, most people that come to America, as far as I know, as far as I observed, come here not to start trouble or make trouble. *They left trouble to come here for a peaceful life. That's why you see the coexistence here.* If we had those people that said, "you know what, let's kill the Christians," there would be a big chaos here. If you had people who killed the Muslims, there would be chaos here. If we had people that said, "you know what, lets kill

all the Hindus," we would have big chaos here. Have you noticed that the Muslim Center is right down the block, right next to the Hindu temple? Have you ever noticed that? So you can tell, most of the people that live in Flushing, basically they are here to live. They want to let their kids go to colleges, they want to have a piece of the American Dream, they want to own houses, businesses. *A lot of stuff happens back home, but you don't find the retaliation to be here. Isn't that true? A lot of stuff happens in the Middle East, but you don't find the Muslims going and trying to retaliate here.*[78]

Nothing had prepared anyone, including the members and leaders of the largest Afghani mosque in the city, for what would happen on September 11, 2001, five days after this interview was given.[79]

As the earlier temples, gurdwaras, and mosques became established in Flushing and grew in membership, they were joined by new places of worship in the 1980s and 1990s. Madhulika Khandelwal notes that "among the urban centers in the United States, New York has the largest concentration of Indians (about 10% of the total 1990 Indian population in the country) . . . [with] 60% in Queens."[80] A recent report by the New York City Department of City Planning demonstrates Flushing's continued significance: from 1990 to 1994 it was the top neighborhood of settlement for Asian Indians, and it also experienced the greatest change in average annual Asian Indian immigration from 1983 through 1994.[81] On Bowne Street, another gurdwara opened up in a storefront by the Swaminarayan temple, and a group of Afghani Hindus later moved into a townhouse near the Ganesha temple. Three more Hindu temples would be established by 2000 in the vicinity, bringing the total in Flushing to seven (eight counting another that moved to nearby Corona-Elmhurst). The Islamic community also grew: as the Muslim Center of New York expanded into an elaborate new mosque, it was joined by two predominantly Afghani mosques. A microcosm of the Indian subcontinent moved to Flushing, and the cross section of different religious groups displayed some of the variety within Hinduism, Sikhism, and Islam.[82] Compressing representatives from all of South Asia into a small section of a community in New York City, however, led to a reality quite different from that of life in India, Pakistan, Nepal, Tibet, Sri Lanka, Bangladesh, and Afghanistan. Although South Asians increasingly use the term *Desi* (Hindi for "people of the *desh,* or country") for solidarity, America (and especially Flushing) brings together South Asians from different religious, regional, and linguistic groups who might not otherwise come into contact back home and forces them to interact in new ways among themselves—and with long-time local residents and other new neighbors.[83]

Religions of Immigrants from East Asia

New York's Second Chinatown

Susan Wu Rathbone, affectionately known as Auntie Wu, remembers when there were only a few Chinese people in Flushing. She grew up in Anhui Province in China, where her father was a local mayor (who was later executed as a revolutionary). After World War II, she married an American soldier in Shanghai and became one of the first war brides to come to the United States. Landing in Texas in 1946, she saw puzzling signs for the ladies' restroom at a train station that said "WHITE" and "COLORED," and she realized that Chinese Americans were also second-class citizens. She and her husband took a train to New York and eventually settled in Flushing in 1949.[84] She recalls feeling disconnected from Chinese culture and traditions: "They were the loneliest days of my life. In Queens at that time, there were only a few Chinese families around. If we didn't receive a letter from home, we didn't even know when it was Chinese New Year's Day."[85] Many years later a large part of central downtown Flushing would become New York's second Chinatown; there would be huge Chinese New Year's parades through downtown Flushing and a new public library with hundreds of titles in every Chinese dialect. In 1949, however, her only connection to China was a Chinese translation of Theodore Dreiser's novel *Sister Carrie,* which she read many times. Yet it was not the somewhat similar tale of a country girl pursuing the American Dream in the big city that captivated her, only the language it was written in: "Every page has my tears on it because I was so homesick for China. This book in my own language was my only comfort."[86] When she happened to meet several other Chinese women in Queens the year after she moved, the group became interested in erasing stereotypes about Chinese Americans and teaching others about Chinese art and culture. Over time, Auntie Wu also established a telephone hotline for Chinese immigrants and a voluntary association called the Chinese Immigrants Service (a benefit society or mutual aid society), both of which helped hundreds of people and continue to operate today.[87]

During World War II, it became embarrassing for the U.S. government to be excluding Chinese immigrants while drafting those who had been in the country nearly a century to fight in China against the Japanese.[88] In 1943, Congress finally repealed the Chinese Exclusion Act of 1882 and replaced it with a quota system of 105 a year. In addition, after World War II, American GIs could bring their Chinese wives back for the first time as part of the War Brides Act. Many refugees from mainland China also had fled to Taiwan and Hong Kong after China's Communist revolution in 1949, and when Congress deracialized immigration quotas in 1965, Chinese from these regions started to come in ever-greater numbers during and after the Cultural Revolution from 1966 to 1976. Like their Indian counterparts from this period, many Chinese immigrants in the first post-1965 wave differed from those who came before and after them in that most were educated professionals and students—what Peter Kwong has referred to as "uptown" Chinese.[89]

Manhattan's early Chinese immigrant community dates back to the mid–nineteenth century, with a discernible Chinatown around Mott Street first referred to in print in 1880, but what is now called the city's second Chinatown did not begin to develop until later in the twentieth century.[90] Like other urban neighborhoods across the country from the late nineteenth century on, there was at least one Chinese "chop suey" restaurant in Flushing as early as 1930.[91] But the dense and diverse Chinese enclave that would dominate much of central downtown Flushing by 2000 did not really begin until the late 1970s.

As Manhattan's Chinatown began to burst at the seams and spread up into Little Italy and over to the Lower East Side, investors from Taiwan and Hong Kong began to look to the outer boroughs for more affordable housing and other business prospects.[92] Like the South Asians before them, this particular wave of Chinese immigrants initially was attracted to Flushing because of its status as the transportation hub of Queens and its diminishing local population, leaving behind vacant apartments, houses, and stores. They also had more money than their Indian counterparts, and Taiwanese businessmen began to buy much of downtown Flushing by the late 1970s and build several new high-rise apartment buildings in the area—helping save Flushing from further decline during one of the city's worst economic slumps. Relatives and friends followed, slowly reviving the area and creating less of a need to go back to the Manhattan Chinatown.[93]

Although those who lived in or visited Flushing in the 1970s and early 1980s remember a microcosm of South Asia as the predominant new immigrant community, others subsequently would observe a downtown central business district that began to look a lot more like Taipei. In the early 1980s, the former Queens borough president Donald R. Manes, along with Representative Gary Ackerman, reportedly placed ads in Taiwanese dailies to encourage migration and investment and get money coming back into Flushing. With as many as every third down-town storefront closed, local politicians and longtime residents wanted to reverse the ghettoization that had begun in the 1970s, which some argue was really a cover-up for deeper racist concerns among white residents who did not want more blacks and Hispanics to settle in Flushing. At first, it was "Thank God the Asians are here and *they* aren't."[94] Over the next decade, wealthy Taiwanese real estate investors like Tommy Huang almost singlehandedly were responsible for giving Flushing a facelift, and many residents initially felt that "the Asians saved Flushing."[95] This cheery sentiment would fade and often turn bitter (with Huang singled out in particular for buying and damaging the landmark RKO Keith's theater), but as downtown Flushing increasingly went in the direction of Chinese-owned businesses, it developed into a "second Chinatown."[96] One report from the Center for an Urban Future notes, "When Fred Fu first moved to Flushing in 1980, the neighborhood had just three Chinese restaurants. 'One was on Main Street, one was on Roosevelt Avenue and one was on Northern Boulevard,' says Fu, president of the Flushing Chinese Business Association. Today, approximately 80 Chinese restaurants dot the streets of downtown Flushing."[97]

There were several differences from the older Chinatown in Manhattan. Whereas the Manhattan Chinatown had come to resemble a very old Cantonese village, with some residents tracing their Chinese American ancestors back to the mid–nineteenth century, Flushing's early Taiwanese residents were already extremely wealthy and educated professionals who came in midlife. Most Chinese immigrants who came later were typically rural, uneducated immigrants from Guangdong and the southern Chinese province of Fujian; they tended to work in restaurants (men) and oppressive sweatshop garment factories (women). Although many more recent Chinese immigrants settled in Manhattan's Chinatown (as well as a third Chinatown in Sunset Park, Brooklyn), in the 1990s these more mainland Chinese began to come to Flushing's then thriving new Chinatown as Manhattan's became overwhelmed (and stretched into Little Italy). Many also were no doubt attracted to the cheaper vacant retail properties and apartments. Some would return to Manhattan for other bilingual services and employment—and, in fact, a busy minivan service developed with vehicles departing about every ten minutes to and from Chinatown in Manhattan for commuters who worked or shopped there but lived in

Flushing and wanted to bypass subways and buses.[98] The explosion of Chinese commerce and the revitalization of Flushing also led to a rebirth of new religious life. As the Flushing Chinese community grew into a self-sufficient second Chinatown, there was a demand for local places of worship so people would not have to make the trek back to Manhattan. As Flushing's Chinese population grew and absorbed individuals with different regional dialects, cultures, and socioeconomic statuses (including Chinese from places outside of China, like Malaysia), the variety of Chinese temples and churches became as diverse as China itself.

Chinese American religious life is often a complex combination of folk traditions, Confucianism, Taoism, Buddhism, and Christianity. The sociologist Fenggang Yang has called this kind of religious syncretism "adhesive identity," which describes the fluidity that many Chinese feel in moving back and forth between one or more of these overlapping spheres throughout their lives.[99] There is a common saying in Taiwan (and perhaps throughout mainland China) that "you are born a Taoist, raised a Confucian, and die a Buddhist," and, some would add, if you are an entrepreneur or migrate to America, you often become Christian.[100] Native traditions would remain deeply popular for many later immigrants, and some had little or no religious beliefs left after Communist Party rule, but a majority of the immigrants from Taiwan and Hong Kong to America were Christian or converted after they arrived.[101] Many of the early Chinese Christian immigrants joined existing congregations in Flushing, made arrangements to share church space and hold separate worship services in Chinese (mostly Taiwanese or Mandarin at first), or made the trek back to churches in Manhattan's Chinatown, but as the Chinese population in Flushing grew (especially with more recent immigrants who spoke little or no English), the desire for Chinese churches in Flushing did too. Among Chinese Christians, the consensus has been that Buddhism, Taoism, and traditional folk practices are superstitions that many leave behind (this was also reinforced by Communist rule), but there are signs that that is not exactly the case—for example, most still observe the Chinese Lunar New Year and even incorporate many of the associated folk traditions into communal activities at their churches. Many Chinese Christians also tend to have relatives who did not convert, so contact with Buddhism and Taoism often continues—sometimes in the same family. Man-Li Lin, one of Flushing's ambassadors of Chinese culture, a Buddhist affiliated with Shaolin Temple, says many Chinese immigrants choose or switch from Christianity or Buddhism depending on their personality:

You have to see your personality. Not everybody can be Buddhist. Because the philosophy's different. Like, Buddhism, you have to depend on yourself. It's not there is a god you can depend on. Okay? So if you feel that you're a more dependable person—you know, like, you like people, you know, [to] help you and guide you, I mean, you should go to the church. It's very hard to be a Buddhist. You have to work by yourself. You have to be responsible for yourself. So I always say you have to see your personality, which one, you know, is suitable for you.[102]

The early Chinese Buddhist and Taoist community in Flushing is difficult to trace, as temples were not built until later in the 1980s and 1990s, and many made pilgrimages to older temples in Manhattan's Chinatown (unlike South Asians, who had no traditional places of worship at all when they arrived). By 2000, there were about a dozen different Chinese Buddhist temples throughout Flushing, each part of the Mahayana ("Great Vehicle or Course") Buddhist lineage, but with different emphases and regional backgrounds.

Established in 1991, the largest Buddhist temple in Flushing was the Fo Guang Shan New York Temple, a branch of the Taiwanese Ch'an (essentially the Chinese precursor to Japanese Zen Buddhism) Buddhist Organization known as the International Buddhist Progress Society.[103] IBPS temples were established by the founder of Fo Kuang Shan, Venerable Master Hsing Yun, with temples in five continents. Yun's objectives were to propagate a humanitarian Buddhism applicable to daily life in the contemporary world and to actualize the mission of establishing the "Pure Land" on earth. Although not quite as palatial as its often newsworthy sibling in California (the Hsi Lai Temple in Hacienda Heights), the New York temple is tucked away in a quiet and peaceful area away from downtown in a massive five-story, fully renovated building encompassing about twenty thousand square feet. Responsible for the entire East Coast and highly organized, it provides facilities such as a large worship hall, a lecture hall, a dining hall and industrial kitchen, a conference room, a library, a meditation hall, classrooms, and a Buddhist culture gift shop. Activities include Buddhist matrimony and funeral services, social welfare events, a women's study group, a youth group, a choir, and a Chinese-language school. Consciously serving as a starting point and gateway to guide young Chinese Americans to participate in mainstream society while maintaining their Buddhist tradition, in October 1995 IBPS

The International Buddhist Progress Society, the New York branch of the Fo Guang Shan Buddhist Order, a Taiwanese Ch'an (Chinese Zen) Buddhist organization.

New York also officially registered the first American Boy Scout troop sponsored by a Chinese Buddhist group.

Two other sizable Buddhist temples were established in the center of downtown for Buddhists wishing to step away from the crowd, commotion, and commerce into a tranquil worship setting. The largest of these was the China Buddhist Association (*Ci Hang Jing She,* in Chinese), an elegant temple established in 1993 devoted to Kuan Yin, the Buddha of Mercy. According to Weishan Huang, "Master Mew Fung was the first Chinese Buddhist minister sponsored by the Taiwanese government to come to the United States. He founded the Buddhist Association of America and established three monasteries: Fa Wang Monastery in Chinatown in 1963, Ci Hang Jing She (CHJS) in Flushing in 1993, and Pine Woods Monastery in Hyde Park, New York."[104]

The Shaolin Temple Overseas Headquarters was founded in 1995 below the tracks of the Long Island Rail Road, first meeting in a makeshift

Shaolin Temple Overseas Headquarters, a center for Ch'an, from Henan (mainland) China, and Shaolin kung fu.

space down the street from the present temple dedicated in 2000. A center for Ch'an and Shaolin kung fu, which is directly descended from the Songshan Shaolin Temple in Henan (mainland) China founded in 495 C.E. during the Wei Dynasty, the Flushing temple seeks to spread "a new Twenty-first Century Shaolin Ch'an Buddhism" by melding Buddhist philosophy with contemporary life. It was the first officially sanctioned Shaolin temple outside of China.[105] The temple was founded by Shifu Shi Guolin, a thirty-fourth-generation Shaolin temple warrior monk who was raised at the Songshan Shaolin temple in China. Uniting Ch'an with martial arts to bring mind and body together through concentration and exercise is thought to help one become immune to distractions from the outside world on the path to enlightenment, and the temple is divided into a Buddhist temple facing the street and kung fu hall in the back. The combination has proved popular, as it attracts a large number of Chinese youth (and, unlike the other Chinese temples, a number of non–Chinese as well) who come initially for martial arts training but also get exposed to Buddhist teachings in the process. The interpreter for the temple monks is Man-Li Lin, who came to Flushing in 1990 from Taiwan. Lin's main job is in the Flushing office of the New York State Department of Labor, where she helps Chinese immigrants who were laid off file for unemployment benefits. But her real passion is with the Shaolin temple

Morning t'ai chi in the park.

and Chinese culture. She has been studying and performing traditional Chinese folk dance since she was a little girl, but when she gave birth to a son she wanted to learn something for and with him. She started learning *kung fu* "because *kung fu* combines grace and power."[106] She has also been teaching ESL to Chinese and Chinese to a diverse swatch of Flushing residents for almost twenty years. As interpreter for the temple and an ambassador of Chinese culture in Flushing, Lin has helped disseminate information about the temple's important history and popular martial arts classes.

As in any Chinese community, there are also many traces of Taoism throughout Flushing. Every morning, groups of Chinese gather early in parks to practice *t'ai chi*, gracefully moving to Chinese folk music on a portable stereo. In the commercial areas, there are a host of Chinese herbalists and acupuncture clinics, as well as tea shops that offer traditional tea ceremonies. Most Chinese restaurants and markets also have shrines with images of Guan Di (alt. Guan Gong), a folk hero and guardian who brings good luck and protection. Guan Gong was a general named Guan Yu in the Three Kingdoms period of China (the third century C.E.) before he earned the posthumous honorific Di, meaning emperor god. But Flushing also gained an actual Taoist temple in the late 1990s—the Temple of Mercy-Charity, which sits on a hill and side street slightly removed from downtown, near Ebenezer Missionary Baptist Church.

Taoist images of Guan Di (alt. Kuan Ti or Kuan Gong), a popular folk hero, guardian, and god of war in shrines at a Chinese market and restaurant to bring good luck and protection. Guan Di was an actual general in the Three Kingdoms period of China (third century C.E.) named Guan Yu before he earned the posthumous honorific Di, meaning emperor god.

The Taoist Temple of Mercy-Charity, with Ebenezer Missionary Baptist Church at left.

Chinese Christians are perhaps an even more diverse lot, in part because of a long and varied history of missionaries and British colonialism in China but also because of the diversity of denominational life in America. Early Chinese Protestants in America date back to the first days of settlement in the nineteenth century.[107] But most Chinese immigrants since the Communist Revolution in China in 1949 who are Buddhist or Christian come from either Hong Kong or Taiwan.

Many Chinese in Flushing belong to Catholic and, especially, Episcopal churches, and there are separate Chinese congregations in large, older institutions like St. Michael's Roman Catholic Church and First Baptist Church. Bowne Street Community Church, once a bastion of Flushing's old-stock Dutch Reformed and Congregationalists, is now dominated by Taiwanese members of the United Church of Christ. One of the more powerful pulpits and signs of change is St. George's Episcopal Church, where the leadership has been Chinese since 1988. Rev. Canon Edmund B. Der was born in Hong Kong in 1936.[108] A fourth-generation Anglican (Episcopalian), he went to college in Taiwan and then to seminary school in the United States at Seabury-Western Theological Seminary in Evanston, Illinois, and at the Church Divinity School of the Pacific in Berkeley, California (affiliated with the Graduate Theological Union, which was just forming at the time). He was ordained in the United States and spent his first five years of ministry in Hong Kong, then ten years in Taiwan, another eight years back in Hong Kong, then fifteen years in Toronto, before coming to Flushing. Both his paternal and maternal grandparents and his paternal great-grandfather had come to America (Arizona and Ohio). His father left the United States in 1925 after his studies (and during a period of intense anti-immigrant sentiment) to start a career in Hong Kong and Shanghai, but Der would grow up intrigued by stories of his Chinese American grandparents, all of whom were Anglicans. The relationship of Hong Kong and the Church of England goes back to China's former days as a British colony. The British missionaries came into Hong Kong first as chaplains to the British command in 1841. By 1849, the British had already built a cathedral there. Although their primary purpose was ministering to the king's subjects, in time they began to serve the local community and started evangelizing. According to Rev. Der:

> The British started schools in Hong Kong for the Chinese. At first it was purely to train clergy, train pastors. But then it expanded. So, the oldest Anglican school in Hong Kong could date back 150 years. That is to say that (St. Paul's was the oldest) as soon as they landed

there, they started—the Bishop of Hong Kong was sent and, at that time, he was the Bishop of South China based in Hong Kong and had to minister to all these. And St. Paul's College was founded, and later on more and more. Now, these schools, some schools there, were founded by wealthy Chinese people locally who ran free schools for poor children. But the real formal schools on the Western curriculum were pioneered by the Anglicans. Even before the Education Department of Hong Kong was formed in 1907. So the Anglican school predates all this. So evangelism is purely mostly done through education. And then following that, about in the 1930s, the social services started—like running a big St. Christopher's home for children. And then, during the 1950s, a whole big scale of social services was started from the church—pioneering before the government ever provided any social services. So the influence of the Anglican contribution to Hong Kong is tremendous. The number of people, Anglicans, as of now is probably over around 30 or 40 thousand registered Anglicans. But they run more than 150 social service centers, more than 150 schools in Hong Kong. So many people study under the Anglican flag. And it permeates through the whole of south China.[109]

Today the total number of Christians (Protestant and Catholic) in Hong Kong is between 18 and 20 percent of the population, with a larger yet indeterminate mix of Buddhists and self-avowed Taoists. Der says most evangelical Chinese Christians are "frightfully fundamentalist" (especially the elderly). Since the 1980s there has been an explosion in the popularity of Chinese evangelical churches with an often fundamentalist orientation.[110] Christian concerts at larger churches like Bowne Street Community Church are reminiscent of emotional revivals and can get crowded when popular singers visit from overseas, and various groups of Chinese missionaries are a regular sight downtown. Der notes that Chinese evangelicals can be categorized by whether they speak Chinese or English (which also determines the liturgy): Chinese speakers tend to sing hymns that date back to the 1870s and 1880s and accept biblical inerrancy; English speakers sing hymns from the 1970s to the present.[111] The complexities of language differences at Chinese churches in general are not only limited to Chinese and English. Fenggang Yang states:

> Probably no other ethnic group in the United States has experienced language problems on the same scale as the Chinese. American Jews are similarly heterogeneous, but at the synagogue there is the common ritual language of Hebrew. Asian Indians have multiple dialects or

Members of the Falun Gong outside the Flushing branch of the New York public library system, on Main Street.

languages, but they do not hold an expectation that all Indians should stick together. Koreans and Japanese, like Chinese people, do hold such an expectation, but they are linguistically homogenous compared to the Chinese in the United States. In Chinese churches, various dialect groups often become contentious about linguistic usages, yet they try to remain in the same church with their Chinese compatriots.[112]

Thus, in many Chinese churches, congregations are often made up of people who speak many different dialects and attend the same service yet cannot understand one another. The situation is similar during Chinese New Year, when Chinese Christians, Buddhists, and Taoists come together with even newer groups like the Falun Gong sect (alt. Falun Dafa) to plan the annual parade—which is further complicated by an ever-growing number of Korean groups who also participate.

Japanese Buddhism in Flushing

Japanese immigrants had been coming to America (mainly to California and other western states) at least since the late nineteenth century, but the majority of New York's Japanese population did not arrive until the last three decades of the twentieth century. Sometime in the early 1970s, thousands of Japanese businessmen on three-to-five-year job assignments from such companies as Sony, Toyota, and Honda began to settle in Flushing and surrounding areas with their families.[113] Although the limited periods meant most would hardly have time to become an active part of the community (yet many did stay), the steady stream of people created one of the largest Japanese communities in America and soon led to efforts to recreate some cultural institutions in the neighborhood. In 1975, the Japanese government and several corporations helped finance the Japanese School of New York for the children of Japanese nationals. First located at the former Parkway School on Grand Central Parkway, the school soon grew and moved to another larger building in Flushing. As the population peaked around 1980, two places of worship were established that mirror modern Japanese religious life.[114] While each derive from mainstream Japanese faiths, both are called "New Religions" because they are religious movements, or sects, that originated and evolved relatively recently in the nineteenth and twentieth centuries. In 1979, a group devoted to the teaching of Tenrikyo founded the Tenrikyo Mission by converting two adjoining houses into a temple complex. Although influenced by Shinto (the ancient indigenous religion of Japan), the founding of Tenrikyo goes back to 1837, when a charismatic Japanese female lay Buddhist of the Pure Land school had messianic visions and claimed she was the medium through which members could achieve salvation by following her basic teachings of altruism. The Flushing mission of approximately one hundred members began with Japanese families but has since attracted a number of European Americans, Koreans, and Chinese. A year after the Tenrikyo mission was established, another group of Japanese families founded the Nichiren Shoshu Daihozan Myosetsu Temple. Starting with a house, the group purchased additional land in 1984 to construct a sleek two-story white building offset more starkly by an imposing tall, black, gated fence. Nichiren Shoshu is based on the teachings of a charismatic thirteenth-century Japanese Buddhist priest who claimed he was a reincarnation of the Bodhisattva of Supreme Action; he stressed the Lotus Sutra as the principal sacred text for followers to realize their Buddha-nature, or salvation. The Flushing temple drew 2,500 when the new building opened in 1984, with a membership only 5 to 10 percent Japanese, approximately 90 percent European American and African American, and the remainder Chinese and Korean.[115] Despite the initial popularity, a schism in 1991 led to a

Nichiren Shoshu Daihozan Myosetsu Temple (est. 1980).

splinter group made up of the Nichiren Shoshu lay organization Soka Gakkai; this faction was excommunicated by the orthodox priesthood for allowing lay members to perform a rite traditionally reserved for priests.[116] A majority at the Flushing temple aligned with Soka Gakkai, but membership plummeted to three hundred within a year—a situation that reflects the lack of priestly support worldwide for Soka Gakkai; also, it had been labeled a cult and would later become enmeshed in controversy. Despite the proximity and shared roots, the Tenrikyo Mission and Nichiren Shoshu Daihozan Myosetsu Temple have had little to do with each other over the years—a principal reason is their different doctrines and rituals; also, the former is mainly Japanese while the latter is not. The two have also interacted very little with their immediate neighborhood, as their membership is mainly composed of either Japanese nationals in town only for several years (in the case of the Tenrikyo Mission) or people commuting to Flushing from the greater New York metropolitan area who are disconnected from local events.[117] The already diminishing Japanese population vanished even faster as more Korean immigrants began to settle in Flushing in ever-growing numbers; the deep, old, mutual animosity between the two cultures led the smaller (and now wealthier) Japanese community to seek solace elsewhere in nearby suburbs.

The Seoul of New York

In November 1947, the General Assembly of the United Nations (which was based from 1946 to 1952 in the former New York City Building of the 1939–1940 World's Fair in Flushing Meadows–Corona Park) established the UN Temporary Commission on Korea (UNTCOK) to facilitate elections for a new Korean government and provide for the withdrawal of occupation forces stationed there after the Japanese surrender on August 15, 1945, and the end of World War II.[118] When separate elections produced dual leaders, war broke out in June 1950, when communist North Korea invaded the Republic of Korea in the south, with the UN Security Council recommending that its members aid the Republic of Korea. North and South Korea together suffered more than three million casualties in the Korean conflict before a truce was negotiated on July 27, 1953.

A small number of Korean immigrants settled in Hawaii starting in 1903, but the Korean War was the pivotal event that led to much larger migration to the United States during the second half of the twentieth century. The close U.S.–South Korean military, political, and economic linkages beginning with the Korean War in 1950 helped many Koreans immigrate to the United States, and most of the Korean immigrants between 1950 and 1964 were wives of U.S. servicemen, war orphans, or international students. Other Korean immigrants came to the United States as a result of the Refugee Relief Act of August 7, 1953, and the Refugee-Escapee Act of September 11, 1957. These early Korean immigrants no doubt were attracted by the proximity of the General Assembly's former location, and a small Korean community began to develop as a number of refugees started to settle in Flushing: educated professionals, students, and many small-business and grocery owners.[119] The third and largest wave began to come after 1965. In addition to Korean newspapers, mutual benefit associations, and schools in New York,

> their most important cultural institutions were many Protestant churches, which claimed more than half the city's Koreans as members. Although a majority of south Koreans are Buddhists, a disproportionate number of Korean immigrants in America are Christians, especially Methodists and Presbyterians. Replacing declining white English-speaking Protestant congregations, they turned a number of these churches into thriving institutions.[120]

The first Korean Christian congregation in Flushing started in the mid-1960s in the First Congregational Church, on Bowne Street, when the progressive leadership of the church welcomed a fledgling Korean congregation to share its space.[121] By 1974, there were two thousand Koreans in Flushing, and Jin Kwan Han, the pastor of the congregation, could boast that "there are 260 families in the parish alone. They like living close to the church and come here for evening English language courses."[122] The Korean American Presbyterian Church of Queens just off of Bowne Street and Franklin Avenue is one of the oldest and biggest Korean churches in the city. What began with a few families in 1973 and a church dedicated in 1983 later blossomed by the 1990s into a 3,500-member congregation in a massive building taking up half a block. Unlike the Chinese (who already had churches in Chinatown), the early Korean community ultimately felt the need to establish their own places of worship sooner, and a staggering number of Korean churches would dot downtown Flushing by the new millennium. In 1980, Koreans were the third-largest Asian immigrant group in downtown Flushing, and there were twenty Korean churches.[123] By 2000, the Korean population in Flushing would double, and there would be over one hundred Korean churches.

After the Civil War, the United States attempted to look for new trade markets in Asia and also sent missionaries. Warships like the *USS Sherman* went up to Korea and tried forcibly to open up Korea for U.S. commerce and trade, and one of the treaties that came out of that was the Treaty of Amity and Friendship, which specifically mandated American missionaries having free rein in the country.[124] These early Protestant missionaries to Korea (Methodists in the south and Presbyterians in the north) planted the seeds for a Korean "Great Awakening" in the postwar 1950s and 1960s, which came about after organized evangelical crusades sparked by Rev. Billy Graham and the Pentecostal World Conference spread the gospel throughout the country while also helping establish hospitals, schools, and universities.[125] While Buddhism would remain strong, the timing of these crusades during and after the devastation of the Korean War created a new appreciation for Christianity and America in general, leading to a pervasive spirit of revival.[126]

By the 1990s, Flushing was home to the largest concentration of Korean Americans on the East Coast. Drawn by the earlier Korean immigrants and the success of Chinese commerce and investment, great numbers of Korean immigrants sought to capitalize on this opportune period of revitalization in Flushing. As Koreans moved in, the earlier Japanese community moved out almost entirely—sushi restaurants that had opened in the 1970s are all owned by Koreans now (an easy transition, as the two cuisines are similar). In their place also came a slew of twenty-four-hour Korean *bulgogi* (barbecue) restaurants, bakeries, *karaoke* nightclubs, Internet cafes, cellular phone franchises, upscale clothing stores, wedding services,

Mi Ju Sung San Church, in a converted house, and New York Full Gospel Love Church in the attached rear garage.

medical clinics, schools, and Korean churches of every kind and size in every conceivable space: *mega, medium, and mini* churches of various denominations have been established in commercial and residential areas, in storefronts, converted warehouses and homes, office space, older defunct churches, and gigantic new structures.

Korean churches became pervasive in Flushing (one almost needs to *see* the multitude to understand the magnitude), and the fact that eighty of the one hundred Korean churches in Flushing were established in the small downtown and surrounding area between 1980 and 2000 gives an idea of the extreme explosion of Korean religious life. Like the Chinese, Koreans share a traditional folk religious mix of shamanistic, Confucian, and Buddhist influences. This mix is widespread and often remains in the background of Korean Christian mentality or somewhere in the family tree. Buddhists actually outnumber Christians in Korea, and although a great number of Korean herbalists, acupuncture clinics, and several Korean Buddhist temples (including the Jun Dung Sa Buddhist temple established in 1980 and the more recent Won Buddhist temple) remain vital parts of the Korean community in Flushing, it is the churches that figure most prominently in Korean American religion.[127]

Although a majority of Korean Christians are Presbyterian or Methodist and virtually all share a conservative theology, a large number also belong to Pentecostal or "Full Gospel" churches, which may be appealing because of a perceived similarity to the spirit world of Korean shamanism.[128] In an industrial area next to a huge New York Police Department lot of repossessed cars, the Full Gospel New York Mission Center (est. 1993) draws a large congregation in a $8.5 million, 140,000-square-foot, nine-story complex on five acres of land with parking for six hundred. Several smaller Korean churches in Flushing include the words "Full Gospel" in their name, but the Full Gospel Mission Center is the largest and most organized. A pastor in New York City since 1977 (and, before that, Berlin), Rev. Nam Soo Kim is a major figure within his denomination and was elected as an executive presbyter of the Assemblies of God USA.[129] Born into a Korean Buddhist family in 1944, he remembers fleeing south with his parents during the Korean war, walking five hundred miles and eating grass and bark from trees to keep from starving. After military service and a business failure, he became a born-again Christian at twenty-six, converting to Christianity and attending seminary school.[130] Although Full Gospel New York is larger than most Korean churches in Flushing, its activities illustrate much about Korean American Christian life. The ministry center is open daily for prayer, Bible studies, senior-citizen social services, counseling, youth meetings, worship services, and theological seminary classes. Monday through Saturday, 150 members gather for prayer at 6:00 in the morning. Sunday worshipers eat dinner together after the morning service, a Korean tradition that strengthens ties. Prepared and served by teams of members, the food is free. The church operates a medical clinic, and a secondhand store sells donated clothing and housewares to raise funds for missions. Weekly radio and television programs beam the gospel to the more than five hundred thousand Koreans living in the metropolitan New York and tristate area. About three hundred converts are baptized annually.

A smaller number of Koreans are Catholic, but the history of Catholicism in Korea goes back much earlier than that of any Protestant denomination. John Choe was born in Seoul and left with his family when he was about five. After earning degrees in history, urban planning, and public policy, he entered New York City politics and served as chief of staff for Councilman John Liu. Choe, who is Catholic, explained that French missionaries brought Catholicism to Korea in the mid–eighteenth century, "but it was seen as a destabilizing force in Korean society, because in the Confucian order there were specific relationships that were kind of preordained, whereas Catholicism in the Korean context focused on the brotherhood of man, so it tended to level a lot of different classes and actually also provided women a role that was not allowed necessarily in Confucian society."[131] This was one of the reasons why Korea closed itself off in the nineteenth century to prevent any future Western religion from coming in.[132] Korean Catholics were persecuted in the early 1800s (partly because they rejected ancestor worship, a central norm of Confucianism), and 102 Korean lay martyrs were later canonized by Pope John Paul in 1984. In 1987 a Korean Catholic church named after one of these martyrs, St. Paul Chong Ha-Sang, was established in Flushing and became the first Korean parish in New York.[133]

Regardless of denomination or size, however, the church serves several important functions in the Korean Christian community. The sociologist Pyong Gap Min has stated that the Korean immigrant church has "four major social functions: 1) providing fellowship for Korean immigrants; 2) maintaining the Korean cultural tradition; 3) providing social services for church members and the Korean community as a whole; and 4) providing status and positions for Korean adult immigrants."[134] The popularity and particularity of establishing a new church or congregation thus led to one hundred different Korean churches in Flushing by 2000. In a study of Korean churches in New York City, Min found that at least a third of these have fifty or fewer members (including children), several have more than five hundred members, but most have about eighty members and are "characterized by a small size."[135] Min explains that "most Korean churches in the United States do not have their own buildings; instead they usually have service and fellowship meetings in American churches."[136] Indeed, the names, leadership, and information of many Korean congregations in Flushing are found on the signs outside most older churches in Flushing alongside names like First Methodist Church, the Unitarian Universalist Church of Flushing, and the Lutheran Church of St. John. Min says the tendency toward small, individual churches "can largely be explained by the need of Korean immigrants for small-group, primary social interactions" and that this is "not unique to the New York Korean community."[137] Yet when this tendency led to one hundred different Korean churches by 2000, certainly an extreme case, other local residents in the neighborhood would begin to wonder why there were so many. Min's explanation about the need of Korean immigrants for "small-group, primary social interactions" may be part of the reason, but another is likely attributable to the simple facts of religious voluntarism and particularism illustrated to an exponential degree by the Korean community in Flushing. As Omar M. McRoberts shows in his study of diverse religious life in a black neighborhood in Boston, congregations can be meaningfully different in a *multitude* of ways, so that people are able to sort themselves into religious communities according to complex bundles of preferences . . . [and] race, national origin, socioeconomic class, lifestyle, level of strictness, size, and internal organization—not to mention religious tradition and denomination—can serve to distinguish institutions in the multicongregational field.[138]

Religions of Immigrants from Latin America

When Fidel Castro came to New York City in April 1959 as part of a goodwill tour to speak at the United Nations just a few months after he assumed power in the Cuban Revolution, he also paid a visit to Flushing. At the time, Flushing had a small Cuban population, and Castro's son Fidel (better known as Fidelito, "little Fidel") had been living in exile with a Flushing family and attending PS 20, John Bowne Elementary School, while his father led an uprising in the Caribbean.[139] To show his gratitude to the school, Castro donated a statue of José Martí, Cuba's first revolutionary hero, and he also posed for pictures with some of Fidelito's classmates at a hotel in Manhattan.[140] Such gestures were short lived, however. U.S.-Cuban relations soured soon after Castro left, and Fidelito went back to live in Cuba.

Cuban refugees began entering the United States soon after Castro took control of Cuba, and they continued to come throughout the 1960s. Although Miami became the center of Cuban American life, many Cubans came to New York as well—and a sizable community developed in Flushing. Local newspapers in the early 1960s occasionally refer to English classes for Cubans at the Church of the Nazarene on Bowne Street (later the site of the Ganesha temple). While the proximity to the former site of the UN General Assembly is the most likely explanation for Castro's son attending school in Flushing, many prominent Latin American families had sent their sons to the Flushing Institute in the nineteenth century, so there is added speculation that Flushing remained in the popular imagination throughout certain privileged parts of Latin America and the Caribbean.

One of the first Cuban immigrants to settle in Flushing was Elena Cata, who arrived in August 1962 and became an active member of St. Michael's Roman Catholic Church, teaching ESL and GED classes for a wide variety of immigrants.[141] Cata was born in 1932 in Havana and left with her family in 1961. When they arrived in New York, there were already a few Cuban families living in Flushing (in fact, she moved into the same building where Fidelito had lived). In 1962, Flushing was "a nice, pleasant place. Many private homes. And it was no accumulation of people, as I'm experiencing now [in 2006]." By September 1968, Cata and about eighteen other Cubans began to be active in the church, holding a Spanish Mass for *Nuestra Señora de la Caridad del Cobre* (Our Lady of Charity, the patron saint of Cuba) in the basement. Up until that time, St. Michael's was principally Irish and Italian. The Cuban members of the congregation were joined by Colombian immigrants who started settling in Flushing in the early 1970s, and these were followed by immigrants from Ecuador, El Salvador, Nicaragua, and Mexico. In addition to the Cuban Mass celebrating *Nuestra Señora de la Caridad del Cobre*, other groups such as the Colombians began holding a large Mass celebrating *El Divino Niño* (the Divine Child Jesus) and a Mass celebrating *Nuestra Señora del Rosario de Chiquinqirá* (Our Lady of Chiquinqirá). Yet despite these different traditions, the shared language and religion proved to be important in uniting everyone. By 1976, it was clear that there was a substantial Hispanic community in the area, so a Spanish Association was formed to represent every nationality.

Although Mexico later would become the source of more newcomers to the United States than any other country, in 1964, the United States and Mexico terminated the *bracero* program that began in 1942 to permit the entry of temporary Mexican laborers. Amendments to the act in 1965 also ended the "Good Neighbor" policy favored by Franklin Delano Roosevelt and put a ceiling on immigrants from the Western Hemisphere, which remained in effect until 1976—when Congress realized the uneven policy had created a tremendous backlog of applications from prospective immigrants.[142] Mexican immigrants to New York would later settle in large numbers mainly in nearby Corona-Elmhurst, Queens, whereas the Hispanic population of Flushing would consist of immigrants from Cuba, Colombia, Ecuador, and other Latin American countries—a trend that was changing the congregational demographics of nearly every Catholic parish, helped along by the Second Vatican Council (1962–1965).[143]

Father José R. Aldegundé came to St. Michael's in the 1990s to serve the growing number of Latin Americans in the congregation. Originally from Galicia, Spain, he emigrated in 1971 when the Catholic Church began to address the great need for more Spanish-speaking priests coinciding with massive Latin American immigration to the United States.[144] Serving first at a church in Bedford-Stuyvesant, Brooklyn, for six years, Aldegundé was transferred to a church in Queens Village for seventeen years, to nearby Jamaica, Queens, and, finally, to Flushing. The diverse Hispanic community has been a challenge, as he explained:

> When you talk about Spanish, it's a very generic term. Spanish are [from] twenty different countries, twenty different musics, twenty different foods, twenty different philosophies, you know? They per-haps agree upon devotion to the Blessed Mother, but otherwise ... when you are talking to an Argentinian and you talk to a Peruvian, you are talking different worlds.[145]

It is for the same reason that the Hispanic community in Flushing is not as organized as other ethnic groups (there are, to be sure, numerous Hispanic leaders in New York City, but there are few pan-Latino organizations that fully represent everyone—the Spanish Association at St. Michael's only represents Hispanic Catholics in the parish). Yet at St. Michael's there is still some sense of unity. The clergy, for instance, tries to avoid songs and liturgy styles from any one country, instead making it more catholic (in the universal sense of the word). In fact, St. Michael's, like the similarly multi-ethnic First Baptist Church, tries to unite the English, Spanish, and Chinese congregations as often as possible. Various functions such as the annual "welcome party" for volunteers, as well as dances and cultural bazaars, bring everyone together for fellowship. Special bilingual holiday masses combine English and Spanish for the homily, or sermon, and readings from the Bible are back to back (Old Testament in English and New Testament in Spanish, with church programs printing in one language what is read in the other language). Aldegundé says, "It's difficult, it's difficult, because you don't please 100 percent of the people, but that's the way to cele-brate certain things like Easter or Christmas, confirmation ceremonies, first communions, and weddings."[146] The one occasion where popular and folk religious traditions come out is for the annual Stations of the Cross procession on Good Friday, before Easter, where a huge crowd from each of the three congregations gathers to reenact the Passion, or crucifixion of Jesus, at different points along a route that winds through downtown Flushing. Each group is responsible for several stations and typically sings totally different songs in their own language and custom. The two-hour walk is then followed by everyone reconvening back at the church for the seven last words of Jesus on the cross, which are read in Spanish.

Outside of the church, Aldegundé says St. Michael's is traditionally "very friendly" with the Free Synagogue of Flushing, but there is "not too much communication" with other groups (except when someone from the church marries someone from another place of worship and the priest has to confer with the other religious leader). Asked about ministering to a Catholic congregation in the midst of such extreme religious diversity in Flushing where the church is but one among many very different places of worship, he said:

> We pray for everybody. We are brothers and sisters, no matter what denomination. I think everybody tries to do what is right but, at the same time, for me to be your friend, I don't have to deny my identity. And also sometimes, you know, it's happened in the Vatican, it happened to us—the politics are always there somehow in the corner. You have to be careful about that, you know, and play by the rules of the game. What I mean is, sometimes you hear . . . about all these things, and sometimes you have to take a look and see what's going on. But you try to be authentic and not do things that are not authentic.[147]

Although the priests at St. Michael's are aware of the diversity around them and may even support ecumenism at the local level, Catholic clergy have to answer to a different authority from most other churches and places of worship in Flushing, so local interaction is limited. Interfaith activity tends to happen mainly on the level of the diocese, in conversation with Jewish groups as well as in "fraternal" relations with the Protestant denominations. But involvement with the community is not nonexistent: the church belongs to a "cluster" of parishes, where different priests and different laypeople gather to discuss neighborhood and housing issues, services, and ethnic relations. For Aldegundé, however, perhaps the biggest concern is not with other world religions but with the people the Catholic Church is losing to evangelical Protestant churches:

> Many evangelical Protestants were Roman Catholics. The Church was cold to them at the beginning—not too welcoming, you know, to Spanish [-speaking people]. It happened to the Italians also: "You are Italian? Go to the other church. You are black? Go to the other church." Pentecostal charismatics [are] mainly increasing in numbers because it's very emotional. Also, you can become a pastor in three months versus twelve years, and you speak their language, sing their songs, they have the same color or face—for that reason, there is a lot of proselytism.[148]

Latinos are still predominantly Catholic, and most go to separate masses in Spanish at St. Michael's (the only Catholic church in the area where services in Spanish are offered regularly). Yet two evangelical churches,

Iglesia Presbiteriana de Flushing and La Promesa, were established in the 1990s, and more will undoubtedly follow as the Hispanic community in Flushing continues to grow.

From Protestant–Catholic–Jew to a Microcosm of World Religions

If Flushing became "a community of churches" in the mid–nineteenth century and Protestant-Catholic-Jewish by the mid–twentieth century, it became a microcosm of world religions by the new millennium—with older churches and synagogues joined by a vast array of Hindu, Sikh, Buddhist, and Taoist temples, mosques, and immigrant churches of every denomination.

Although it is tempting to explain this remarkable transformation by linking Flushing's colonial heritage of religious freedom to the present (as some do), the extreme religious diversity in modern Flushing actually came about by accident thanks to a mix of factors (outlined earlier in this chapter) that encouraged settlement during a period of decline in Flushing's history to create fertile ground for transplanting new immigrant groups and their places of worship. Longtime residents and politicians did not seem to realize exactly why or how the proliferation of places of worship came about until after the neighborhood had visibly changed, and Flushing's heritage of religious freedom turned from a blessing to a curse in the minds of some—testing the local tradition of tolerance celebrated in midcentury and forcing modern residents of Flushing to figure out how to live with pluralism.

4

A Blessing and a Curse?
The Possibilities and Limits of Religious Pluralism

If one religion only were allowed in England,
the Government would very possibly become
arbitrary; if there were but two, the people
would cut one another's throats; but as there
such a multitude, they all live happy and
in peace.

— *Voltaire, Letters on the English or* Lettres Philosophiques,
c. 1778, Letter VI: On the Presbyterians

Religious pluralism is against the will of God.
But it is the human condition; it is written
into the script of history. It will not somehow
marvelously cease to trouble the City.

—*John Courtney Murray, SJ,* We Hold These Truths, *1960*

When the designers of the 1939–1940 New York World's Fair set about building the "World of Tomorrow" by transforming a gigantic ash dump into a sparkling wonderland of the future, their own Temple of Religion pavilion was limited to the Protestant-Catholic-Jewish America they knew at the time. Establishing the temporary headquarters of the United Nations General Assembly in a converted building from the fair began to bring foreign dignitaries from around the globe to Flushing between 1946 and 1952, and though the subsequent 1964–1965 New York World's Fair also attracted a greater variety of international exhibits, religious traditions other than Christianity and Judaism remained largely exotic or unknown to most Americans. The country was on the cusp of great changes to come with the passage of the Immigration Act of 1965, but its effects and the future were still far away.

Sixty years after the 1939–1940 World's Fair, visitors to Flushing, Queens, might declare that the World of Tomorrow is here today. Modern Flushing, however, may not be what the designers of the World's Fairs had in mind for their vision of the future: immigration since 1965 has led to such a dense variety of ethnic businesses and places of worship that the urban landscape more closely resembles futuristic scenes from the science-fiction film *Blade Runner* than the orderly and planned community of Greenbelt, Maryland, touted in a film by the American Institute of City Planners at the 1939–1940 fair called *The City*.[1]

In the thirty-five years since the Immigration Act of 1965, America experienced levels of peak immigration that would surpass other periods, and again there were signs of growing pains. The figures rose to the highest ever in the 1990s, a decade that was also marked by new immigration hysteria. Those concerned were not just reacting to numbers but to the ethnic and religious differences of new immigrant groups they feared were inassimilable.[2] Looking back, we see that such outbreaks are nothing new and that it is possible to discern patterns of nativism, or "intense opposition to an internal minority on the ground of its foreign (i.e., 'un-American') connections," in American history—an atavistic phenomenon that appears in times of crisis, disappears in times of confidence, and reappears again in new times of crisis.[3] Reflecting on his classic study of nativism, *Strangers in the Land,* the historian John Higham noted in 2000:

> Now an acrid odor of the 1920s is again in the air. It rises from vast fortunes accumulating around new technology; from a grasping individualism eroding traditional constraints on the market; from a reckless hedonism in popular culture and a resurgent religious conservatism mobilizing against it; from a profound distrust of the state, a reviving isolationism, a baffled concern over illegal immigration, and a deadlock in race relations.[4]

The difference between the post-1965 period and earlier periods of peak immigration in U.S. history is that most recent newcomers are not other Christians or Jews from Europe but people from other parts of the world who represent entirely different (that is, non-Western) religious traditions—in addition to Christians from Asia, Latin America, the Caribbean, and Africa.

The recent history of Flushing illustrates how these changes since 1965 have played out locally in what has become perhaps the most remarkable case of religious pluralism in the world. In this vibrant and bustling commercial district and residential neighborhood, smaller than 2.5 square miles, there are half a dozen Hindu temples; two Sikh gurdwaras; several mosques; Japanese, Chinese, and Korean Buddhist temples; Taoist temples; over one hundred Korean churches; Latin American evangelical churches; Falun Gong practitioners; Jehovah's Witnesses; Mormons . . . as well as some of the oldest churches and synagogues in the city—in all, over two hundred different places of worship densely concentrated in a heavily populated and busy urban neighborhood.

"Is this not," as the theologian H. Richard Niebuhr once said, "religious chaos?"[5] What happens when a microcosm of world religions is compressed into an area of roughly 2.5 square miles? How do people get along in such a neighborhood? To return to the central question of this book, in the words of John Courtney Murray SJ:

> How much pluralism and what kinds of pluralism can a pluralist society stand? And conversely, how much unity and what kind of unity does a pluralist society need in order to be a society at all?[6]

The dramatic and rapid change in Flushing's religious landscape caused by the waves of immigration from 1965 to 2000 created a striking laboratory of pluralism. As I put it rather simply in the Introduction, I answer Murray's question by arguing that there is good news and bad news. The good news is that the absence of widespread religious conflict (with the exception of occasional but rare bias-related crimes and hostility) suggests that there is no limit to how much pluralism a pluralist society can stand. This demonstrates the remarkable possibilities of pluralism for civil society—that a pluralist society committed to democracy and religious freedom can accommodate an enormous amount of diversity. On the other hand, there are in fact some real limits of pluralism too—spatial limits, social limits, structural limits, and theological limits—and these limits illustrate the challenge of trying to find unity in a pluralist community or society.

Earlier migrants to Flushing, longtime residents, and each of the different religious groups within each new immigrant community whose early history was documented in Chapter 3 all responded in different ways over time to their increasingly diverse neighborhood. Tracing this range of different responses to diversity illustrates what pluralism really is: the coexistence of diverse groups in a community and the spectrum of social behavior caused by living in such a community. The history of Flushing during the final third of the twentieth century is a story of conflict and cooperation, of interaction and noninteraction, and it sheds light on different facets of pluralism: its possibilities and its limits.[7]

The Limits of Religious Pluralism

Growing Pains: Testing a Tradition of Tolerance in a Microcosm of World Religions

Residents and visitors to Flushing in the late twentieth century would find it hard to overlook a dizzying new religious diversity. The rapid, dramatic change in the religious landscape of Flushing ultimately led to certain spatial and practical issues that affected its day-to-day quality of life. What began with a few modest and generally unnoticed structures tucked away in various corners steadily grew and spread to commercial areas downtown as well as residential areas throughout the neighborhood: soon congregations of nearly every conceivable religious tradition had moved into converted storefronts, office spaces, buildings and warehouses, single-family homes, townhouses, and defunct churches. Perhaps the most symbolic snapshot of these changes is on Bowne Street. In an interesting twist on Flushing's founding vision, Bowne House, an old Dutch Reformed/Congregational church, and an Orthodox synagogue have been joined by many new places of worship introduced by successive waves of immigrants among the rows of single-family homes, townhouses, and apartment complexes: a Latino/Korean Presbyterian church sits a few blocks from three Hindu temples, a Sikh gurdwara, a Chinese evangelical church, and a gigantic Korean Presbyterian church. Venturing just off of Bowne Street would lead one past a seventeenth-century Quaker meeting house, other older and newer churches, Reformed and Conservative synagogues, Buddhist temples, another Sikh gurdwara and two more Hindu temples, and several mosques.[8] Over time, the "religious presence" of so many places of worship would not only change the visual landscape of the neighborhood and reduce space for housing and commerce; it would affect the nature of living in such an environment through the activities of all the people who come and go for worship.[9]

When certain kinds of urban areas begin to attract this kind of dense religious life, they sometimes become what the sociologist Omar M. McRoberts has called a "religious *district*, where the most commonplace and the most unusual faith communities exist literally side by side."[10] According to McRoberts, religious districts tend to form in depressed urban neighborhoods with vacant commercial spaces, which become perfect places to host places of worship, leading to "dense religious ecologies."[11] This understanding arises from

> the idea that urban forms give rise to religious forms [which] originated in the religious ecological tradition of congregational studies. This tradition in turn grew out of the Chicago School of Urban

Sociology, which understood the city as a system analogous to a natural ecology with concentric zones and local communities serving unique functions in the organic whole.[12]

McRoberts' study focused on Four Corners, a predominantly African American neighborhood in Boston composed of Holiness-Pentecostal-Apostolic and "mainline" (Baptist, Catholic, and United Methodist) congregations but also numerous black Caribbean and Hispanic immigrant churches. While most members of the various congregations lived elsewhere in Boston and commuted to Four Corners for worship, the churches that opened up in vacant properties, by their activism and sheer religious presence, helped revitalize and save a ghetto otherwise destined for further urban decay. Sociologist Katie Day explores a similar situation on a street in Philadelphia where she highlights the sometimes imperceptible impact of religious congregations on an urban neighborhood, which contrasts with the common perception that religious institutions do not benefit the city because they take up residential/commercial space and are tax exempt.[13]

The concept of the religious district would seem to apply not just to other urban poor black neighborhoods with many churches but also to many immigrant neighborhoods in general—which, after 1965, include churches and synagogues as well as non-Western places of worship from the world's other major religions. In the 1970s and 1980s, downtown Flushing declined and attracted new immigrants who bought vacant property to open small businesses and, eventually, places of worship. Yet despite the bad economy, Flushing was always a commercial center and the main transportation hub of Queens, with a large residential population that grew exponentially after 1965 with the influx of new immigrants. Several distinct commercial areas sprang up where one ethnic or regional group formed an enclave (Little India, Chinatown, etc.), but the residential area where most of the new places of worship opened was more scattered, mixed, and without boundaries. As Flushing grew more radically diverse in the 1980s and 1990s, it became not so much a religious district as *a microcosm of world religions*—a true global village that forces people from different countries and faiths to encounter one another in a little world and interact more than they might in other areas where groups are separate and distinct. Though similar microcosms of world religions are found in other urban areas (albeit to a lesser extreme), New York City is unlike some other cities in America (such as Los Angeles, Phoenix, or Houston), where people generally have to drive to distant spaces to go to their respective places of worship.[14] New Yorkers, by contrast, are very densely concentrated and thrown together in a relatively small area: they walk a lot, bump into one another, and ride a sprawling yet efficient mass transit system that puts them in literal contact when packed into subway cars. So although many worshippers do commute from outside, most people live in Flushing and walk to their neighborhood church, synagogue, temple, gurdwara, or mosque.

The sociologist Robert J. Sampson has shown how recent immigration has helped revitalize urban neighborhoods, but the initial gratitude that many longtime residents of Flushing may have felt toward their new Asian American neighbors for helping save the area from further economic decline gradually gave way to occasional bitterness, nativism, and outright hostility in the 1980s and 1990s, as the neighborhood changed from a primarily residential area to one riddled with religious institutions that tested the limits of the neighborhood's celebrated heritage of religious freedom and tolerance.[15] One of the greatest blessings of Flushing became, for some, a curse: "We have them all over the damn place, like chicken pox. They really converge from very far-flung areas into a very residential neighborhood and it does make for trouble for the people who live there."[16] There are so many Korean churches in particular (over one hundred) that scholars of religious congregations would call the area "overchurched." Korean Americans have their own reasons for the plethora of churches, but this does not change their staggering numbers and effects on the community. Councilwoman Julia Harrison had stirred controversy and news in the late 1990s when she said in an interview that the sudden and transforming arrival of Asian Americans was "an invasion, not an assimilation":

> Those new immigrants were not like my grandfather, who arrived hungry at Ellis Island early in the century from Transylvania. They did not come because of a potato famine or because some czar was conducting a pogrom. They were more like colonizers than immigrants. They sure as hell had a lot of money, and they sure as hell knew how to buy property and jack up rents of retail shops and drive people out. The money came first. The paupers followed, smuggled in and bilked by their own kind.
>
> It's very discombobulating, very upsetting. We all recognize that change is part of life, but it doesn't sit well.[17]

A longtime resident of Flushing, Harrison got her start in politics organizing for Eugene J. McCarthy's presidential run in 1968 and later became a vocal defender and lightning rod of the community in her long tenure as a local City Council member (from 1986 to 2000). Harrison may have made headlines and may be remembered for her blunt and sometimes alienating comments, but the press was somewhat unfair and extreme in its depiction—missing part of the bigger, complex picture with a simplistic desire to cast new versus old, good versus bad, during a time when immigration hysteria was already in the national news.[18] A progressive, liberal Democrat who was fond of quoting James Madison in her community newsletters, Harrison was really just a tough fighter who spoke her mind and was decidedly not a Pollyanna when it came to calling attention to real problems that arose from massive immigration to the area. For example, she made it a requirement that Chinese and Korean businesses make their signs bilingual by including an English translation.[19] This was not done just because the signs made longtime residents feel like foreigners themselves; it was an actual public safety issue: a store was robbed on Union Street, but the police could not find it—it was fifty feet away from the 109th precinct of the NYPD, but the sign was in Korean.[20] While some of Harrison's rhetoric was inflammatory, the same exasperation was echoed by other longtime residents and leaders such as the district director of Community Board 7, who said, "You're taking a beautiful neighborhood and decimating it."[21] Areas once lined with attractive old homes have been drastically changed by the addition of religious institutions, and the phrase "Not In *My* Back Yard" took on new meaning. In the forty-four square blocks in eastern Flushing that make up the Holly Civic Association's territory, for instance, there were now twenty-three houses of worship—a fact that was frustrating to the organization's zoning and land use chairwoman:

> They came gradually, so at first we didn't notice, until now they are all over. It's just too much. They're taking over the neighborhood. We believe in the right to worship as you want; I mean, Flushing is the *birthplace* of religious freedom. But what about our rights as residents? These churches don't even look like real churches. You know, a Hindu temple just doesn't fit into our architecture here.[22]

Such statements reveal the sometimes hypocritical nature of Flushing's "old guard" that often expressed pride in Flushing's heritage but also ignorance while grumbling about change. The aesthetic conflict over neighborhood architectural styles would remain a sore spot into the new millennium. The use of "we" and "our" also might lead one to believe that longtime residents of Flushing still represented a clear majority in 1990, but this had been changing steadily since the 1970s, and such complaints barely cloaked a more basic nativistic reaction, a fear of foreignness and otherness. This sentiment also coincided with a significant increase in crime from the mid–1980s to the mid–1990s and no doubt compounded the sense of crisis. The early center of downtown Flushing along Northern Boulevard by Main Street had become a scary ghost zone: the old RKO Keith's theater closed after sixty years, the Flushing Armory was turned into a homeless shelter, and Town Hall became a crack house with prostitutes outside. Gangs were so widespread they made it into the national news and a book.[23] Some residents also expressed a paranoid fear that many new places of worship belonged to groups who did not even live in Flushing: "They're not local parishioners. That's the problem. Some of these churches are not serving the community."[24] In reality, a number of places of worship did serve people who lived elsewhere, but most were actually neighborhood institutions that were integral to the new immigrant communities: some people drove, but most could walk to their place of worship. The local presence of new immigrants as residents would be illustrated by the 2000 U.S. Census, after continuous waves of immigrants to Flushing had brought about a sea change in local demographics. Asian Americans now outnumbered whites. But there were other more legitimate gripes. Resentment grew from new parking problems in particular:

> It's very frustrating for the people who live here. When you have people flipping you off when they park in front of your driveway on a Sunday morning and cursing at you when you tell them "Please move your car out of my driveway." People literally have parked *in* our driveway, gotten out of their car and gone to church saying "Oh, we'll just be forty-five minutes!" What?! This is *outrageous*. I mean, *no one* should tolerate that kind of thing.[25]

Parking indeed had become a major problem, as the largely residential area was jammed on weekends and during certain festivals, when crowds of people in cars frantically look for parking spaces but often end up double parking and clogging the streets, sidewalks, and neighbors' driveways. As one reporter for the *New York Times* observed: "There is a stretch of Flushing, Queens, where Christians, Muslims, and Hindus worship within blocks of one another without sectarian strife. When it comes to parking spaces, though, it is an all-out war."[26] Old zoning laws from 1961 required places of worship to provide a parking space for every fixed pew that seats six, but many immigrant churches get around this by using folding chairs, and most non Judeo-Christian places of worship (Hindu and Buddhist temples, Sikh gurdwaras, and mosques) have no seats at all—people sit on the floor. Local activists say the solution lies in changing the outdated zoning code to make parking spaces related to occupancy: "If they had to put in the amount of parking that they need for the amount of people that are coming to worship, they wouldn't be able to do what they're doing here. It's that simple."[27] With so many places of worship already established, however, such changes would be difficult to enforce or make retroactive.

But how did it all come about in the first place? As outlined in greater detail in Chapter 3, Flushing was first chosen by new immigrants after 1965 for five reasons. First, Flushing was one of the top destinations for many upwardly mobile New Yorkers and new immigrants arriving after 1965 who were looking to escape overcrowding in Manhattan and have more space and perhaps a yard. Second, it was also already widely known as the site of two Worlds' Fairs and temporary home of the United Nations General Assembly in nearby Flushing Meadows. Third, it was (and still is) centrally located, with the largest intermodal transportation point in the city. Fourth, an exodus of many older residents beginning later in the 1960s left a lot of vacant property, commercial space, and available housing by the 1970s. In a 1993 report on fifty-five communities, Flushing/Whitestone ranked first in all of New York City for the number of immigrant-occupied housing units.[28] Finally, a very flexible zoning law from 1961 allowed many different immigrant groups to build so-called community facilities (which includes religious institutions) in residential neighborhoods as long as they met Department of Buildings fire codes. By the 1980s, as more new places of worship had become established parts of the community, the area had become fairly well known as a safe and good place for a wide range of immigrants to live, open ethnic grocery markets and restaurants, and open their own places of worship. The gradual integration of the early new immigrant community into Flushing created a certain buzz about Flushing in the new immigrant community around the region and abroad, and the growth was also fed by the phenomenon of chain migration. Few religious leaders in the various new immigrant communities in Flushing had heard of its colonial history and heritage of religious freedom and tolerance before or soon after arriving in Flushing—most would hear about it later, after they settled and learned more about the area. Recent celebrations of Flushing's history, such as the loan by the New York State Archives of the Flushing Remonstrance for two different exhibits at the Flushing branch of the New York Public Library, has led to greater awareness of local history. Many religious leaders at the mosques, Hindu and Buddhist temples, Sikh gurdwaras, and many ethnic churches now commonly claim this history as part of their own and see their inclusion as part of an unfolding legacy of religious freedom in Flushing.

The unchecked proliferation of places of worship remained a major issue in the 1990s and into the new millennium, and the reason that came up most in the local newspapers and community board meetings was the fifth reason mentioned above: the as-of-right loophole in the Land Use Resolution of 1961, amended 1973, as it pertains to Chapter 6–Community Facilities, which allowed an unlimited number of community facilities (religious institutions, schools, nursing homes, or medical offices, which are intended to serve the local population) to be built in residential neighborhoods. As a long-time resident and member of the North Flushing Civic Association noted,

> The zoning resolution that was adopted in 1961 (but a product of the '30s, '40s and '50s) was written to encourage a doctor, a church, a school, etc. to locate in the immediate area because a certain amount of public facilities is necessary to serve the local community. This was a time when land was still plentiful, local public facilities served the local community, and the facilities created were in keeping with their neighbors. This is no longer the case. The proliferation and over-building of public facilities have caused local residents to experience ongoing traffic congestion, additional noise, stressed public services and overcrowded conditions.[29]

Most new community facilities in Flushing since 1961 have been places of worship, and a variety of other religious groups and religious architecture styles from around the world have been built within a neighborhood of older churches and synagogues, leading to quite a different landscape over the last fifty years. Nowhere else in metropolitan New York have religious groups been able to do this to such a degree: they either had to build in commercial areas or put up ten feet of landscaping in residential areas to soften the juxtaposition with adjoining houses. Community facilities are also allowed to build larger structures than allowed for purely commercial or residential uses, without lengthy approval processes, and many fundraising new immigrant groups would eventually demolish temporary religious centers in converted old houses for large new structures.[30] The situation became so attractive to aggressive religious organizations that they reportedly sometimes joined forces with real estate companies to hound people into selling their houses—with some groups even pretending to be families who would then flip the house back to a religious organization.[31] By 2000, even some Asian American residents who had grown up in Flushing agreed that the unchecked proliferation of new places of worship was forever changing a neighborhood: John Liu, the Taiwanese American former president of the North Flushing Civic

(*above*) Bowne House, "A National Shrine to Religious Freedom," built in 1661.

Remonstrance
Of the Inhabitants of the Towne of Flushing
To Governor Peter Stuyvesant
December 27, 1657

(*left*) On loan from the state archives in Albany for the first time since 1957, the Flushing Remonstrance returned to Flushing and remained on display at the Queens Library, Flushing Branch, from November 19 to December 23, 1999. The Remonstrance was also on display at the Queens Museum of Art from April 6 to June 29, 2008, for the 350th anniversary of its signing on December 27, 1657.

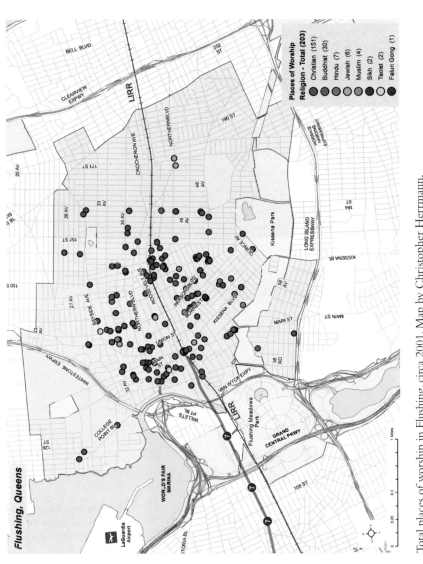

Total places of worship in Flushing, circa 2001. Map by Christopher Herrmann, Law and Police Science Department, CUNY John Jay College of Criminal Justice.

The storefront Gurdwara Singh Sabha sits directly across from the Boon Church of Oversea Chinese Mission on Bowne Street. The Boon Church bookstore (now closed) later removed the Christian mural, which offended its Sikh neighbors, who eventually bought the property and expanded.

Ratha yatra (chariot) procession during the annual Ganesh Chaturthi celebration of the Hindu Temple Society of North America passing Kissena Jewish Center and other places of worship along Bowne Street and downtown Flushing.

(left) Hindu women and children share a neighbor's porch during Ganesh Chaturthi on Bowne Street.

(below) Most Latinos are Catholic and go to churches like St. Michael's R.C.C., but a growing minority attend small evangelical Protestant churches like Iglesia Presbiteriana de Flushing on Bowne Street, which now shares space with a group of Korean Presbyterians.

The 3,500-member Korean American Presbyterian (mega-)Church of Queens on the corner of Franklin and Bowne streets.

Mormon Elders of the Church of Jesus Christ of Latter-Day Saints on Union Street.

(left) Removing graffiti from the World Buddhist Ch'an Jing temple on Main Street.

(below) A woman praying to Kuan Yin, the Buddha of Mercy, inside the China Buddhist Association just off Main Street on 39th Avenue.

The displacement of African American residents in 1951 and a new Flushing Parking Field in 1953 stripped Macedonia A.M.E. (est. 1811) of its old neighborhood community and left the church (rebuilt in 1957) surrounded by cars in a barren concrete lot.

The annual Lunar New Year parade in downtown Flushing passing a stretch of Korean businesses along Union Street.

The cars and crowd after *Jumu'ah* (Friday *Salat*, or prayers) outside the Muslim Center of New York on Geranium Avenue. Established in 1975 (construction of the current building began in 1990), it is the oldest mosque in Queens.

Memorial to victims of the World Trade Center attacks, September 11, 2001, Queens Library, Flushing Branch.

Association who would replace Harrison in the local City Council office in 2001, said: "We are not railing against community facilities. Our main beef is that zoning regulations encourage community facilities to locate in single-family areas."[32] In the 1990s and early 2000s, there were numerous initiatives to alter the 1961 city zoning laws (led especially by Liu and City Councilman Tony Avella, now a New York State senator), finally leading to the Community Facilities Text Reform Bill, which became law on September 9, 2004, and was aimed at protecting the quality of life in residential communities.[33] While the reform bill prohibits medical and dental offices from being built in residential zones designed for single-family homes, religious institutions are more complicated because of a recent federal law, the Religious Land Use and Institutionalized Persons Act of 2000, which was enacted by Congress "to protect religious liberty, and for other purposes."[34] Furthermore, despite recent initiatives to reverse course, the dramatic changes in the local religious landscape already had taken place: for better or worse, Flushing was stuck with its particular case of religious pluralism and would have to learn to live with it.

In addition to the kinds of legal, linguistic, and practical limits that affected the day-to-day quality of life in Flushing and sometimes led to nativism and hostility, other less obvious limits of pluralism developed. As the neighborhood struggled to adapt to rapid demographic change in the last decades of the twentieth century, social, structural, and theological limits of pluralism would further complicate efforts to achieve and sustain a sense of community or unity in Flushing.

Public/Private Urban Space and the Social Limits of Religious Pluralism

> The tolerance, the room for great differences among neighbors— differences that often go far deeper than differences in color—which are possible and normal in intensely urban life, but which are so foreign to suburbs and pseudosuburbs, are possible and normal only when streets of great cities have built-in equipment allowing strangers to dwell in peace together on civilized but essentially dignified and reserved terms.
>
> Jane Jacobs, *The Death and Life of Great American Cities*, 1961

In Robert Orsi's introduction to *Gods of the City: Religion and the American Urban Landscape,* he noted that "ever since the publication in 1938 of Louis Wirth's influential article 'Urbanism as a Way of Life,' American sociologists and urban scholars have debated whether the conditions of urban life ... give rise to distinct subjectivities. Is there a characteristic city self? Does the city [because of its large size, density, and heterogeneity] ... make people more or less tolerant, more or less nervous?"[35] Although Wirth's theory (and the study of the city as an urban ecology popularized by Wirth and other scholars associated with the Chicago School of sociology) has been challenged and disputed by some, even critics acknowledge the essay has shown remarkable staying power as the most cited article about the city of all time.[36] One of the arguments in Wirth's essay is that while city people regularly come into contact with many other people in public, their relations tend to be impersonal because of a desire to protect their personal, private space. He says that "in relation to the number of people whom they see and with whom they rub elbows in the course of daily life, they [urban inhabitants] know a smaller proportion, and of these they have less intensive knowledge. The contacts of the city may indeed be face to face, but they are nevertheless impersonal, superficial, transitory, and segmental."[37] Wirth was no doubt influenced by the German social theorist Georg Simmel, who wrote another influential essay, "The Metropolis and Mental Life," in 1903. In the following passage, Simmel describes the "reserve" that urban residents develop and the range of responses it can lead to:

> The mental attitude of the people of the metropolis to one another may be designated formally as one of reserve. If the unceasing external contact of numbers of persons in the city should be met by the same number of inner reactions as in the small town, in which one knows almost every person he meets and to each of whom he has a positive relationship, one would be completely atomized internally and would fall into an unthinkable mental condition. Partly this psychological circumstance and partly the privilege of suspicion which we have in the face of the elements of metropolitan life (which are constantly touching one another in fleeting contact) necessitates in us that reserve, in consequence of which we do not know by sight neighbors of years standing and which permits us to appear to small-town folk so often as cold and uncongenial. Indeed, if I am not mistaken, the inner side of this external reserve is not only indifference but more frequently than we believe, it is a slight aversion, a mutual strangeness and repulsion which, in a close contact which has arisen any way whatever, can break out into hatred and conflict.[38]

A decade before Wirth, his fellow Chicago sociologist Robert E. Park made a similar observation when he suggested that "the mobility of city life, with its increase in the number and intensity of stimulations" makes people behave "much as people do in some great hotel, meeting but not knowing one another. The processes of segregation establish moral distances which make the city *a mosaic of little worlds* which touch but do not interpenetrate."[39] Another scholar in the urban ecological tradition, Jane Jacobs, picked up this theme in 1961 in her book *The Death and Life of Great American Cities,* further developing these theories with her ideas about the uses of sidewalks for safety and contact in city neighborhoods. Jacobs insisted that because "cities are, by definition, full of strangers," one of the qualities for a successful city neighborhood is that, in order for people to feel safe, there should be a clear demarcation between public and private space—and that "a good city street neighborhood achieves a marvel of balance between its people's determination to have essential privacy and their simultaneous wishes for differing degrees of contact."[40] Jacobs had critics too (actually, the same people who had disagreed with Wirth), but her book also has proven to be one of the great classics.[41] Jacobs's ideas can be extended to think about religious pluralism and help shed more light on the interactions of residents in religiously diverse urban neighborhoods. Scholarship on the "public and private dichotomy" goes back at least to the late nineteenth century (judging from a search of titles on JSTOR).[42] Few, if any, scholars, however, have sought to apply such ideas about urban public and private space to the study of interaction among different religious groups or studies of religious pluralism, though other urban sociologists since Jacobs also have focused on the topic of a city of strangers.[43] There is a fairly extensive literature in sociology of religion and church history on the public/private distinction as it relates to urban congregational studies and social ministry—one of the most comprehensive recent books is Lowell Livezey's edited volume *Public Religion and Urban Transformation.*[44] Such work began with the sociologist Peter Berger, who was among the first to examine the division between the public and private *spheres* (followed much later by Jürgen Habermas) and to what extent urban religious congregations tend toward expressions of private faith or public action.[45] I would like to suggest that the topic of public religion is a separate area of study and furthermore that there is a difference between the public/private *spheres* as understood in such work and public/private *space*. The distinction between public/private space as expressed by Jacobs and later sociologists help explain why, in the most densely populated and diverse urban neighborhoods, individuals and groups with different religious backgrounds may encounter one another daily but generally do not interact.

Jacobs's idea about the importance of a clear demarcation between public and private space for successful city neighborhoods and its usefulness for understanding the social limits of religious pluralism is perhaps best illustrated by contrasting two very different types of religious interaction: public encounters with urban religious street parades or festivals and interfaith dialogue. These two types of interaction reinforce what Jacobs meant by "that almost unconsciously enforced, well-balanced line . . . between the city public world and the world of privacy."[46] For instance, examples of religious encounters familiar to residents of urban neighborhoods with different immigrant or ethnic communities might include watching a raucous, religious street festival, parade, or procession pass by one's apartment building, or perhaps accepting a pamphlet from a Mormon missionary or Jehovah's Witness on a streetcorner or subway exit.[47] These kinds of urban religious street and sidewalk life are, in general, somehow acceptable to city people because they do not typically have to involve much interaction—such displays are simply, as the urban historian Lewis Mumford once said, part of living in a city as "a theater of social action." Jacobs notes, "It is possible to be on excellent sidewalk terms with people who are different from oneself, and even, as time passes, on familiar public terms with them."[48] A similar observation was made by Wirth:

> The contacts of the city may indeed be face to face, but they are nevertheless impersonal, superficial, transitory, and segmental. The reserve, the indifference, and the blasé outlook which urbanites manifest in their relationships may thus be regarded as devices for immunizing themselves against the personal claims and expectations of others.[49]

As Jacobs and Wirth suggest, urban inhabitants deal with everyday life in a dense and diverse neighborhood by adopting and practicing various strategies in public to protect their personal space. New Yorkers are somewhat conditioned to accept diversity because they encounter such a wide range of different people in public and are generally forced to do so more than other areas that are not as densely populated and more spread out, but the interaction is often superficial. As Wirth and Jacobs suggest, city people value their privacy, so while residents of Flushing may live, work, and worship *near* one another, overall there is not much meaningful, lasting interaction among different ethnic/racial/religious groups—in large apartment buildings, next-door neighbors of different faiths and cultures sometimes never get to know each other. As one resident remarked, "Flushing is the twenty-first-century Babel—it's a place where seventy different ethnic groups *don't* get along and hold hands like 'Free to Be You and Me' but instead fight for scarce resources and space and *overlap* each other like a transparency but never quite commingle."[50]

Living in a densely populated urban area seems to force people to adopt certain coping mechanisms to deal with crowding. The geographer Yi-Fu Tuan suggests that working and living closely with others can lead to the avoidance of contact:

> Crowding is a condition known to all people at one time or another. People live in society. Whether one is an Eskimo or a New Yorker, occasions will arise when he has to work or live closely with others. Of the New Yorker this is obviously true, but even Eskimos do not always move on the broad open stage of the Tundra; in the course of many dark and long nights they have to bear with each other's company in ill-ventilated huts. The Eskimo, though less often than the New Yorker, must on occasion screen the stimulus of other people by turning them into shadows and objects. Etiquette and rudeness are opposite means to the same end: helping people avoid contact when such contact threatens to be too intense.[51]

Such behavior is perhaps most obvious on crowded public transportation: for instance, subway riders are often forced to get very close to people they might otherwise never meet, but most do not interact—instead, commuters typically put up a shield or mask with their newspapers, books, smartphones, and sunglasses to protect whatever personal space they have from homeless people asking for change, musicians going from car to car, rowdy children going home from school, or other intrusions. But the same behavior is obvious on the streets and sidewalks of diverse urban neighborhoods too during the kinds of religious encounters described above. Often it is just the simple need for privacy that can explain why there is so little interaction among residents of different religious backgrounds in a diverse urban neighborhood. Consider another passage from Jacobs:

> Privacy is precious in cities. It is indispensable. Perhaps it is precious and indispensable everywhere, but most places you cannot get it. In small settlements everyone knows your affairs. In the city everyone does not—only those you choose to tell will know much about you. This is one of the attributes of cities that is precious to most city people, whether their incomes are high or their incomes are low, whether they are white or [black], whether they are old inhabitants or new, and it is a gift of great city life deeply cherished and jealously guarded.[52]

It is not difficult to see how this might be applied to the religious practices of city people—especially in a densely populated and diverse urban
neighborhood where there seems to be an even greater need for space
and privacy. This may help explain why not only interaction but also interfaith efforts sometimes fail or go against the grain; as Jacobs adds, "The
requirement that much shall be shared drives city people apart."[53] Ironi-
cally, however, the same factors that keep people apart also help preserve
a kind of order, as the maintenance of this demarcation of public/private
space not only protects personal religious space but can help contribute
to a kind of religious pluralism where civil coexistence in diverse and
densely populated communities like Flushing, Queens, prevails.

Race, Ethnicity, and Class: Structural Limits of Pluralism

In 1964, the sociologist Milton M. Gordon analyzed the role of race,
religion, and national origins in American life and advanced a theory
of "structural pluralism" to explain why "relations between members
of different racial and religious groups in the United States remain at a
minimal level. This structural separation provides for the preservation of
the communal nature of the ethnic group, and, in the case of the major
religious denominations, makes for the retention of a core of differentiated religious beliefs, values, and historical symbols important to the loyal
members of the faith."[54] Gordon contrasted this with the related goal of
cultural pluralism, which he said was "to maintain enough subsocietal
separation to guarantee the continuance of the ethnic cultural tradition
and the existence of the group, without at the same time interfering with
the carrying out of standard responsibilities to the general American civic
life."[55] Though the United States would start to become much more
diverse the year after Gordon wrote his book with the passage of the
Immigration Act of 1965, Gordon's focus on the structural limits of pluralism is still relevant.

The racial limits of pluralism have been evident in Flushing and in
American society in general since the days of slavery, and race would continue to matter amid the increasingly diverse pluralism of the late twentieth century. The Immigration Act of 1965 was passed in the same year as
the Voting Rights Act of 1965 and just a year after the Civil Rights Act
of 1964 (all part of President Johnson's Great Society programs), which
together, one hundred years after the end of the Civil War, finally and
formally ended Jim Crow laws of legalized segregation and voting discrimination. Despite the optimism and successes of the civil rights move-

ment in the southern United States during the 1950s and early 1960s that culminated with this landmark legislation, racial tension remained widespread in American cities and led to race riots starting in 1965 in the Watts neighborhood of Los Angeles. A majority of blacks had moved away from the South to urban areas in the North during the Great Migration to escape Jim Crow laws and find work in factories. After World War II, however, many factories began to close down or move to the suburbs, where many whites were now moving as well—leaving a majority of blacks and other minorities trapped in the deindustrialized inner city with fewer job prospects and living in old neighborhoods that often faced redevelopment to make way for new bridges, roads, and housing projects.[56]

As discussed in Chapter 1, the black population in Flushing was first recorded in the 1690s (according to a census in 1698) and grew large enough by the early nineteenth century to support the founding of Macedonia AME church in 1811—eventually leading to a thriving, largely middle-class black community around Macedonia in the center of downtown until the 1950s. Yet, as discussed in Chapter 3, a much larger number of blacks came from other parts of the city in the 1950s through the 1970s, when several new housing projects were built. Over the next several decades, most African Americans in Flushing would end up living in these buildings where they were essentially segregated up to the present.

Catherine and Jay Williams were born in Flushing in the early 1930s, and they have been active members of Macedonia AME for their entire lives: Mr. Williams is the church historian who regularly presents a slide show of its history to new members; Mrs. Williams is church secretary. They have lived in a house on Bowne Street for many years (a block from the Ganesha temple) and can remember when there was a thriving black community all around Macedonia, including fourteen black-owned businesses.[57] Flushing was segregated then, however, and Mr. Williams recalls that he and other blacks could not go in the YMCA to swim. They both also remember, as discussed in Chapter 2, when the city decided to displace the black community around Macedonia in 1951 to make way for a large parking lot that now encircles the church, forcing many to relocate to the new Bland Housing Development on the western periphery of downtown (and later to Latimer Housing Development on the northern side of Northern Boulevard). As Rev. Nicholas Genevieve-Tweed, a pastor at Macedonia, would later remark: Flushing may be the most diverse place, but it is also "one of the most segregated places."[58] African Americans in Flushing frequently report the lack of affordable housing and the difficulty of finding work in local businesses owned by Asian Americans—sometimes of even being served in Asian American businesses. The problem, according to the Williams and Rev. Tweed, has been that the same new immigrant entrepreneurs who helped save Flushing's economy starting in the 1970s often did not seem to care about the effects their businesses might have on the existing community as much as they did about individual profit.[59] The focus on investment gains over local concerns has led to a downtown commercial district where longtime residents (white and black) report feeling like strangers in their hometown, given the gradual disappearance of familiar businesses like delis, diners, bars, and grocery stores with Western foods since the area's rapid transformation in the 1980s and 1990s. It also has meant that the success enjoyed by new immigrant entrepreneurs has not been shared by others in the community—especially blacks and Hispanic immigrants, who have considerably less power in the local Flushing economy and politics. Perhaps for such reasons, Macedonia AME continues to fulfill the role churches have always served in the black community as a trusted institution for self-help, religious devotion, and fellowship. At the same time, Macedonia has always been engaged with the community outside its doors as well—serving not just its congregation (which has grown to include some white, South Asian, and Chinese congregants among its five hundred active members) but also the community at large with a daycare and soup kitchen that are both popular with new immigrants. The leadership at Macedonia also has always been involved in local interfaith activities. Rev. Tweed, who has been especially active in the community, summed up his perspective on pluralism in Flushing this way:

> Pluralism is an aspiration that is informed by our religious convictions and represents our best hopes for building community. But in practical terms it has been disconnected from a social–political context so that the goal of pluralism has been unhinged from the building of community. And I think that as long as people are motivated by material interests that it becomes increasingly more difficult to create a truly pluralistic community. Our religious convictions are formed in communities where our religious practice is determined on the basis of race and ethnicity. The goals are universal in terms of ideals but in practice divided along racial, ethnic, and cultural lines.[60]

There are some signs such division may be fading somewhat in the twenty-first century, though: for example, the development corporation of Macedonia broke ground in January 2010 next door to the church on an impressive new building called Macedonia Plaza. Offering affordable residential and commercial units to reflect and enhance the community, Macedonia may help reverse some of lingering racial limits in Flushing in the years ahead.

Besides race, the structural limits of ethnicity and culture have affected intergroup relations in Flushing in other ways. One of the most obvious limits tied to ethnicity has been language. Ethnic businesses that seek to cater mainly to their own community and bearing signs with no English translation have created animosity among longtime white and black residents. In the 1980s and 1990s, Chinese and Korean businesses in downtown Flushing often placed signs outside only in Chinese or Korean, which led to many longtime residents feeling unwelcome in "their" neighborhood. It has also led to serious safety issues—as mentioned earlier, in at least one case, the police of the 109th precinct was notified about a crime but could not make it there in time because they simply could not read the sign to find the store where the incident had occurred. This linguistic limit of pluralism in Flushing was compounded by the gradual disappearance of many "familiar" grocery stores, delis, bars, and restaurants; they were largely replaced by Chinese, Korean, and Indo-Pak-Bangla markets, shops, and restaurants by 2000. The commercial landscape of downtown Flushing changed at the same time as did the religious landscape.

Places of worship are also separated by language: in churches with multiethnic congregations there are separate services for different languages, but there are, of course, also many different places of worship that exist to serve immigrant communities in their native language, not to mention particular regional-linguistic groups *within* each community. The half-dozen Hindu temples in Flushing represent different traditions and communities divided along regional-linguistic lines in India, and a similar ethnolinguistic diversity exists in other religious traditions represented in Flushing: there are separate mosques that cater mainly to Pakistani or Afghan immigrants; dozens of Buddhist temples serve either Chinese (Taiwan and mainland), Korean, or Japanese immigrants. Similarly, the Korean Christian immigrant community is represented by many separate churches—over one hundred out of the two hundred total number of places of worship in Flushing.

The Swaminarayan Hindu temple (also known as Bochasanwasi Akshar Puroshottam Sanstha, or BAPS) was established two blocks down Bowne Street from the Ganesha temple, but the two often seem as far away as Chennai (Madras) in South India is from Ahmedabad in the western Indian state of Gujarat.[61] Devotees at the Swaminarayan temple say they customarily slow down when driving past the Ganesha temple out of respect, and some refer to Bowne Street as *"Bawa* Street" (Saint Street) because of its diverse religious life. Many are loosely involved with activities in other Hindu temples, yet other Hindus do not often visit the Swaminarayan temple because they do not understand Gujarati. Several women and men with whom I spoke pointed out that even though they do associate with other Hindus and worship some of the same major Hindu deities, their primary allegiance is to Swaminarayan, whom they regard as an incarnation of the god Krishna. They call this *pativratani bhakti* (literally, "one husband devotion"), meaning you should respect all religions but follow one. A priest further explained that relations with other places of worship take place on three different levels: priest to priest, manager to manager, and president to president.

Language and culture also help explain the staggering number of Korean churches in Flushing. Despite the success of several megachurches, the vast majority of the hundred-plus Korean churches in Flushing are very small—which leads to the question: why are there so many? Older residents of Flushing have been frustrated and baffled, and most do not understand why Koreans cannot just join existing churches rather than build new ones.[62] There are a few exceptions where Koreans have merged with other congregations, like the now multiethnic First Methodist Church, but most are exclusively Korean. As is the case with any new immigrant group, language is one factor; another part of the explanation involves groups taking advantage of the 1960s zoning law that permits religious organizations to establish places of worship as community facilities. Indeed, Korean Christian groups seem to have benefited from this loophole more than any other group, and some have abused it—a few churches were found to be operating as businesses and exploiting their tax-exempt status.[63] But these explanations miss a larger matrix of cultural reasons. A common impression of Koreans in Flushing is that they can sometimes seem exclusionary, cold, and insensitive to the rest of the community—some Korean stores have been criticized for refusing to serve non-Koreans, and some cashiers at Korean delicatessens still follow a traditional Korean practice of avoiding eye contact and not placing change in the customer's hand. Until the late nineteenth century, Korea was a very closed nation and had a culture virtually untouched by external influence. The twentieth century brought Korea into greater contact with the rest of the world, but a majority of Koreans retain a lingering distrust of outsiders, which people tend to see as a closed and guarded arrogance toward strangers, making it difficult for Koreans to merge with other congregations and participate in community life. Yanghee Hahn, a city government employee active in Flushing's civic life for fifteen years who grew up in one of the first Christian families in South Korea (her maternal grandmother was the first female elder of the first Methodist church in Korea) says: "It reflects a characteristic of Koreans: Koreans are very individualistic players compared to Chinese, so they don't like or they're not very good at group playing—individually they're very strong, talented, bright people and able, but unable to work in a team or group. We acknowledge that ourselves as our weakness."[64] But Hahn also feels the reason for the large number of churches may go beyond basic cultural differences in social interaction. First, many Korean men simply want to be ministers because they connect much of South Korea's recent post-war redevelopment and renewed prosperity with the legacy of Protestant missionaries, so Christianity and Westernization are generally viewed as the salvation of Korea and Koreans—especially among those who decide to emigrate.[65] Non-Christian Koreans are actually viewed by their Christian peers as "having less vitality, being more subdued and laid back, less open, less progressive, less driven, and less achieving."[66] Despite a majority of men who are drawn to a career in the church for deep spiritual reasons, some may have other motives. A large number of less-affluent or less-educated Korean immigrants tend to work long, hard hours in small labor-intensive Korean businesses like delicatessens and cornershops where they are never recognized as upper-class members of society. The ministry, on the other hand, is widely recognized and respected in Korean culture, and it may have become an attractive alternative to those without much of an education and no business aspirations:

> Some people are getting into it to make an easier and more honorable living, because otherwise the option is you have to get into running a business and hard labor. It's not an easy life, and you're not really honored and recognized as a small business owner in Korea. So some men may see becoming a minister and running a church [as an opportunity to] make a decent, comfortable living—and you get social recognition, so that some people actually may choose that as a more secular interest and motivation rather than really a sacred sense of calling.[67]

It is of course impossible to gauge how often this may be the reason a Korean man becomes a minister, but some critically minded Koreans suspect that it does occur. Whatever the case may be, when all of these students graduate from theological seminaries, each pastor wants his own church (again, this is related to Korean individualism), and many opt to start out with a small church rather than join a larger one.

The second phenomenon behind the explosion of churches is that, as these smaller new churches grow, factions develop, and they fight—ultimately causing one or more factions to depart from the congregation and establish other small churches, each with a brand-new minister. I am told this happens many times.[68] With such a huge number from which to choose, many Korean Americans in Flushing have the possibility of selecting a church based on personal taste, a pastor's personality, and different styles of worship. Some feel the family-style approach of smaller churches has more to offer than the hierarchical organization of bigger ones, but with so many smaller churches, the majority are not likely to last beyond the first generation of immigrants who established them (although these could be replaced again by new churches). Meanwhile, however, the proliferation of Korean churches in Flushing has continued virtually unchecked for over a decade and threatens to destroy the fabric of a once largely residential neighborhood. There is growing awareness of the problem among Koreans, and more are beginning to cooperate with neighbors about other social issues as well. Hahn says, "it's getting better due to rapid Western exposure. Also, most of all, Christianity, because Christianity opens up their psyche—opens up their heart and soul, because Christians have to witness Christ for other people. So that's what they actually try to practice, [and it is] rapidly changing their way of life and their psyche as well."[69] A number of residents interviewed felt the Korean American community in Flushing could be more sensitive to the surrounding neighborhood by monitoring the addition of new churches and immediately finding better parking solutions. But those I spoke to in the Korean community said they tend to be very reluctant to talk badly about other Koreans in public; it is not honorable to air other people's "dirty laundry."[70] It seems this tendency, along with other cultural-behavioral explanations described earlier (which are also common among other first-generation immigrant groups), combined with the popularity of seminary school and lax zoning laws and led to the problem. A few first- and several second-generation Korean church and community leaders in Flushing participate in community board and interfaith meetings, however, and there is hope that they will guide the Korean community into better relations with the rest of Flushing.[71]

Theological Limits of Pluralism

> It is impossible to live in peace with those one believes to be damned.
> Rousseau, "On Civil Religion," *The Social Contract*

Finally, religious difference also affects why some people do not interact and would not want to participate in any dialogue or interaction—because they believe "the Other" is wrong and/or evil or some kind of threat to be avoided. It is clear that not everyone in Flushing is eager to jump on the interfaith bandwagon, and it seems religious groups involved in mission work are the least likely to get involved—a fact that also ultimately keeps them from joining other groups in community-related civic projects.

The theological limits of pluralism are perhaps best illustrated by those groups that exhibit the extreme but fairly uncommon sentiment expressed by Rousseau. For instance, when the hall across the street that Gurdwara Singh Sabha on Bowne Street had first used was purchased by a Chinese evangelical group, tension soon followed. A branch with headquarters in Manhattan's Chinatown, the Boon Church of Oversea Chinese Mission (OCM) soon converted the space and swelled in membership, later opening the Christian Witness Theological Seminary of New York and Boon Church Christian Bookstore across the street in a building adjacent to the gurdwara. Relations were civil until the church added a large bold mural outside that proclaimed "Jesus is Lord!" The Sikhs objected, but the mural was not removed until 1996, when the gurdwara acquired the building next door and expanded. One of the pastors at OCM later shared that he was waging "a spiritual battle for souls on Bowne Street" against the "devil Hindu churches" across the street and nearby. Evidently, he believed the Sikh gurdwara, the Swaminarayan Hindu temple, and the Ganesha temple were all the same.

In another case, the same church that prides itself on its "multiethnic, multicultural, multilingual," and racially integrated congregation is very exclusive when it comes to religion.[72] When I asked Rev. Gary Domiano if First Baptist Church ever participated in interfaith activities with non-Christians, for instance, he replied: "No, we have not done that . . . we don't go into the debate settings. They are not profitable. But we have not yet done that or had the opportunity to sit down with another religious leader in dialogue about our beliefs, our differences."[73] Similarly, although several Korean American residents and ministers have participated in the NIH, the pastor at Full Gospel New York Mission Center explained that there are "different conceptions of God and different goals—we respect individual people but not necessarily their religions."[74]

And, if you are an evangelical Christian who lives in a diverse place like Flushing where you believe everyone else is damned, the natural inclination (the biblical commandment, they believe) for some is to share the "good news" of Jesus Christ and "save" your neighbors through proselytism and mission work.[75]

"A Missiological Gold Mine"

At some point in the 1990s, word must have spread in certain circles that Flushing was a ripe new site for proselytizing, and more and more missionaries began to appear on streetcorners all over. The sociologist R. Stephen Warner has said that "locations with high rates of in-migration . . . offer attractive markets for aggressive religious organizations," and it seems that some groups actually watch for developing immigrant meccas.[76] Several very different groups now have active missionary drives throughout Flushing, and the spiritual battle for souls is often waged every day of the week (especially when the weather is nice) by competing Baptists and Pentecostal groups, Jehovah's Witnesses, Mormons, Korean Presbyterians, Chinese evangelicals, and the Falun Gong. Occasionally, modern-day circuit riders of a more fundamentalist bent also visit from distant home bases (Georgia, for instance), with flyers and briefcases full of videos about the Apocalypse. Outside the Flushing branch of the New York Public Library, music often fills the air like an urban street revival: Chinese women belt out emotional hymns over a portable stereo while, just a few yards away, a European American youth minister does the same on an acoustic guitar. Some passersby stop, listen, talk to the missionaries, and join them in an impromptu prayer while exchanging information. There is a real sense of urgency and determination among the groups, almost like miners descending upon a gold rush (except the gold here involves the *souls* of pedestrians and people entering and exiting the subway and buses in New York City on their way to and from work, home, and shopping). Mission work is always bold business, as dogmatic individuals often confront people from different faiths as sure of the truth of their own religion as the missionaries are themselves. Expecting recent immigrants who feel lost in a strange new land and perhaps with little English, missionaries specially trained to deal with every kind of response often lure newcomers with ESL classes and other needed services, with the ulterior plan of gradual indoctrination. But it is very difficult to attract new immigrants who have already invested time and money in establishing their own places of worship, which most immigrant groups tend to do fairly quickly. A missionary's only real hope

Members of Free Living Water Church with "Jesus Loves You" vests outside of the Flushing branch of the New York public library system, on Main Street.

is to happen upon an immigrant who has either just arrived or has not yet joined or found a place of worship—and this is not a common thing in a place like Flushing. For every rare instance of friendly exchange that leads to further contact (much less conversion), there is a much greater amount of rejection, hostility, and pamphlets tossed in the trash. Some missionaries are even out to convert each other, leading to interesting street debates full of opposing but equal convictions. Other parts of the world suffer from bloodshed and war because of religious and ethnic conflict stemming from territorial disputes and tyranny; in densely populated and diverse urban neighborhoods like Flushing evangelical groups encounter other world religions and express their zeal through mission work, services, festivals, and parades.

Various religious and ethnic processions and parades criss-cross the same streets on similar routes, each group proudly and loudly asserting itself, but on different and separate days and times of the year. Police officers in the Community Affairs Unit of the local 109th precinct often act as a liaison to the different ethnic and religious groups in Flushing. Before all street parades, festivals, and other functions, places of worship send a

Hispanic women from the Jehovah's Witnesses, with free copies of the *Watchtower* for people entering and exiting the subway, wait next to newspaper vendors.

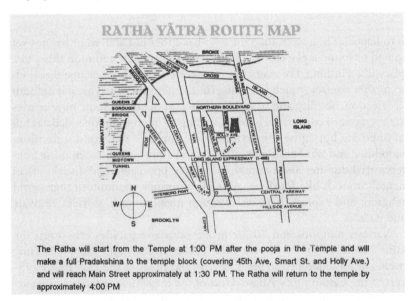

Ratha Yatra route map for the annual Ganesh Chaturthi parade.

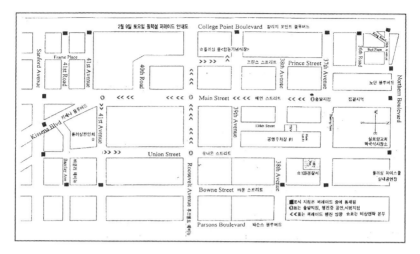

2002 Lunar New Year parade route.

letter to the precinct with dates, times, and planned routes in advance of an event, and a number of officers are then sent as a free service to monitor activities.[77] The streets of Flushing might be a kind of battleground if such events were ever scheduled for the same time, but instead it seems the various parades and processions take place quite literally on common ground.

Though other groups in Flushing work the same crowd, no one organizes a more aggressive and systematic missionary drive than the Church of Jesus Christ of Latter-Day Saints (LDS). Young Mormons (nineteen years of age for males, twenty-one for females) who apply to undertake missions and earn the title of elder spend months at a missionary training center in Provo, Utah, before embarking on the eighteen-month proselytizing journey, which usually sends them across the world to spread the gospel. Traditionally, missionaries have been assigned to a specific country, and they learn the language during training, but the church has added domestic missions to certain concentrated urban areas ("zones") as immigration since 1965 has brought people from all over the world much closer to Salt Lake City. The Flushing ward (congregation) is the most diverse zone LDS missionaries work in New York City in terms of languages spoken by elders. Whereas Korean Presbyterians and Chinese evangelical groups mainly target coethnics and in fact usually only approach Koreans and Chinese,

MARCH FOR JESUS ROUTE MAP & PRAYER POINTS

I will give you every place where you set your foot" Joshua 1:3

1. **Boro Pregnancy Counseling Center**
Pray for effective Christ centered outreach to young women in need.

2. **Psychic Club at Flushing Free Synagogue**
Pray for a revelation of Jesus as Messiah to be given to our Jewish neighbors and that this false altar come down.

3. **Downtown Prayer Station Site*****
Pray for the many Flushing Churches as they witness at this major intersection. Pray that signs and wonders will be released through the Prayer Station ministries!

4. **Flushing Commercial/Transportation Hub**
Pray blessing on businesses, & commuters on buses, LIRR & 7 Train. The Federal Government has designated the 7 train as a Millennial Trail used by peoples from all nations.

5. **Wendy's Massacre Site*****
Pray for healing, restoration, and cleansing the land.

6. **Northern Blvd. as Gate to Flushing**
From the Flushing River, Northern Blvd. was an ancient pathway into Flushing originally used by native Americans. Pray that this gate be lifted up for the King to enter!

7. **RKO Keith: Historic Landmark**
Pray for the resolution of the decade old court tie-up over the building's usage. Pray for the property owner to come to know Jesus and use the property for Kingdom purposes.

8. **Abortion Clinic Site*****
Pray for grace & mercy toward those who are taking human lives. Pray that the clinic goes out of business, and for young women in crisis be directed to Boro Pregnancy Counseling Center! The building owner is the same as point 7 above.

9. **Quaker Meeting House**
Oldest standing house of worship in the USA. Pray for redigging of wells of evangelical teaching and tearing down the altars of Universalism which have spread throughout Flushing.

10. **Flushing Obelisk/Former Masonic Lodge Site**
Pray against the ancient & deceiving spirit of Freemasonry historically established at the gates of Flushing.

11. **Town Hall**
Pray for community leaders and the 107 Precinct as Town Hall served as the seat of Flushing Government and its Police Station for many years. Pray for Creative Arts to glorify God!

12. **Armory/Flushing Remonstrance Site of 1657*****
Pray that Flushing fulfills its destiny. Hailed as the birthplace of Religious Freedom "in Christ Jesus," pray that all men will be drawn to Jesus as He is now lifted up in this most multi-national of communities!

13. **Flushing High School*****
Pray for this historic first high school in NY State (1875) as representative of all high schools in the region.

14. **Flushing YMCA*****
Pray for a release of God's purposes in the "Y" as Flushing pastors meet with the "Y" Director on a monthly basis.

15. **Bowne Street/Fox Rock**
This was the site from which George Fox held open-air meetings and preached the gospel to crowds in the 1672. Pray for the "River of God" to again flow publicly in Flushing!

16. **John Bowne House**
Underground Railroad site before Civil War. Pray that Flushing will always extend compassion, justice and welcome to the oppressed and immigrant.

17. **Public School 20**
Pray for summer outreaches to schoolchildren on the streets, in parks and through VBS's.

18. **Bowne Playground*****
Pray for a visitation of the Holy Spirit today that will remain after the rally with many coming to Christ throughout the summer and into the fall!

Highlighted points indicate special prayer stops

March for Jesus route map, 2001.

respectively, LDS elders are a multilingual group (replenished continuously by new recruits) that systematically divides the Flushing zone by each ethnic enclave—focusing on each with careful precision and relentlessly, patiently keeping at their task nearly every day of their mission. They live together in apartments rented by the church, following a strict regimen and meeting regularly to compare experiences, bolster confidence, and pray together. Such support is necessary: they come from school in Utah (where 70 percent of the population is Mormon), and missions to other countries are hard enough. But pluralistic places like Flushing present new difficulties, as it not just a one-on-one dynamic (for example, Mormons versus Muslims in Indonesia); instead, the elders are surrounded not only by many other faiths, but they are also competing with other missionaries. One would think a mission in America would be easier, but Flushing is one of the most challenging postings even for bright, idealistic young adults—a test not only of one's ability as a missionary but also sometimes of the preconceived boundaries and absolute truth of one's beliefs.

Elders Packer and Harrison were mission partners in Flushing beginning in 2000, and both had been trained to speak Chinese (as well as a
little Spanish and Korean). I asked them to run me through a typical day:

> EH: We get up out of bed no later than 6:30, and from 6:30 to 9:30
> we spend an hour studying together about the Gospel of Jesus
> Christ and also Chinese. And then we have an hour to study by
> ourselves, and that's kind of split up as well. And then an hour
> to get ready to go. And then, by 9:30, we are out on the streets
> talking to people; or, a lot of times, we come to the church to
> teach people. And if we don't have any appointments, we are just
> outside all the time trying to invite people to come to church
> and to try and teach them something about the Gospel. And
> then we have about an hour for lunch and an hour for dinner.
> Other than that, we are missionaries all the way until 9:30 at
> night—that's when we go home, and we are sleeping by 10:30.[78]

Though they are called "preparation days," Mondays are their only break.
Then elders have time to relax, be tourists, wash clothes (they always
appear neatly dressed with official nametags—men wear crisp white shirts
with ties; women wear similarly modest semiformal outfits), buy the
things they need for the week, and generally get ready to hit the streets
again. I asked how a typical encounter might go:

> EH: Well, the first thing is we just try and catch their attention, get
> them to notice something about us . . . I don't know. Sometimes
> all we have to say is "Hello" in their language and they look at
> us like "Wow, this is a white guy speaking Chinese." And some
> of them are pretty amazed by that and they want to talk to us
> and see if that's all we know or if we know how to say a little
> bit more. So that gets a lot of people's attention, if they haven't
> met us before. And then we'll just get to know them, get to find
> out where they are from, find out about their families, how long
> they've been here, what they're doing, if they are students, or . . .
> all that kind of stuff. And then, what I'll try and do is, I'll try
> and take some part of the Gospel of Jesus Christ and liken it to
> their lives and kind of teach them a little bit about it. And then,
> if they have interest, then we can continue to either talk about it
> right then; or, if they don't have any time, we'll get their phone
> number and address and come back later. That's basically what
> it is.[79]

They have to be prepared for every kind of reaction, as experiences can run from good to bad:

> EH: It ranges from talking to people who are half crazy to people who already know all about your religion and don't want anything to do with it. The only thing that's really coming to my mind right now actually is a really good one. There was this one time when I talked to this lady on the street, and she'd actually been to Salt Lake City and seen the Headquarters of the Church. And she'd been interested in it at that point. She was already Christian. And she hadn't been going to church for a while. But she felt like, when she talked to us as missionaries, that that was kind of God's way of getting her to come back to church. So she was very interested from the start. We wrote down her phone number and got in touch with her later and later she was baptized. So, that was a really good one.
>
> EP: Well, if people don't want to talk to us, they don't want to talk to us. There's not much we can do about it ... so they'll walk by, wave at us. Maybe if we try a little harder, if we give them strike two, then they'll tell us "Sorry, I'm in a rush—don't have the time." But I've never ... I'm sure we'll have some people that might be religious or whatever, or opposed to whatever it is that we are doing on the streets. But, for the most part, the Chinese people are very kind and loving people, and they are willing to talk with you even if it's just about their family and their life.[80]

The success rate is not exactly encouraging, but it is measured in different ways. Elders estimate maybe one in twenty people will provide them with contact information and allow them to follow up; out of this percentage, maybe one in ten of these will visit the church or come to learn more. It takes patience and perseverance, but the elders seem to take it in stride:

> EH: I'd say that, if we are just saying hi to people as they walk by and seeing their reaction to that, its smaller. But if we are actually just walking up to people and shaking their hand and saying "Hi, I'm Elder Harrison"—something like that, then they are more likely to say "OK" and at least talk with you for a little while. You speak a little Chinese at them and they are a little bit interested, or at least they are not going to be real rude right then. So I'd say most of the people that you go up to like that will talk to you. There are a few that will just say, "I know who you are, and I've talked

to you, I don't want to come to church, and I don't want to talk to you"—and that's it. But I'd say most of the people that you talk to like that will stop and talk with you.

EP: It's kind of like, I don't know, shooting baskets. Or playing baseball. You don't get a hit every time you play. The more chances you get to hit, or the more chances you get to shoot, the more they'll fall in . . . eventually.[81]

When they do have the opportunity to follow up, the elders first visit people in their apartments and homes. But often the exchange is mutual:

EP: Well, one thing I've really loved is getting welcomed into their homes and them being so willing to share their culture with us, teach us about what it's like in China, and also cooking their food, letting us taste it and use chopsticks and hang out in their house with them. That's one of my favorite parts, just learning about their culture. Because it's so different and it's on the other side of the world and something that I think a lot of people in the Western Hemisphere really don't understand because it's kind of an interesting place.

EH: Yeah . . . I think it's interesting because people who wouldn't have anything to do with the church will invite you over to eat. They'll say, "Yeah, you know, I'd like to take you to China with me. I'd show you around and . . ." and they are just the nicest people you could ever want to meet, *even if they don't have even a speck of interest in what you're doing*. Well . . . that doesn't happen all the time, but there are people who will do that. Or, we'll end up teaching, but they are really not interested in what we have to say, but they'll say, "You can come over and eat anytime" or something! And they love to teach *us* about their culture.[82]

Learning about the culture can be advantageous for later encounters with other people, but sometimes the table is turned and something different happens. Day after day of walking by and interacting with people from different churches, synagogues, temples, gurdwaras, and mosques also can have an effect:

EH: Well, I'd say that there are a lot of people who want to tell you about *their* religion. You know, that's what *you* are doing, and so they think, "Well, yeah . . . I should be able to share with you too." I'd say as far as hearing what anybody else . . . and about their beliefs, I think it's fun to learn about them, and I think that it gives me more of a respect for what they believe in, and for who they are as people.

EP: I think it's pretty interesting, you know, how you know no matter where they are from, or what religion they claim, they all believe in a Supreme Being. And no matter what they call the Supreme Being, we can all kind of believe together that that's our Creator, that that's something that leads and guides and directs us and something that we all share in common. And through that, we can also understand that we are very similar no matter what our culture is, we are all kind of brothers and sisters.[83]

Missionaries in Flushing, especially Mormon elders who spend a great deal of time in dialogue with the people they are trying to convert, sometimes change themselves by the time their mission ends and they leave. Not only have they learned more about another culture, but the idealism and unquestioned beliefs they had when they arrived also occasionally gives way to a more balanced understanding of world religions.

Meanwhile, back at First Baptist, the church leadership continued its past commitment to "seizing the opportunities for mission at our doorstep" by reaching out in different ways to everyone it possibly could at home. Realizing the vast number of non-Christian new immigrants in the area, the assistant pastor wrote to seminary colleagues that "We are sitting on a 'missiological gold mine' here in our community with the 100 language groups."[84] Although less organized than the Mormons, First Baptist and other evangelical partner churches throughout Queens display an equal amount of zeal in their activities. Every year the church sponsors a missions conference and emphasizes missions for an entire month in the congregations. Outreach takes several forms.

Classes in English as a second language are one of the more subtle lures, as Rev. Domiano explained:

And when you hang an ESL sign on the gate of your church, that's going to draw people. We put the advertisement in some of the local newspapers, language newspapers, shop windows where people visit, Laundromats, and then word of mouth. And few churches in the area actually have ESL programs. So that's one way of us connecting meaningfully with the community. We do that as a ministry to the community. As an opportunity not only to teach English, but make a connection with the community and introduce them along the way to Jesus Christ if possible.[85]

Every year, once a year, the whole church also participates in the production of a festival (actually more like a revival or old-time evangelical camp
meeting), which is a more communal and public medium. Renting park
space across the street, they set up tables with the different ministries and
support groups the church offers, and a stage provides a platform for pup-
pets, preachers, testimonies, and diverse Christian musical performances.
But the most direct means of mission work is actually going out in the
street and trying to convert people. Like all evangelicals, many people in
the congregation and the leadership at First Baptist feel it is their duty as
Christians to do mission work—they see it, in fact, as a biblical commandment, as Domiano pointed out:

> Well, Jesus said, his last command was "Go into all the world and preach
> the gospel to all nations, baptizing them in the name of the Father and
> the Son and the Holy Spirit." All through the Bible, one thing that
> stands out about God's character is that He is a Missionary God. He's
> seeking the lost. And when Christ left, He leaves this great commission
> with the church—go into all the world, preach the gospel to all nations.

The reference to "all the nations" has a particular resonance in Flushing, as
missionaries apply it to the many new immigrant communities transplanted
from all over the world. Domiano also finds other acts of Jesus to follow by
example that relate to engaging people that others shy away from:

> [One] Sunday I preached on John 4, where Jesus reaches the woman
> at the well. She was a Samaritan, which means she was a mixed-race
> person, half-Jew/half-Gentile. She was a woman, so there was the
> gender barrier, there was a religious barrier, there was the ethnic
> barrier. And most Jews, all Jews, they would avoid Samaria like the
> plague—when traveling from south to north, they would go around.
> Jesus says he has to go through Samaria, and then he engages this
> woman in conversation. She believes, brings her whole town, and
> they all believe in Jesus. Over and over, Jesus models that—the Gos-
> pel goes to all people. When you read the Book of Acts, Paul is a
> missionary. The Apostles are missionaries. And that just carries down
> to the church, biblically. That, whether we live here or whether we
> live in Tucson, Arizona, or Orlando, Florida, our responsibility as
> believers is to proclaim the gospel to those that . . . to those who
> are around us. So, we happen to live in an extremely challenging
> community, because of the diversity. It just means that we still need
> to do it—we may just need to be more equipped.[86]

But it can be a real challenge sometimes to become familiar enough with someone from an entirely different culture—much less attempt to change something as deeply embedded as religious beliefs. It involves not only knowing a good deal about another religion and how to navigate certain cultural customs but also persuading someone that their religion is backward or untrue, that they risk eternal damnation, that they can be saved if they only jettison their previous traditions and beliefs and accept Jesus Christ as their personal savior—yet doing all of this while also somehow being very sensitive.

The congregational members of First Baptist are very devout, with very strong, firmly held beliefs, but just across the street and down every block you have Jews, Hindus, Sikhs, Muslims, and Buddhists who also believe in their traditions with similar fervor and claims to truth. What does it mean to people involved in mission work to be surrounded by such a large number of other world religions and faiths? I asked Domiano if that is seen as a challenge in any way: "No, as a *responsibility*, a challenge . . . yes. But a responsibility—we have a responsibility to reach out to our community no matter how diverse."[87] He noted that there are a few people in the congregation who were Hindus, Muslims, and Buddhists, but that such conversions take time. One outreach effort to Muslims and Hindus in Flushing and Jackson Heights involved interviewing people on the street with survey forms. After asking questions about someone's faith (what they believe, what their religion meant to them personally), the missionaries then asked if they could share a little bit about what Christ and Christianity meant to them. Domiano said, "We had marvelous conversations. But it's hard for people like that to come to Christ right away. It's a process."[88] Asked if being surrounded by so many other faiths ever felt unbearable to him or members of the church, Domiano replied:

> No. Personally, I love it. And we love it. There's something about diversity that really makes life exciting. So nobody sees it as adversity—just a challenge. I think I used the word earlier, it's *challenging*—how do you . . . because the same gospel has to be packaged kind of differently if you are talking to a Hindu woman or a Muslim man. Or a Mormon who is in from Utah for two years. So, it's the same message, but somehow you have to know who you are talking to, kind of have to know a little bit about what they believe, and what's their culturally acceptable way of approaching them. Like if I were to walk down to the Hindu temple on Bowne Street, and kind of just walk in to the temple shoes on, dressed the wrong way, nobody would talk to me.

I would not effectively go up to a Muslim woman on the street and engage her in conversation. It's taboo. So there are different skills and different things you should develop.[89]

There may be no adversity in diversity, but it can be challenging—especially for missionaries in Flushing. It requires a new kind of multicultural or religious literacy, but for the sake of disproving different beliefs and traditions, not tolerating them. High school and college students in the congregation participate in three-month training programs and are then given the opportunity to undertake mission work. Mission-minded folk from First Baptist may not undertake eighteen-month mission journeys devoted solely to gaining converts, but many also take their mission with them to school and work. The church tries to give enough encouragement, enough biblical instruction, and enough training so that when people encounter others as they conduct their daily lives, they will effectively be able to begin conversations and speak to people about the gospel wherever they are. With such comprehensive, ongoing dedication it would seem that the end goal of groups like First Baptist is a totalizing mission to Christianize Flushing. That might be, but the leadership is also realistic, as Domiano explained:

> Well, my theological convictions come from what Jesus said in Matthew 7: the road to life is a narrow road, and few find it; and the road to destruction is broad, and most are on that road. So theologically, even with the Old Testament Israelites, there was always just a remnant who were truly saved and in the right relationship with God. So theologically, no matter where you are, there will always be a minority of Christians in the world. Whatever that number is, there will always be a minority. So I don't make any mistake about that.
>
> Seldom do you see a place turn entirely Christian. A place as diverse as Flushing, probably not. If you go, let's say, into a village in a part of Asia or Africa where there's a tribal chief or a main leader, it's almost "as goes the leader, so go the people." So sometimes if someone in a key position like that comes to faith in Christ, he or she has tremendous influence over those who follow. But when in such diversity, you don't have that domino effect. People who have done Muslim missions know that it is difficult soil to plow. There are just so many barriers to hurdle. So many misconceptions to clear up. So it's really a stronghold. And theologically, why people are blind, spiritually blind, is: people are religious by nature, so they will gravitate toward something. And that's why you see it.[90]

First Baptist may gain a small number of converts from other faiths over the years, but the process will be gradual and doubtfully very extensive. Flushing will probably always remain an extremely diverse place of many very different religions because each has the freedom to flourish and each has had time to become an established part of the community and the communities they serve.

The Possibilities of Religious Pluralism

Yet for all of the spatial, social, structural, and theological limits of pluralism, the story of Flushing suggests there may be no limit to how *much* pluralism a pluralist society can stand. In general, this small, densely populated neighborhood with over two hundred different places of worship has not been torn apart by ethnic and religious conflict but instead has been characterized mainly by a history of civil coexistence. To be sure, fault lines of tension stemming from the various limits of pluralism lie just under the surface, and there are occasional tremors. Parking problems and changes in the landscape of neighborhoods have generated nativist sentiment and isolated incidents of hostility, and the area has at times been plagued by gang activity over turf—but there has never been the kind of ethnic and religious strife or war found in other parts of the world. This demonstrates the remarkable possibilities of pluralism for civil society—that a pluralistic society committed to democracy and religious freedom can accommodate an enormous amount of diversity, though it can still be a real test for a diverse community to *live* with pluralism. As in every community across America, this test will continue, but the story of Flushing suggests we have reason to be hopeful.

Bridges of Dialogue or Tower of Babel?

> But now what is most remarkable is, that over this confused diversity there broods after all a higher unity, and that in this chaos of peoples the traces of a specifically American national character may be discerned.
>
> Philip Schaff, *America: A Sketch of its Political,*
> *Social, and Religious Character*, 1855

By the late twentieth century, not only Flushing but much of America was caught up in wondering how much pluralism a pluralist society could stand. Diversity had begun to test the capacity of institutions and traditions to accommodate to such a degree that many perceived an overall decline of civil society, or "the connections between citizens and the nation's collective need for discussion of the common good."[91] Pointing to a general sense of widening societal fragmentation since the 1950s, Jean Bethke Elshtain remarked: "It is no longer possible for us to speak to one another. We, quite literally, inhabit our own little islands of bristling difference where we comport with those just like ourselves."[92] As immigration peaked again in the early 1990s, many descended into another bout of related hysteria and sought to place blame on the record numbers of newcomers.[93] Increasing indifference was also perceived to be a factor, as John Higham noted: "The eclipse of liberal nationalism since the 1960s has deprived all the nation's minorities of a powerful means of affirming their fraternity with others and exploring their relations to a common Americanism."[94] Immigration and diversity may have accelerated this splintering, but the reactionary reform and nativist impulses to restrict immigration in the 1990s because it was seen as the root problem were largely unfounded: wiser voices knew the real problem lay in unaddressed social conditions of inequality and marginalization.[95]

Meanwhile, as critics were busy blaming immigrants for society's woes, a different dynamic was taking place in the religious institutions of many new immigrant communities, a dynamic that not only empowered them but may also ultimately help restore faith in diversity. Recent studies have shown that religious institutions are one of the most important places where people can learn civic skills, particularly those who are otherwise disadvantaged socioeconomically. Because they sometimes provide exposure to requests for political activity, religious institutions have a potential to act as a compensatory factor for civic participation, a slight counterbalance to the overwhelming weight of socioeconomic status.[96] Americans also tend to give more of their time, money, and energy to religious institutions than to secular political or nonpolitical activities (for example, labor unions)—an important fact given that fewer workers today are union members and so many are church members.[97] As Robert Wuthnow has explained: "Active church members are likely to be exposed to religious teachings about loving their neighbor and being responsible citizens, they are more likely to have social capital in the form of ties to fellow congregants that can be used to mobilize their energies, and they are more likely to be aware of needs and opportunities in their communities as a result of attending services in their congregations."[98] In the 1960s, many younger Americans abandoned their parents' houses of worship, and more were turned off in the 1980s as churches gained a more conservative evangelical and fundamentalist bent; at the same time, new immigrant communities were thriving with religious life and vitality. R. Stephen Warner has noted: "Their religious institutions and cultures had not yet forgotten that new generations need to be nurtured, [and] it is the sociological wisdom of their religious institutions that is setting the tone for the cultural role of U.S. religion at the end of the twentieth century."[99] As immigrants from different religious traditions learn civic skills and join forces with long-time residents in their communities, they give new life to local voluntary organizations, and "the ability of religious people to create innovative partnerships with nonreligious community agencies, volunteer centers, and nonprofit corporations may be the greatest test of their role in mobilizing civic engagement."[100]

On December 20, 1986, three young African American men were driving when their car broke down near the predominantly white area of Howard Beach, Queens—about ten miles south of, but a world away from, Flushing. Wandering into a pizza parlor for a slice, the three young black men were confronted by four young white men, who shouted, "You don't belong here!" Chasing them out, pursuing, and beating them, the assailants trailed one, Michael Griffith, in their car. Griffith fled on foot onto the busy Shore Parkway, where he was crushed to death by a car. The incident shocked New York and the nation, and the director Spike Lee based some of his film *Do the Right Thing* on the violent racial outbreak.

Less than three weeks after the Howard Beach incident, newly elected Julia Harrison established the Network for Intergroup Harmony (NIH) as one of her first acts in office as the New York City Council member for District 20 in Flushing. Meeting for the first time on January 8, 1987, at the historic Macedonia African Methodist Episcopal church, a diverse group of local community leaders and residents gathered to discuss the purpose of the network, which, as stated in its new constitution and bylaws, was "to promote harmony, cooperation, and understanding among the various religious, racial, ethnic, and cultural groups in Queens."[101] Although NIH was sponsored initially as a political committee of the Coalition for a Planned Flushing, its power over the following decade would depend on its effectiveness as a voluntary organization. Two years after its founding, the network was honored by Mayor Ed Koch in December 1988 with a plaque for being "one of the few groups organized after the Howard Beach incident to bring harmony and understanding between groups that is still meeting."[102]

Memory of the Howard Beach incident remained raw through the 1990s, but the network also discovered new ways to focus its energies in the community. Annual Interfaith services that coincided with the birthday of Rev. Dr. Martin Luther King Jr. were held at different places of worship throughout Flushing and became the highlight each year, but the network also sponsored a conference each fall on different themes with workshops on communication skills for multicultural and interfaith dialogue and conflict resolution. NIH board meetings every month became a regular forum to discuss current issues of common concern—including Korean and Chinese signage, cultural differences, ethnic and racial relations, bias crimes, and gangs. The leadership started out diverse and became increasingly more so as the network methodically reached out to every religious and ethnic group in mass mailings, newspapers (including ethnic newspapers), telephone calls, and visits. Chairs of the board over the years included a Chinese American woman, three African American pastors of Macedonia AME, and a Chinese American rector of St. George's Episcopal church.[103] While it is difficult to measure success, NIH did make significant progress on serious issues of the times: easing Black-Jewish relations, bringing greater sensitivity to Korean merchants and conflicting conceptions of community, and changing the Chinese New Year parade into the Lunar New Year parade to include Taiwanese and Koreans. In 1996, the network also received a grant of over ten thousand dollars from the Citizens' Committee for New York City to found Youth for Intergroup Harmony (YIH), which began recruiting high school students for training who, in turn, then facilitated workshops for other youth.

As memory of the Howard Beach incident faded, however, the network struggled to redefine its mission in the new millennium. Most grassroots groups start out with volunteers but eventually need more structure, incorporation and nonprofit status, and a paid staff. They also need to find common issues that will bring diverse groups together and have long-term significance that require follow up: coalitions that come together only in crisis do not last long. The original approach of bringing diverse groups together to get to know one another, seek understanding, and forge relationships based on mutual respect to create a network where people already knew one another in a positive context that could prevent future conflicts had been fairly successful. But by 2000, Flushing was so accustomed to its diversity that tolerance was already quite widespread, and the network often found itself just sitting around waiting for something bad to happen. The leadership now wondered whether NIH should be "principle and issue driven" or "people driven"—that is, should it be an advocacy group or one that was more informational and educational. Societal problems remained: quality-of-life concerns such as sanitation problems, signage, parking, drugs, facilities in residential areas, economic development, and lack of business diversity. But these were structural and social issues that the city was best equipped to deal with, not NIH. In the end, the leadership decided that groups would come together on such issues as education, police, economic opportunities, affordable housing, and healthcare; it also rededicated itself to collaborating with the diverse sections of the community and identifying common concerns. With a relative lack of community crises it felt it could address, however, NIH meetings became increasingly perfunctory—yet it continued to meet and keep a vigilant eye on the street just in case until finally disbanding after 9/11, when larger interfaith coalitions would form.[104]

Outside of NIH, there have been a few other surprising alliances. As the Ganesha temple on Bowne Street was the first Hindu temple on the block (actually, the first in the country), the leadership had always made an effort to fit in as much as possible and actively take part in community affairs and interfaith opportunities—even placing an ecumenical symbol on the exterior of the temple. Meanwhile, the Bowne House Historical Society on the other end of Bowne Street had begun to include more representatives of Flushing diverse religious community to its annual July 4 celebration of John Bowne's story and reading of the Flushing Remonstrance, and in 1999, the traditional Protestant, Catholic, and Jewish mix was joined by the temple's president, who wore a colorful *sari* and discussed the history of the temple and Hinduism in general. Across town on Prince Street, a surprisingly amicable situation also developed between the Korean members of the New York Philadelphia Presbyterian Church and the African American members of the Ebenezer Baptist Missionary Church, located in the adjacent building. Unlike areas where blacks outnumber Koreans such as Flatbush, Brooklyn, or the section of Los Angeles where Korean stores were looted during the riots of 1992 after the Rodney King incident, Flushing has a higher Korean population than blacks (approximately 15 percent compared with 6 percent of population). Normally, the only interaction between these groups would be at a Korean deli or store where there have been misunderstandings about simple things like placing a customer's change in their hands or, worse, refusing to serve non-Koreans at all. But because Ebenezer had rented the building next door to the Korean church, the two unlikely partners had more occasions to meet—becoming friends over the years and often joining together for worship services.[105]

Some groups will never jump on the interfaith bandwagon, but if NIH and a rising younger crop of Flushing politicians are any sign, there may be a bright future ahead. Most community leaders now agree that something must be done about the unchecked proliferation of religious institutions taking advantage of outdated zoning laws and parking regulations. Yet, for better or worse, whether it is a blessing or a curse, the reality of religious pluralism is already well established in Flushing, and residents will have to live with it and make the best of it. Voluntary organizations like the Network for Intergroup Harmony have shown how effective they can be at uniting a fragmented community through civic engagement and dialogue.

Finally, although it is easier to measure interfaith involvement at the group or leadership level, I occasionally met individuals whose lives seem to have been transformed through their own personal spiritual journeys. Elena Cata, the Cuban American woman interviewed in Chapter 3, had this to say about life in her apartment building:

> On my floor, I have my neighbor from Korea, very good people. We are friends. On the other side, it's Chinese from China; they don't speak English, but they're very nice to me, and I'm also nice to them. Every morning, they see me, and they open the door for me, and I tell you—I think they are very family oriented, sir. Yes.
>
> Well, I tell you something. One thing I always say, one of the things I was happy to come—to want to get into this country first of all: we can live in freedom, and I can practice my religion, you know, in freedom also. But another thing that I was very good to be is that we live in the different races—how you say—different communities that—you learn from each other. You learn. You really—it's a good experience, to live with different communities, different races, I believe, because you learn—I think we learn from each other. But one of my reasons I'm happy about that is because you experience something, some other—how you say—the word don't come to me, but the different customs, you know, different ways. Yes. And you appreciate that we are all the same, no matter what race, what religion. We should respect each other, just being human beings, you know. Yes.[106]

Though Ms. Cata's perspective seems like an isolated exception, survey research through questionnaires most likely would reveal that at least a small percentage of the population felt the same way. In general, however, as I argued earlier in this chapter, efforts to interact and create community in a densely populated, religiously diverse urban neighborhood also still seem to operate against a powerful tendency not to—that is, to remain private.

First Baptist Church, a multiethnic, multicultural, multilingual church.

Multiethnic Churches and Congregations

Rev. Dr. Martin Luther King Jr. observed that "eleven o'clock Sunday morning is the most segregated hour in America." While this was no doubt also largely true in Flushing during the 1960s, many integrated, multiethnic congregations developed in the following years—and they were not just black and white. A handful of radically multiethnic congregations in Flushing offer a glimpse into a new world of twenty-first-century denominational life.[107] Gradually forming within established churches as one person or family attracted another, many mainline Protestant and Catholic congregations absorbed so many Chinese and Hispanic members that Sundays were divided up into separate services by language. As many new immigrants with little English remained in Chinese and Spanish (and other) services while taking ESL classes, those who knew more began to make the English services much more diverse. Finally, many churches also began to unite the separate services into one congregation for certain holidays and special occasions that brought everyone together. Studies have shown that predominantly white churches in changing neighborhoods are often unwilling to reach out to new residents, and, by failing to open their doors actively to ethnic minorities, they eventually become culturally isolated and irrelevant dying congregations.[108] The multiethnic churches in Flushing demonstrate how embracing diversity can lead to church vitality.

First Baptist's sign stands out: "A Multi-ethnic, Multi-cultural, Multi-lingual Church." People notice it and are drawn to the church because of its message. Founded in 1857 and later switching its affiliation to the Conservative Baptist denomination when it broke ties with the American Baptists over concerns of "liberal theology," the church has seen a lot of changes over the years.[109] With a predominantly European American congregation of three hundred to four hundred people for the first half of its life, First Baptist began to integrate in 1945 when a family originally from Barbados began to attend. During the 1950s people from different countries were attracted to the church, especially with the United Nations General Assembly nearby in Flushing Meadows Park and then the new waves of immigration after 1965. From the 1960s on, as more people from around the world were drawn to New York, the church championed a philosophy of ministry that stressed doing mission work at home. Still primarily homogeneous, the new focus caused a deep struggle, and the church split over the missions issue, but the leadership continued to embrace the view of missions at home even as many people in the congregation were moving toward retirement. By 1978, when Rev. Russ Rosser came to First Baptist Church, the congregation had dwindled to 142 people—leaving a remaining core group of European Americans, along with a growing number of West Indians, African Americans, Filipinos, Hispanics, Armenians, second-generation Chinese, and others. To Rosser, the way to move forward was obvious: the church would become intentionally multiethnic and multilingual, reflecting the community. By September 1980, First Baptist had three congregations functioning as one church with integrated assets and leadership teams: one English speaking, one Chinese speaking, and one Spanish speaking. As Rev. Gary Domiano, the present pastor, commented:

> First Baptist church: it's a unique model. There are three congregations. But they are only divided based on language. It's one church, not three. That's the unique part. There are a lot of churches in the city where the church will have another congregation and share the building. So you may have a Spanish congregation, Ukrainian congregation . . . but they're not one church—they are two churches in one building. *We* are really one church. So when I speak of the congregation, I don't simply mean the English speaking; I would be referring to the whole.[110]

Rosser retired in 1999, but, in twenty years, First Baptist became the most diverse congregation in Flushing—and it was thriving more than ever before.[111] Assistant Pastor Rev. McKenzie Pier wrote in a seminary paper about First Baptist:

> If there is one word to describe the church, it is *heterogeneous*. The church's diversity strikes you at every level—linguistically, more than twenty languages could be spoken; ethnically—more than sixty nations have been represented; and economically—we have had homeless and medical doctors in the same sanctuary. The church has been a home to immigrants, with 75% of its current congregants being foreign-born.[112]

Like many places of worship in Flushing, First Baptist is a community or neighborhood church—with nearly half of the congregation living in the immediate zip code. Yet it is also simultaneously a "niche" church, where people come together along lines of class, ethnicity, or interest. Most multiethnic churches tend to be commuter churches with congregants coming in from various outside destinations; niche churches tend to form in ethnic enclaves. That First Baptist could be both is something quite new.

Rev. Domiano, or Pastor Gary as he is more commonly known to most at the church, first came to First Baptist in 1987 as a member of the congregation upon graduating from college. He grew up in an all-white neighborhood in nearby Jackson Heights, Queens, where he remembers signs spray painted on the local candy store wall that said "Keep the Heights White" (the neighborhood is now much more diverse). He was raised in an Italian-German Catholic family but never felt the Catholic Church satisfied his spiritual needs—it was more of a tradition, he said. He felt that the problem with the Catholic Church was that the Bible was buried under church tradition and the church fathers, so that their teachings really were on par with, if not above, the Bible as the word of God. As an older teenager Domiano looked for a church that upheld biblical inerrancy and the literal interpretation of the Bible. He did not really become a Christian, he said, until he was nineteen, when his fundamentalist quest ended and he was born again in a Pentecostal church. It was the diversity of First Baptist that personally drew him to it as well. His wife is from Barbados, and there were already several interracial couples when he first visited in 1987: "I said, 'Wow,' and I knew that this was a place where we were welcome. And that's the experience of a lot of people when they come—wherever they come from, no matter who they are."[113] Domiano was a member of First Baptist from 1987 until 1990, when he became a student at Eastern Baptist Theological Seminary, a Conservative Baptist school that had just opened a New York branch. After receiving his master's in divinity in 1993, he became church intern and youth director at First Baptist. As youth pastor, he oversaw children from many different ethnic and racial groups all together, and he never heard racial slurs: "You didn't see anything. You just saw these kids kind of cross-pollinating together."[114]

In 2000, Domiano became the English pastor at a time when multiethnic churches seem destined to be the wave of the future. There are many religious options, even for Christians, in Flushing; there are even a number of other multiethnic churches, but First Baptist has been the most successful. I asked him what it was about First Baptist that attracts people the most. Why has it worked?

> I think one reason . . . let me give you some important components of the church. Number one: no group stands out as superior to another. That's important. If a group suddenly feels like they are welcome in the church but they are inferior in some way, you lose them. That's number one. So in this church, the ground is level. There is not a white congregation. The English-speaking congregation may be the largest numerically, but it is one of three. We have one leadership board, one board of deacons for the church. It's made up of men from all three congregations. We have a trustee board—men from all three congregations. We have a weekly staff meeting with all the pastors and staff that come from all different congregations. Everything we do, we do together. That's one reason it works. The keys to this church are respect and, I guess, tolerance. That makes it work—a commitment to prayer and a commitment to unity. We value the biblical teachings on "We are one in Christ." John 17: Jesus prayed "Lord, make them one even as we are one." We value the teaching on Christian unity. We preach it, we live it, we model it, and people come.[115]

There are also times when the English, Chinese, and Spanish congregations all join. There are four all-church prayer events in the year—where, on a Sunday, right after services around 12:00 or 12:15, all the congregations gather for forty-five minutes of prayer. The pastor states the themes and the areas of prayer, and people pray in their own languages. They also have joint services two to three times a year. Domiano says these are "very hard to pull off space-wise and translation-wise, so we try as best we can."[116] Children's programs are all-church events, and cantatas, Easter, and Christmas are open to the whole church. The Spanish congregation leads a sunrise Easter service, and all the congregations are invited to that service and a communal breakfast afterward. Finally, the outreach each year is an all-church event: in 2001, everyone from the church joined numerous other churches throughout Queens to sponsor a "March for Jesus" in downtown Flushing.

From his vantage point as preacher in the pulpit, I asked Domiano if there were certain passages from the Bible he had meditated on when he looked out over his diverse congregation:

> Yes. There are a couple of passages. There are three that stand out. One is Acts 13:1–3, the church in Antioch. Antioch was the northern part of Israel. And it says the church in Antioch in Acts 13 was comprised of a leadership team where men came from different continents. You had Paul, who was from Asia. You had two African leaders. You had a Jew. You had, I believe, a European. And when we look at the church in Antioch, and we look at the leadership team of that church, it was diverse. It was a diverse church. And it was in Antioch that Christians were first called "Christians"—they didn't know what else to call them. Because they weren't Jews; they were diverse. And so they were Christians—followers of Christ. Another passage is Ephesians 2, where it talks about the wall of hostility—the dividing wall between Jew and gentile has broken down. When you talk about barriers throughout the ages, one of the main barriers was always between Jews and gentiles. And, in Christ, that wall came down. So that in the church Paul says "We are one in Christ." Christ has brought these two groups near and made them new men. That's in Ephesians 2. Another passage would be from Revelation 7 (and 5) where it talks about how Christ has gathered to himself people from every tribe, culture, tongue, nation, people group—by His blood He has brought all of these people near. And, of course, John 3:16, "God so loved the world"—not God so loved Europeans, God so loved Africans, God so loved Chinese . . . God loves the world. So, those are the passages that . . . you cannot as a Christian conclude that 11:00 Sunday morning should be a segregated time. And we see it. We've seen it all through the country. It's the most segregated hour in America in a lot of places. That is absolutely contrary to Scripture. Or if they bring in another group, they bring them in as second class. They don't have a nice facility, or they don't have, let's say, leadership authority in the church. That's the stuff that kills a church. But here it's equal.[117]

The church is already fairly well known throughout the nation as a unique model, and numerous pastors and seminary professors have visited to take notes.[118] But First Baptist is also self-reflexive and keenly aware of future issues it faces, among them demographic shifts in the community and communicating more with an increasingly foreign-born population; class issues and balancing the needs of less affluent members of the congregation who live nearby with wealthier members who commute from further away; reaching out to youth and stressing that they be competitive by becoming technologically literate, multilingual, and possessing multicultural sensitivities; and continued mission work at home and abroad.[119] Domiano ended with these final thoughts:

> You know, as a church . . . historically, a church always lags behind the culture. They are always a little bit behind. It's important for a church to stay contemporary and contextual. So, I believe the church will always reflect the community it's in. That's important for this church. We will not deviate from the vision of this church to be a church of all nations, because we live in a community of all nations. Whether we always have these three congregations, whether we add a fourth congregation, a Korean congregation, or something else, that remains to be seen. But the leadership of this church is very committed to always thinking towards the future. What do we see God doing, and how can we join in? Do we buy this building right across the lot here? That's a possibility—and expand our facility. Do we cut off a segment of the church and plant another church somewhere in Flushing or somewhere in the city? Do we add a second service, a certain service that will reach a certain group of people that we are not now reaching? But the church is always looking to grow outwardly, because we believe again that the great commission is: we are not an inward-facing church; we want to be an outward-facing church and reach the community and the world that's here. So that's the direction we continue to move in.[120]

Revitalization by embracing the idea of a multiethnic congregation has also involved synagogues welcoming the many Russian Jews who emigrated from the former Soviet Union after the end of the Cold War. Although most Russian Jews flocked to Brighton Beach in Brooklyn, many sought to escape that crowded neighborhood for more room in Forest Hills, Kew Gardens, and Flushing. With such a large number of new members not seen since World War II, the increase in membership breathed new life into local synagogues such as Temple Gates of Prayer. Rabbi Albert Thaler explained that in the mid- and late 1980s he mobilized the congregation to invite Soviet Jewish immigrants. He had been active in this regard for over a decade. After the 1967 Six-Day War, Thaler was chairman of a committee that organized a mass rally at Madison Square Garden in 1970 to free Soviet Jewry—the "Jews of Silence" (Jews who were living in the Soviet Union but had to suppress their beliefs and identity).Years later, when Thaler came to Temple Gates of Prayer in 1980, he said there was an influx of Soviet Jews to Flushing at the time: "we invited them. We had evenings for them—meaning we even conferred honorary membership upon them. We gave them *mezuzot,* and I taught them with a booklet in Russian and in English how to affix it to their doors."[121] With older members of the congregation already beginning moving to Florida, such openness to a multiethnic congregation breathed new life into Temple Gates and added thirty-five new members.

Modern Flushing and Pluralism

How Pluralism "Works"

What factors help explain the lack of conflict in Flushing? Local residents like to invoke Flushing's heritage of religious freedom and tolerance, but this is not the reason—for one thing, fewer people in Flushing today know about its history than in the 1940s and 1950s, when it was something of a "community ideology," as described in Chapter 2. Even during such a time of greater community cohesion (when knowledge and celebration of local history was at an all-time high, in addition to Cold War pressure to conform and demonstrate religious faith), it is doubtful that residents of Flushing consciously pledged to live together in peace, as had the signers of the Flushing Remonstrance in 1657. Instead, we must look for other explanations. The absence of conflict among immigrants who were traditional enemies in their native countries is partially explained by the fact that historic territorial disputes overseas are not always carried over and somehow reinscribed on American soil. Furthermore, histories of animosity between various groups are often rendered irrelevant and replaced by a new, shared American history where everyone is on common ground. Part of the answer also lies in the particular urban nature of Flushing, where the same social limits that keep people apart also preserve a kind of order, as the maintenance of this demarcation of public/private space not only protects personal religious space but can contribute to a kind of religious pluralism where civil coexistence in diverse and densely populated urban communities like Flushing, Queens, prevails. Finally, law enforcement generally ensures that order is upheld. But there are also larger reasons that have to do with basic principles of American democracy.

As local colonial policies of religious freedom and tolerance like Flushing's were superseded by a nationally guaranteed right in the First Amendment in 1791, the voluntary principle inherent in disestablishment (separation of church and state) ensured that no religion would have coercive primacy; instead, churches essentially became voluntary associations free and independent of the state, assuming a different organizational form. The church historian Sidney E. Mead has called this *denominationalism*.[122] Touring the young nation in the 1830s, Alexis de Tocqueville noted (among many other observations) that the variety of Protestant denominations did not die out because they lacked political support after the separation of church and state; rather, all religious groups small and large were able to grow and thrive throughout the nineteenth century.[123] This voluntary principle still guides American religious life because it still explains how any religious congregation or institution operates in the United States. For individuals, the proliferation of religious institutions has meant that people have the freedom to choose among many different options (or no religion at all) in a kind of religious open market that thrives thanks to healthy competition—a phenomenon that some modern sociologists of religion have termed "rational choice" theory, to contrast with the earlier "secularization" theory, which argued that pluralism weakens the plausibility of religion.[124] Instead, the theory goes, pluralism helps different congregations enjoy greater vitality because their religious particularism permits them to cater to specific, localized groups (such as the large number of Korean churches in Flushing) in a kind of "*de facto* congregationalism" where people are not forced to adhere to parish-like boundaries but rather assemble together wherever they happen to live.[125]

Coexistence in even the most diverse communities in America is made possible by another corollary of religious freedom—a phenomenon described by Thomas Jefferson in his *Notes on the State of Virginia* and by James Madison in *Federalist Papers* (nos. 10 and 51), which speak of society so broken up into such a "multiplicity of sects" spread out over a large area that there is little danger of one faction acting as an oppressive majority for long.[126] In Flushing, the population is now so diverse that everyone is a minority—it is an area that city demographers call a "melting-pot neighborhood" because no one ethnic or racial group is dominant and many are represented.[127] Instead, it is nondiversity that tends to lead to conflict when a new and different group suddenly moves into a place that has been relatively homogeneous for a long time—and Flushing certainly experienced periods of nativism during intense immigration when new-comers who stood out (for example, Hindus) moved into the area for the first time. But it follows that the more diverse a place becomes, the more tolerant it becomes over time.

After a certain point, however, how diverse a community is starts to lose its salience—in other words, the issues are essentially the same whether there are twenty or two hundred places of worship next door to one another. The American religious historian Martin E. Marty offers a helpful way of understanding how pluralism "works" at the national level. He uses a sports metaphor and suggests there are four elements or con-ditions in pluralism: "'any number can play,' a considerable number does play, there are at least minimal 'rules of the game,' and the game devel-ops an observable ethos."[128] Flushing's extremely high number of places of worship in a small urban neighborhood certainly confirms the first two conditions. Marty notes that Madison liked to quote Voltaire's ob-servation (one of the two epigraphs at the beginning of this chapter): "If one religion only were allowed in England, the Government would very possibly become arbitrary; if there were but two, the people would cut one another's throats; but as there such a multitude, they all live happy and in peace." And Jefferson, recycling a passage from John Locke's "Letter Concerning Toleration," stated something similar in his *Notes on the State of Virginia*: "But it does me no injury for my neighbor to say there are twenty gods or no God." The "rules of the game" in the United States are the twenty words in Article VI of the Constitution and the sixteen words in the First Amendment, which read: "No religious test shall ever be re-quired as a Qualification to any Office or public Trust under the United States" and "Congress shall make no law respecting an establishment of religion or prohibiting the free exercise thereof." Marty goes on to say the "observable ethos" of the game are the kinds of binding customs that lead residents to say certain things are "done" or "not done" in their commu-nity. Though Marty's discussion focuses on the national and even interna-tional levels, the "pluralism game" seems applicable at the local level too.

So how does (religious) pluralism "work" at the local level? When plu-ralism is discussed with regard to religion, theologians and philosophers of religion often employ an exclusivist-inclusivist-pluralist typology to describe the basic responses to religious diversity, but these are generally abstract thoughts at the macro level and do not give us a full picture of pluralism itself in a community and of the reality of intergroup relations

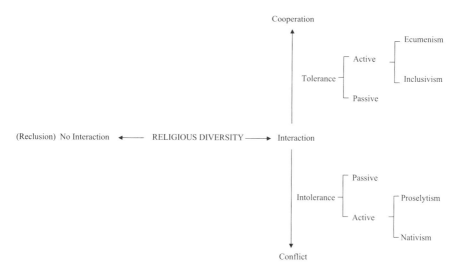

Conceptual model of religious pluralism in Flushing (diagram represents the range of different individual and group responses to religious diversity).

in a microcosm of world religions such as Flushing.[129] Such a perspective is necessary to understand the complex range of different responses to the religious diversity in Flushing, with different levels of engagement and different gradations of each level all taking place simultaneously within a small area. Taken as a whole, then, this spectrum of social behavior is what is meant by religious pluralism: *the range of responses to living in a diverse religious community, or the state of living in such a community.*

To understand better the particular social dynamics at play, the different responses to religious diversity in Flushing described in the history of groups and individuals in the preceding pages can be plotted in a diagram to show a conceptual model of religious pluralism with a comprehensive mapping out of the possibilities and limits of pluralism. Responses to religious diversity are either characterized by interaction or noninteraction, with interaction (or association across and within religious, ethnic, or racial boundaries) leading to some form of cooperation or conflict.

Noninteraction: Reclusion

Individuals or groups who fall under noninteraction tend toward *reclusion* (if not *exclusion*) and are essentially neutral with regard to cooperation and conflict—they don't choose to "play" in the pluralism game.[130] This could describe, for instance, those in the Korean immigrant community in Flushing who prefer to live, shop, work, and worship only with other Koreans and who do not yet generally engage with the larger community in local civic and political affairs. It could also describe many other immigrant communities in the early stages of their history (for example, during the first and second generation), where the familiarity of the ethnic enclave is of primary importance. Finally, it could also describe any person or group that seeks to avoid others for religious/theological reasons.

Interaction: Cooperation, Conflict, and Passive/Active Forms of Tolerance and Intolerance

Groups and individuals who are characterized by interaction present a much more complex range of behavior, with varying degrees of cooperation or conflict. *Cooperative interaction* stems from tolerance, but tolerance itself can be active or passive.[131] Passive tolerance does not lead to any further interaction (this could describe a great number of residents in Flushing who have a "live and let live" mentality stemming from the social limits of pluralism in urban areas discussed earlier in the chapter), whereas active tolerance is more constructive and can lead to a kind of *inclusivism* in which one might seek to understand another religious perspective (for example, a Hindu welcoming a Christian who is interested in attending a Hindu ceremony or festival just to learn more about it, a Jewish parent inviting their son's Sikh friend to his *bar mitzvah*, or a Christian welcoming a Buddhist or Muslim to a Christmas candlelight service) or *ecumenism* (not simply designating the unification of Protestant denominations or all Christians but a broader interfaith dialogue—for example, the Network for Intergroup Harmony in Flushing).[132] *Conflictive interaction* stems from intolerance, which can also be passive or active. Passive intolerance might be simple prejudice that is perhaps voiced in private but not acted on, whereas active intolerance is more destructive and can lead to *proselytism* (the most overt form of exclusivism) or *nativism* (hostility and violence).[133]

In each of these types there are also, of course, exceptions—individuals who stray from their group's overall mentality and may be closer to another type of response. In fact, we see that it is very difficult to speak in general terms about groups even in a "micro" study such as Flushing; it is even more problematic to do so on a "macro" scale, as it is harder to account for individual or small-group variation. Most populations are also fluid and experience movement, shifting, and cultural exchange as a matter of daily life—individuals are not static; they are dynamic agents in a complex and constantly changing world of local, national, and transnational dimensions that is affected by particular historical contexts.

Finally, intermarriage can add further complexity.[134] As politicians and demographers in an increasingly pluralistic American society strive to develop a grammar that accurately reflects multiracial ancestry on U.S. Census forms, so will theologians and other scholars of religion. Whereas earlier instances of exogamy may have once consisted primarily of unions between people descended from various European nationalities, African Americans, and native Americans, immigration since 1965 has brought about many new combinations: interethnic, interracial, and interfaith marriages that join not only various Christian denominations with another, with one of several branches of Judaism, or with any number of native traditions, but now also with every conceivable world religion. Again, there is a range of responses to this new religious diversity and theological mixing, with many cleaving to orthodoxy and notions of ethnic, racial, and religious purity. Yet, as the news commentator Richard Rodriguez has noted: "The other possibility is we are entering an age of astonishing ecumenism—religious traditions flowing into one another, deepening and enlivening one another, within the soul of a single child."[135] Indeed, the future of religions may depend on how well each can tolerate religious hybridity in a new, more cosmopolitan world of religious pluralism.

5
Flushing Since September 11, 2001

> The city, for the first time in its long history,
> is destructible. A single flight of planes no
> bigger than a wedge of geese can quickly end
> this island fantasy, burn the towers, crumble
> the bridges, turn the underground passages
> into lethal chambers, cremate the millions.
> The intimation of mortality is part of New
> York now: in the sound of jets overhead, in
> the black headlines of the latest edition.
>
> All dwellers in cities must live with the
> stubborn fact of annihilation; in New York
> the fact is somewhat more concentrated
> because of the concentration of the city itself,
> and because, of all targets, New York has a
> certain clear priority. In the mind of whatever
> perverted dreamer might loose the lightning,
> New York must hold a steady, irresistible charm.
>
> —*E. B. White, "Here Is New York," 1949*

I was having a cup of coffee when my mother called a few minutes after the first plane hit the World Trade Center. As I joined the whole world to watch the unfolding terror of September 11, 2001, on the news, I was eerily reminded of the forgotten footage from 1940 of U.S. Army planes demonstrating a new precautionary World War II defense maneuver of covering lower Manhattan's skyscrapers in a smokescreen (see Chapter 2), and later of E. B. White's extremely prescient observation. As soon as it became clear that Osama bin Laden and Al Qaeda were responsible (and that President Bush would not distinguish between "terrorists and those that harbor them"—that is, the Taliban in Afghanistan), I immediately thought of the Afghan community in Flushing—the largest in New York City. I had interviewed and taped an oral history of Assistant Imam Ah-mad Wais Afzali at Masjid-I-Abubakr just five days before 9/11 on one of my final research trips back to Flushing (after living in Flushing for two years to do fieldwork and research, I had moved to Providence, Rhode Island, in the summer of 2001 for a postdoctoral fellowship at Brown University). I tried to call the mosque all day, but the phone just rang and rang. When I finally reached Imam Afzali late on Friday, he sounded shaken but said everything was fine. They had just had a special prayer service that afternoon for *Jumu'ah*, and he shared some verses from the Qur'an that he had discussed in his *khutba* (sermon):

> In the name of Allah, most benevolent, ever-merciful.
>
> Say: "We believe in God and what has been sent down to us, and what had been revealed to Abraham and Ishmael and Isaac and Jacob and their progeny, and that which was given to Moses and Christ, and to all other prophets by the Lord. We make no distinction among them, and we submit to Him." 2:136
>
> Piety does not lie in turning your face to East or West: Piety lies in believing in God, the Last Day and the angels, the Scriptures and the prophets, and disbursing your wealth out of love for God among your kin and the orphans, the wayfarers and mendicants, freeing the slaves, observing your devotional obligations, and in paying the *zakat* [giving of alms] and fulfilling a pledge you have given, and being patient in hardship, adversity, and times of peril. These are the men who affirm the truth, and they are those who follow the straight path. 2:177
>
> Do not argue with the people of the Book unless in a fair way, apart from those who act wrongly, and say to them: "We believe what has been sent down to you. Our God and your God is one, and to Him we submit." 29:46
>
> Among other signs of His is the creation of the heavens and the earth, and the variety of your tongues and complexions. Surely there are signs in this for those who understand. 30:22
>
> God does not forbid you from being kind and acting justly towards those who did not fight over faith with you, nor expelled you from your homes. God indeed loves those who are just. 60:8

I had heard the phrase "people of the book" (*al-Kitab* in Arabic) before and knew it referred to the shared history of Jews, Christians, and Mus-lims. I had spoken with Afzali about it when we met, and he stressed it now for obvious reasons.

I drove down to New York from Providence that weekend, and many weekends afterward. I knew I needed to talk to people and see how the community reacted right after the attacks. As I got closer to New York, I passed more and more flags and posters hanging from overpasses along the highway; crossing the Whitestone Bridge, I could still see the smoke rising from the Financial District in lower Manhattan. It was Sunday, September 16. First I drove by the Afghan mosques, and I was relieved to see officers from the New York Police Department stationed outside in patrol vehicles (they stayed on rotating duty 24/7 for several weeks). One Afghan restaurant had been vandalized, but the officers reported no trouble at the mosques. Sikhs, on the other hand, were being attacked in Queens and all over the country because their turbans and beards led many ignorant and vengeful persons to mistake them for Taliban.[1] Like the rest of New York City and much of the country, there were flags and memorials all over Flushing. Chinese street vendors on Main Street were already selling patriotic T-shirts, bumper stickers, and pictures of the World Trade Center, and I wondered how they were able to think of this particular enterprise so quickly. A young Pakistani man, a Muslim, was passing out flyers for an interfaith prayer service the following week, and *every* single place of worship I passed had organized special prayer services.

Typically, I would visit many places of worship every Sunday (and throughout the week) for my research, attending as many services as possible. I had many choices that day, but I felt especially drawn to the old Friends Meeting House (Flushing's first place of worship built in 1694) because the quiet assembly and historic pacifism of Quakers seemed like the best company in light of the recent tragedy and growing talk of war. I was not the only outside visitor that day either: the rabbi and several other Jews from Flushing Free Synagogue had come. The diverse congregation was unusually large, with approximately forty people (nowhere near the size it was in the eighteenth century), and I learned that this had been common during similar times of crisis in the past. Normally, the reverent silence of a Quaker meeting is interrupted only when people are spontaneously moved by the divine Light within them to speak and offer a prayer or message that has come out of the silence, but that morning a widowed mother of two children wept uncontrollably as her son tried to comfort her. Those who did rise to speak cited scriptural references and wrestled with the Islamic concept of *jihad* (holy war), but most returned to themes of faith, hope, and love.

Ten days after September 11, nearly one hundred Afghan Muslims marched from Masjid Hazrat-I-Abubakr through downtown Flushing

Friends Meeting House, September 16, 2001.

chanting "Death to bin Laden," hoisting signs that said "Islam is a religion of peace," and proclaiming their support for the United States.[2] One
woman wearing a *hijab* (veil) carried her child and screamed, "Why don't
you believe us? We are not terrorists!" There were no confrontations, but
the local police precinct arranged for city buses to transport the group
back to the mosque after the march out of fear for their safety. A month
later, members of the Network for Intergroup Harmony and the Flushing
Jewish Community Council met at the mosque to announce the forma-
tion of the Coalition of Religious Leaders of Greater Flushing, whose mission was to establish within Flushing "an interfaith discourse on all levels."[3]

The Changing of the Guard: Immigration, Religion, and Local Politics

By the mid-1990s, the political tide was turning in Flushing as the established and still-growing Asian American community began to mobilize
into voting blocs that would soon take on the older status quo. Sol Nache-
min, an eighty-two-year-old son of Russian immigrants who had lived in
Flushing since 1954, said his kind was dying out, and, as inevitably as earlier
immigrants had theirs, the Asians' turn was coming: "I got to tell you, I

have a sneaking admiration for them. They're hard-working. They're good business people. At the library, I see all these Oriental kids sitting around the table doing their homework. It reminds me of the Jewish kids of my generation. I have no doubt. They'll start feeling their oats politically. And one of these days, you'll see a Korean or Chinese Councilman."[4]

In *Native Speaker,* Chang-Rae Lee's novel about Korean American New York, the main character is a young aide to the fictitious City Councilman John Kwang, a Flushing native (and elder at the Korean Presbyterian Church of Queens) who wins election after a second attempt and becomes so widely popular in his district, the city, and to the media that he considers running for mayor.[5] Writing in 1995, Lee's book came out when Asian Americans were first breaking into city politics, and it foreshadowed what would eventually transpire in the new millennium. In reality, Asian American civic groups were not yet fully organized to teach enough people about the electoral process and voter registration, and Julia Harrison actually remained in office until December 31, 2001, but the writing had been on the wall for several years. Although the future had not yet happened, Lee had imagined what it might look like.

It turned out that he was not far from the truth: in 2001, the Taiwanese American John Liu was elected to City Council District 20 on his second attempt.[6] The son of a banker and a garment worker, Liu has already been dubbed "the new voice of the city's Asian-Americans" by the media and city officials alike.[7] So many political heavyweights (including Senator Charles Schumer and Senator Hillary Rodham Clinton) showed up for his inauguration at the Flushing library that Representative Gary Ackerman remarked: "This doesn't look like an installation. This looks like a coronation of a new emperor!"[8] In the weeks that followed his swearing-in, Liu could also boast of his friendly relationship with the new mayor, Michael Bloomberg. For the first time since its last heyday from 1939 to 1965 (when the World's Fairs, Bowne House, and UN General Assembly focused attention on the area), the spotlight had returned to Flushing.

With so much political power and potential, Flushing seems poised for rebirth. If the popular maxim is true that "every neighborhood in New York City changes every thirty years," local politicians have a real opportunity to help shape Flushing's future. One of the most important legacies they could leave would be to solve the problems created by Flushing's religious pluralism. Paul Graziano, who grew up in Flushing and went on to do graduate work in city planning before becoming the youngest candidate to run for City Council in 2001 (and also one of the few Green

Party candidates in the city), has been an active defender of the neighborhood's historic houses and vocal critic of zoning issues, but he also has suggested that greater unity in the community is not unimaginable:

> This is a brave new world here, man. We are in a community unlike any other place in the world—*right now* we are in the future, you know, we *are* the future of America here. You know it, and I know it. This is going to happen in many other places—it's already happening in other places, just not to this extreme. And I think people should be *watching*: they should look at what's wrong, and they should look at what's right. Let's celebrate the good things, but let's try to fix the things that are bad. I'm tired of people holding hands and saying, "And the diversity. . . ." For most newspaper reporters, it's, "Look at these fascinating natives! Look how they groom each other!" I mean, the *New York Times* writes as if we were in American Samoa! And it bothers me. Well, you know what? This is my *town, this is where I grew up*. It is different than it was thirty years ago, but it's not . . . the dynamics of people wanting a good life and people wanting to raise a family, and people wanting good schools, these are universal things and these are the things that can bind people together—they're very *easy* things to bind people together.[9]

Graziano raises an interesting point that casual visitors to Flushing and the media often miss: while Flushing may offer a glimpse of the future, it is important not to be merely dazzled by its diversity; *it is what the community does with this diversity, and what diversity does to the community*, that is most important. John Liu (who won the 2001 City Council race) shared Graziano's concerns about zoning and said: "The church is a good thing. But too much of a good thing makes it less desirable."[10] As I discuss in more detail in Chapter 4, Liu took a firm stand against the unchecked proliferation of places of worship during his time in office, and he argued that the community at large should have a say in where and how "community facilities" are established.[11] Other residents and Queens politicians such as New York State Senator Tony Avella also have worked hard to address zoning and land-use reform (culminating in the 2004 Community Facilities Text Reform Bill), but it will be interesting to see what Liu's successor, Peter A. Koo, and others will do to monitor change and try to maintain a better balance and quality of life (after serving as city councilman for eight years, Liu ran successfully for city comptroller in 2009 and ran for mayor in 2013).

The question for the twenty-first century is: Will Flushing and other diverse communities in America like it come together in new and lasting ways to build bridges of dialogue, or will they further fragment into a Tower of Babel? Much of this book has focused on the theologian John Courtney Murray's provocative question: "How much pluralism, and what kinds of pluralism, can a pluralist society stand?" But I would like to stress the second part of Murray's question here now: "And, conversely, how much unity, and what kinds of unity, does a pluralist society need in order to be a society at all?" Interfaith groups point the way toward more meaningful possibilities of civil society and community, but the problem is that many of these efforts often do not last beyond the crisis or incident that led to their creation. There are model interfaith organizations elsewhere, and if Flushing's religious, ethnic, and civic leaders are able to organize and maintain an effective network of dialogue at the local level to solve common problems in the community, Flushing really could be a new "city on a hill." A handful of multiethnic church congregations in Flushing also offer hope that longtime residents and new immigrants can come together, and such congregations demonstrate how embracing diversity can lead to new life for older places of worship. Students in the local schools who are growing up with diversity may yield a new generation whose members are more comfortable with one another. On the other hand, the limits of pluralism in a densely populated and diverse urban neighborhood may prohibit *the many* from ever really wanting to interact as *one*. Is Flushing so diverse now that it is impossible to have a shared sense of community and history, or are there still some common topics of mutual concern that can bring people together? I did not see a lot of evidence before 2001 (when I ended my study) that there was much meaningful, organized interaction going on aside from Community Board meetings, which are perhaps the only regularly scheduled times when community-wide representation and attendance can be expected. But there are signs that this lack of overall interaction among the different groups in the community that I perceived may be changing.

While the sociologist Robert J. Sampson has shown that recent immigration has helped revitalize urban neighborhoods, the political scientist Robert D. Putnam has argued that ethnically diverse communities suffer from more general distrust, greater isolation, and poorer civic participation than homogenous ones.[12] Newspaper reporters and some alarmists seized on Putnam's initial observation to conclude that diversity hurts civic activism and community.[13] This was the kind of impression one might have had of intergroup relations in Flushing during the 1980s and 1990s, when the neighborhood population was changing rapidly and Flushing became more fragmented. Putnam says this is only in the short to medium term, however, and eventually, over time, recent immigrant groups do form new, more encompassing identities—that is, it really only applies to recent or first-generation immigrants. This makes sense, as the sociologist Stephen Steinberg has noted, because recent immigrants need this space of being separate to decompress, build their own networks, stores, religious centers, and institutions, and get organized—the first steps of assimilation.[14] This is what you see on a large scale in Flushing among Korean American immigrants, for instance, who have a disproportionate amount of churches. But the second part of Putnam's analysis is worth noting, as it applies to the second, third, and later generations of recent immigrant groups: as they continue the process of assimilation, they will form more encompassing identities—that is, many will in fact get more involved locally as time goes on. Putnam's study is significant because it speaks to the recent lack of community in diverse places like Flushing while also showing that this is only a temporary state—that what you eventually see is more participation and civic engagement after several generations. A similar conclusion was reached in 1964 by the sociologist Milton M. Gordon, who also saw minimal interaction among persons of different ethnic background up through the 1950s, but he predicted that would change:

> The achievement in full or civil rights for all groups—creates situations on the job, in the neighborhood, in the school, and in the civic arena, which place persons of different ethnic background into secondary, frequently equal-status, contacts with each other. These secondary contacts will not necessarily lead to primary group relationships, such as clique friendships, common membership in small organizations, dating, and intermarriage, and in the immediate or intermediate future will probably not seriously disturb the basic outlines of ethnic communality which have been shown to exist in America. However, over a sufficiently extended period of time, these new secondary group relationships between people of diverse ethnic backgrounds will presumably lead to an increase in warm, personal friendships across ethnic lines, a broadening of cultural perspective, an appreciation of diverse values, and in some degree a rise in the rate of interethnic marriage.[15]

Gordon was no doubt inspired by the optimism and achievements of the civil rights movement by the time his book was published, yet his predictions and Putnam's work seem to reflect what in fact has been developing in Flushing during the first decade of the twenty-first century: representatives from many of the different groups in the neighborhood have come together regularly at Community Board meetings and neighborhood civic association meetings for years, in addition to the efforts of local interfaith leaders before and after 9/11. And there have been still other efforts to bring the community together in the new millennium. In 2007 the first Flushing Forum was held entitled "Building Bridges: Flushing Community"—a very well organized workshop for a wide range of community leaders in downtown Flushing sponsored by former Councilman Liu, the Queens General Assembly of Borough President Helen Marshall, and the Korean American Community Foundation. Representation of Flushing's different religious communities was very high as judged by attendance, and it was the most promising development I saw in over twenty years of studying Flushing. I hope the efforts of individuals and groups interested in building community will continue, yet such interaction seems to run up against a more common tendency among city people to remain private or in their own "tribes." Many religious leaders I interviewed also simply said they often just do not have much time for these kinds of activities—especially new immigrants who are so busy just trying to survive and serve their own communities.

During all the flux in Flushing from 1965 to 2010, the "old guard" of longtime residents still held onto local traditions and sought to renew them in the face of so much change. With pluralism pushing people to their limits, it was perhaps only natural for some to seek refuge in memory and memorials. Numerous events and exhibits paraded the past, but often only to a limited audience. Pre-1965 Flushing may have had a stronger sense of community and Flushing's heritage, but it has taken time to translate this effectively for new immigrant neighbors: Asian immigrants outnumbered whites by 2000, but many knew little about local history. Efforts to revive Flushing's heritage began in the 1980s when local history–minded folk persuaded City Planning officials to affix several little red "Flushing Freedom Trail" markers to street signs at various historic sites throughout Flushing. The Queens Historical Society elaborated upon this in 1999 by printing and distributing a map called "The Flushing Freedom Mile Historic Tour" and also published a book on the history of the Underground Railroad in Flushing and Long Island.[16] A newly revamped Flushing Town Hall also opened with great fanfare, featuring regular music and cultural programs, exhibits, and a map of the Queens Jazz Trail.[17] And while the two time capsules from the 1939–1940 and

1964–1965 World's Fairs remain buried in Flushing Meadows–Corona Park for five thousand years, Town Hall decided to unveil its own time capsule, which had been deposited in a cornerstone of the building in 1862 and had not surfaced since a 1962 centennial.[18] In 1999, the Flushing Remonstrance returned to Flushing from the New York State Archives in Albany for an exhibit at the popular new multilingual Flushing library (the busiest branch in the nation's busiest library system, thanks to the large immigrant population that obviously believes in education for success), where it was seen by a fairly wide swath of residents.[19] Some local history buffs actually wanted to fight to keep the Flushing Remonstrance in Flushing, where they argued it would resonate more than in the State Archives in Albany, but the archives refused (rightly, I think) for fear of the document's care and preservation.[20] Despite this struggle, the occasional loan of the Flushing Remonstrance for anniversaries and exhibits helps it live on and may also help create some larger sense of community in Flushing. The Flushing Remonstrance returned to Queens again in 2007 for its 350th anniversary, and the State Archives organized a year's worth of festivities around the city and state to mark the occasion.[21] Not since the 300th anniversaries of Flushing in 1945 and the Flushing Remonstrance in 1957 had this level of attention been focused on Flushing's history. Bowne House also has been a fairly active part of the community since it opened as a museum in 1945, featuring tours, student volunteer programs, an annual July 4 celebration where the Flushing Remonstrance is read and local religious leaders, politicians, or scholars give speeches. In my two years of living across the street from it, I would see children of immigrants who grew up in Flushing walk by Bowne House every day; many adults occasionally paused outside to read the sign, and some would enter the yard to inquire about a tour.[22] All of these kinds of local history events need to be inclusive to continue, and they could expand by placing even more emphasis on disseminating news of events in multiple languages and sending invitations to various neighborhood religious, ethnic, and civic institutions.

Several leaders at the newer places of worship also have become aware of Flushing's heritage of religious freedom and tolerance since moving in and sometimes appropriate or invoke it in their own history, but this is still quite rare. To keep the memory of Flushing's important history alive, community leaders will need to keep it relevant to the changing times—addressing language barriers, creating more opportunities for inclusion, and stressing more local history in the public schools. In a microcosm of world religions, the time would seem to be ripe for a revival of

A small sign on the traffic light post at the intersection of Bowne Street at Northern Boulevard directs visitors along the "Flushing Freedom Trail."

Flushing's heritage of religious freedom and tolerance to leave a lasting legacy.

In fact, most recently, it is the second generation from the Chinese immigrant community in particular that is beginning to assume new ownership of Flushing's history and help propel it to new heights—just as Putnam predicted. In 2014, U.S. Representative Grace Meng (D–Queens), who was born and raised in Queens, sponsored a bill in Congress called the Flushing Remonstrance Study Act, which was signed into law by President Obama in December 2014 and may lead to Bowne House and Friends Meeting House becoming a National Historic Park or a National Historic Site because of their association with the Flushing Remonstrance and its national significance.[23] In 2008 Meng was elected to New York's 22nd Assembly district and in 2013 was elected to the U.S. House of Representatives—becoming the first Asian American to represent part of New York in Congress. Politics, it seems, runs in the family, as Meng's father, Jimmy Meng (who was born in the Shandong province in China and emigrated to the United States from Taiwan in 1975), also was elected to New York's 22nd assembly district in 2004 and was the first Asian American to be elected to the legislature in New York State history.[24]

In addition to local history, there are still several other major areas that immigration policy analysts recommend that leaders of large diverse urban communities pay attention to and work on to ensure their stability. As Brian Ray at the Migration Policy Institute put it:

> History demonstrates that diversity is not a sufficient condition to bring about the sustained inclusion of the different groups that populate a city. The collapse into inter-ethnic conflict of once relatively harmonious multicultural cities like pre–World War I Vienna, pre–World War II Warsaw, and in more recent decades Beirut, Sarajevo, and Srebrenica, highlights the fragility of cultural diversity. Learning to live with cultural diversity, managing cultural exchanges among people, organizations, and institutions, and dealing directly with inequities and discrimination are challenges that cities must face if they are to be socially inclusive and culturally diverse. For most cities, efforts to decrease social polarization and manage diversity rely on the "bedrock" social policies of public education, health care, and income support that are usually the responsibility of national and state, provincial or regional governments. But social inclusion also depends on the quality of the countless interactions that occur among the kaleidoscope of individuals, social groups, and institutions that exist in a city. In this respect, city governments also have a responsibility to develop local policies that manage diversity and integrate newcomers and long-established residents into dynamic social, economic, and political environments.[25]

Ray mentions the following areas of concern for

> inclusive urban environments: street design, pricing and availability of public transportation, location and accessibility of employment, management of schools, management of police services, economic development that benefits a range of social groups, enforcement of employment codes, commercial regulations, and by-laws, garbage removal, licensing street vendors and public market spaces, pricing and servicing industrial land.[26]

He also recognizes that immigrants have a range of needs: "from housing to education to language instruction to efficient public transportation for accessing jobs spread over vast metropolitan areas." Many of these areas have been addressed by local politicians and a variety of immigrant organizations, but there is room for improvement. On the other hand, in urban neighborhoods like Flushing where rapid demographic change has led to new immigrant restaurants and businesses largely replacing once-cherished institutions like familiar diners, pubs, delis, and department stores, longtime residents report feeling like strangers in the community where they have always lived. While many old-timers have come to enjoy the incredible array of ethnic cuisine and appreciate the economic vitality that new immigrant entrepreneurs have brought back to Flushing since the 1980s, others grumble about the changes, signage that they cannot read, and not feeling welcome anymore. Local political and civic leaders would find that efforts to preserve and encourage a greater range of businesses in the downtown area would likely be met with great enthusiasm. Likewise, new and sustained attention needs to be paid to the zoning laws that helped create a favorable environment for pluralism by allowing for the virtually unchecked proliferation of religious institutions as "community facilities."

One way that diverse urban communities like Flushing can and do strive toward greater inclusion and vitality is by working more closely with the Department of City Planning and the local Community Board. In his book *Cosmopolis II,* the urban planning theorist Leonie Sandercock has discussed several case studies of city governments and planners who have been able

> to "manage" difference with respect to integrating immigrants— efforts to think through the implications of multiculturalism not only symbolically, but street by street, neighbourhood by neighbourhood, neither ignoring the fears aroused by the presence of strangers, nor the fears experienced by the strangers themselves as they struggle to accommodate to a new environment and develop new attachments to a strange place.[27]

Cities that are successful at this is what Sandercock calls a "cosmopolis: cities in which there is an acceptance of, connection with, a respect and space for 'the stranger,' the possibility of working together on matters of common destiny and forging new hybrid cultures and urban projects and ways of living."[28] One example in the United States that she gives is the story of the Oak Park neighborhood in the western suburbs of Chicago, where residents in an area in the path of outward-moving black expansion embraced the goal of residential racial openness rather than white flight in the 1960s. The Oak Park Housing Center (OPHC) was instrumental in attracting new residents who wanted to live in a diverse community: Sandercock says the OPHC "worked in a very detail and people-oriented way, anticipating and managing fears as best it could, apartment complex by apartment complex, and block by block. This included escorting potential renters to apartment blocks, introducing them to residents, and speaking honestly about community responses to racial minorities."[29] Other research has focused on the similar neighborhood history of West Mt. Airy in Philadelphia, which also has been noted as a model of stable racial integration.[30] Flushing did not follow the same trajectory as Oak Park or Mt. Airy and, as I relate in Chapter 3, many whites did leave downtown Flushing in the last quarter of the twentieth century—population density maps drawn from Census 2000 data by race/ethnicity show that downtown Flushing is now primarily Asian, intermingled with Hispanic enclaves and isolated areas of blacks, whereas whites have largely moved to the periphery. Instead, Flushing became what the director of the population division in the New York City Department of City Planning Joseph J. Salvo calls a "'melting-pot tract,' in which no single group dominates" and where there are similar percentages of Hispanic, white, Asian, and black populations in the community.[31] Salvo believes what's happening in Queens is "probably the greatest social experiment in history," and Flushing shows how this has played out in terms of the religious pluralism brought about by new immigration.

While several local interfaith and multicultural organizations and groups have come and gone in Flushing, from the Network for Intergroup Harmony in the late 1980s to the Coalition of Religious Leaders of Greater Flushing after 9/11, Flushing (like most other urban communities in the United States) has not had a permanent agency devoted specifically to issues of diversity in the community. Such entities are rare, but the cities of Fremont, California, and Leicester in the United Kingdom show how some communities have made an organized effort to devote personnel, office space, and time to interfaith and multicultural affairs. Leicester was the first planning authority in the United Kingdom, and also in Europe, to produce in 1977 a policy on places of worship, and it benefits from an office of the Council of Faiths and a Society for Inter-Cultural Understanding; Fremont has its own Human Relations Commission and is part of the Tri-City Interfaith Council—enabling it to institute more structured and lasting organizations to bring city religious leaders together more regularly.[32] Other national organizations, such as Eboo Patel's Interfaith Youth Core (based in Chicago), offer a model and training programs for communities to develop, and the Pluralism Project at Harvard

University has begun to chart America's emerging interfaith infrastructure. Diverse neighborhoods and interested leaders everywhere should take note to see what they can learn and apply to their own communities.[33]

As Paul Graziano noted above, if wanting a good life, raising a family, and having good schools are among the common concerns of longtime residents and new immigrants alike, focusing on education would seem to be one of the most crucial ways to bind a diverse place like Flushing together. Most immigrant parents will communicate that a major reason for immigration has to do with the welfare of their children. Likewise, native-born families stay in or choose an area to raise their children often because of its schools.

Recent work in developmental psychology has stressed the importance of middle childhood (ages six to fourteen) as a crucial stage: this is when children have their first encounters with different institutions and contexts outside their family and begin to navigate their own ways through societal structures.[34] Furthermore, immigrant children also face added experiences of exclusion, devaluation, invisibility, discrimination, and racism for the first time, which in turn influence their interactions with and reactions to "mainstream" society.[35] Indeed, middle childhood is such a formative period that it not only affects how successful children will be in school (and whether they attend college) but also may directly affect the future social dynamics of intergroup relations in any area.

When children are taught to hate other racial, ethnic, and religious groups, they often do so as adults; conversely, the opposite is also true. Recent intellectuals have pushed "cosmopolitan education," but teaching children to be young citizens of the world with no national identity may prove to be a confusing and vague enterprise. Perhaps the best we can hope for are new educational initiatives that stress multicultural and interfaith literacy and voluntary organizations like Flushing's (now defunct) Youth for Intergroup Harmony. Such efforts could begin in basic social studies courses in elementary school, be revisited in junior high, and move into more advanced material by high school (not to mention college). Among scholars of religion, there is already a growing movement to introduce religion into the classrooms in a way that is constitutionally permissible and educationally sound.[36]

The future of Flushing, and America, rests largely on the well-being of its youth and children of today. On one hand, there is a greater need for knowledge of local history and customs so immigrant children can feel like they are a part of the community and the still-unfolding narrative and special heritage of Flushing and the nation, but the opportunity in a diverse society to teach a new multicultural and interfaith literacy to all may be even more urgent.[37] Children growing up today have seen or been exposed to so many recent world conflicts stemming from religious and ethnic difference, and they are bound to have questions. Parents need to have good answers and not propagate prejudice, but schools can also help with new initiatives that go beyond mere tolerance and instead point toward a pluralistic civil society built on mutual understanding and respect.

I have noticed that when an effort is made to teach children of recent immigrants about the area, many are fascinated and begin to see themselves and their own culture and religion as part of a larger narrative (one they may have felt excluded from before). In 2006, a new public high school called the East-West School was established in Flushing that requires students to study one East Asian language for at least four years—illustrating the school's belief that the next generation must have a more global awareness. At the same time, the East-West School also embraces the local: in 2009, forty students in the school's Student Leadership Initiative participated in a program called "Touring World Religions in Flushing," in which they visited and studied the Muslim Center of New York, the Sikh Center of New York, Buddha's Light International Association of New York, Macedonia AME Church, and the Free Synagogue of Flushing.

Religious Pluralism in New York City and America

> On the holy mount stands the city he founded; the Lord loves the gates of Zion more than all the dwelling places of Jacob. Glorious things are spoken of you, O city of God.
>
> Psalm 87: 1–3

> And the city has no need of sun or moon to shine upon it, for the glory of God is its light . . .
>
> By its light shall the nations walk; and the kings of the earth shall bring their glory into it, and its gates shall never be shut by day—and there shall be no night there; they shall bring into it the glory and honor of the nations.
>
> Revelation 21:23–26

The "City of God" in the Psalms is Jerusalem; in the Book of Revelation it is the Heavenly City. St. Augustine wrote after the fall of Rome and distinguished between the two separate spheres, the Earthly City

and the Heavenly City. And to the novelist E. L. Doctorow, the City of
God was New York City. Indeed, reading the passage from Revelation
by itself does sound like New York—the diversity, "the city that never
sleeps," Times Square with its bright lights always on . . . But Doctorow's
novel, even though set in the late twentieth century, does not resemble
New York City in all of its complexity. Doctorow's New York is still a
Judeo-Christian city, with no mention of the modern religious pluralism
that characterizes it today. Perhaps this is because Doctorow's novel takes
place largely on the Upper West Side of Manhattan. The story might have
been different had the author branched out to other boroughs and included areas like Flushing (or even if he had looked around a bit more in
Manhattan itself to notice its own mosques, Buddhist and Hindu temples,
and other religious institutions). It is for this reason that I chose "City of
Gods" for my title—to draw attention to the plural form of the word:
the many different religions and conceptions of God (and gods) in New
York and, especially, in that small part of it in Flushing, Queens. In this
sense, the City of Gods in New York or microcosm of world religions in
Flushing reflects what Stephen Prothero has referred to as "a nation of
religions" in which "U.S. religions are many, not one; that American religious experience comes in all shapes and sizes; and that the meanings of
each are polysemous and contested."[38]

But to what extent does a neighborhood in New York City mirror the
rest of the United States? The microcosm of world religions in Flushing
may be a unique, extreme case, but its story runs parallel to the larger
American story and reflects something that, to some extent, is happening, or will happen, almost everywhere. Many Americans in the countless predominantly Christian communities across the country have not
had reason to think much about religious pluralism before, although this
is changing almost everywhere. There are suburbs and towns and vast
stretches of land that have been comparatively devoid of religious diversity or where whatever new immigrant religious group that may exist is
often largely unknown to most locals—perhaps sited modestly in a storefront, converted house, or building. To be sure, New York City is different
from most places in America, and Flushing even more so—some would
say New York City is more of an island off the coast of America than it
is America writ large. As I discussed in Chapter 4, urban areas are funda-
mentally different from suburban and rural areas in terms of population
density, size, and heterogeneity, and this can give rise to different forms
of religious life and behavior. But there is a saying that whatever happens
in New York happens ten years later everywhere else. Indeed, much of

America is already more diverse than it was before 1965, from other cities like Chicago to suburbs and small rural towns coast to coast.[39] As other areas across the country begin to notice their own growing immigrant communities, they may find Flushing more relevant—and an especially good model to contrast with places outside the United States torn by religious and ethnic conflict. That is, the "good news"—the great possibility of pluralism—is that Flushing, and ultimately any community in America or in any country committed to principles of religious freedom, immigration, and democracy, can absorb a tremendous amount of diversity and, as Voltaire said, they will all live happy and in peace. The history of Flushing also shifts attention from the standard New England Puritan narrative of British colonial America to the brief but arguably more important Dutch period of New Netherland (as well as the history of the Middle Atlantic region in general)—in part thanks to new work based on the transcription of early documents from the period.[40]

Shortly after 9/11, the columnist Joyce Purnick suggested in the *New York Times* that New York's characteristic diversity is what makes conservative evangelical Christians and Americans from more suburban or rural parts of the country nervous and what also "infuriates the terrorists." She went on to say:

> It's a big part of what normally makes the country so dislike the city that it now purports to admire (surely not for long). New Yorkers do not all love each other. The city has endured riots and racial tensions over the years; since the bombings, Muslims and those who appear to be from the Middle East have been victims of slurs, threats and some attacks, though other parts of the country have reported more, and more violent, hate crimes. The fact is, while New Yorkers are no strangers to bigotry, most people tolerate each other. Some celebrate diversity, others just live with it, if only as a survival mechanism. People are thrown together on subways, in buses, on the streets, instead of being isolated in cars. New Yorkers are so used to seeing people in black coats or turbans or dreadlocks that it takes a lot to make them blink.[41]

In this sense, too, New York is different from other parts of the country. As the historian Thomas Bender has noted: "The New York experience and the outlook associated with that experience posit a political and cultural life based upon difference, while the myth of rural and small-town America excludes difference from politics and culture."[42] At the same time, Bender adds that "the historic cosmopolitanism of New York . . .

[is also increasingly becoming the reality for] other cities in the United States."[43]

September 11 tested the limits of this cosmopolitan tolerance of pluralism among New Yorkers and Americans. After the expected wave of hate crimes against American Muslims immediately following September 11 subsided, another reaction started to surface. For weeks and months after the attacks, many Americans seemed to be more interested in learning more about Islam and other world religions than they ever did before. A new ecumenical spirit of interfaith understanding seemed to pervade not just Flushing but much of the country—as well as a renewal of respect for the wisdom of the founding principle of religious freedom. Such binding sentiment was limited, however, and temporary—especially in light of more recent controversy and hysteria over Imam Feisal Abdul Rauf and the proposed construction in 2010 of an Islamic community center named Cordoba House several blocks from Ground Zero and the World Trade Center site. During a time when many Americans unfairly equate Islam with terrorism after 9/11 and the threat of ISIS, and as hysteria continues over how to secure U.S. borders from illegal immigration, it is important to remember that immigration and religious diversity have always been major themes in the nation's, and especially New York's, history—and that they have been sources of strength. When the people of Flushing stood up for Quakers by signing the Flushing Remonstrance of 1657, they also spoke of "the law of love, peace and liberty . . . extending to Jews, Turks and Egyptians, as they are considered sons of Adam" and that "whatsoever form, name or title hee appears in, whether Presbyterian, Independent, Baptist or Quaker, but shall be glad to see anything of God in any of them." As Eboo Patel has written, "the Flushing Remonstrance belongs in the tradition of imagining America as a *beloved community*, a country that welcomes the contributions of all people."[44]

The story of Flushing is more relevant now than ever, as it demonstrates at the neighborhood level how religious pluralism works in a nation committed to the fundamental human right of religious freedom.[45] When Bowne House was dedicated as a "national shrine to religious freedom" in 1945 for the 300th anniversary of Flushing, Mayor La Guardia had no idea how much his words would still ring true in 2015: "It belongs to our country because it is typical of America, and it belongs to the world because it is a symbol of what the world is looking for today."[46]

Appendixes

Appendix A
Note on Methods

My initial background in ethnography and oral, or life, history (and recording techniques) was informed by working as a research and office assistant to the legendary folklorist Alan Lomax in New York. My research in New York for the Pluralism Project at Harvard also included basic ethnographic training geared toward the goals of the project—essentially two-page ethnographies to document each place of worship, in addition to records, interviews, and photographs (slides)—but I had to learn largely by trial and error and rely on common sense and intuition. At the University of Chicago, I began to refine my method as I gained more exposure to ethnography through courses in cultural anthropology and ethnographic narrative with John Comaroff and James Fernandez and courses in urban sociology with Gerald Suttles. Finally, as an exchange scholar at Columbia University again after my MA, I received further graduate training in oral history from Ronald J. Grele, director of the Oral History Research Office.

I had to adopt a comparative approach to study all of the communities in the diverse community of Flushing, Queens, yet I developed a significant amount of expertise in Asian American history, culture, and religion because the Asian American community in Flushing is so big and diverse itself. Already aware of most major terms and concepts in world religions, I acquired some basic Tamil, Hindi, Urdu, Arabic, Chinese, and Korean (I am also fluent in German and can read and speak basic French and Spanish), but it would have been impossible for me to learn all of the languages spoken in Flushing for the interviews and oral history I did for my research and fieldwork; consequently, I sought out English speakers and relied on translators when necessary.

Using a topical outline for each interview instead of a survey-oriented list of questions, my interviews for oral histories in general traced the life of each informant (dwelling especially on their particular contribution to the history of Flushing), and the topical outline focused on two sets of questions that addressed each person's view of interaction and their own response to religious and ethnic diversity in Flushing: how have the different religious and ethnic groups in Flushing associated with others across boundaries over time, and what are the different places where and when conflict or cooperation have arisen? I also asked those I interviewed to describe what they considered to be the boundaries of Flushing, their daily walking route(s), areas they avoided, etc., to gain an even deeper understanding of the neighborhood.[1]

A project description and preliminary list of sample questions to be used in interviews first was approved by the Institutional Review Board (IRB) of the Committee on the Protection of Human Subjects Rights at the University of Chicago on August 13, 1998: Notice of Exemption from Institutional Review Board (IRB) Review, IRB Identification Number 98088, based on the following 45 CFR 46.101 (b): interview procedures. Historians who do oral history tend to use the real names of the people they interview, whereas sociologists often assign pseudonyms to protect privacy and confidentiality. Every person interviewed in this book gave me permission to record an interview and use their actual name.

Since 1994, I have conducted approximately fifty recorded interviews, with hundreds of additional informal interviews (members of congregations, residents, etc.) through phone calls, impromptu meetings on the street, in places of worship, and all over Flushing in general.[2] During the course of my research, I spoke with religious and community leaders, local historians, shopkeepers, police, residents, children . . . and anyone else who *they* felt I should talk to—a technique of selecting informants called "snowball" sampling. It is a fairly intuitive process: you start with what and whom you already know, and it takes off from there. After interviewing someone, you ask them if there is someone else they know who might be relevant (and whose experiences are relevant to your research). This, in turn, introduces the researcher to different circles and provides a way to tap into a pool of potential informants that you otherwise might not have access to. As the snowball imagery implies, before you know it you have quite a large sample of people. The sampling suggests that this is a statistical method in the domain of sociology, but the search for qualitative aspects of social networks would interest anthropologists (and like-minded historians) as well. It is actually not a good method for statisticians, but it can be effective for ethnographers who need to look at certain populations and take advantage of existing social networks in order to make contact with more people to interview. Alternative methods might be more random, but these also have their own drawbacks. Snowball sampling is easier than picking addresses and sending invitations: it cuts down on rejection rates because future informants know someone you have already interviewed.

I decided to add a substantial amount of complementary visual material partly because there were virtually unknown images in archives but also because ethnographic photography seemed especially relevant to this particular project—you almost need to *see* how diverse Flushing is to comprehend it. I had been taking pictures (mostly color slide film—this was before digital) ever since my work for the Pluralism Project began in 1994, and, living in Flushing for two years, I constantly carried a camera to document things as they happened or occurred to me, and sometimes just because the lighting or time of day happened to be right. I also primarily walked or used a bicycle to get around during the two years I lived there, so I was mobile and had my own kind of regular patrol of the neighborhood. Even though some of my pictures show some of the dense concentration and juxtaposed proximity of diverse religious institutions in Flushing, it is only possible to see this fully in person, in a film, or perhaps with the kind of panoramic interactive views possible with Virtual Reality (VR) for an immersive online experience—please look for details on www.rscotthanson.com and empirestateeditions.com. I have also explored the possibility of a documentary film based on the book.

Appendix B
Population Tables

The following tables are meant to accompany Chapters 3 through 5. They provide a range of Flushing population figures for most of the twentieth century but focus most on the postwar years (1950–2000). Earlier population figures can be found in Chapters 1 and 2.

Table 1. Flushing population, 1910–2000

Year	Population
1910	17,349
1930	54,527
1950	85,093
1960	118,509
1970	141,481
1980	139,601
1990	152,812
2000	177,299

Table 2. Flushing population by race, 1950–2000

	1950		1960		1970	
White	88,477	98%	123,782	97%	142,378	95%
Negro	2,069	2%	2,534	2%	3,551	2%
Other Nonwhite	155	0%	843	1%	2,719	2%
Spanish American					1,867	1%
	90,701		127,159		150,515	

	1980		1990		2000	
White	118,394	78%	98,705	60%	77,610	37%
Black	9,830	7%	10,091	6%	7,141	3%
Hispanic	16,118	11%			34,009	16%
Asian	6,522	4%	55,372	34%	80,672	38%
Other			454	0%	12,854	6%
Total Population	150,864		164,622		212,286	

Table 3. Flushing population by Asian origin, 1980–2000

Population	1980		1990	
Japanese	1,087	6%	551	1%
Chinese	6,011	36%	19,829	42%
Filipino	1,194	7%	1,951	4%
Korean	4,558	27%	17,022	36%
Asian Indian	3,788	23%	6,937	15%
Vietnamese	182	1%	344	1%
Other Asian			157	0%
Total Asian Population	16,820		46,791	

	2000	
Japanese	491	1%
Chinese	41,729	46%
Filipino	2,498	3%
Korean	25,858	29%
Asian Indian	11,618	13%
Vietnamese	710	1%
Bangladeshi	518	1%
Malaysian	445	0%
Pakistani	2,077	2%
Taiwanese	1,478	2%
Other Asian	2,356	3%
Total Asian Population	89,778	

Table 4. Flushing population by Hispanic origin, 1970–2000

Population	1970		1980		1990		2000	
Cuban	2,347	94%	1	0%	1,689	20%	1,112	3%
Mexican	147	6%	9,870	98%	705	8%	1,489	4%
Puerto Rican			181	2%	6,173	72%	5,597	15%
Dominican							3,064	8%
Central American							3,563	10%
South American							11,973	33%
Other Hispanic							9,622	26%
Total Hispanic Population	2,494		10,052		8,567		36,420	

Notes

Introduction

1. I am recycling and slightly revising a rather famous opening line (translated from Dutch) from Johan Huizinga, *The Waning of the Middle Ages,* trans. F. Hopman (1919; New York, 1954), 9; cf. Johan Huizinga, *The Autumn of the Middle Ages,* trans. Rodney J. Payton and Ulrich Mammitzsch (Chicago: University of Chicago Press, 1996), 1.

2. St. Augustine, *City of God* (413–427; New York: Penguin, 1984).

3. Robert A. Markus, *Saeculum: History and Society in the Theology of St. Augustine* (Cambridge: Cambridge University Press, 1970), 47–55; see also Robert A. Markus, *Christianity and the Secular* (Notre Dame, Ind.: University of Notre Dame Press, 2006).

4. Markus, *Saeculum,* 53, 173.

5. Augustine, *City of God,* 18.54. Cited by Markus, *Christianity and the Secular,* 67–68.

6. Markus, *Christianity and the Secular,* 65.

7. Somini Sengupta, "Some Hear a Screech, Others America's Story: For Aiding Immigration, No. 7 Line Is Named a Historic Trail. Who Knew?" *New York Times* (July 1, 1999).

8. See Jeff Pearlman, "At Full Blast: Shooting Outrageously from the Lip, Braves Closer John Rocker Bangs Away at His Favorite Targets" *Sports Illustrated* (December 22, 1999).

9. Vivian S. Toy, "Bustling Queens Library Speaks in Many Tongues," *New York Times* (May 31, 1998).

10. Martin E. Marty, *Pilgrims in Their Own Land: Five Hundred Years of Religion in America* (New York: Little, Brown, 1984), 71.

11. Somini Sengupta, "A Snapshot of World Faith: On One Queens Block, Many Prayers Are Spoken," *New York Times* (November 7, 1999).

12. Diana L. Eck, *A New Religious America: How a "Christian Country" Has Become the World's Most Religiously Diverse Nation* (New York: HarperCollins, 2001), 1.

13. Will Herberg, *Protestant-Catholic-Jew: An Essay in American Religious Sociology* (Chicago: University of Chicago Press, 1955).

14. The marketing information firm Claritas Inc. (now part of the Nielsen Company) analyzed U.S. Census figures from 1990 and 2000 to generate a report in 2001 on the most diverse counties in the United States. The demographer Ken Hodges, who was part of that study, explained that they applied a basic diversity index to 1990 and 2000 census race/ethnicity data for all U.S. counties, but the rankings were limited to counties with populations over 250,000. The measure used is called "Simpson's D," which Hodges described as the likelihood that two persons chosen at random from the population would be from different groups. So a score of 0.7636 (on a scale ranging from a low of 0.0 to a maximum of 1.0) means that a second person chosen at random would have a roughly 76 percent chance of being of a different race/ethnic category than the first. The study was widely cited in the media, especially in New York. Hodges generated a similar unpublished report for the author in 2015 based on the 2010 U.S. Census and found that Queens is still the most diverse county among those with a population over 250,000. The same conclusion was reached by the demographers Arun Peter Lobo and Joseph J. Salvo of the New York City Department of City Planning in "A Portrait of New York's Immigrant Mélange," in *One Out of Three: Immigrant New York in the Twenty-First Century,* ed. Nancy Foner (New York: Columbia University Press, 2013), 41. Also see Lobo and Salvo's periodic series, *The Newest New Yorkers,* published by the New York City Department of City Planning in 1996, 2005, and 2013. Finally, it also should be noted (and both Hodges and Salvo have stressed) that there are many ways to measure race/ethnic diversity (and different ways to measure race and ethnicity), but Queens still ranks as the most diverse by many measures or common measures.

15. See Susan Levine, "A Place for Those Who Pray; Along Montgomery's 'Highway to Heaven,' Diverse Acts of Faith," *Washington Post* (August 3, 1997); Bob Keeler, "Religion Row: Ecumenical Diversity Rules on This Two-Mile Stretch of Deer Park Avenue," *New York Newsday* (April 12, 1998); Lowell W. Livezey, "Communities and Enclaves: Where Jews, Christians, Hindus, and Muslims Share the Neighborhoods," in *Public Religion and Urban Transformation: Faith in the City,* ed. Lowell W. Livezey (New York: NYU Press, 2000); and the documentary film *Fremont, U.S.A.*, directed by Elinor Pierce and Rachel Antell, Pluralism Project at Harvard University, 2008.

16. See Richard Bonney and R. Scott Hanson, "Understanding and Celebrating Religious Diversity in Britain: A Case Study of Leicester Since 1970 Making Comparison with Flushing, Queens County, New York City," *Encounters* 9, no. 2 (2003).

17. Alexis de Tocqueville, *Democracy in America* (1848; New York: Harper & Row, 1966), 290–295.

18. John Courtney Murray, *We Hold These Truths: Catholic Reflections on the American Proposition* (New York: Sheed and Ward, 1960), 132.

19. "Rev. John Courtney Murray, 62, Leading Jesuit Theologian, Dies," *New York Times* (August 17, 1967).

20. The only exception being very isolated and rare bias/hate crimes over time.

21. Jon Butler, "Theory and God in Gotham," *History and Theory, Theme Issue* 45 (December 2006).

22. In particular, see Omar M. McRoberts, *Streets of Glory: Church and Community in a Black Urban Neighborhood* (Chicago: University of Chicago Press, 2003). McRoberts focuses on a black neighborhood in Boston that is home to a large and diverse number of churches—a type of urban area he calls the "religious district," which shares some things in common with the "microcosm of world religions" I discuss in Flushing.

23. Martin E. Marty has dealt with this subject in many of his writings, and the American historians Philip Gleason and John Higham have been painstakingly thorough in their helpful clarifications of the many twists and turns in discussions of ethnicity and conceptions or models of ethnic relations in American history (e.g., acculturation, assimilation, the "melting pot," pluralism, cosmopolitanism). See Martin E. Marty, *The One and the Many: America's Struggle for the Common Good* (Cambridge, Mass.: Harvard University Press, 1997); Philip Gleason, *Speaking of Diversity: Language and Ethnicity in Twentieth-Century America* (Baltimore, Md.: Johns Hopkins University Press, 1992); John Higham, "Ethnic Pluralism in American Thought," in *Send These to Me: Immigrants in Urban America, rev. ed.* (Baltimore, Md.: Johns Hopkins University Press, 1984). Also see Philip Gleason, "American Identity and Americanization," in *Harvard Encyclopedia of American Ethnic Groups,* ed. Stephan Thernstrom et al. (Cambridge, Mass.: Harvard University Press, 1980). Other examples of macro studies of religious pluralism include Eck, *A New Religious America;* William R. Hutchison, *Religious Pluralism in America: The Contentious History of a Founding Ideal* (New Haven, Conn.: Yale University Press, 2003); and Robert Wuthnow, *America and the Challenges of Religious Diversity* (Princeton, N.J.: Princeton University Press, 2005).

24. Clifford Geertz, *Islam Observed: Religious Development in Morocco and Indonesia* (Chicago: University of Chicago Press, 1968), 4.

25. These questions guided the overall project as well as interviews and oral histories recorded during the course of my research. See Appendix for more on method.

26. Fred Kniss and Paul D. Numrich, *Sacred Assemblies and Civic Engagement: How Religion Matters for America's Newest Immigrants* (New Brunswick, N.J.: Rutgers University Press, 2007), 10, 21–22, 34.

27. Emile Durkheim, *The Elementary Forms of the Religious Life* (1915; New York: Free Press, 1965), 22.

28. I am building here on some of David A. Hollinger's language in *Postethnic America: Beyond Multiculturalism* (New York: Basic Books, 1995). Hollinger speaks of "ethno-racial blocs" in his book, but I would amend this to factor in religion as tied to the other two components of identity.

29. For the most thorough intellectual history of pluralism, particularly as it contrasts with assimilation, see Philip Gleason, "The Odd Couple: Pluralism and Assimilation," in *Speaking of Diversity: Language and Ethnicity in Twentieth-Century America* (Baltimore, Md.: Johns Hopkins University Press, 1992). Also see Higham, "Ethnic Pluralism in American Thought."

30. For the longer discussion of the history and changing meaning of these terms, see my essay "Pluralism and Cosmopolitanism in American Thought," *Journal of American Ethnic History* (under review).

31. For a more detailed discussion of Flushing's boundaries before consolidation, see Chapter 1.

32. Two exceptions, both about Corona-Elmhurst, are: Roger Sanjek, *The Future of Us All: Race and Neighborhood Politics in New York City* (Ithaca, N.Y.: Cornell University Press, 1998); and Steven Gregory, *Black Corona: Race and the Politics of Place in an Urban Community* (Princeton, N.J.: Princeton University Press, 1998). Corona-Elmhurst, although similarly diverse (11373 is actually *the* most diverse zip code in the country), does not have as many different places of worship densely concentrated in its neighborhoods as Flushing—religion is not as striking a factor there as is race and ethnicity, and its religious history is not particularly significant. A majority of immigrants in Corona-Elmhurst are from the many countries of Latin America (this is what accounts for the diverse zip code), with comparatively fewer Asian immigrants, and they are either Catholics or evangelical Protestants with many who also regularly frequent the numerous *botanicas*.

33. New Yorkers, perhaps to a greater degree than residents of many other cities, often form strong opinions about one another based on the five boroughs of the city and its many neighborhoods. One of the first questions at a party or social event in Manhattan might be: "So, where do you live?" The answer to this question can reveal something about one's class, status, and position in New York society, and it drives a kind of Manhattan snobbery that has given rise to epithets like "bridge and tunnel," which refers to anyone commuting to Manhattan—essentially lumping the outer boroughs together with people from New Jersey and Connecticut. But even the outer boroughs themselves have a kind of hierarchy: Brooklyn is probably number one (or two, after Manhattan) with its brownstones, hipster neighborhoods, memories of Ebbets Field and the Dodgers; Queens is second; the Bronx has Yankee Stadium; and Staten Island comes in last because it is connected to the city only by the Staten Island Ferry and Verrazano–Narrows Bridge—and because much of Manhattan's trash has

been dumped in the massive Fresh Kills landfill there for years (not surprisingly, Staten Islanders have wanted to secede). Yet a clothing store in Brooklyn has been selling T-shirts emblazoned with the number 718—a trend that may (or may not) be a sign of an emerging outer borough solidarity tied to the 718 telephone area code, which residents of Brooklyn, Queens, the Bronx, and Staten Island all share.

34. Kirk Semple, "Tourists Have Landed in Queens. They're Staying," *New York Times* (August 25, 2015).

35. Marcia Biederman, "Library Thrives with a Common Touch: Queens Stresses Popular Taste, Not Scholarship," *New York Times* (September 12, 1999).

36. Produced by Norman Lear, the CBS show ran from January 1971 to April 1979 and became one of the most influential programs in the history of American television.

37. A review of indices to the *American Historical Review, Journal of American History,* and *New York History* turned up only one reference to Bowne or Flushing: an article in the latter journal by Milton M. Klein, "New York in the American Colonies: A New Look," *New York History* 53, no. 2 (April 1972). The only recent scholarship on Flushing is a sociological study of its demographic and economic changes in the 1990s. See Christopher J. Smith, "Asian New York: The Geography and Politics of Diversity," *International Migration Review* 29, no. 1 (Spring 1995); and Christopher J. Smith and John R. Logan, "Flushing 2000," in *From Urban Enclave to Ethnic Suburb: New Asian Communities in Pacific Rim Countries,* ed. Wei Li (Honolulu: University of Hawai'i Press, 2006).

38. In particular, see Henry D. Waller, *History of the Town of Flushing, Long Island* (Flushing, 1899); and Rev. G. Henry Mandeville, *Flushing, Past and Present: A Historical Sketch* (Flushing, 1860). Also see W. W. Munsell & Co., *History of Queens County, New York with Illustrations, Portraits, & Sketches of Prominent Families and Individuals* (New York, 1882); and Benjamin F. Thompson, *History of Long Island: From Its Discovery and Settlement to the Present Time* (1839; New York, 1918). There is also a wealth of information in the Queens Historical Society, *Angels of Deliverance: The Underground Railroad in Queens, Long Island, and Beyond* (Flushing, 1999). Finally, also see Vincent F. Seyfried, *The Civil War Era in Flushing* (Garden City, N.Y., 2002).

39. For instance, there is an entry for John Bowne in the *Dictionary of American Biography.* As for histories of New York, Bowne and Flushing appear in such works as Michael Kammen's *Colonial New York* in 1975, Kenneth T. Jackson's *Encyclopedia of New York City* in 1995, and Edwin G. Burrows and Mike Wallace's *Gotham: A History of New York City to 1898* in 1999. In American religious history, Bowne and Flushing appear in such works as Leonard Woolsey Bacon's *A History of American Christianity* in 1898, Frederick J. Zwierlein's *Religion in New Netherland* in 1910, William Warren Sweet's *The Story of Religions in America* in 1930, and Martin E. Marty's *Pilgrims in Their Own Land* in 1984.

40. See, for example, Sydney E. Ahlstrom, *A Religious History of the American People 1972.* Flushing also received no mention whatsoever in Ric Burns's

otherwise excellent 1999 megadocumentary history series *New York: A Documentary Film* (in fact, in one scene during "The Country and the City, 1609–1825: Part One," Burns took a letter from the Dutch West India Company to Governor Stuyvesant in 1663 about John Bowne out of context and did not mention Bowne or Quakers at all—incorrectly saying that the letter was about the fledgling Sephardic Jewish community in New Amsterdam).

41. See Russell Shorto, *The Island at the Center of the World: The Epic Story of Dutch Manhattan and the Forgotten Colony That Shaped America* (New York: Vintage, 2004); and Randall Balmer and Mark Silk, eds., *Religion and Public Life in the Middle Atlantic Region: The Fount of Diversity* (Lanham, Md.: AltaMira, 2006).

42. For more on this topic, see my essay "Religious Pluralism and the Canon of American Religious History," *Religion and American Culture: A Journal of Interpretation* (forthcoming).

43. David G. Hackett, ed., *Religion and American Culture: A Reader* (New York, 1995), ix.

44. Martin E. Marty, "The American Religious History Canon," *Social Research* 53, no. 3 (Autumn 1986): 518.

45. See Hanson, "Religious Pluralism and the Canon of American Religious History." For a sample of recent work, see Jay P. Dolan, "Immigration and American Christianity: A History of Their Histories," in *A Century of Church History: The Legacy of Philip Schaff,* ed. Henry W. Bowden (Carbondale: Southern Illinois University Press, 1988); Jay P. Dolan, "The Immigrants and Their Gods: A New Perspective in American Religious History," *Church History* 57 (March 1988), reprinted in *Religion in American History: A Reader,* ed. Jon Butler and Harry S. Stout (New York: Oxford University Press, 1998); Thomas A. Tweed and Stephen Prothero, eds., *Asian Religions in America: A Documentary History* (New York: Oxford University Press, 1999); Raymond B. Williams, *Religions of Immigrants from India and Pakistan: New Threads in the American Tapestry* (Cambridge: Cambridge University Press, 1988); Yvonne Yazbeck Haddad, ed., *The Muslims of America* (New York: Oxford University Press, 1991); Rick Fields, *How the Swans Came to the Lake: A Narrative History of Buddhism in America* (Boston: Shambhala, 1992); Thomas A. Tweed, *The American Encounter with Buddhism, 1844–1912: Victorian Culture and the Limits of Dissent* (Chapel Hill: University of North Carolina Press, 1992); Stephen Prothero, *The White Buddhist: The Asian Odyssey of Henry Steel Olcott* (Bloomington: Indiana University Press, 1996); Thomas A. Tweed, "Asian Religions in the United States: Reflections on an Emerging Sub-Field," in *Religious Diversity and American Religious History: Studies in Traditions and Cultures,* ed. Walter Conser and Sumner Twiss (Athens: University of Georgia Press, 1997); Diana L. Eck, *On Common Ground: World Religions in America* (New York: Columbia University Press, 1997); R. Stephen Warner and Judith G. Wittner, eds., *Gatherings in Diaspora: Religious Communities and the New Immigration* (Philadelphia: Temple University Press, 1998); and David K. Yoo, ed., *New Spiritual Homes: Religion and Asian Americans* (Honolulu: University of Hawai'i Press, 1999).

46. R. Scott Hanson, "Neighborhood Narratives in the City of Gods: Religious Freedom, Immigration, and Pluralism in Flushing, New York," paper presented at the 2001 Annual Meeting of the American Historical Association, in a session cosponsored by the Immigration and Ethnic History Society entitled "New Narratives for an Old Story: Moments of Peak Immigration Over Three Centuries of U.S. History."

47. See Peter Brimelow, *Alien Nation: Common Sense About America's Immigration Disaster* (New York: Random House, 1995); Arthur M. Schlesinger Jr., *The Disuniting of America: Reflections on a Multicultural Society* (New York: Norton, 1992); Lawrence W. Levine, *The Opening of the American Mind: Canons, Culture, and History* (Boston: Beacon, 1996); David M. Reimers, *Unwelcome Strangers: American Identity and the Turn Against Immigration* (New York: Columbia University Press, 1998); and Neil J. Smelser and Jeffrey C. Alexander, eds., *Diversity and Its Discontents: Cultural Conflict and Common Ground in Contemporary American Society* (Princeton, N.J.: Princeton University Press, 1999).

48. Ric Burns, interview with Aaron Brown for CNN (October 5, 2001), http://transcripts.cnn.com/TRANSCRIPTS/0110/05/se.14.html.

49. John Higham, "Ethnicity and American Protestants: Collective Identity in the Mainstream," in *New Directions in American Religious History*, ed. Harry S. Stout and D. G. Hart (New York: Oxford University Press, 1997), 242. Two notable recent works include Shirley J. Yee, *An Immigrant Neighborhood: Interethnic and Interracial Encounters in New York Before 1930* (Philadelphia: Temple University Press, 2012); and Allison J. Varzally, *Making a Non-White America: Californians Coloring Outside Ethnic Lines, 1925–1955* (Berkeley: University of California Press, 2008).

50. See George M. Stephenson, *The Religious Aspects of Swedish Immigration* (Minneapolis: University of Minnesota Press, 1932); William I. Thomas and Florian Znaniecki, *The Polish Peasant in Europe and America* (Urbana: University of Illinois Press, 1918–1920); Nathan Glazer and Daniel P. Moynihan, *Beyond the Melting Pot: The Negroes, Puerto Ricans, Jews, Italians, and Irish of New York City* (Cambridge, Mass.: MIT Press, 1963); Milton M. Gordon, *Assimilation in American Life: The Role of Race, Religion, and National Origins* (New York: Oxford University Press, 1964); Rudolph J. Vecoli, "Ethnicity: A Neglected Dimension of American History," in *The State of American History*, ed. Herbert J. Bass (Chicago: University of Chicago Press, 1970); Martin E. Marty, "Ethnicity: The Skeleton of Religion in America," *Church History* 41 (March 1972); Harry S. Stout, "Ethnicity: The Vital Center of Religion in America," *Ethnicity* 2, no. 2 (June 1975); Timothy L. Smith, "Religion and Ethnicity in America," *American Historical Review* 83 (December 1978); Kathleen Neils Conzen, "Community Studies, Urban History, and American Local History," in *The Past Before Us: Contemporary Historical Writing in the United States*, ed. Michael Kammen (Ithaca, N.Y.: Cornell University Press, 1980); Kathleen Neils Conzen, "Immigrants, Immigrant Neighborhoods, and Ethnic Identity: Historical Issues," *Journal of American History* 66, no. 3 (December 1979); Ronald Takaki, *Strangers from*

a Different Shore: A History of Asian Americans (New York: Back Bay, 1989); Ronald Takaki, *A Different Mirror: A History of Multicultural America* (Boston: Back Bay, 1993); Roger Daniels, "No Lamps Were Lit for Them: Angel Island and the Historiography of Asian American Immigration," *Journal of American Ethnic History* 17, no. 1 (Fall 1997); Rudolph J. Vecoli, "Immigration, Ethnicity, and Religion," in *A Selected Bibliography on American Immigration and Ethnicity (Revised)* (St. Paul, 1998), 18; and Roger Daniels, "Asian American History's Overdue Emergence," *Chronicle Review* (December 7, 2001): B7–B9.

51. See, for instance, Josef J. Barton, *Peasants and Strangers: Italians, Rumanians, and Slovaks in an American City* (Cambridge, Mass.: Harvard University Press, 1975); David A. Gerber, *The Making of an American Pluralism: Buffalo, New York, 1825–1860* (Urbana: University of Illinois Press, 1989); Richard White, *The Middle Ground: Indians, Empires, and Republics in the Great Lakes Region, 1650–1815* (New York: Cambridge University Press, 1991); Ramón Gutiérrez, *When Jesus Came the Corn Mothers Went Away: Marriage, Sexuality, and Power in New Mexico, 1500–1846* (Stanford, Calif.: Stanford University Press, 1991); John Demos, *The Unredeemed Captive: A Family Story from Early America* (New York: Vintage, 1994); Jon Gjerde, *The Minds of the West: Ethnocultural Evolution in the Rural Middle West, 1830–1917* (Chapel Hill: University of North Carolina Press, 1997). Also see Catherine L. Albanese, "Exchanging Selves, Exchanging Souls: Contact, Combination, and American Religious History," in *Retelling U.S. Religious History,* ed. Thomas A. Tweed (Berkeley: University of California Press, 1997).

52. See Peter Berger, ed., *The Desecularization of the World: Resurgent Religion and World Politics* (New York: Eerdmans, 1999).

53. Butler, "Theory and God in Gotham," 57.

54. Robert A. Orsi, "Introduction: Crossing the City Line," in *Gods of the City: Religion and the American Urban Landscape,* ed. Robert A. Orsi (Bloomington: Indiana University Press, 1999), 41.

55. See, for instance, Robert J. Sampson, *Great American City: Chicago and the Enduring Neighborhood Effect* (Chicago: University of Chicago Press, 2014); and Kenneth T. Jackson, "The End of Sprawl: The City Beckons Once Again," lecture for Columbia University Alumni Association, Philadelphia, June 20, 2009.

56. See, for example, Thomas J. Sugrue, *The Origins of the Urban Crisis: Race and Inequality in Postwar Detroit* (Princeton, N.J.: Princeton University Press, 1996); Elijah Anderson, *Code of the Street: Decency, Violence, and the Moral Life of the Inner City* (New York: Norton, 1999); and Kenneth T. Jackson, *Crabgrass Frontier: The Suburbanization of the United States* (New York: Oxford University Press, 1985).

57. Louis Wirth, "Urbanism as a Way of Life," *American Journal of Sociology* 44, no. 1 (July 1938): 1–24.

58. Jane Jacobs, *The Death and Life of Great American Cities* (New York: Vintage, 1961), 35, 59.

59. Mary Pipher, *The Middle of Everywhere: The World's Refugees Come to Our Town* (New York: Harcourt, 2002); and Stephen G. Bloom, *Postville: A Clash of Cultures in Heartland America* (Orlando, Fla.: Harcourt, 2000).

60. Arthur M. Schlesinger, "The City in American History," *Mississippi Valley Historical Review* 27 (June 1940).

61. For more on Roger Williams's "lively experiment" and the Rhode Island charter of 1663, see Sidney E. Mead, "When 'Wise Men Hoped': An Examination of the Mind and Spirit of the National Period," in *The Lively Experiment: The Shaping of Christianity in America* (New York, 1963), 91. Mead borrowed the title of his book from the text of Rhode Island's charter of 1663 to describe the concept of free churches (i.e., churches under a system of separation of church and state, or disestablishment—in other words, churches as voluntary associations). Mead also refers to this as "the great experiment" and notes that Jefferson referred to "the fair experiment" in his *Notes on the State of Virginia* (1781). Similarly, William Penn referred to the colony of Pennsylvania as a "holy experiment."

62. See the Appendix for a more detailed discussion of how I conducted my research.

63. See Richard Wightman Fox, "Experience and Explanation in Twentieth-Century American Religious History," in *New Directions in American Religious History,* ed. Harry S. Stout and D. G. Hart (New York: Oxford University Press, 1997); Suzanne Desan, "Crowds, Community, and Ritual in the Work of E. P. Thompson and Natalie Davis," in *The New Cultural History,* ed. Lynn Hunt (Berkeley: University of California Press, 1989); and Karen Halttunen, "Cultural History and the Challenge of Narrativity," in *Beyond the Cultural Turn: New Directions in the Study of Society and Culture,* ed. Victoria E. Bonnell and Lynn Hunt (Berkeley: University of California Press, 1999), 167. As the oral historian Paul Thompson has noted: "Reality is complex and many-sided; and it is a primary merit of oral history that to a much greater extent than most sources it allows the original multiplicity of standpoints to be recreated." Paul Thompson, *The Voice of the Past: Oral History* (1978; New York: Oxford University Press, 1988), 5.

64. Michel-Rolph Trouillot, *Silencing the Past: Power and the Production of History* (Boston: Beacon, 1995), 49.

65. Pierre Bourdieu, "The Biographical Illusion," *Working Papers and Proceedings of the Center for Psychosocial Studies* 14 (Chicago, 1987).

66. For more discussion of my oral history interviews, see the Appendix.

67. Robert A. Orsi, *The Madonna of 115th Street: Faith and Community in Italian Harlem, 1880–1950* (New Haven, Conn.: Yale University Press, 1985). For an extended look at the history of religion and the American city, see Robert A. Orsi, "Introduction: Crossing the City Line," in *Gods of the City: Religion and the American Urban Landscape,* ed. Robert A. Orsi (Bloomington: Indiana University Press, 1999).

68. See, for example, Rhys Isaac, *The Transformation of Virginia, 1740–1790* (Chapel Hill: University of North Carolina Press, 1982); and Natalie Zemon Davis, *Society and Culture in Early Modern France* (Stanford, Calif.: Stanford University Press, 1975). For more on the history of history and ethnography, see Ronald G. Waters, "Signs of the Times: Clifford Geertz and Historians," *Social Research* 47 (1980); Bernard S. Cohn, John W. Adams, Natalie Z. Davis,

and Carlo Ginzburg, "Anthropology and History in the 1980s," *Journal of Interdisciplinary History* 12 (1981); Clifford Geertz, "History and Anthropology," *New Literary History 21* (1989–1990); Lynn Hunt, ed., *The New Cultural History* (Berkeley: University of California Press, 1989); John and Jean Comaroff, *Ethnography and the Historical Imagination* (Boulder, Colo.: Westview, 1992).

69. Emmanuel LeRoy Ladurie, *Montaillou: The Promised Land of Error* (New York: Vintage, 1979).

70. Orsi, *The Madonna of 115th Street,* xix–xx.

71. Ibid., xxiii.

72. David M. Hummon, *Commonplaces: Community Ideology and Identity in American Culture* (Albany: SUNY Press, 1990).

73. Roger Chartier, *Cultural History: Between Practices and Representations* (Ithaca, N.Y.: Cornell University Press, 1988). Peter Burke adds that "Encounters and interactions should therefore join the practices and representations which Chartier has described as the principal objects of the new cultural history." See Peter Burke, *Varieties of Cultural History* (Ithaca, N.Y.: Cornell University Press, 1997), 203.

74. See the Appendix for a more detailed account.

75. Only when there was much repetition with a group (there are over one hundred Korean churches) did I instead choose a sample.

76. Anderson, *Code of the Street,* 11.

77. In addition to scholarly texts about the world's religious traditions, I also referred to Arthur J. Magida, ed., *How to Be a Perfect Stranger: A Guide to Etiquette in Other People's Religious Ceremonies* (Woodstock, Vt.: Jewish Lights, 1996).

78. Robert A. Orsi, *Between Heaven and Earth: The Religious Worlds People Make and the Scholars Who Study Them* (Princeton, N.J.: Princeton University Press, 2005), 3. For another thought-provoking look into the relationship of the ethnographer to one's subject(s), see Allison Lurie, *Imaginary Friends* (New York: Coward-McCann, 1967).

1. Religion in Vlissingen (Flushing) from 1645 to 1945

1. "Tercentenary Keynote to Be Free Worship: Plans for Flushing Fete to Be Drafted on National Scope," *Long Island Star Journal* (April 9, 1945). Colden was a descendant of Lieut. Gov. Cadwallader Colden (1688–1776) who retired in Flushing.

2. "Oaks of Flushing to Form Symbols: 300th Anniversary Celebration of Charter to Name Trees for United Nations," *New York Times* (May 27, 1945).

3. "Flushing Gets New Park and Mayor's Salute: On 300th Anniversary, He Broadcasts from Bowne House, Tolerance Shrine," *New York Herald Tribune* (October 8, 1945).

4. "Mayor Opens Flushing Tercentenary Celebration," *Press* (October 8, 1945).

5. "Flushing Tercentenary to Be Carried to Nation," *Long Island Star-Journal* (September 11, 1945); "Army to Send Out News of Tercentenary," *Long Island Star-Journal* (July 30, 1945).

6. "Old Flushing Home Becomes a Shrine: Bowne House Is Dedicated to Religious Freedom on 300th Anniversary of Community," *New York Times* (October 11, 1945).

7. "Race Prejudice Will Be Theme at Town Rally: Educators Give Talks at Flushing High School," *Long Island Star-Journal* (October 11, 1945).

8. "3,000 Parade for Flushing Tercentenary," *Long Island Star-Journal* (October 13, 1945).

9. "Tercentenary to Be Celebrated by Flushing in Week of Oct. 7: Ceremonies Marking Signing of Charter in 1645 Will Include Concerts, Costume Ball, and Parade," *New York Times* (July 22, 1945). Local history and fiction also flourished around this time in Flushing. See Haynes Trebor, *Colonial Flushing* (Flushing, N.Y., 1945); Cornelia Mitchell Parsons, *The Quaker Cross: A Tale of Old Bowne House* (Flushing, N.Y., 1911); and Stella E. Asling-Riis, *Star Over Flushing* (Flushing, N.Y., 1939).

10. "Tolerance in Flushing," *New York Times* (October 12, 1945).

11. *Historical Documents XIV,* 15. Cited in Henry D. Waller, *History of the Town of Flushing Long Island, New York* (Flushing, N.Y., 1899), 11–14.

12. I am indebted to the urban geographer and my former neighbor Jack Eichenbaum for impressing upon me the topographical significance of Flushing in a lecture entitled "The Ups and Downs of Queens" at the Queens Historical Society, March 1, 2000. Also see Jack Eichenbaum, "The Evolution of Lawn Guyland," *New York Times* (March 29, 1998). In the 1930s–1960s, Parks Commissioner Robert Moses also recognized that Flushing Meadows–Corona Park was the geographical center of New York City, and he chose the area for two World's Fairs and park space.

13. Frederick Van Wyck, *Select Patents of New York Towns* (New York, 1938), 5–6. Also see Jerrold Seymann, *Colonial Charters, Patents, and Grants to the Communities Comprising the City of New York* (New York, 1939).

14. Haynes Trebor, *The Flushing Remonstrance (The Origin of Religious Freedom in America)* (Flushing, N.Y., 1957), 6–8.

15. Henry Onderdonk Jr., "The Rise of the Society of Friends in Flushing," in *Original Journal of John Bowne of Flushing, L.I. (1627–1695), containing entries of Births, Marriages and Deaths in the family from 1649–1676 with Vol. Of Extracts from Journal and Newspaper cuttings of contributions to Flushing's Centennial,* by Henry Onderdonk Jr., 2 vols., 12 mo., manuscripts collection, the Library of the New-York Historical Society. Library note: "Vol. of newspaper cuttings being extracts from Journal of JB edited by Onderdonk, a chronicler who lived in the nineteenth century and worked as headmaster at Union Hall academy in nearby Jamaica, Queens. Journal entries span 1656–1702 (JB and Samuel Bowne, son); articles span 1700–1801 and may be a combination of Bowne

material, Onderdonk articles for the original Flushing Times (a Civil War era paper that preceded the current eponymous one), and church records from the Friends Meeting House. The 'Centennial' referred to is most likely Flushing's *Bi*-Centennial in 1845, as Onderdonk lived 1804–1886. Onderdonk notes that 'in 1789 the records of Flushing were burnt. This loss . . . is mitigated by the preservation of an old account book of John Bowne and his son Samuel, extending from 1656–1702.'"

16. Evan Haefeli, *New Netherland and the Dutch Origins of American Religious Liberty* (Philadelphia: University of Pennsylvania Press, 2012), 21, 10. Also see Carla Gardina Pestana, *Liberty of Conscience and the Growth of Religious Diversity in Early America, 1636–1786* (Providence, R.I., 1986). Pestana's book was a catalogue derived from an exhibition of the same name at the John Carter Brown Library, Brown University, May 1–September 30, 1986, in honor of the 350th anniversary of the founding of the state of Rhode Island.

17. Maarten Prak, *The Dutch Republic in the Seventeenth Century,* trans. Diane Webb (Cambridge: Cambridge University Press, 2005), 219–220; cited in Haefeli, *New Netherland and the Dutch Origins of American Religious Liberty,* 13.

18. Haefeli, *New Netherland and the Dutch Origins of American Religious Liberty,* 4.

19. Jeremy Dupertuis Bangs, "Dutch Contributions to Religious Toleration," *Church History* 79, no. 3 (2010): 585–613; cited in Haefeli, *New Netherland and the Dutch Origins of American Religious Liberty,* 12–13.

20. Haefeli, *New Netherland and the Dutch Origins of American Religious Liberty,* 13.

21. Hugh Hastings, *Ecclesiastical Records of the State of New York* (New York, 1901), 1:352.

22. Waller, *History of the Town of Flushing Long Island,* 20–21.

23. Onderdonk, "The Rise of the Society of Friends in Flushing."

24. Waller, *History of the Town of Flushing Long Island,* 25–28.

25. Ibid. There seems to have been a kind of pipeline between Flushing and Rhode Island in the mid–seventeenth century (indeed, tracing the history of each reveals a religious freedom trail), as John Bowne also later recorded in his journal on June 11, 1661: "we went from our house at Flushing towards Rhode Island, to the General Meeting, where we stayed 9 days time."

26. Ibid.

27. Please refer to the reproduction of *The Flushing Remonstrance.*

28. David William Voorhees, "The 1657 Flushing Remonstrance in Historical Perspective," paper given at the New York State History Conference, June 2007.

29. See Evan Haefeli, "The Text of the Flushing Remonstrance," paper presented to the Center for Ethical Culture, November 15, 2007. Haefeli argues that Stuyvesant was simply following orders by cracking down on anyone practicing any religion but Dutch Reformed in public until he was rebuked by the Dutch West India Company after Bowne's appeal.

30. Edith King Wilson, *Bowne Family of Flushing, Long Island* (New York, 1987). Hannah was the cousin of the third town sheriff of Flushing, Tobias Feake (who delivered the Flushing Remonstrance to Stuyvesant), a daughter of Elizabeth Fones Winthrop Feake (cofounder of Greenwich, Connecticut), and daughter-in-law through her first marriage of John Winthrop (first governor of the Massachusetts Bay Colony).

31. Onderdonk, Extracts from the State's Office, Albany, in "The Rise of the Society of Friends in Flushing."

32. Michael Kammen, *Colonial New York: A History* (New York: Scribners, 1975), 63.

33. John Bowne of Flushing, L.I. (1627–1695), from the *Original Journal of 1649–1676*, manuscripts collection, the Library of the New-York Historical Society. See note 15.

34. Voorhees, "The 1657 Flushing Remonstrance in Historical Perspective."

35. Hastings, *Ecclesiastical Records*, 1:530. Dispatch from The Directors of the W I Company—Amsterdam addressed to the Governor and Council of New Netherland dated 16 of April 1663.

36. *Historical Documents I*, 425, cited by Waller, *History of the Town of Flushing Long Island*, 28.

37. George L. Smith has addressed the conflicting interests of the Dutch West India Company by focusing on the Dutch understanding of "connivance" in *Religion and Trade in New Netherland: Dutch Origins and American Development* (Ithaca, N.Y.: Cornell University Press, 1973).

38. Martin E. Marty, *Pilgrims in Their Own Land: Five Hundred Years of Religion in America* (New York: Little, Brown, 1984), 71–72.

39. Bowne already had begun to anglicize Vlissingen by writing "Vlishing" in his journal. "Flushing" is used in later records at least as early as 1664.

40. Hastings, *Ecclesiastical Records*, 1:545.

41. Haefeli, *New Netherland and the Dutch Origins of American Religious Liberty*, 254.

42. Ibid., 256–257, 260.

43. Ibid., 261.

44. The spot is now marked by a large slab of inscribed rock on Bowne Street where the "Fox Oaks" used to stand. Fox later recalled: "We had a very large meeting, many hundreds of people being there, some of whom came 30 miles to it. A glorious and heavenly meeting it was and the people were much satisfied." Onderdonk, "The Rise of the Religious Society of Friends in Flushing."

45. Hastings, *Ecclesiastical Records of the State of New York*, 2:864. Queens County itself was made one of the counties of the Province of New York on November 1, 1683, and named after Queen Catherine of Braganza (Queen of Charles II of England, r. 1660–1685). Governor Dongan also approved a new treaty in 1684 with the local native Americans that was drawn up by Bowne and eight others and signed by Takapousha, sachem of the Matinecoc tribe.

46. Rev. G. Du Bois to the Classis of Amsterdam, May 14, 1741, in *Ecclesiastical Records,* 4:2756; cited by Milton M. Klein, "New York in the American Colonies: A New Look," *New York History* 53, no. 2 (April 1972): 146.

47. Constitution of the State of New York, 1777. Italics added.

48. There is no doubt that the social contexts surrounding the Portsmouth Compact make it an important document of early colonial America, but it is brief, and any religious freedom is vague: "We whose names are underwritten do hereby solemnly in the presence of Jehovah incorporate ourselves into a Bodie Politick and as He shall help, will submit our persons, lives and estates unto our Lord Jesus Christ, the King of Kings, and Lord of Lords, and to all those perfect and most absolute laws of His given in His Holy Word of truth, to be guided and judged thereby."

49. Pestana, *Liberty of Conscience and the Growth of Religious Diversity in Early America,* 45–46.

50. Thomas Jefferson, *Notes on the State of Virginia,* ed. William Peden (Chapel Hill: University of North Carolina Press, 1954), 157–161. Also see Charles B. Sanford, *The Religious Life of Thomas Jefferson* (Charlottesville: University of Virginia Press, 1984).

51. See Russell Shorto, *The Island at the Center of the World: The Epic Story of Dutch Manhattan and the Forgotten Colony That Shaped America* (New York: Vintage, 2004); Randall Balmer and Mark Silk, eds., *Religion and Public Life in the Middle Atlantic Region: The Fount of Diversity* (Lanham, Md.: AltaMira, 2006).

52. "The Exact List of All Ye Inhabitants' Names Within Ye Town of Flushing and Precincts, of Old and Young Freemen and Servants, White and Black, etc., 1698," Long Island Division, Queens Borough Public Library, Jamaica Branch.

53. Onderdonk, "The Rise of the Society of Friends in Flushing." The Meeting House kept records of sufferings of Friends throughout the seventeenth and eighteenth centuries, which these clippings reflect.

54. Sydney E. Ahlstrom, *A Religious History of the American People* (New Haven, Conn.: Yale University Press, 1972), 210.

55. Onderdonk, "The Rise of the Society of Friends in Flushing." The footnote from the Meeting House record adds: "The Act of Parliament allowed Friends the privilege of worshiping God without molestation provided the place of worship be certified to the justices of the peace at the Sessions, and recorded, and that the meeting be held without the doors locked, barred, or bolted. In 1704 3d mo. John Rodman, Samuel Haight and Thos. Stevenson were desired to present our meeting houses and places to Court to be recorded."

56. Jon Butler, *Awash in a Sea of Faith: Christianizing the American People* (Cambridge, Mass.: Harvard University Press, 1990), 175, 164–165.

57. Ibid., 182.

58. Letter from Rev. Thomas Colgan to the Secretary of the Society for the Propagation of the Gospel, November 22, 1740, in *Documentary History of the State of New-York,* ed. E. B. Callaghan (Albany, N.Y., 1850), 3:316–317.

59. Ibid., September 29, 1746.

60. Letter from Rev. Samuel Seabury to the Secretary of the Society for the Propagation of the Gospel, October 10, 1759, in *Documentary History of the State of New-York,* ed. E. B. Callaghan (Albany, N.Y., 1850), 3:321.

61. Ibid., March 28, 1760.

62. Onderdonk, "The Rise of the Society of Friends in Flushing."

63. Ibid.

64. See Edmund A. Stanley Jr., *Of Men and Dreams: The Story of the People of Bowne & Co. and the Fulfillment of Their Dreams in the Company's Two Hundred Years from 1775 to 1975* (New York, 1975).

65. Historical Commission of Macedonia African Methodist Episcopal Church, Journal on "The History of Macedonia" commemorating History Day at the church on January 16, 1977. Also see Richard Newman, *Freedom's Prophet: Bishop Richard Allen, the AME Church, and the Black Founding Fathers* (New York: NYU Press, 2009).

66. Ibid. Also see Marty, *Pilgrims in Their Own Land,* 238–239. Ahlstrom offers this explanation on the Methodist Episcopal connection: "The Methodist predicament was entwined with the Anglican because it originated as a revival movement within the Church of England." *A Religious History of the American People,* 370.

67. Historical Commission of Macedonia African Methodist Episcopal Church, Journal on "The History of Macedonia."

68. Ibid.

69. The Queens Historical Society, *Angels of Deliverance: The Underground Railroad in Queens, Long Island, and Beyond* (Flushing, N.Y., 1999).

70. See Kathleen G. Velsor, "Quaker Families and Their Connections: The Long Island Origins of the Anti-Slavery Movement" and "The Queens Freedom Trail," in Queens Historical Society, *Angels of Deliverance.*

71. Samuel Bowne Parsons obituary, *Brooklyn Eagle* (January 5, 1906). Cited in James Driscoll, "Flushing in the Early Nineteenth Century," in Queens Historical Society, *Angels of Deliverance,* 81.

72. For more on Quaker pacifism, see Meredith Baldwin Weddle, *Walking in the Way of Peace: Quaker Pacifism in the Seventeenth Century* (New York: Oxford University Press, 2001).

73. Ibid. The charter was later revised and village boundaries expanded in 1839 and 1873, changing to current limits with consolidation into the city in 1898.

74. Ibid.

75. Vincent F. Seyfried, *The Civil War Era in Flushing* (Garden City, N.Y., 2002), 1.

76. For more on Bowne's mayoralty, see City of New York, *Minutes of the Common Council of the City of New York, 1784–1831,* vol. XVII–XVIII (New York, 1917).

77. Flushing, Old Town Records, 1833–1863, in the New York City Municipal Archives.

78. *Flushing Journal* (July 12, 1862); cited by Seyfried, *The Civil War Era in Flushing,* 117. The *Flushing Journal* began in 1842 and was the major local paper throughout the nineteenth century. The Queens historian Vincent F. Seyfried has laboriously indexed the entire span of the paper and made it available to the Long Island Division at the Queens Borough Public Library, Jamaica Branch.

79. See Butler, *Awash in a Sea of Faith,* 221, 257–258, 268–270; and Sidney E. Mead, "Denominationalism: The Shape of Protestantism in America," in *The Lively Experiment: The Shaping of Christianity in America* (New York: Harper and Row, 1963).

80. *Flushing Journal* (August 4, 1854): 2. Cited in James Driscoll, "Flushing in the Early Nineteenth Century," in Queens Historical Society, *Angels of Deliverance,* 83.

81. G. Henry Mandeville, *Flushing, Past and Present: A Historical Sketch* (Flushing, N.Y., 1860), 169. Mandeville notes: "It is a singular circumstance that a church of this denomination should not have existed here at an earlier date; particularly when we remember that the first religious teacher in Flushing [William Wickenden] entertained their views in relation to the ordinance of Baptism."

82. Flushing Bible Society, *Third Annual Report* (Flushing, N.Y., 1857), 8–12. For the report, the society enlisted the services of a Mr. Alfred Cauldwell, who visited 1,764 families in Flushing and conducted an informal religious census as he distributed Bibles and religious tracts in English and German (for the large number of German immigrants).

83. *Flushing Journal* (September 16, 1854).

84. *Flushing Journal* (April 7, 1855). For more on the Know-Nothings, see Tyler Anbinder, *Nativism and Slavery: The Northern Know Nothings and the Politics of the 1850s* (New York: Oxford University Press, 1992).

85. Ahlstrom, *A Religious History of the American People,* 629–631.

86. This was quite a different stance than a century earlier, when much of Queens County was loyalist during the American Revolution, except New-town. On August 7, 1776, in the Battle of Long Island, British forces defeated Washington, who retreated to Manhattan. The British then occupied Queens for seven years until they were completely evacuated in November 1783, leaving a ravaged countryside. In Flushing, the Friends Meeting House was taken over briefly by British troops and used as a hospital.

87. *Flushing Journal* (March 22, 1862).

88. *Flushing Journal* (December 24, 1864).

89. Seyfried, *The Civil War Era in Flushing,* 153. Mainly, Seyfried says, this meant renovation, change of ministers, etc.; also adding that "these events are sparingly chronicled."

90. *Flushing Journal* (January 4, 1862); cited by Seyfried.

91. *Flushing Journal* (October 19, 1861); cited by Seyfried. For more on First Baptist, see Rev. MacKenzie Pier, "First Baptist Church of Flushing: A Portrait of Heaven," Community Transformation Papers for Eastern Baptist Theological Seminary (October 1998).

92. Flushing, Old Town Records, in the New York City Municipal Archives. For an excellent study of a similarly diverse city's struggle with pluralism in the nineteenth century in which Irish and German Catholic immigrants also staged a major political turnaround, see David A. Gerber, *The Making of an American Pluralism: Buffalo, New York, 1825–60* (Urbana: University of Illinois Press, 1989).

93. Jim Driscoll, Research Director of Queens Historical Society, interview with author, March 20, 2001.

94. Mandeville, *Flushing, Past and Present*.

95. J. Carpenter Smith, *History of Saint George's Parish, Flushing Long Island* (Flushing, N.Y., 1897); Henry D. Waller, *History of the Town of Flushing Long Island, New York* (Flushing, N.Y., 1899).

96. Rev. Hubert S. Wood, sermon at St. George's Episcopal Church on the occasion of Flushing's Centennial celebration as an incorporated village in 1837; cited in the *Long Island Daily Star* (November 8, 1937).

2. Heralding the "World of Tomorrow": Religion and Community in Flushing, 1898–1965

1. Jon A. Peterson and Vincent F. Seyfried, "A Research Guide to the History of the Borough of Queens: Bibliography, Chronology, and Other Aids," Department of History, Queens College (Flushing, N.Y., 1987).

2. Darby Richardson, "Illustrated Flushing and Vicinity," Businessmen's Association of Flushing (1917).

3. Alison Isenberg, *Downtown America: A History of the Place and the People Who Made It* (Chicago: University of Chicago Press, 2004), 142.

4. Flushing Chamber of Commerce, "So This Is Flushing" (June 1941).

5. Thomas Merton, *The Seven Storey Mountain: An Autobiography of Faith* (New York: Harcourt Brace, 1948), 8–13.

6. Donald Miller, *Lewis Mumford: A Life* (New York: Grove, 2002), 4, 11.

7. Rabbi Albert Thaler, "Temple Gates of Prayer . . . One Hundred Years," Flushing Jewish Community Council News, *Tishrei-Cheshvan* 5760 (September–December 1999).

8. Bernard Rosenwald, President of Kissena Jewish Center, interview with author, July 1999.

9. Madeline B. Valles, "A History of Flushing," MA thesis, Columbia University (Flushing, N.Y., 1938), 113–114.

10. Robert A. Caro, *The Power Broker: Robert Moses and the Fall of New York* (New York: Knopf, 1974), 1082.

11. Ibid., 1083.

12. F. Scott Fitzgerald, *The Great Gatsby* (1925; New York, 1991), 27–28.

13. Tom Johnson and Lance Bird, producers and directors, "The World of Tomorrow," an American Portrait video by Direct Cinema Limited, narrated by Jason Robards (1984).

14. Robert W. Rydell, *All the World's a Fair: Visions of Empire at American International Expositions, 1876–1916* (Chicago: University of Chicago Press, 1984), 237.

15. Robert W. Rydell, *World of Fairs: The Century-of-Progress Expositions* (Chicago: University of Chicago Press, 1993), 8–11.

16. Warren I. Susman, "The People's Fair: Cultural Contradictions of a Consumer Society," in *Dawn of a New Day: The New York World's Fair, 1939/40,* ed. Helen A. Harrison (New York: NYU Press, 1980), 19; Warren I. Susman, ed., *Culture and Commitment, 1929–1945* (New York: Braziller, 1973).

17. Rydell, *World of Fairs*, 132–133.

18. Ibid., 3.

19. J. Terry Todd, "Imagining the Future of American Religion at the New York World's Fair, 1939–40," Ph.D. diss., Columbia University (New York, 1996); J. Terry Todd, "The Temple of Religion and the Politics of Religious Pluralism: Judeo-Christian America at the 1939–1940 New York World's Fair," in *After Pluralism: Reimagining Religious Engagement,* ed. Courtney Bender and Pamela E. Klassen (New York: Columbia University Press, 2010).

20. Todd, "Imagining the Future of American Religion at the New York World's Fair."

21. Temple of Religion, Officially Licensed Post Card of the New York World's Fair 1939.

22. Todd, "Imagining the Future of American Religion at the New York World's Fair," 99.

23. *Official Guide Book of the New York World's Fair 1939*, 2nd ed., 136.

24. Todd, "Imagining the Future of American Religion at the New York World's Fair." Also see Deborah Dash Moore, *GI Jews: How World War II Changed a Generation* (Cambridge, Mass., 2004); and David Gelernter, *1939, The Lost World of the Fair* (New York: Free Press, 1995), 49–51. Gelernter points to American "civic religion" and the "American Way of Life" in his discussion of religion around the 1939–1940 fair, but he is unaware of the origins of the terms.

25. John Higham, *History: Professional Scholarship in America* (Baltimore, Md., 1965), 221–224. Also see Martin E. Marty, *The One and the Many: America's Struggle for the Common Good* (Cambridge, Mass.: Harvard University Press, 1997), 83–85; Bernard Sternsher, *Consensus, Conflict, and American Historians* (Bloomington: Indiana University Press, 1975); and R. Stephen Warner, "Changes in the Civic Role of Religion," in *Diversity and Its Discontents: Cultural Conflict and Common Ground in Contemporary American Society,* ed. Neil J. Smelser and Jeffrey C. Alexander (Princeton, N.J.: Princeton University Press, 1999).

26. Will Herberg, *Protestant-Catholic-Jew: An Essay in American Religious Sociology* (Chicago: University of Chicago Press, 1955); Oscar Handlin, *The Uprooted: The Epic Story of the Great Migrations That Made the American People* (New York: Little, Brown, 1951).

27. Herberg, *Protestant-Catholic-Jew,* 84.

28. Robert Wuthnow, "Mobilizing Civic Engagement: The Changing Impact of Religious Involvement," in *Civic Engagement in American Democracy,* ed. Theda Skocpol and Morris P. Fiorina (Washington, D.C.: Brookings Institution, 1999), 331–332.

29. "Historical Background of Flushing Meadows Revealed by Halleran: Site of Revolutionary Days and Early Colonization of Long Island," *North Shore Daily Journal* (May 21, 1937).

30. Jesse T. Todd, research notes from "Imagining the Future of American Religion at the New York World's Fair, 1939–40."

31. *New York Times* (April 30, 1937); cited by Todd, "Imagining the Future of American Religion at the New York World's Fair," 85–86.

32. Rydell, *All the World's a Fair,* 5.

33. Neil Harris, "Great American Fairs and American Cities: The Role of Chicago's Columbian Exposition," in *Cultural Excursions: Marketing Appetites and Cultural Tastes in America* (Chicago: University of Chicago Press, 1990), 125.

34. Rydell, *All the World's a Fair,* 39–40, 235–237.

35. Johnson and Bird, "The World of Tomorrow."

36. Rabbi Albert Thaler, interview with author, October 23, 2007.

37. Paul Graziano, 2001 Green Party candidate for City Council District 20, interview with author, July 29, 2001.

38. Henry Steele Commager, *The Search for a Usable Past and Other Essays in Historiography* (New York: Knopf, 1967). Also see Eric Hobsbawm and Terence Ranger, eds., *The Invention of Tradition* (Cambridge: Cambridge University Press, 1983); Michael Kammen, *Mystic Chords of Memory: The Transformation of Tradition in American Culture* (New York: Knopf, 1991); and John Bodnar, *Remaking America: Public Memory, Commemoration, and Patriotism in the Twentieth Century* (Princeton, N.J.: Princeton University Press, 1992).

39. John Higham, "The Ethnic Historical Society in Changing Times," *Journal of American Ethnic History,* 13, no. 2 (Winter 1994): 31. Also see Edward N. Saveth, *American Historians and European Immigrants, 1875–1925* (New York: Columbia University Press, 1948); David J. Russo, *Keepers of Our Past: Local Historical Writing in the United States, 1820s–1930s* (Westport, Conn.: Greenwood, 1988); John J. Appel, *Immigrant Historical Societies in the United States, 1880–1950* (New York: Arno, 1980); Leslie W. Dunlap, *American Historical Societies, 1790–1860* (Madison, Wis., 1944); and Lana Ruegamer, "Historical Societies and Professional Historians: Another Part of the Forest," *OAH Newsletter* (August 1985).

40. David M. Hummon, *Commonplaces: Community Ideology and Identity in American Culture* (Albany: SUNY Press, 1990), 5.

41. Ibid.

42. Final Report of the New York State Joint Legislative Committee for the Celebration of the 300th Anniversary of the Signing of the Flushing Remonstrance, State of New York, Legislative Document (1958), no. 37.

43. "President Joins in Tribute to Remonstrance: 3,000 Hear Message at Bowne House," *Long Island Star-Journal* (October 11, 1957).

44. Caro, *The Power Broker,* 1091–1093.

45. Ileen Sheppard, "Icons and Images: The Cultural Legacy of the 1965/65 World's Fair," in *Remembering the Future: The New York World's Fair from 1939 to 1964,* ed. *Queens Museum* (New York, 1989), 179.

46. Morris Dickstein, "From the Thirties to the Sixties: The New York World's Fair in Its Own Time," in *Remembering the Future: The New York World's Fair from 1939 to 1964,* ed. *Queens Museum* (New York, 1989), 26.

47. Ibid., 38.

48. Katherine Kuh, "The Day Pop Art Died," *Design in America* (May 23, 1964); cited by Sheppard, "Icons and Images," 172.

49. Sheppard, "Icons and Images," 180.

50. Ibid.

51. Dickstein, "From the Thirties to the Sixties," 34.

52. "Flushing's Parking Woes: 6,000 Women Shoppers Demand City Build Field Before Christmas," *Long Island Star Journal* (August 14, 1951); "Official Ground Breaking! Welcome . . . the Flushing Parking Field! [advertisement sponsored by the Flushing Merchants Association, Inc.]," *Long Island Star Journal* (June 2, 1953); "Congregation Fears Progress Is Putting the Squeeze on It," *Newsday* (September 20, 1985). Also based on my recording of Mr. Jay Williams's history and slide show of Macedonia AME on May 11, 2001, which is given regularly to new members of the church after ninety days of attendance and orientation; and Rev. Nicholas Genevieve-Tweed, pastor of Macedonia AME, interview with author, May 10, 2001.

53. Robert W. Rydell, "African Americans in the World of Tomorrow," in Rydell, *World of Fairs.*

54. Flushing Town Hall, Flushing Town Council on Culture and the Arts, "The Queens Jazz Trail," 2nd ed. (Flushing, N.Y., 1998).

3. Beyond Protestant-Catholic-Jew: The Immigration Act of 1965 and the Religions of New Immigrants in Flushing

1. Portions of this chapter were presented at the 2001 Annual Meeting of the American Historical Association in a paper entitled "Neighborhood Narratives in the City of Gods: Religious Freedom, Immigration, and Pluralism in Flushing, New York," for a session cosponsored by the Immigration and Ethnic History Society entitled "New Narratives for an Old Story: Moments of Peak Immigration Over Three Centuries of U.S. History." Session participants

included Jon Gjerde, David A. Gerber, Suzanne Sinke, R. Scott Hanson, and Douglas M. Bradburn. For more thorough discussion of this section in general, see Philip Gleason, "American Identity and Americanization" in *Harvard Encyclopedia of American Ethnic Groups,* ed. Stephan Thernstrom (Cambridge, Mass.: Harvard University Press, 1980); and Philip Gleason, *Speaking of Diversity: Language and Ethnicity in Twentieth-Century America* (Baltimore, Md.: Johns Hopkins University Press, 1992).

2. For more on this period, see David M. Reimers, *Unwelcome Strangers: American Identity and the Turn Against Immigration* (New York: Columbia University Press, 1998), 25–26; and Thomas Alexander Aleinikoff, David A. Martin, and Hiroshi Motomura, eds., *Immigration and Citizenship: Process and Policy,* 4th ed., American Casebook Series (St. Paul, Minn.: West Group, 1998), 168–171.

3. Reimers, *Unwelcome Strangers,* 26–27.

4. See note 14 in the Introduction for sources and explanation of these studies.

5. See Scott Cummings, *Left Behind in Rosedale: Race Relations and the Collapse of Community Institutions* (Boulder, Colo.: Westview, 1998).

6. For a more detailed discussion of this trend, see Alison Isenberg, *Downtown America: A History of the Place and People Who Made It* (Chicago: University of Chicago Press, 2004).

7. Ibid., 10.

8. Rev. Dr. Timothy P. Mitchell, Ebenezer Missionary Baptist Church, interview with author, August 17, 2001. Also see "Tricentennial Celebration: African Americans in Flushing, New York—1694–1994," in *An African American Heritage Project of the Ebenezer Missionary Baptist Church Historical Commission, 1992–1994.*

9. "Minister Says Urban Renewal Only Means Negro Removal," *Long Island Star Journal* (May 1, 1968).

10. Evangeline Egglezos, executive director of Bowne House Historical Society, interview with author, June 29, 2001.

11. Robert Kalish, "Flushing Center: A Study and a Proposal with Recommendations and a Design Solution for a Transportation Center and the Improvement of Pedestrian Movement with Suggestions Concerning the Currently Proposed Bus Terminal," MA paper, Graduate School of Architecture, Pratt Institute (Brooklyn, 1973). Also based on my interview with Julia Harrison, former member of the Council of the City of New York (1986–2000), 20th Council District, July 3, 2001. I am indebted to Mrs. Harrison for sharing a copy of this report.

12. Ibid.

13. For more on community facilities, see the "Growing Pains" section of Chapter 4.

14. See, for instance, Walter Laidlaw, ed., *Population of the City of New York, 1890–1930* (New York, 1932); Works Progress Administration (WPA) Federal Writer's Project, Historic Records Survey, Church Records Series, 1936–1942, published as *Inventory of Church Archives* and *Guide to Vital Statistics in the City*

of New York Churches (New York, 1942). Also see Kevin J. Christiano, *Religious Diversity and Social Change: American Cities, 1890–1906* (New York: Cambridge University Press, 1987); and Jon Butler, "Protestant Success in the New American City, 1870–1920: The Anxious Secrets of Rev. Walter Laidlaw, Ph.D." in *New Directions in American Religious History,* ed. Harry S. Stout and D. G. Hart (New York: Oxford University Press, 1997).

15. "Religious Census Taken in Flushing," *Long Island Star Journal* (August 11, 1962). I am indebted to Ms. Joanne Claasen, former secretary of the Protestant Reformed Dutch Church, and former pastor Rev. Dr. Elton J. Bruins for their help in locating a copy of Mr. Van Elk's "Religious Census Report"— now in the Hope College Collection of the Joint Archives of Holland at Hope College, in Holland, Michigan (where Rev. Dr. Bruins has been a professor of Old Testament studies). Mr. Van Elk went on to become Rev. Paul Van Elk and served as pastor of Bradley Gardens Reformed Church in Bridgewater, New Jersey, for many years.

16. Portions of this section were presented in a paper entitled "Intra- and Extra-Religioethnic Encounters: Responses to Plurality Among Hindu Temples on Bowne Street in Flushing, New York," for a session on "Hinduism in America: Constructing Sacred Space and Collective Identity" in the North American Religions Section of the 1999 Annual Meeting of the American Academy of Religion. Session participants included Diana L. Eck, Vasudha Narayanan, Mary McGee, R. Scott Hanson, Prema Kurien, and Raymond B. Williams. Also see R. Scott Hanson, "Temples and Mosques of New York City," Pluralism Project Research Notes, in the multimedia CD-ROM by Diana L. Eck, *On Common Ground: World Religions in America* (New York, 1997).

17. For more on the Vedanta Society, see Carl T. Jackson, *Vedanta for the West: The Ramakrishna Movement in the U.S.* (Bloomington: Indiana University Press, 1994).

18. Emanuel Kanter, "Racial Groups in New York I," Record Sub-Series #410649, "Hindus in New York: Contributions to American Culture," WPA Federal Writers' Project, NYC Unit, March 20, 1936.

19. See Karen Isaksen Leonard, *Making Ethnic Choices: California's Punjabi Mexican Americans* (Philadelphia: Temple University Press, 1992); and Vivek Bald, *Bengali Harlem and the Lost Histories of South Asian America* (Cambridge, Mass.: Harvard University Press, 2013). For more on Sikhism in the United States, also see John Stratton Hawley and Gurinder Singh Mann, eds., *Studying the Sikhs: Issues for North America* (Albany: SUNY Press, 1993).

20. For more on South Asians in New York, see Maxine P. Fisher, *The Indians of New York City: A Study of Immigrants from India* (New York: Columbia University Press, 1980); and Madhulika S. Khandelwal, "Indian Immigrants in Queens, New York City: Patterns of Spatial Concentration and Distribution, 1965–90," in *Nation and Migration: The Politics of Space in the South Asian Diaspora,* ed. Peter van der Veer (Philadelphia: University of Pennsylvania Press, 1995). Also see Johanna Lessinger, *From the Ganges to the Hudson: Indian Immigrants in New York City* (Boston: Allyn

and Bacon, 1995); and John Stratton Hawley, "Global Hinduism in Gotham," in *Asian-American Religion: The Making and Remaking of Borders and Boundaries,* ed. Tony Carnes and Fenggang Yang (New York: NYU Press, 2004).

21. Khandelwal, "Indian Immigrants in Queens," 184.

22. Ibid., 186–187.

23. Portions of this section were presented in a paper entitled "Intra- and Extra-Religioethnic Encounters: Responses to Plurality Among Hindu Temples on Bowne Street in Flushing, New York." See note 16, above.

24. Bharati Mukherjee, *Jasmine* (New York: Grove, 1989), 146.

25. Ibid., 142.

26. Ibid.

27. Rekha Malhotra, interview with author, April 25, 2001.

28. Ibid. There is a common misconception that Jackson Heights (not Flushing) is the center of Indian New York, but, as Malhotra explains, it is really just a commercial area: "I've always been proud of being from Flushing. I've always, like, it's always represented an Indian community to me. I've always hated the fact that Jackson Heights gets a lot of [credit], because it's just a shopping center when people live in Flushing. And I hate when like, you know, high-brow, second-generation Indian academics keep looking to Jackson Heights and miss the mark—they miss it, they don't get it. And I always say, it's not Jackson Heights—people *shop* in Jackson Heights, people *live* in Flushing. You need to go to Flushing to find out what's really going on. You know, Jackson Heights is so arbitrary, I don't even know how it happened."

29. For a more detailed history of the Ganesha temple, see R. Scott Hanson, "Sri Maha Vallabha Ganapati Devasthanam of Flushing, New York" in *Hindu Diasporas: Global Perspectives,* ed. T. S. Rukmani (Montreal: Concordia University Press, 1999). The book grew out of the International Conference on the Hindu Diaspora that was held in August 1997 at Concordia University in Montreal.

30. The stone sanctum of Ganesha was made in India and transported to be reassembled in New York. It is the only stone sanctum in the United States; all others are brick and mortar.

31. Henry D. Waller, *History of the Town of Flushing, Long Island* (Flushing, N.Y., 1899), 201. Also see the *Belcher Atlas of the Borough of Queens, Third Ward, City of New York,* vol. 3 (New York, 1904), double-page plate no. 8, 2nd page. I am indebted to Jim Driscoll, research director of the Queens Historical Society, for these references.

32. See "First Church of Nazarene Opens Building Drive," *Long Island Press* (November 20, 1954); and "Wanna Buy a Church? Russian Orthodox Building for Sale," *Long Island Star Journal* (December 27, 1971). I am indebted to Jim Driscoll, research director of the Queens Historical Society, for these references.

33. For a discussion of his association with Dr. Alagappan and the temple, see C. V. Narasimhan, *The United Nations at Fifty: Recollections* (Delhi: Konark, 1996), 242.

34. Dr. Alagappa Alagappan, interview with author, June 30, 1997.

35. Dr. Alagappa Alagappan, interview with author, July 1994.

36. Ibid.

37. Raymond Brady Williams, "Training Religious Specialists for a Transnational Hinduism," *Journal of the American Academy of Religion* 66, no. 4 (Winter 1998): 842. For a complete treatment of Swaminarayan religion, see Raymond Brady Williams, *A New Face of Hinduism: The Swaminarayan Religion* (New York: Cambridge University Press, 1984).

38. This was also around the same time as the "dotbuster" incident of 1987 in Jersey City, New Jersey, when a gang of young white men and women focused horrific nativism on the *bindi* (the traditional decorative dot Hindu women wear on their forehead) and perpetuated racial violence on South Asians in the area. One man was murdered; another was beaten in front of a fire station and left for dead. The violence subsided when six suspects were successfully prosecuted, but the case changed many lives and sparked major activism in the South Asian community.

39. Anita Oberwiler, interview with author, October 31, 1999.

40. For a full account of Swaminarayan "transnational ethnicity," see Williams, "Training Religious Specialists for a Transnational Hinduism." For a discussion of NRIs, see Madhulika S. Khandelwal, "Indian Networks in the United States: Class and Transnational Identities," in *Immigrants and Immigration Policy: Individual Skills, Family Ties, and Group Identities,* ed. Duleep and Wunnava (Greenwich, Conn.: JAI, 1996), 128.

41. Based on interviews with Mr. Giri Chabra, president of the Hindu Center. Also see http://www.hinducenter.com/about/history.htm.

42. The present office of the temple also used to be the national headquarters for another Hindu temple: the Shri Vishwa Seva Ashram (a group devoted to the teachings of a saint from Uijjain in the state of Madhya Pradesh), which later moved to nearby Corona-Elmhurst.

43. Dr. Uma Mysorekar, in Somini Sengupta, "A Snapshot of World Faith: On One Queens Block, Many Prayers Are Spoken," *New York Times* (November 7, 1999).

44. Wilma Treadwell, in Ji-Yeon Yuh, "The Call to Worship Testing Tolerance; Neighbors Ask Church Limits," *Newsday, Queens Edition* (February 23, 1990).

45. Rosemary Thomson, in ibid.

46. Associated Press, "Baptists Say Hindus Need Prayers," *New York Times* (October 22, 1999). Also see Gustav Niebuhr, "Baptists' Ardor for Evangelism Angers Some Jews and Hindus," *New York Times* (December 4, 1999).

47. Roshni Abayasekara, "The New New Yorker/Enriching a Borough's Spirit: Ganesha Temple Serves as Bridge for Hindus and Others in Queens," *Newsday* (January 31, 2001).

48. http://www.indianet.com/ganesh/.

49. Dr. Alagappa Alagappan, interview with author, June 30, 1997.

50. See Dr. Alagappa Alagappan, "Some Guidelines for Management of Hindu Temples in North America: Relevance of New York Ganesha Temple Experience," first presented to the Council of Temples as a background document in May 1994 (revised May 1997).

51. Alagappan, interview with author, July 1994.

52. Ibid.

53. Douglas Martin, "Alagappa Alagappan, 88, Dies; Founded Hindu Temples Across U.S.," *New York Times* (November 1, 2014).

54. Raymond Brady Williams, *Religions of Immigrants from India and Pakistan: New Threads in the American Tapestry* (Cambridge: Cambridge University Press, 1988), 63.

55. Madhulika S. Khandelwal, "Hindu Religious Activities in Queens," *Asian/American Center Working Papers,* Queens College/CUNY (New York, 1989), 55.

56. Rekha Malhotra, interview with author, April 25, 2001.

57. Ibid. The *kara* is one of the "five K's of Sikhism" that devout Sikhs (initiated *Khalsa* Sikhs) always wear: the other four are the *kachha* (underpants), *kanga* (comb), *kesh* (uncut hair), and *kirpan* (ceremonial dagger). But *all* Sikhs (and many Punjabi Hindus) wear the *kara*.

58. The Richmond Hill gurdwara was destroyed in a fire on March 8, 2002—a tragedy made worse by a rash of Sikh bashing following September 11, 2001, when ignorant vindictive individuals mistook turban-wearing Sikhs for Arab Muslims because they "look like Osama bin Laden." See Jacob H. Fries, "Fire Destroys a Sikh Temple in Queens, Injuring 6 Priests," *New York Times* (March 9, 2002).

59. Rekha Malhotra, interview with author, April 25, 2001. While caste may not enter into everyday Indian American life, there are still some manifestations and vestiges. Another temple in nearby Woodside, Queens, the Sri Guru Ravidas Sabha, was founded later by members of the so-called Untouchable *Camar* caste of leatherworkers who are devoted to the teachings of the sixteenth-century North Indian poet-saint Ravidas, who rejected the hierarchically variegated Hindu worldview of caste distinctions. For more on Ravidas, see John Stratton Hawley and Mark Juergensmeyer, *Songs of the Saints of India* (New York: Oxford University Press, 1988).

60. Ibid.

61. For a look at (mostly Latino) gangs in Flushing in the 1980s and 1990s, see National Public Radio correspondent Maria Hinojosa, *Crews: Gang Members Talk to Maria Hinojosa* (New York: Harcourt, 1995).

62. Rekha Malhotra, interview with author, April 25, 2001.

63. For more info on Basement Bhangra, see http://www.sangament.com. Rekha also appeared in the recent film *American Desi* and in a PBS video for WNET/Channel 13, *Desi: South Asians in New York*.

64. This section is based on my interviews with Pritpal "Paul" Singh of Gurdwara Singh Sabha.

65. Susan Saulny, "In Aftermath of Temple Fire, Sikhs Pray, and Share Sorrow," *New York Times* (March 10, 2002).

66. For more on Islam in America, see Williams, *Religions of Immigrants from India and Pakistan*; and Yvonne Yazbeck Haddad, ed., *The Muslims of America* (New York: Oxford University Press, 1991).

67. Information from this section is taken from interviews with Mohammad T. Sherwani, director of the Muslim Center of New York, as well as from issues of *Markaz, the* journal of the Muslim Center of New York, and "History" at http://www.muslimcenter.org/.

68. Masjid Al Haram is the most sacred mosque in Islam, which Muslims try to make a pilgrimage to once in their lifetime. It contains the *Ka'ba*, the cube-shaped chamber to which all Muslims turn to face in prayer five times a day.

69. *Markaz,* journal of the Muslim Center of New York, "Ground Breaking Special," vol. 12, no. 1 (February 1990).

70. *Markaz,* journal of the Muslim Center of New York, "Inauguration Special," vol. 17, no. 5 (October 1997).

71. David M. Herszenhorn, "New Skyline View: A Minaret Rises Over Main Street," *New York Times* (September 1997).

72. Anonymous interview outside MCNY during *Jumu'ah,* August 25, 2000.

73. Ahmad Wais Afzali, assistant imam of Masjid Hazrat-I-Abubakr, interview with author, September 6, 2001.

74. The smaller mosque is named after Al-Sayyid Mohammad Jamal al-Din Afghani, a nineteenth-century Afghani Islamic philosopher, writer, orator, and journalist who led reform, liberation, and pan-Islamic movements and stressed modernization.

75. Ahmad Wais Afzali, interview with author, September 6, 2001.

76. Ibid.

77. Ibid. Italics added.

78. Ibid. Italics added.

79. Also see Chapter 5 for post–September 11 reactions.

80. Madhulika S. Khandelwal, "Indian Immigrants in Queens, New York City: Patterns of Spatial Concentration and Distribution, 1965–90," in *Nation and Migration: The Politics of Space in the South Asian Diaspora,* ed. Peter van der Veer (Philadelphia: University of Pennsylvania Press, 1995), 181.

81. Arun Peter Lobo, Joseph J. Salvo, and Vicky Virgin, *The Newest New Yorkers, 1990–1994: An Analysis of Immigration to NYC in the Early 1990s* (New York: New York City Department of City Planning, 1996), 133.

82. Corona-Elmhurst, Queens, though less extreme and more recent than Flushing, is another nearby mini–South Asia. See Aseem Chhabra, "A Calm Corner Keeps an Eye on a Violent Subcontinent," *New York Times* (March 10, 2002).

83. The term has gained more currency in the United States with recent films like *American Desi* and *ABCD: American-Born Confused Desi* (in which the

Hindu Center in Flushing was featured), as well as PBS videos like *Desi: South Asians in New York*.

84. Susan Wu Rathbone, interview with author, October 26, 2006.

85. Susan Woo Rathbone, "Flushing's 'Auntie Wu' Remembers Her First Chinese New Year in America," *Flushing Times* (February 10, 1994).

86. Ibid.

87. Susan Wu Rathbone, "Social and Political Changes in Queens Chinese Immigrant Women From 1946 to 1989," paper presented at the Fourth International Interdisciplinary Congress on Women, June 3–7, 1990.

88. John Kuo Wei Tchen, in *Harmony & Spirit: Chinese Americans in New York*, WNET/Channel 13 PBS video (New York, 1997); also see Frederick M. Binder and David M. Reimers, *All the Nations Under Heaven: An Ethnic and Racial History of New York City* (New York: Columbia University Press, 1995), 231–232. For an excellent study of attitudes about China prior to the first Chinese immigrants, see John Kuo Wei Tchen, *New York Before Chinatown: Orientalism and the Shaping of American Culture, 1776–1882* (Baltimore, Md.: Johns Hopkins University Press, 1999).

89. Peter Kwong, *The New Chinatown* (New York: Noonday, 1987).

90. For the early history of Chinese in New York, see Tchen, *New York Before Chinatown*; and Tyler Anbinder, *Five Points: The Nineteenth-Century New York City Neighborhood That Invented Tap Dance, Stole Elections, and Became the World's Most Notorious Slum* (New York: Plume, 2002).

91. A "Chop Suey" sign is visible (with magnification) just north of Roosevelt Avenue on Main Street between a Western Union and a Florsheim Shoes store in a picture from August 9, 1930. A widely popular Chinese American restaurant called Lum's opened in the early 1960s and was considered by many to be the best in town (until more authentic Chinese restaurants began to open in the 1980s and 1990s). For a longer history of Chinese restaurants in America, see Gish Jen, "A Short History of the Chinese Restaurant," *Slate.com* (April 27, 2005). Jen's article was based on an exhibit entitled "Have You Eaten Yet?" at New York's Museum of Chinese in the Americas.

92. Ibid. Also see Hsiang-Shui Chen, *Chinatown No More: Taiwan Immigrants in Contemporary New York* (Ithaca, N.Y.: Cornell University Press, 1992).

93. Binder and Reimers, *All the Nations Under Heaven*, 232. Also see Fiona Chi-Hsin Yung, "The Far East," *Time Out New York 285* (March 8–15, 2001): 22–23.

94. Paul Graziano, 2001 Green Party candidate for City Council District 20, interview with author, July 29, 2001.

95. Evangeline Egglezos, executive director of Bowne House Historical Society, interview with author, June 29, 2001.

96. Tchen, in *Harmony & Spirit: Chinese Americans in New York*; Binder and Reimers, *All the Nations Under Heaven*, 231–232; Peter Kwong, *The New Chinatown*; Chen, *Chinatown No More*; Amanda Hesser, "A Hungry Explorer in New York's 3 Chinatowns," *New York Times* (May 2, 2001).

97. Center for an Urban Future, "A World of Opportunity," February 2007. http://www.nycfuture.org.

98. Yung, "The Far East," 22–23.

99. Fenggang Yang, *Chinese Christians in America: Conversion, Assimilation, and Adhesive Identities* (University Park: Pennsylvania State University Press, 1999).

100. Rev. Canon Edmund B. Der, interim rector of St. George's Episcopal Church, interview with author, September 6, 2001.

101. For a discussion of the preceding period, see Timothy Tseng, "Chinese Protestant Nationalism in the United States, 1880–1927," in *New Spiritual Homes: Religion and Asian Americans,* ed. David K. Yoo (Honolulu: University of Hawai'i Press, 1999). Also see Carolyn E. Chen, "Getting Saved in America: Religious Conversion to Evangelical Protestantism Among Taiwanese Immigrants," dissertation, University of California at Berkeley, Department of Sociology, 2000.

102. Man-Li Lin, interview with author, November 4, 2006.

103. For more on the Fo Guang Shan temple, see http://www.ibps.org/newyork/English/e-aboutus.htm. For the Hsi Lai Temple, also see Irene Lin, "Journey to the Far West: Chinese Buddhism in America," in *New Spiritual Homes: Religion and Asian Americans,* ed. David K. Yoo (Honolulu: University of Hawai'i Press, 1999); and Chen, "Getting Saved in America." For a good general history of Buddhism in America, see Rick Fields, *How the Swans Came to the Lake: A Narrative History of Buddhism in America* (1981; Boston: Shambhala, 1992); and, for the earlier period, see Thomas A. Tweed, *The American Encounter with Buddhism, 1844–1912: Victorian Culture and the Limits of Dissent* (1992; Chapel Hill: University of North Carolina Press, 2000).

104. Weishan Huang, "The Making of a Promised Land: Religious Responses to Gentrification and Neighborhood Ethnic Diversity," September 22, 2008, http://www.thefreelibrary.com.

105. Eileen Markey, "Buddhist Sect Flowers in Flushing: First Official Shaolin Temple Outside China," *Newsday* (April 17, 2000).

106. Man-Li Lin, interview with author, November 4, 2006.

107. Timothy Tseng, "Chinese Protestant Nationalism in the United States, 1880–1927," in *New Spiritual Homes: Religion and Asian Americans,* ed. David K. Yoo (Honolulu: University of Hawai'i Press, 1999).

108. Rev. Canon Edmund B. Der, interim rector of St. George's Episcopal Church, interview with author, September 6, 2001.

109. Ibid.

110. Chen, "Getting Saved in America." Chen found that conversion to ethnic religious institutions facilitates the adjustment of many Taiwanese immigrants to the United States and that many parents often turn to Chinese Christian churches to deal with family issues.

111. Ibid.

112. Fenggang Yang, "Tenacious Unity in a Contentious Community: Cultural and Religious Dynamics in a Chinese Christian Church," in *Gatherings in*

Diaspora: Religious Communities and the New Immigration, ed. R. Stephen Warner and Judith G. Wittner (Philadelphia: Temple University Press, 1998), 342–345.

113. Rev. David M. Kelley, interview with author, July 2001. Rev. Kelley, a former minister at First Congregational Church, had lived in Japan in the early 1960s and became acquainted with Japanese immigrants upon his return to Flushing.

114. Marleen Kassel, "Two Japanese New Religions in Flushing: The Tenrikyo Mission and the Nichiren Shoshu Daihozan Myosetsu Temple," *Long Island Historical Journal 5, no. 1* (Fall 1992): 82.

115. Ibid., 87.

116. For more on Soka Gakkai, see Phillip Hammond and David Machacek, *Soka Gakkai In America: Accommodation and Conversion* (New York: Oxford University Press, 1999).

117. Kassel, "Two Japanese New Religions," 87–88.

118. For a helpful overview of this chapter of the UN General Assembly's history, see the 1939–1940/1964–1965 World's Fair Exhibit in the permanent collection of the Queens Museum of Art, located in the former site of the General Assembly and New York City Building of the 1939 World's Fair in Flushing Meadows–Corona Park.

119. Illsoo Kim, "The Koreans: Small Business in an Urban Frontier," in *New Immigrants in New York,* ed. Nancy Foner (New York: Columbia University Press, 1987).

120. Binder and Reimers, *All the Nations Under Heaven,* 235–236.

121. Rev. David M. Kelley, interview with author, July 2001.

122. "East Meets West at Flushing—Fair Spurred Migration," *Sunday News* (June 16, 1974).

123. Rosalia Bacarella, "A Family of Nations Settles in Flushing," *Queens Tribune* (June 5–11, 1980). The 1980 Census of Population and Housing shows there were 5,209 Chinese, 4,246 Indians, and 3,524 Koreans in Flushing at the time.

124. John Choe, interview with author, April 11, 2009.

125. Rev. Nam Soo Kim, Full Gospel New York Church, interview with author, July 26, 2001.

126. Jin-Hong Kim, "The Great Christian Revival in Korea," in *The Asian Christian History Reader,* 2 vols., ed. Jin-Hong Kim (Flushing, N.Y., 1999); Ho-Youn Kwon, Kwang Chung Kim, and R. Stephen Warner, eds., *Korean Americans and Their Religions: Pilgrims and Missionaries from a Different Shore* (University Park: Pennsylvania State University Press, 2001). Also based on my interview with Rev. Nam Soo Kim, Full Gospel New York Church, July 26, 2001.

127. For more on Won Buddhism (Won is Korean for circle), see Bok In Kim, "Won Buddhism in the United States," in *Korean Americans and Their Religions: Pilgrims and Missionaries from a Different Shore,* ed. Ho-Youn Kwon et al. (University Park: Pennsylvania State University Press, 2001).

128. Ho-Youn Kwon, Kwang Chung Kim, and R. Stephen Warner, "Korean American Religion in International Perspective," in *Korean Americans and Their Religions: Pilgrims and Missionaries from a Different Shore,* ed. Ho-Youn Kwon et al. (University Park: Pennsylvania State University Press, 2001), 8.

129. Assemblies of God USA and Assemblies of God organizations around the world make up the world's largest Pentecostal denomination, with some thirty-eight million members and adherents.

130. Rev. Nam Soo Kim, Full Gospel New York Church, interview with author, July 26, 2001.

131. John Choe, interview with author, April 11, 2009.

132. Ibid.

133. Sister Eve Gilchrist OP, "First Korean Parish Is Planned for Flushing," *Tablet* (August 22, 1987).

134. Pyong Gap Min, "The Structure and Social Functions of Korean Immigrant Churches in the United States," *International Migration Review* 26, no. 4 (Winter 1992): 1370–1394. It should be noted that Min is the expert on Koreans in Flushing (if not Korean Americans in general): he also lives in Flushing and teaches at Queens College.

135. Ibid.

136. Ibid.

137. Ibid.

138. Omar M. McRoberts, *Streets of Glory: Church and Community in a Black Urban Neighborhood* (Chicago: University of Chicago Press, 2003), 59. Also see my discussion of "*de facto* congregationalism" in the section "How Pluralism 'Works'" in Chapter 4.

139. "Bust of Cuban Hero: Castro's P.S. 20 Gift Stirs Controversy," *Long Island Star-Journal* (August 10, 1960).

140. Nicholas Hirshon, "Recalling How Queens Kids Met (and Liked) Dictator Fidel Castro in 1959," *Daily News* (March 9, 2008).

141. Elena Cata, interview with author, October 26, 2006.

142. Aleinikoff et al., *Immigration and Citizenship,* 169.

143. For more on Vatican II and Hispanics, see Jay P. Dolan, *The American Catholic Experience: A History from the Colonial Times to the Present* (Notre Dame, Ind.: University of Notre Dame Press, 1992), 427–428.

144. Father José R. Aldegundé, St. Michael's Roman Catholic Church, interview with author, August 17, 2001. Also based on information from "Centenary of St. Michael's Church, 1833–1933" and St. Michael's "Memory Book" of 1962.

145. Ibid.

146. Ibid.

147. Ibid.

148. Ibid.

4. A Blessing and a Curse? The Possibilities and Limits of Religious Pluralism

1. See Toni Schlesinger, "Shelter," *Village Voice* (November 10, 1998). Schlesinger, who is not alone in this characterization, mentions "Flushing, which is so *Blade Runner* with all the Asian and Spanish signs and the planes flying low." Also see *The City* (American Institute of City Planners, 1939).

2. Lawrence W. Levine charts the intellectual contexts and background of this heated period in "The Search for American Identity," part 3 of *The Opening of the American Mind: Canons, Culture, and History* (Boston:Beacon Press, 1996).

3. John Higham, *Strangers in the Land: Patterns of American Nativism, 1860–1925* (1955; New Brunswick, N.J.: Rutgers University Press, 1988), 4.

4. John Higham, "Instead of a Sequel, or How I Lost My Subject," *Reviews in American History* 28, no. 2 (June 2000): 327–328; Higham, *Strangers in the Land.* Also see Kathleen Neils Conzen, "Thomas and Znaniecki and the Historiography of American Immigration," *Journal of American Ethnic History* 16, no. 1 (Fall 1996): 16. Conzen refers to the 1990s as "a time when issues of immigration, pluralism, and national integration are once more at the center of national debate."

5. H. Richard Niebuhr, *The Kingdom of God in America* (New York: Harper & Brothers, 1937), 3.

6. John Courtney Murray, *We Hold These Truths: Catholic Reflections on the American Proposition* (New York: Sheed and Ward, 1960), 132.

7. For a longer account of my understanding of pluralism, see R. Scott Hanson, "Pluralism and Cosmopolitanism in American Thought," *History and Theory* (under review).

8. Somini Sengupta, "A Snapshot of World Faith: On One Queens Block, Many Prayers Are Spoken," *New York Times* (November 7, 1999). Also see J. H. Oppenheimer, "Religious Freedom: Where It Started and Where It Continues," *Queens Courier* (August 15, 1996): 14.

9. David A. Roozen, William McInney, and Jackson W. Carroll, *Varieties of Religious Presence* (New York, 1988); Robert Wuthnow, *The Restructuring of American Religion* (Princeton, N.J.: Princeton University Press, 1988).

10. Omar M. McRoberts, *Streets of Glory: Church and Community in a Black Urban Neighborhood* (Chicago: University of Chicago Press, 2003), 7.

11. Ibid., 9.

12. Ibid., 9–10.

13. Katie Day, *Faith on the Avenue: Religion on a City Street* (New York: Oxford University Press, 2014), 60–64.

14. I am reminded of the opening scene from the 2005 film *Crash*: "It's the sense of touch. . . . Any real city, you walk, you know? You brush past people, people bump into you. In LA, nobody touches you. Always behind this metal and glass. I think that we miss that touch so much, we crash into each other just so we can feel something."

15. See Robert J. Sampson, *Great American City: Chicago and the Enduring Neighborhood Effect* (Chicago: University of Chicago Press, 2014).

16. Julia Harrison, member of City Council District 20, in Jessica Kowal, "The Religion Zone: Flushing Residents Fed Up with Flocks of Faithful," *Newsday* (July 18, 1999).

17. Celia W. Dugger, "Queens Old-Timers Uneasy as Asian Influence Grows," *New York Times* (March 31, 1996). Also see Jonathan P. Hicks, "Anti-Asian Remarks an Issue in Primary," *New York Times* (September 4, 1997).

18. See Peter Brimelow, *Alien Nation: Common Sense About America's Immigration Disaster* (New York, 1995); Arthur M. Schlesinger Jr., *The Disuniting of America: Reflections on a Multicultural Society* (New York, 1992); Levine, *The Opening of the American Mind*; David M. Reimers, *Unwelcome Strangers: American Identity and the Turn Against Immigration* (New York, 1998); and Neil J. Smelser and Jeffrey C. Alexander, eds., *Diversity and Its Discontents: Cultural Conflict and Common Ground in Contemporary American Society* (Princeton, N.J.: Princeton University Press, 1999).

19. Julia Harrison, former member of the Council of the City of New York (1986–2000), 20th Council District, interview with author, July 3, 2001.

20. Paul Graziano, 2001 Green Party candidate for City Council District 20, interview with author, July 29, 2001.

21. Marilyn Bitterman, district director of Community Board 7, in Sengupta, "A Snapshot of World Faith."

22. Helen Dunn, in Ji-Yeon Yuh, "The Call to Worship Testing Tolerance; Neighbors Ask Church Limits," *Newsday, Queens Edition* (February 23, 1990).

23. For a look at (mostly Latino) gangs in Flushing in the 1980s and 1990s, see National Public Radio correspondent Maria Hinojosa, *Crews: Gang Members Talk to Maria Hinojosa* (New York, 1995). Flushing gangs actually are almost as diverse as the community, with Latino, black, white, South Asian, Chinese, and Korean groups all vying for turf.

24. Marilyn Bitterman, district director of Community Board 7, in Sengupta, "A Snapshot of World Faith."

25. Paul Graziano, 2001 Green Party candidate for City Council District 20, interview with author, July 29, 2001.

26. Robert F. Worth, "In Queens, Religious Rites Are Welcomed; Parking Rights Are Thornier," *New York Times* (March 29, 2004).

27. Ibid.

28. 1993 New York City Housing and Vacancy Survey, table 6.1, "Recently Turned-Over Housing Units by Accessibility and Immigrant Occupancy."

29. Tyler Cassell, "Zoning Battle Serves to Preserve Residential Neighborhoods," *Times-Ledger* (April 17, 2003).

30. Paul Graziano, 2001 Green Party candidate for City Council District 20, interview with author, July 29, 2001. Also see Corey Kilgannon, "Wary of an Invasion of Cars, Street Shuns New Neighbor," *New York Times* (October 31,

1999); and David W. Dunlap, "A Delicate Balance: Community Facilities and Communities," *New York Times* (October 27, 2002).

31. Ibid.

32. Sengupta, "A Snapshot of World Faith."

33. Joe Amoroso, "The Test of Community Facilities Zoning Text," *Times-Ledger* (November 4, 2004).

34. David W. Dunlap, "God, Caesar, and Zoning," *New York Times* (August 27, 2000).

35. This section is adapted from R. Scott Hanson, "Public/Private Urban Space and the Social Limits of Religious Pluralism," paper presented at American Academy of Religion, San Diego, Calif., 2007. Robert A. Orsi, ed., *Gods of the City: Religion and the American Urban Landscape* (Bloomington: Indiana University Press, 1999), 5.

36. Herbert Gans, "Urbanism and Suburbanism as Ways of Life: A Reevaluation of Definitions," in *People, Plans, and Policies: Essays on Poverty, Racism, and Other National Urban Problems* (1962; New York: Columbia University Press, 1991), 66.

37. Louis Wirth, "Urbanism as a Way of Life," *American Journal of Sociology* (1938).

38. Georg Simmel, "The Metropolis and Mental Life" (1903), in *On Individuality and Social Forms,* ed. Donald N. Levine (Chicago: University of Chicago Press, 1971), 331.

39. Robert E. Park, "The City: Suggestions for the Investigation of Human Behavior in the Urban Environment," in *The City,* ed. Robert E. Park and Ernest W. Burgess (Chicago: University of Chicago Press, 1925), 40, 59. Emphasis added.

40. Jane Jacobs, *The Death and Life of Great American Cities* (New York: Vintage, 1961), 30, 35, 59.

41. Herbert Gans, "Urban Vitality and the Fallacy of Physical Determinism," in *People, Plans, and Policies: Essays on Poverty, Racism, and Other National Urban Problems* (1962; New York: Columbia University Press, 1991).

42. Jeff Weintraub and Krishan Kumar, eds., *Public and Private in Thought and Practice: Perspectives on a Grand Dichotomy* (Chicago: University of Chicago Press, 1997).

43. See Lyn H. Lofland, *A World of Strangers: Order and Action in Urban Public Spaces* (Prospect Heights, Ill.: Waveland, 1973); Claude S. Fischer, "The Public and Private Worlds of City Life," *American Sociological Review* 46, no. 3 (June 1981): 306–316. Fischer builds on Lofland (who builds on Simmel and Wirth and Jacobs) by arguing that "urbanism produces estrangement from, and even conflict with, the unknown, socially dissimilar, and potentially threatening people and subcultures who make up the city" (315). Also see Claude S. Fischer, "Toward a Subcultural Theory of Urbanism," *American Journal of Sociology* 80, no. 6 (May 1975): 1319–1341. Fischer notes that "the greater ethnic variety of

cities means that they will exhibit greater amounts of unconventionality based on ethnicity. For example, simply because of this population distribution, cities will tend to have more dissident and unusual forms of religious behavior. The greater 'intensity' of ethnic groups, which tends to be associated with urbanism (especially because of group size), means that minority group members will be more able and willing to maintain their unconventional behaviors and beliefs" (1333). Also see Claude S. Fischer, "The Subcultural Theory of Urbanism: A Twentieth-Year Assessment," *American Journal of Sociology* 101, no. 3 (November 1995): 543–577.

44. In particular, see Lowell W. Livezey, ed., *Public Religion and Urban Transformation: Faith in the City* (New York: NYU Press, 2000); Clarke E. Cochran, *Religion in Public and Private Life* (New York: Routledge, 1990); Nancy T. Ammerman, "Organized Religion in a Voluntaristic Society," *Sociology of Religion* 58, no. 3 (1997): 203–215; and Penny Edgell Becker, *Congregations in Conflict: Cultural Models of Local Religious Life* (Cambridge: Cambridge University Press, 1999).

45. Martin E. Marty, "Public and Private: Congregation as Meeting Place," in *American Congregations, vol. 2: New Perspectives in the Study of Congregations,* ed. James P. Wind and James W. Lewis (Chicago: University of Chicago Press, 1994), 134.

46. Ibid., 62.

47. For more on parades, see Kathleen Neils Conzen et al., "The Invention of Ethnicity," *Journal of American Ethnic History* 12 (1992): 3–41; Kathleen Neils Conzen et al., "Ethnicity as Festive Culture: German-America on Parade," in *The Invention of Ethnicity*, ed. Werner Sollors (Oxford University Press, 1989), 44–76.

48. Jacobs, *Death and Life,* 62.

49. Wirth, "Urbanism as a Way of Life."

50. Paul Graziano, 2001 Green Party candidate for City Council District 20, interview with author, July 29, 2001.

51. Yi-Fu Tuan, *Place and Space: The Perspective of Experience* (Minneapolis: University of Minnesota Press, 1977).

52. Jacobs, *Death and Life,* 58.

53. Ibid., 62.

54. Milton M. Gordon, *Assimilation in American Life: The Role of Race, Religion, and National Origins* (New York: Oxford University Press, 1964), 239.

55. Ibid., 158.

56. For more on the effects of deindustrialization on the inner-city black community, see Thomas J. Sugrue, *The Origins of the Urban Crisis: Race and Inequality in Postwar Detroit* (Princeton, N.J.: Princeton University Press, 1996); and Elijah Anderson, *Code of the Street: Decency, Violence, and the Moral Life of the Inner City* (New York: Norton, 1999), 107–110.

57. Catherine and Jay Williams, interview with author, September 7, 2006.

58. Rev. Nicholas Genevieve-Tweed, interview with author, May 10, 2001.

59. This was a common complaint in my interviews with longtime residents outside of the Asian immigrant community. Similar observations were made by Christopher J. Smith and John R. Logan in their essay "Flushing 2000: Geographic Explorations in Asian New York," in *From Urban Enclave to Ethnic Suburb: New Asian Communities in Pacific Rim Countries,* ed. Wei Lei (Honolulu: University of Hawai'i Press, 2006).

60. Rev. Nicholas Genevieve-Tweed, interview with author, April 4, 2009.

61. I am grateful to Raymond B. Williams (the pioneer in the study of South Asian religion in America and the expert on Swaminarayan Hinduism in particular) for sharing many valuable contacts and information on the Swamina-rayan temple. For a detailed study of the group, see his *A New Face of Hinduism: The Swaminarayan Religion* (Cambridge, 1984). Williams also documents the less widely known Indian Christian immigrants in *Christian Pluralism in the United States: The Indian Immigrant Experience* (Cambridge, 1996).

62. Sajan P. Kuriakos, "Holy Land: The Growth of Korean Churches in Flushing Sparks Community Tensions," *Village Voice* (February 20, 2001).

63. Paul Graziano, 2001 Green Party candidate for City Council District 20, interview with author, July 29, 2001.

64. Also see Young Pai, Deloras Pemberton, and John Worley, *Findings on Korean American Early Adolescents and Adolescents* (Kansas City, 1987), "Appendix: Differences Between American and Korean Cultures."

65. Rev. Nam Soo Kim, Full Gospel New York Church, interview with author, July 26, 2001; Yanghee Hahn, human rights specialist, New York City Commission on Human Rights, Neighborhood Human Rights Program, interview with author, July 25, 2001.

66. Yanghee Hahn, human rights specialist, New York City Commission on Human Rights, Neighborhood Human Rights Program, interview with author, July 25, 2001.

67. Ibid.

68. Ibid. Also see Eui Hang Shin and Hyung Park, "An Analysis of Causes and Schisms in Ethnic Churches: The Case of Korean-American Churches," *Sociological Analysis* 49 (Fall 1988): 234–248; Kwang Chung Kim and Shin Kim, "Ethnic Roles of Korean Immigrant Churches in the United States," in *Korean Americans and Their Religions: Pilgrims and Missionaries from a Different Shore,* ed. Ho-Youn Kwon et al. (University Park, Penn., 2001).

69. Ibid.

70. Ibid.

71. Also see recent bulletin board discussions by Korean clergy about Flushing at http://www.emmanuelchurch.net/bbs/messages/77.html.

72. By contrast, Macedonia AME is exclusively black but is very active in the community (with a free soup kitchen every week that is popular not just with low-income or homeless African Americans but also many new immi-grants), and the leadership participates regularly in interfaith activities.

73. Rev. Gary Domiano, First Baptist Church of Flushing, interview with author, May 8, 2001.

74. Rev. Nam Soo Kim, Full Gospel New York Church, interview with author, July 26, 2001.

75. McRoberts notes that many African American Christians in urban neighborhoods also would rather avoid contact and engagement with the local community due to fears of negative influence from those outside the fold ("the street as evil other"). See McRoberts, *Streets of Glory,* 83–86.

76. R. Stephen Warner, "Work in Progress Toward a New Paradigm for the Sociological Study of Religion in the United States," *American Journal of Sociology* 98, no. 5 (March 1993): 1064.

77. Officer Henry Sookhu and Detective Steve Poholski, Community Affairs Unit, New York Police Department, 109th Precinct, interviews with author, May 11, 2001; June 22, 2001.

78. Elders Packer and Harrison, Church of Jesus Christ of Latter-Day Saints, group interview with author, August 17, 2001.

79. Ibid.

80. Ibid.

81. Ibid.

82. Ibid.

83. Ibid.

84. Rev. McKenzie Pier, cover letter to "11355: The Soul of Flushing."

85. Rev. Gary Domiano, First Baptist Church of Flushing, interview with author, May 8, 2001.

86. Ibid.

87. Ibid.

88. Ibid.

89. Ibid.

90. Ibid.

91. Robert Wuthnow, "The Culture of Discontent: Democratic Liberalism and the Challenge of Diversity in Late-Twentieth-Century America," in *Diversity and Its Discontents: Cultural Conflict and Common Ground in Contemporary American Society,* ed. Neil J. Smelser and Jeffrey C. Alexander (Princeton, N.J.: Princeton University Press, 1999).

92. Jean Bethke Elshtain, *Democracy on Trial* (New York, 1995), xi.

93. See, for instance, Peter Brimelow, *Alien Nation: Common Sense About America's Immigration Disaster* (New York, 1995); Arthur M. Schlesinger Jr., *The Disuniting of America: Reflections on a Multicultural Society* (New York, 1992). Also compare Lawrence W. Levine, *The Opening of the American Mind: Canons, Culture, and History* (Boston, 1996); David M. Reimers, *Unwelcome Strangers: American Identity and the Turn Against Immigration* (New York, 1998).

94. John Higham, "Cultural Responses to Immigration," in *Diversity and Its Discontents: Cultural Conflict and Common Ground in Contemporary American*

Society, ed. Neil J. Smelser and Jeffrey C. Alexander (Princeton, N.J.: Princeton University Press, 1999), 57.

95. Wuthnow, "The Culture of Discontent," 30–34.

96. Sidney Verba, Kay Lehman Schlozman, and Henry E. Brady, *Voice and Equality: Civic Voluntarism in American Politics* (Cambridge, Mass.: Harvard University Press, 1995), 518–521.

97. Ibid.

98. Robert Wuthnow, "Mobilizing Civic Engagement: The Changing Impact of Religious Involvement," in *Civic Engagement in American Democracy,* ed. Theda Skocpol and Morris P. Fiorina (Washington, D.C.: Brookings Institution, 1999), 334.

99. R. Stephen Warner, "Changes in the Civic Role of Religion," in *Diversity and Its Discontents: Cultural Conflict and Common Ground in Contemporary American Society,* ed. Neil J. Smelser and Jeffrey C. Alexander (Princeton, N.J.: Princeton University Press, 1999), 239.

100. Wuthnow, "Mobilizing Civic Engagement," 362.

101. I am grateful to Rita Cassel, recording secretary of the Network for Intergroup Harmony, for letting me borrow her folder of network meeting minutes and records since its inception in 1986.

102. Ibid.

103. Jane H. Lii, "Warlord's Son Pursues Peace as a Rector," *New York Times* (October 27, 1996).

104. Paul Engel, executive director, Flushing Jewish Community Council, interview with author, July 28, 2009. Engel, a longtime member of NIH, said "it just burned out by 2004, especially after the active and vocal secretary, Rita Cassel (who had kept meeting minutes), passed away."

105. Bruce Stanley, "Neighbors Coexist in a State of Grace," *Newsday* (November 17, 1991). Also based on my interview with Rev. Dr. Timothy P. Mitchell, pastor of Ebenezer Baptist Missionary Church, August 17, 2001.

106. Elena Cata, interview with author, October 26, 2006.

107. Although they often have multiethnic "congregations" also, I do not include mosques and temples in this category because their worship services are rarely offered in more than one language.

108. For studies of multiethnic congregations and congregations in general, see Nancy T. Ammerman, "Adaptation: Integrating Across Cultures" in *Congregation and Community* (New Brunswick, N.J.: Rutgers University Press, 1997). Also see Penny Edgell Becker, *Congregations in Conflict: Cultural Models of Local Religious Life* (Cambridge: Cambridge University Press, 1999); Nancy L. Eiesland, *A Particular Place: Urban Restructuring and Religious Ecology in a Southern Exurb* (New Brunswick, N.J.: Rutgers University Press, 2000); Omar M. McRoberts, *Streets of Glory: Church and Community in a Black Urban Neighborhood* (Chicago: University of Chicago Press, 2003); Gerardo Marti, *A Mosaic of Believers: Diversity and Innovation in a Multiethnic Church* (Bloomington: Indiana

University Press, 2004); Michael O. Emerson, *People of the Dream: Multiracial Congregations in the United States* (Princeton, N.J.: Princeton University Press, 2006); and Kathleen Garces-Foley, *Crossing the Ethnic Divide: The Multiethnic Church on a Mission* (New York: Oxford University Press, 2007).

109. I am indebted to Assistant Pastor Rev. McKenzie Pier at First Baptist for sharing two very helpful research papers from his seminary days, "11355: The Soul of Flushing" and "First Baptist Church of Flushing: A Portrait of Heaven," *Community Transformation Papers for Eastern Baptist Theological Seminary* (October 1998). For his papers, Pier conducted a three-hundred-person congregational survey in three languages, eight community ethnographic interviews, and six local church interviews. The papers have been presented to the national Conservative Baptist leadership to initiate a conversation about developing an urban training institute and missions training center in partnership with First Baptist.

110. Rev. Gary Domiano, First Baptist Church of Flushing, interview with author, May 8, 2001.

111. Ibid.

112. Pier, "First Baptist Church of Flushing: A Portrait of Heaven."

113. Rev. Gary Domiano, First Baptist Church of Flushing, interview with author, May 8, 2001.

114. Ibid.

115. Ibid.

116. Ibid.

117. Rev. Gary Domiano, First Baptist Church of Flushing, interview with author, May 8, 2001.

118. See John M. Perkins and Jo Kadlecek, *Resurrecting Hope: Powerful Stories of How God Is Moving to Reach Our Cities* (Ventura, Calif.: Regal, 1995). Also see Jo Kadlecek, "Shattering Your Church's Color Barriers: Here's a Look at What Successful Multiethnic Congregations Have Done to Breach Racial and Ethnic Barriers," http://members.aol.com/FBCFlushing/docs/article.html (originally on ministriestoday.com).

119. Pier, "First Baptist Church of Flushing: A Portrait of Heaven."

120. Rev. Gary Domiano, First Baptist Church of Flushing, interview with author, May 8, 2001.

121. Rabbi Albert Thaler, interview with author, November 3, 2006.

122. Sidney E. Mead, "Denominationalism: The Shape of Protestantism in America," in *The Lively Experiment* (New York: Harper & Row, 1963), 103–133.

123. Alexis de Tocqueville, "The Main Causes That Make Religion Powerful in America," in *Democracy in America* (1848; New York: Harper & Row, 1966), 294–301.

124. See R. Stephen Warner, "Work in Progress Toward a New Paradigm for the Sociological Study of Religion in the United States," *American Journal of Sociology* 98, no. 5 (March 1993); Nancy T. Ammerman, *Congregation and*

Community (New Brunswick, N.J.: Rutgers University Press, 1997); and Nancy T. Ammerman, "Religious Choice and Religious Vitality: The Market and Beyond," in *Rational Choice Theory and Religion: Summary and Assessment,* ed. Lawrence A. Young (New York: Psychology Press, 1997). For the classic secularization theory text (now renounced by its author), see Peter Berger, *The Sacred Canopy* (New York: Doubleday, 1969).

125. Ibid.

126. For a concise overview of these themes, see Martin E. Marty, "Anticipating Pluralism: The Founder's Vision" (Providence, 1986), address delivered at the Annual Meeting of the Associates of the John Carter Brown Library, Brown University, May 2, 1986.

127. Joseph Berger, "Brooklyn's Technicolor Dream Quilt," *New York Times* (May 29, 2005).

128. Martin E. Marty, *When Faiths Collide* (Malden, Mass.: Blackwell, 2005), 72–76.

129. As I note in the Introduction, for more on the changing meaning of "pluralism" see my essay "Pluralism and Cosmopolitanism in American Thought."

130. This is similar to the term "isolated" that the Gallup organization used in polls on American attitudes toward adherents of other religions to describe "those who tend to believe in the truth of their perspective above all others." See Albert L. Winseman, "Religious Tolerance Score Edged Up in 2004," http://www.gallup.com/poll/15253/Religious-Tolerance-Score-Edged-2004 .aspx. Cited by Paul D. Numrich in *The Faith Next Door: American Christians and Their New Religious Neighbors* (New York: Oxford University Press, 2009), 159.

131. Ibid. What the Gallup poll refers to merely as "tolerance" I refer to as passive tolerance, and what I refer to as active tolerance (inclusivism or ecumenism) the Gallup poll calls "integrated."

132. What I call "ecumenism" is similar to what Diana L. Eck calls "pluralism," and what I call "cooperative interaction" is similar to what Martin E. Marty calls "civil pluralism." See Diana L. Eck, *A New Religious America: How a "Christian Country" Has Become the World's Most Religiously Diverse Nation* (New York: HarperCollins, 2001); Martin E. Marty, *The One and the Many: America's Struggle for the Common Good* (Cambridge, Mass.: Harvard University Press, 1997).

133. Missionaries will no doubt disagree with the characterization of proselytism as a form of intolerance, and I do not mean to discount the positive side of mission work when people voluntarily seek out or *choose* to learn more about a faith outside of their own. But the truth is many people are offended by the aggressive tactics of missionaries, and conversion necessarily involves the repudiation of someone else's religious beliefs.

134. If time had permitted, I would have compiled a sample of public marriage licenses in Flushing from 1965 to 2000 to analyze rates of endogamy and exogamy.

135. Richard Rodriguez, "Theological Curry," *NewsHour with Jim Lehrer* (June 27, 2000).

5. Flushing Since September 11, 2001

1. For a moving account of the treatment of Sikhs after 9/11, see the documentary film *Divided We Fall: Americans in the Aftermath,* dir. Sharat Raju and Valarie Kaur, New Moon Productions (2008).

2. Alexander Dworkowitz, "Flushing Afghanis March in Unity Against Terrorism," *Flushing Times* (September 21, 2001).

3. Alexander Dworkowitz, "Flushing Religious Leaders Join Forces After Sept. 11," *Flushing Times* (November 15, 2001).

4. Celia W. Dugger, "Queens Old-Timers Uneasy as Asian Influence Grows," *New York Times* (March 31, 1996). Also see Jonathan P. Hicks, "Anti-Asian Remarks an Issue in Primary," *New York Times* (September 4, 1997); and Andrew Hsiao, "New New York vs. Old," *Village Voice* (September 9, 1997).

5. Chang-Rae Lee, *Native Speaker* (New York: Berkley, 1995).

6. Alexander Dworkowitz, "Liu Becomes the First Asian Elected to City Council," *Flushing Times* (November 8, 2001).

7. Denny Lee, "A Kid from Flushing Becomes the Voice of the Asian Community," *New York Times* (February 17, 2002).

8. Alexander Dworkowitz, "Liu Sworn in for Council as First Asian-American," *Flushing Times* (January 3, 2002).

9. Paul Graziano, 2001 Green Party candidate for City Council District 20, interview with author, July 29, 2001.

10. Sajan P. Kuriakos, "Holy Land: The Growth of Korean Churches in Flushing Sparks Community Tensions," *Village Voice* (February 20, 2001).

11. Sengupta, "A Snapshot of World Faith."

12. Robert J. Sampson, *Great American City: Chicago and the Enduring Neighborhood Effect* (Chicago: University of Chicago Press, 2014); Robert D. Putnam, "*E Pluribus Unum:* Diversity and Community in the Twenty-First Century," *Scandinavian Political Studies* 30, no. 2 (2007); Robert D. Putnam and David E. Campbell, *American Grace: How Religion Unites and Divides Us* (New York: Simon & Schuster, 2010).

13. See, for instance, Patrick J. Buchanan, "Robert Putnam: Diversity Is Our Destruction," *VDARE.com* (September 2007).

14. Stephen Steinberg, "The Melting Pot Is NOT Broken," *San Francisco Chronicle* (October 9, 2007).

15. Milton M. Gordon, *Assimilation in American Life: The Role of Race, Religion, and National Origins* (New York: Oxford University Press, 1964), 253.

16. Queens Historical Society, "The Flushing Freedom Mile Historic Tour" (1999); Queens Historical Society, *Angels of Deliverance: The Underground Railroad in Queens, Long Island, and Beyond* (Flushing, N.Y., 1999).

17. Flushing Council of the Arts, Flushing Town Hall, "The Queens Jazz Trail: A Full-Color Illustrated Map," 2nd ed. (1998).

18. Flushing Council of the Arts, Flushing Town Hall, "Remembrances of Civil War Flushing: Unveiling the 1862 Town Hall Time Capsule" (2001).

19. Vivian S. Toy, "Bustling Queens Library Speaks in Many Tongues," *New York Times* (May 31, 1998). Also see Marcia Biederman, "Making It Work: Library Thrives with a Common Touch," *New York Times* (September 12, 1999); Dean E. Murphy, "Queens Library Moves Past 'Shh' (and Books)," *New York Times* (March 7, 2001).

20. Glenn Collins, "In Flushing, a Return to History: Seeking Permanent Custody of a Declaration of Its Own," *New York Times* (January 28, 2000).

21. http://www.flushingremonstrance.info. Among the other events for the celebration, I gave talks at the Museum of the City of New York and the Queens Museum of Art, and the historian Kenneth T. Jackson wrote an op-ed piece about the significance of the Flushing Remonstrance for the *New York Times* on the actual day of the remonstrance's 350th anniversary: Kenneth T. Jackson, "A Colony with a Conscience," *New York Times* (December 27, 2007).

22. George Fox Stone (the giant slab of inscribed stone marking the site where two large oak trees once stood to provide shade for George Fox, founder of the Society of Friends, who preached outside Bowne House in 1672) also sat right outside my apartment building, but it has not proved to be as successful a historical landmark at communicating its message as Bowne House. I conducted an informal site survey of people passing by when I lived in the neighborhood as a kind of barometer of local memory and community ideology. The stone is now largely a curiosity to immigrant adults and an odd boulder for kids to clamber on. When I asked people, "Have you ever stopped to read the inscription about Fox and the Society of Friends—you know, the Quakers?" most would say, "what's a Quaker?"

23. http://meng.house.gov/media-center/press-releases/meng-bill-seeking-to-make-queens-historic-sites-part-of-national-park. On May 17, 2015, Congresswoman Meng, City Councilman Peter Koo, and the author gave speeches at Bowne House for the New York Landmarks Conservancy Sacred Sites Open House Weekend "Celebrating New York's Diverse Houses of Worship."

24. http://www.chinadaily.com.cn/english/doc/2004-11/05/content_389005.htm.

25. Brian Ray, "The Role of Cities in Immigrant Integration," Migration Policy Institute (October 1, 2003). http://www.migrationpolicy.org/article/role-cities-immigrant-integration/.

26. Ibid.

27. Leonie Sandercock, *Cosmopolis II: Mongrel Cities of the Twenty-First Century* (London: Continuum, 2003), 134. This is somewhat similar to the urban spaces that the sociologist Elijah Anderson has described in *The Cosmopolitan Canopy: Race and Civility in Everyday Life* (New York: Norton, 2011).

28. Ibid., 127.

29. Ibid., 146–147.

30. Barbara Ferman, Theresa Singleton, and Don DeMarco, "West Mount Airy, Philadelphia," *Cityscape: A Journal of Policy Development and Research* 4, no. 2 (1998), U.S. Department of Housing and Urban Development, Office of Policy Development and Research.

31. Suketu Mehta, "The Meltingist Pot," *New York Times* (October 5, 2003).

32. See Richard Bonney and R. Scott Hanson, "Understanding and Celebrating Religious Diversity in Britain: A Case Study of Leicester Since 1970 Making Comparison with Flushing, Queens County, New York City," *Encounters* 9, no. 2 (2003); *Fremont, U.S.A.*: A City's Encounter with Religious Diversity, dir. Elinor Pierce and Rachel Antell (2008). Also see Gustav Niebuhr, *Beyond Tolerance: Searching for Interfaith Understanding in America* (New York: Viking, 2008).

33. See http://www.ifyc.org/ and http://www.pluralism.org/interfaith/.

34. For the importance of middle childhood in children's development, see J. S. Eccles, "The Development of children Ages 6 to 14," *The Future of Children* 9, no. 2 (1999); S. M. Quintana, "A Model of Ethnic Perspective-Taking Ability Applied to Mexican-American Children," *Journal of Intercultural Relations* 18, no. 4 (1994); and U. Bronfenbrenner, "Ecology of the Family as a Context for Human Development: Research Perspectives," *Developmental Psychology* 22 (1986). Also see John Modell, "How May Children's Development Be Seen Historically?" *Childhood* 7, no. 1 (2000).

35. For a discussion of how experiences within the family, institutions, and communities create particular realities in the lives of immigrant children, see C. Suárez-Orozco and M. M. Suárez-Orozco, *Transformations: Migration, Family life, and Achievement Motivation Among Latino Adolescents* (Stanford, Calif., 1995); and C. Suárez-Orozco and M. M. Suárez-Orozco, *Children of Immigration* (Cambridge, 2001). For a discussion of how children learn to navigate multiple worlds, see C. R. Cooper et al., "Multiple Selves, Multiple Worlds: Three Useful Strategies for Research with Ethnic Minority Youth on Identity, Relationships, and Opportunity Structures," in *Conceptual and Methodological Issues in the Study of Minority Adolescents and Their Families,* ed. V. McLloyd and L. Steinberg (Hillsdale, N.J., 1998). For a discussion of how developmental and contextual processes impinge in the development of adaptation, see Cynthia García-Coll and K. Magnuson, "The Psychological Experience of Immigration: A Developmental Perspective," in *Immigration and the Family: Research and Policy on U.S. Immigrants,* ed. A. Booth et al. (Mahwah, N.J., 1998); A. J. Fuligni, "Adolescents from Immigrant Families," in *Studying Minority Adolescents,* ed. V. C. McLoyd and L. Steinberg (Mahwah, N.J., 1998).

36. See Bruce Grelle and D. Keith Naylor, eds., "Spotlight on Teaching About Religion in the Schools," *AAR Religious Studies News* 17, no. 2 (March 2002); the Oxford University Press series on *Religion in American Life* edited

by Jon Butler and Harry S. Stout; audiovisual material such as Diana Eck's CD-ROM *On Common Ground: World Religions in America* (New York: Columbia University Press, 2002); and Stephen Prothero, *Religious Literacy: What Every American Needs To Know—and Doesn't* (New York: HarperCollins, 2008).

37. In interviews with local elementary and high school teachers, I learned that in New York City fourth grade is the most geared toward local history before junior high social studies courses and high school history courses. Besides a few veteran teachers who stress Flushing's history and incorporate field trips to Bowne House, however, there is very little in the way of local history at the present.

38. Stephen Prothero, "Introduction," in *A Nation of Religions: The Politics of Pluralism in Multireligious America* (Chapel Hill: University of North Carolina Press, 2006), 5.

39. See, for instance, Paul D. Numrich, *The Faith Next Door: American Christians and Their New Religious Neighbors* (New York: Oxford University Press, 2009); Mary Pipher, *The Middle of Everywhere: The World's Refugees Come to Our Town* (New York: Harcourt, 2002); and Stephen G. Bloom, *Postville: A Clash of Cultures in Heartland America* (Orlando, Fla.: Harcourt, 2000). Further, more widespread coverage of the new religious landscape of America is presented in Diana L. Eck, *A New Religious America: How a "Christian Country" Has Become the World's Most Religiously Diverse Nation* (New York: HarperCollins, 2001); also see Eck's comprehensive Pluralism Project website at http://www.pluralism.org.

40. See Russell Shorto, *The Island at the Center of the World: The Epic Story of Dutch Manhattan and The Forgotten Colony That Shaped America* (New York: Vintage, 2004). Shorto's book is based on the transcription work of the historian Charles Gehring at the New York State Archives in Albany. For more on Gehring's work, see Danny Hakim, "His Specialty? Making Old New York Talk in Dutch," *New York Times* (December 26, 2009). Also see Evan Haefeli, *New Netherland and the Dutch Origins of American Religious Liberty* (Philadelphia: University of Pennsylvania Press, 2013).

41. Joyce Purnick, "Our Daily Tribute to Differences Provokes Dislike Among Many," *New York Times* (September 20, 2001).

42. Thomas Bender, "New York as a Center of Difference," in *The Unfinished City: New York and the Metropolitan Idea* (New York: The New Press, 2002), 186.

43. Ibid.

44. Eboo Patel, *Sacred Ground: Pluralism, Prejudice, and the Promise of America* (Boston: Beacon, 2012), 12–14. Emphasis added.

45. New York newspapers and local radio have been reporting on Flushing for some time, but the U.S. State Department is now too: a series of articles for America.gov have put Flushing's story on the web and U.S. embassy websites around the world. See http://www.america.gov/st/diversity-english/2008/August/20080825143428xlrennef0.4305994.html.

46. "Flushing Gets New Park and Mayor's Salute: On 300th Anniversary, He Broadcasts from Bowne House, Tolerance Shrine," *New York Herald Tribune* (October 8, 1945).

Appendix A: Note on Methods

1. Answers to such questions often reflected insights about neighborhood safety and urban life outlined in such works as Jane Jacobs, *The Death and Life of Great American Cities* (New York: Vintage, 1961); Kevin Lynch, *The Image of the City* (Cambridge, Mass.: MIT Press, 1960); and the chapter on "Walking in the City" by Michel de Certeau in his book *The Practice of Everyday Life* (Berkeley: University of California Press, 1984).

2. Initial interviews were recorded on a professional cassette tape recorder, but I later switched to a portable digital MiniDisc recorder (state of the art in the mid- and late 1990s but rare these days) for even better audio and archival quality. All interviews have since been imported and converted to mp3 audio files.

Bibliography

Ahlstrom, Sydney E. *A Religious History of the American People.* New Haven, Conn.: Yale University Press, 1972.

Alba, Richard D. *Ethnic Identity: The Transformation of White America.* New Haven, Conn.,: Yale University Press, 1990.

Albanese, Catherine L. *America: Religions and Religion.* 5th ed. Belmont, Calif.: Wadsworth, 2012.

Aleinikoff, Thomas Alexander, David A. Martin, and Hiroshi Motomura, eds. *Immigration and Citizenship: Process and Policy.* 4th ed. American Casebook Series. St. Paul, 1998.

Ammerman, Nancy T. *Congregation and Community.* New Brunswick, N.J.: Rutgers University Press, 1997.

———. "Organized Religion in a Voluntaristic Society." *Sociology of Religion* 58, no. 3 (1997).

———. "Religious Choice and Religious Vitality: The Market and Beyond." In *Rational Choice Theory and Religion: Summary and Assessment,* ed. Lawrence A. Young. New York: Routledge, 1997.

Anbinder, Tyler. *Five Points: The Nineteenth-Century New York City Neighborhood That Invented Tap Dance, Stole Elections, and Became the World's Most Notorious Slum.* New York: Plume, 2002.

———. *Nativism and Slavery: The Northern Know Nothings and the Politics of the 1850s.* New York: Oxford University Press, 1992.

Anderson, Elijah. *Code of the Street: Decency, Violence, and the Moral Life of the Inner City.* New York: Norton, 1999.

———. *The Cosmopolitan Canopy: Race and Civility in Everyday Life.* New York: Norton, 2011.

Appadurai, Arjun. *Modernity at Large: Cultural Dimensions of Globalization.* Minneapolis, Minn.: University of Minnesota Press, 1996.

Appel, John J. *Immigrant Historical Societies in the United States, 1880–1950.* New York: Ayer, 1980.

Ariarajah, S. Wesley. *The Bible and People of Other Faiths.* Geneva: Wipf & Stock, 1985.

Augustine. *City of God [413–427].* New York: Penguin, 1984.

———. *Of True Religion* [390]. Washington, D.C.: Henry Regnery, 1959.

Bacon, Leonard Woolsey. *A History of American Christianity.* New York: Charles Scribner Sons, 1900.

Bald, Vivek. *Bengali Harlem and the Lost Histories of South Asian America.* Cambridge, Mass.: Harvard University Press, 2013.

Balmer, Randall, and Mark Silk, eds. *Religion and Public Life in the Middle Atlantic Region: The Fount of Diversity.* Lanham, Md.: AltaMira, 2006.

Barth, Karl. *Church Dogmatics.* Edinburgh: T&T Clark, 1961.

Barton, Josef J. *Peasants and Strangers: Italians, Rumanians, and Slovaks in an American City.* Cambridge, Mass.: Harvard University Press, 1975.

Becker, Penny Edgell. *Congregations in Conflict: Cultural Models of Local Religious Life.* Cambridge: Cambridge University Press, 1999.

Bender, Courtney, and Pamela E. Klassen. *After Pluralism: Reimagining Religious Engagement.* New York: Columbia University Press, 2010.

Bender, Thomas. "New York as a Center of Difference." In *The Unfinished City: New York and the Metropolitan Idea.* New York: New Press, 2002.

———. "Wholes and Parts: The Need for Synthesis in American History." *Journal of American History* 73 (1986).

Berger, Peter. *The Sacred Canopy.* New York: Anchor, 1969.

Berger, Peter, ed., *The Desecularization of the World: Resurgent Religion and World Politics.* New York: Eerdmans, 1999.

Bhabha, Homi K. "Editor's Introduction: Minority Maneuvers and Unsettled Negotiations." *Critical Inquiry* 23, no. 3 (Spring 1997).

———. *The Location of Culture.* New York: Routledge, 1994.

———. "Unsatisfied: Notes on Vernacular Cosmopolitanism." In *Text and Nation,* ed. Peter C. Pfeiffer and Laura García-Moreno. New York: Columbia University Press, 1996.

Binder, Frederick M., and David M. Reimers. *All the Nations Under Heaven: An Ethnic and Racial History of New York City.* New York: Columbia University Press, 1995.

Bloom, Stephen G. *Postville: A Clash of Cultures in Heartland America.* Orlando, Fla.: Mariner, 2000).

Bodnar, John. *Remaking America: Public Memory, Commemoration, and Patriotism in the Twentieth Century.* Princeton, N.J.: Princeton University Press, 1992.

Bonney, Richard, and R. Scott Hanson. "Understanding and Celebrating Religious Diversity in Britain: A Case Study of Leicester Since 1970 Making

Comparison with Flushing, Queens County, New York City." *Encounters* 9, no. 2 (2003).

Bourdieu, Pierre. "The Biographical Illusion." *Working Papers and Proceedings of the Center for Psychosocial Studies* 14. Chicago, 1987.

Bourne, Randolph. "Trans-National America." *Atlantic Monthly* 118 (July 1916).

Bowne, John, of Flushing, L.I. (1627–1695). *Original Journal* of, containing entries of Births, Marriages and Deaths in the family from 1649–1676 with Vol. of Extracts from Journal and Newspaper cuttings of contributions to Flushing's Centennial by Henry Onderdonk Jr. 2 vols. 12 mo. Manuscripts collection, Library of the New-York Historical Society.

Breckenridge, Carol A., Sheldon Pollock, Homi K. Bhabha, and Dipesh Chakrabarty, eds. "Cosmopolitanism: Millennial Quartet." *Public Culture: Society for Transnational Cultural Studies* 12, no. 3 (Fall 2000).

Brimelow, Peter. *Alien Nation: Common Sense About America's Immigration Disaster.* New York: Harper, 1995.

Bronfenbrenner, U. "Ecology of the Family as a Context for Human Development: Research Perspectives." *Developmental Psychology* 22 (1986).

Brown, Karen McCarthy. *Mama Lola: A Vodou Priestess in Brooklyn.* Berkeley, Calif.: University of California Press, 1991.

Burke, Peter. *Varieties of Cultural History.* Ithaca, N.Y.: Cornell University Press, 1997.

Burrows, Edwin G., and Mike Wallace. *Gotham: A History of New York City to 1898.* New York: Oxford University Press, 1999.

Butler, Jon. *Awash in a Sea of Faith: Christianizing the American People.* Cambridge, Mass.: Harvard University Press, 1990.

———. "Protestant Success in the New American City, 1870–1920: The Anxious Secrets of Rev. Walter Laidlaw, Ph.D." In *New Directions in American Religious History,* ed. Harry S. Stout and D. G. Hart. New York, 1997.

———. "Theory and God in Gotham." *History and Theory* 45 (December 2006).

Callaghan, E. B., ed. *Documentary History of the State of New-York.* Vol. 3. Albany, N.Y.: Weed, Parsons & Co., 1850.

Caro, Robert A. *The Power Broker: Robert Moses and the Fall of New York.* New York: Vintage, 1974.

Chartier, Roger. *Cultural History: Between Practices and Representations.* Ithaca, N.Y.: Cornell University Press, 1988.

Cheah, Pheng, and Bruce Robbins, eds. *Cosmopolitics.* Minneapolis, Minn.: University of Minnesota Press, 1998.

Chen, Carolyn E. "Getting Saved in America: Religious Conversion to Evangelical Protestantism Among Taiwanese Immigrants." Ph.D. diss. Department of Sociology, University of California at Berkeley, 2000.

Chen, Hsiang-Shui. *Chinatown No More: Taiwan Immigrants in Contemporary New York.* Ithaca, N.Y.: Cornell University Press, 1992.

Christiano, Kevin J. *Religious Diversity and Social Change: American Cities, 1890–1906.* Cambridge: Cambridge University Press, 1987.

Clooney, Francis X. *Theology After Vedanta: An Experiment in Comparative Theology.* Albany, N.Y.: SUNY Press, 1993.

Cochran, Clarke E. *Religion in Public and Private Life.* New York: Routledge, 1990.

Cohen, Charles L., and Ronald L. Numbers, eds., *Gods in America: Religious Pluralism in the United States.* New York: Oxford University Press, 2013.

Cohn, Bernard S., John W. Adams, Natalie Z. Davis, and Carlo Ginzburg. "Anthropology and History in the 1980s." *Journal of Interdisciplinary History* 12 (1981).

Comaroff, John, and Jean Comaroff. *Ethnography and the Historical Imagination.* Boulder, Colo.: Westview, 1992.

Commager, Henry Steele. *The Search for a Usable Past and Other Essays in Historiography.* New York: Knopf, 1967.

Conzen, Kathleen Neils. "Community Studies, Urban History, and American Local History." In *The Past Before Us: Contemporary Historical Writing in the United States,* ed. Michael Kammen. Ithaca, N.Y.: Cornell University Press, 1980.

———. "Ethnicity as Festive Culture: German-America on Parade." In *The Invention of Ethnicity,* ed. Werner Sollors. Oxford, 1989.

———. "Immigrants, Immigrant Neighborhoods, and Ethnic Identity: Historical Issues." *Journal of American History* 66, no. 3 (December 1979).

———. "Thomas and Znaniecki and the Historiography of American Immigration." *Journal of American Ethnic History* 16, no. 1 (Fall 1996).

Conzen, Kathleen Neils, David A. Gerber, Ewa Morawska, George E. Pozzetta, and Rudolph J. Vecoli. "The Invention of Ethnicity." *Journal of American Ethnic History* 12 (1992).

Crèvecœur, J. Hector St. John de. *Letters from an American Farmer and Sketches of Eighteenth-Century America* [1782]. New York: Penguin, 1980.

Cummings, Scott. *Left Behind in Rosedale: Race Relations and the Collapse of Community Institutions.* Boulder, Colo.: Westview, 1998.

Cusa, Nicholas of. *De Pace Fidei.* [1453]. Lewiston, N.Y.: Edwin Mellen, 1991.

D'Costa, Gavin. *Theology and Religious Pluralism.* New York: Oxford University Press, 1986.

Daniels, Roger. "Asian American History's Overdue Emergence." *Chronicle Review* (December 7, 2001).

———. "No Lamps Were Lit for Them: Angel Island and the Historiography of Asian American Immigration." *Journal of American Ethnic History* 17, no. 1 (Fall 1997).

Davis, Natalie Z. *Society and Culture in Early Modern France.* Stanford, Calif.: Stanford University Press, 1975.

Day, Katie. *Faith on the Avenue: Religion on a City Street.* New York: Oxford University Press, 2014.

de Tocqueville, Alexis. *Democracy in America* [1848]. New York: HarperCollins, 1988.

Demos, John. *The Unredeemed Captive: A Family Story from Early America.* New York: Vintage, 1994.

Desan, Suzanne. "Crowds, Community, and Ritual in the Work of E. P. Thompson and Natalie Davis." In *The New Cultural History,* ed. Lynn Hunt. Berkeley, Calif.: University of California Press, 1989.

Dewey, John. "Pluralism." In *Dictionary of Philosophy and Psychology,* vol. 2, ed. James Mark Baldwin. New York: Macmillan, 1901.

Dolan, Jay P. *The American Catholic Experience: A History from the Colonial Times to the Present.* Notre Dame, Ind.: University of Notre Dame Press, 1992.

———. "The Immigrants and Their Gods: A New Perspective in American Religious History." *Church History* 57 (March 1988). Reprinted in Jon Butler and Harry S. Stout, eds. *Religion in American History: A Reader.* New York: Oxford University Press, 1998.

———. "Immigration and American Christianity: A History of Their Histories." In *A Century of Church History: The Legacy of Philip Schaff,* ed. Henry W. Bowden. Carbondale: Southern Illinois University Press, 1988.

Dunlap, Leslie W. *American Historical Societies, 1790–1860.* Madison, Wis.: Cantwell Printing Co., 1944.

Durkhem, Emile. *The Elementary Forms of the Religious Life* [1915]. New York: Free Press, 1965.

Eccles, J. S. "The Development of children Ages 6 to 14." *The Future of Children* 9, no. 2 (1999).

Eck, Diana L. *Encountering God: A Spiritual Journey from Bozeman to Banaras.* Boston: Beacon, 1993.

———. *A New Religious America: How a "Christian Country" Has Become the World's Most Religiously Diverse Nation.* San Francisco, 2001.

———. *On Common Ground: World Religions in America* [1997]. New York, 2002. CD-ROM.

Eiesland, Nancy L. *A Particular Place: Urban Restructuring and Religious Ecology in a Southern Exurb.* New Brunswick, N.J.: Rutgers University Press, 2000.

Elshtain, Jean Bethke. *Democracy on Trial.* New York: Basic Books, 1995.

Emerson, Michael O. *People of the Dream: Multiracial Congregations in the United States.* Princeton, N.J.: Princeton University Press, 2006.

Fields, Rick. *How the Swans Came to The Lake: A Narrative History of Buddhism in America.* Boston: Shambhala, 1992.

Fischer, Claude S. "The Public and Private Worlds of City Life." *American Sociological Review* 46, no. 3 (June 1981).

———. "The Subcultural Theory of Urbanism: A Twentieth-Year Assessment." *American Journal of Sociology* 101, no. 3 (November 1995).

———. "Toward a Subcultural Theory of Urbanism." *American Journal of Sociology* 80, no. 6 (May 1975).

Fisher, Maxine P. *The Indians of New York City: A Study of Immigrants from India.* New York: Columbia University Press, 1980.

Fitzgerald, F. Scott. *The Great Gatsby* [1925]. New York: Scribner, 1991.

Foner, Nancy, ed. *One Out of Three: Immigrant New York in the Twenty-First Century.* New York: Columbia University Press, 2013.

Foucault, Michel. *The Archaeology of Knowledge and The Discourse on Language.* New York: Vintage, 1972.

Fox, Richard Wightman. "Experience and Explanation in Twentieth-Century American Religious History." In *New Directions in American Religious History,* ed. Harry S. Stout and D. G. Hart. New York: Oxford University Press, 1997.

Fuchs, Lawrence H. *The American Kaleidoscope: Race, Ethnicity, and the Civic Culture.* Middletown, Conn.: Wesleyan University Press, 1990.

Gans, Herbert. *People, Plans, and Policies: Essays on Poverty, Racism, and Other National Urban Problems* [1962]. New York: Columbia University Press, 1991.

Garces-Foley, Kathleen. *Crossing the Ethnic Divide: The Multiethnic Church on a Mission.* New York: Oxford University Press, 2007.

Garcia-Coll, Cynthia, and K. Magnuson. "The Psychological Experience of Immigration: A Developmental Perspective." In *Immigration and the Family: Research and Policy on U.S. Immigrants,* ed. A. Booth, A. Couter, and N. Landale. New York: Routledge, 1997.

Geertz, Clifford. "History and Anthropology." *New Literary History 21* (1989–1990).

———. *Islam Observed: Religious Development in Morocco and Indonesia.* Chicago: University of Chicago Press, 1968.

Gelernter, David. *1939: The Lost World of the Fair.* New York: Free Press, 1995.

Gerber, David A. *The Making of an American Pluralism: Buffalo, New York, 1825–1860.* Urbana: University of Illinois Press, 1989.

Gerstle, Gary. "Liberty, Coercion, and the Making of Americans." *Journal of American History* 84, no. 2 (September 1997).

———. "The Power of Nations." *Journal of American History* 84, no. 2 (September 1997).

Gjerde, Jon. *The Minds of the West: Ethnocultural Evolution in the Rural Middle West, 1830–1917.* Chapel Hill, N.C.: University of North Carolina Press, 1997.

Glazer, Nathan, and Daniel P. Moynihan. *Beyond the Melting Pot.* Cambridge, Mass.: Harvard University Press, 1963.

Gleason, Philip. "American Identity and Americanization." In *Harvard Encyclopedia of American Ethnic Groups,* ed. Stephan Thernstrom, Ann Orlov, and Oscar Handlin. Cambridge, Mass.: Harvard University Press, 1980.

———. *Speaking of Diversity: Language and Ethnicity in Twentieth-Century America.* Baltimore, Md.: Johns Hopkins University Press, 1992.

Gordon, Milton M. *Assimilation in American Life: The Role of Race, Religion, and National Origins.* New York: Oxford University Press, 1964.

———. "Models of Pluralism: The New American Dilemma." *Annals* 454 (March 1981).

Gregory, Steven. *Black Corona: Race and the Politics of Place in an Urban Community.* Princeton, N.J.: Princeton University Press, 1998.

Grelle, Bruce, and D. Keith Naylor, eds. "Spotlight on Teaching About Religion in the Schools." *AAR Religious Studies News* 17, no. 2 (March 2002).

Gutiérrez, Ramón. *When Jesus Came the Corn Mothers Went Away: Marriage, Sexuality, and Power in New Mexico, 1500–1846.* Stanford, Calif.: Stanford University Press, 1991.

Hackett, David G., ed. *Religion and American Culture: A Reader.* New York: Routledge, 1995.

Haddad, Yvonne Yazbeck, ed. *The Muslims of America.* New York: Oxford University Press, 1991.

Haefeli, Evan. *New Netherland and the Dutch Origins of American Religious Liberty.* Philadelphia: University of Pennsylvania Press, 2013.

Hall, Stuart. "Culture and Power." Interview by Peter Osborne and Lynne Segal. *Radical Philosophy* 86 (November/December 1997).

Halttunen, Karen. "Cultural History and the Challenge of Narrativity." In *Beyond the Cultural Turn: New Directions in the Study of Society and Culture,* ed. Victoria E. Bonnell and Lynn Hunt. Berkeley, Calif.: University of California Press, 1999.

Hammond, Phillip, and David Machacek. *Soka Gakkai in America: Accommodation and Conversion.* New York: Oxford University Press, 1999.

Handlin, Oscar. *The Uprooted: The Epic Story of the Great Migrations That Made the American People.* New York: Little, Brown & Co., 1973.

Hanson, R. Scott. "Intra- and Extra-Religioethnic Encounters: Responses to Plurality Among Hindu Temples on Bowne Street in Flushing, New York." Paper presented at a session on "Hinduism in America: Constructing Sacred Space and Collective Identity," North American Religions Section, 1999 Annual Meeting of the American Academy of Religion.

———. "Neighborhood Narratives in the City of Gods: Religious Freedom, Immigration, and Pluralism in Flushing, New York." Paper presented at the 2001 Annual Meeting of the American Historical Association in a session cosponsored by the Immigration and Ethnic History Society entitled "New Narratives for an Old Story: Moments of Peak Immigration Over Three Centuries of U.S. History."

———. "Pluralism and Cosmopolitanism in American Thought." *Journal of American Ethnic History* (under review).

———. "Public/Private Urban Space and the Social Limits of Religious Pluralism." Paper presented at American Academy of Religion, San Diego, Calif., 2007.

———. "Religious Pluralism and the Canon of American Religious History." *Religion and American Culture: A Journal of Interpretation* (under review).

———. "Sri Maha Vallabha Ganapati Devasthanam of Flushing, New York." In *Hindu Diasporas: Global Perspectives,* ed. T. S. Rukmani. Montreal: Munshirm Manoharlal, 1999.

———. "Temples and Mosques of New York City." Pluralism Project Research Notes. In *On Common Ground: World Religions in America,* by Diana L. Eck. New York, 1997.

Harris, Neil. *Cultural Excursions: Marketing Appetites and Cultural Tastes in America.* Chicago: University of Chicago Press, 1990.

Hastings, Hugh. *Ecclesiastical Records of the State of New York,* vol. 1. New York: J. B. Lyon, 1901.

Hawley, John Stratton. "Global Hinduism in Gotham." In *Asian-American Religion: Borders and Boundaries,* ed. Tony Carnes and Fenggang Yang. New York: New York University Press, 2004.

Hawley, John Stratton, and Mark Juergensmeyer. *Songs of the Saints of India.* New York: Oxford University Press, 1988.

Hawley, John Stratton, and Gurinder Singh Mann, eds. *Studying the Sikhs: Issues for North America.* Albany, N.Y.: SUNY Press, 1993.

Heim, S. Mark. *Salvations: Truth and Difference in Religion.* Maryknoll, N.Y.: Orbis, 1995.

Herberg, Will. *Protestant-Catholic-Jew: An Essay in American Religious Sociology.* Chicago: University of Chicago Press, 1955.

Hick, John. *God Has Many Names.* Louisville: Westminster John Knox Press, 1982.

———. *An Interpretation of Religion: Human Responses to the Transcendent.* New Haven, Conn.: Yale University Press, 1989.

Higham, John. "The Ethnic Historical Society in Changing Times." *Journal of American Ethnic History* 13, no. 2 (Winter 1994).

———, "Ethnicity and American Protestants: Collective Identity in the Mainstream." In *New Directions in American Religious History,* ed. Harry S. Stout and D. G. Hart. New York: Oxford University Press, 1997.

———. *History: Professional Scholarship in America.* Baltimore, Md.: Johns Hopkins University Press, 1965.

———. "Instead of a Sequel, or How I Lost My Subject." *Reviews in American History* 28, no. 2 (June 2000).

———. *Send These to Me: Immigrants in Urban America [1975].* Rev. ed. Baltimore, Md.: Johns Hopkins University Press, 1984.

———. *Strangers in the Land: Patterns of American Nativism, 1860–1925* [1955]. New Brunswick, N.J.: Rutgers University Press, 1988.

Hinojosa, Maria. *Crews: Gang Members Talk to Maria Hinojosa.* New York: Harcourt, 1995.

Hobsbawm, Eric, and Terence Ranger, eds. *The Invention of Tradition.* Cambridge: Cambridge University Press, 1983.

Hollinger, David A. *Postethnic America: Beyond Multiculturalism.* New York: Basic Books, 1995.

Huizinga, Johan. *The Waning of the Middle Ages [1919].* Trans. F. Hopman. New York, 1954. Cf. Johan Huizinga. *The Autumn of the Middle Ages.* Trans. Rodney J. Payton and Ulrich Mammitzsch. Chicago: University of Chicago Press, 1996.

Hummon, David M. *Commonplaces: Community Ideology and Identity in American Culture.* Albany, N.Y.: SUNY Press, 1990.

Hunt, Lynn, ed. *The New Cultural History.* Berkeley, Calif.: University of California Press, 1989.

Hutchison, William R. *Religious Pluralism in America: The Contentious History of a Founding Ideal.* New Haven, Conn.: Yale University Press, 2003.

Isaac, Rhys. *The Transformation of Virginia, 1740–1790.* Chapel Hill, N.C.: University of North Carolina Press, 1982.

Jackson, Carl T. *Vedanta for the West: The Ramakrishna Movement in the U.S.* Bloomington: Indiana University Press, 1994.

Jackson, Kenneth T. *Crabgrass Frontier: The Suburbanization of the United States.* New York: Oxford University Press, 1985.

———. "The End of Sprawl: The City Beckons Once Again." Lecture for Columbia University Alumni Association, Philadelphia, Penn., June 20, 2009.

Jackson, Kenneth T., ed. *Encyclopedia of New York City.* New Haven, Conn.: Yale University Press, 1995.

Jacobs, Jane. *The Death and Life of Great American Cities.* New York: Vintage, 1961.

James, William. *A Pluralistic Universe.* New York: Longmans, Green & Co., 1909.

———. *The Will to Believe and Other Essays in Popular Philosophy.* New York: Longmans, Green & Co., 1897.

Jefferson, Thomas. *Notes on the State of Virginia.* Ed. William Peden. Chapel Hill: University of North Carolina Press, 1954.

Johnson, Tom, and Lance Bird. *The World of Tomorrow.* An American Portrait video by Direct Cinema Limited. Narrated by Jason Robards. 1984.

Kallen, Horace M. "Democracy *Versus* the Melting-Pot." *The Nation* 100 (February 18, 25, 1915): 190–194, 217–220. Reprinted in *Culture and Democracy in the United States.* New York: Boni and Liveright, 1924.

Kammen, Michael. *Colonial New York: A History.* New York: Scribners, 1975.

———. *Mystic Chords of Memory: The Transformation of Tradition in American Culture.* New York: Vintage, 1991.

Kant, Immanuel. "Idea for a Universal History from a Cosmopolitan Point of View." *Berlinische Monatsschrift* (December, 1784). Reprinted in *On History.* New York: Pearson, 1963.

Kassel, Marleen. "Two Japanese New Religions in Flushing: The Tenrikyo Mission and the Nichiren Shoshu Daihozan Myosetsu Temple." *Long Island Historical Journal 5, no. 1 (*Fall 1992).

Kazal, Russell A. "Revisiting Assimilation: The Rise, Fall, and Reappraisal of a Concept in American Ethnic History." *American Historical Review* 100, no. 2 (April 1995).

Khandelwal, Madhulika S. *Becoming American, Being Indian: An Immigrant Community in New York City.* Ithaca, N.Y.: Cornell University Press, 2002.

———. "Hindu Religious Activities in Queens." *Asian/American Center Working Papers.* Queens College/CUNY. New York, 1989.

———. "Indian Immigrants in Queens, New York City: Patterns of Spatial Concentration and Distribution, 1965–90." In *Nation and Migration: The Poli-*

tics of Space in the South Asian Diaspora, ed. Peter van der Veer. Philadelphia: University of Pennsylvania Press, 1995.

———. "Indian Networks in the United States: Class and Transnational Identities." In *Immigrants and Immigration Policy: Individual Skills, Family Ties, and Group Identities,* ed. Duleep and Wunnava. JAI Press, 1996.

Kim, Illsoo. "The Koreans: Small Business in an Urban Frontier." In *New Immigrants in New York,* ed. Nancy Foner. New York: Columbia University Press, 1987.

Kim, Jin-Hong. "The Great Christian Revival in Korea." In *The Asian Christian History Reader,* 2 vols., ed. Jin-Hong Kim. Flushing, N.Y., 1999.

Klein, Milton M. "New York in the American Colonies: A New Look." *New York History* 53, no. 2 (April 1972).

Kniss, Fred, and Paul D. Numrich. *Sacred Assemblies and Civic Engagement: How Religion Matters for America's Newest Immigrants.* New Brunswick, N.J.: Rutgers University Press, 2007.

Knitter, Paul. *No Other Name? A Critical Survey of Christian Attitudes Toward the World Religions.* Maryknoll, N.Y.: Orbis, 1985.

Küng, Hans. *Christianity and the World's Religions.* Maryknoll, N.Y.: Orbis, 1986.

Kwon, Ho-Youn, Kwang Chung Kim, and R. Stephen Warner, eds. *Korean Americans and Their Religions: Pilgrims and Missionaries from a Different Shore.* University Park: Pennsylvania State University Press, 2001.

Kwong, Peter. *The New Chinatown.* New York: Hill and Wang, 1987.

Ladurie, Emmanuel L. *Montaillou: The Promised Land of Error.* New York: George Braziller, 1979.

Laidlaw, Walter, ed. *Population of the City of New York, 1890–1930.* Albany: New York State, 1932.

Lee, Chang-Rae. *Native Speaker.* New York: Riverhead, 1995.

Leonard, Karen Isaksen. *Making Ethnic Choices: California's Punjabi Mexican Americans.* Philadelphia: Temple University Press, 1992.

Lessinger, Johanna. *From the Ganges to the Hudson: Indian Immigrants in New York City.* Boston: Pearson, 1995.

Levine, Lawrence W. *The Opening of the American Mind: Canons, Culture, and History.* Boston: Beacon, 1996.

Lindbeck, George A. *The Nature of Doctrine: Religion and Theology in a Postliberal Age.* Louisville: Westminster John Knox, 1984.

Livezey, Lowell W., ed. *Public Religion and Urban Transformation: Faith in the City.* New York: New York University Press, 2000.

Lobo, Arun Peter, and Joseph J. Salvo. *The Newest New Yorkers, 1990–1994: An Analysis of Immigration to NYC in the Early 1990s.* New York: New York City Department of City Planning, 1996.

———. *The Newest New Yorkers, 2000: Immigrant New York in the New Millennium.* New York: New York City Department of City Planning, 2005.

———. *The Newest New Yorkers, 2013 Edition: Characteristics of the City's Foreign-Born Population.* New York: New York City Department of City Planning, 2013.

Lofland, Lyn H. *A World of Strangers: Order and Action in Urban Public Spaces.* Prospect Heights, Ill.: Waveland, 1973.

Lurie, Allison. *Imaginary Friends.* New York: Coward McCann, 1967.

Magida, Arthur J., ed. *How to Be a Perfect Stranger: A Guide to Etiquette in Other People's Religious Ceremonies.* Woodstock, Vt.: Gemstone, 1996.

Mandeville, Rev. G. Henry. *Flushing, Past and Present: A Historical Sketch.* Flushing, N.Y., 1860.

Markus, Robert A. *Christianity and the Secular.* Notre Dame, Ind.: University of Notre Dame Press, 2006.

———. *Saeculum: History and Society in the Theology of St. Augustine.* Cambridge: Cambridge University Press, 1970.

Marti, Gerardo. *A Mosaic of Believers: Diversity and Innovation in a Multiethnic Church.* Bloomington: Indiana University Press, 2004.

Marty, Martin E. "The American Religious History Canon." *Social Research* 53, no. 3 (Autumn 1986).

———. "Anticipating Pluralism: The Founder's Vision." Address delivered at the Annual Meeting of the Associates of the John Carter Brown Library, Brown University, Providence, R.I., May 2, 1986.

———. "Ethnicity: The Skeleton of Religion in America." *Church History* 41 (March 1972).

———. *Modern American Religion. Vol. 1: The Irony of It All, 1893–1919.* Chicago: University of Chicago Press, 1986.

———. *The One and the Many: America's Struggle for the Common Good.* Cambridge, Mass.: Harvard University Press, 1997.

———. *Pilgrims in Their Own Land: Five Hundred Years of Religion in America.* New York: Little, Brown, 1984.

———. "Public and Private: Congregation as Meeting Place." In *American Congregations, vol. 2: New Perspectives in the Study of Congregations,* ed. James P. Wind and James W. Lewis. Chicago: University of Chicago Press, 1994.

———. *Religion and Republic: The American Circumstance.* Boston: Beacon, 1987.

———. *When Faiths Collide.* Malden, Mass.: Wiley-Blackwell, 2005.

May, John D'Arcy., ed. *Pluralism and the Religions: The Theological and Political Dimensions.* London: Cassell, 1998.

McLoyd, V., and L. Steinberg, ed. *Studying Minority Adolescents: Conceptual, Methodological, and Theoretical Issues.* Mahwah, N.J.: Lawrence Erlbaum Associates, 1998.

McRoberts, Omar M. *Streets of Glory: Church and Community in a Black Urban Neighborhood.* Chicago: University of Chicago Press, 2003.

Mead, Sidney E. *The Lively Experiment: The Shaping of Christianity in America.* New York: Harper and Row, 1963.

Min, Pyong Gap. "The Structure and Social Functions of Korean Immigrant Churches in the United States." *International Migration Review* 26, no. 4 (Winter 1992).

Modell, John. "How May Children's Development Be Seen Historically?" *Childhood* 7, no. 1 (2000).

Mukherjee, Bharati. *Jasmine*. New York: Grove, 1989.

Murray, John Courtney. *We Hold These Truths: Catholic Reflections on the American Proposition*. New York: Sheed and Ward, 1960.

Narasimhan, C. V. *The United Nations at Fifty: Recollections*. Delhi: Konark, 1996.

Newman, Richard. *Freedom's Prophet: Bishop Richard Allen, the AME Church, and the Black Founding Fathers*. New York: New York University Press, 2009.

Niebuhr, Gustav. *Beyond Tolerance: Searching for Interfaith Understanding in America*. New York: Viking, 2008.

Niebuhr, H. Richard. *The Kingdom of God in America*. Middletown, Conn.: Wesleyan, 1988.

Novak, Michael. *The Rise of the Unmeltable Ethnics: The New Political Force of the Seventies*. New York: Macmillan, 1971.

Numrich, Paul D. *The Faith Next Door: American Christians and Their New Religious Neighbors*. New York: Oxford University Press, 2009.

Nussbaum, Martha C., et al. *For Love of Country: Debating the Limits of Patriotism*. Boston: Beacon, 1996.

Ogden, Schubert M. *Is There Only One True Religion or Are There Many?* Dallas, Tex.: SMU Press, 1992.

Orsi, Robert A. *Between Heaven and Earth: The Religious Worlds People Make and the Scholars Who Study Them*. Princeton, N.J.: Princeton University Press, 2005.

———, ed. *Gods of the City: Religion and the American Urban Landscape*. Bloomington: Indiana University Press, 1999.

———. *The Madonna of 115th Street: Faith and Community in Italian Harlem, 1880–1950*. New Haven, Conn.: Yale University Press, 1985.

Oxtoby, Willard G., ed. *Religious Diversity: Essays by Wilfred Cantwell Smith*. New York: HarperCollins, 1976.

Pai, Young, Delores Pemberton, and John Worley. *Findings on Korean American Early Adolescents and Adolescents*. Kansas City, Mo.: University of Missouri Press, 1987.

Panikkar, Raimundo. *The Intrareligious Dialogue*. New York: Paulist Press, 1978.

Patel, Eboo. *Sacred Ground: Pluralism, Prejudice, and the Promise of America*. Boston: Beacon, 2012.

Perkins, John M., and Jo Kadlecek. *Resurrecting Hope: Powerful Stories of How God Is Moving to Reach Our Cities*. Ventura, Calif.: Regal, 1995.

Pestana, Carla Gardina. *Liberty of Conscience and the Growth of Religious Diversity in Early America, 1636–1786*. Foreword by Martin E. Marty. Providence: John Carter Brown Library, 1986.

Peterson, Jon A., and Vincent F. Seyfried. "A Research Guide to the History of the Borough of Queens: Bibliography, Chronology, and Other Aids." Department of History, Queens College. Flushing, N.Y., 1987.

Pierce, Elinor, and Rachel Antell, dirs. *Fremont, U.S.A.* The Pluralism Project at Harvard University. Cambridge, Mass., 2008.

Pipher, Mary. *The Middle of Everywhere: The World's Refugees Come to Our Town.* New York: Houghton Mifflin Harcourt, 2002.

Prothero, Stephen. *A Nation of Religions: The Politics of Pluralism in Multireligious America.* Chapel Hill: University of North Carolina Press, 2006.

———. *Religious Literacy: What Every American Needs To Know—and Doesn't.* New York: HarperOne, 2008.

———. *The White Buddhist: The Asian Odyssey of Henry Steel Olcott.* Bloomington: Indiana University Press, 1996.

Putnam, Robert D. "*E Pluribus Unum*: Diversity and Community in the Twenty-First Century." *Scandinavian Political Studies* 30, no. 2 (2007).

Putnam, Robert D., and David E. Campbell. *American Grace: How Religion Unites and Divides Us.* New York: Simon & Schuster, 2010.

Queens Council on the Arts. *The International Express: A Guide to Communities Along the 7 Train.* Woodhaven, N.Y., 2000.

Queens Historical Society. *Angels of Deliverance: The Underground Railroad in Queens, Long Island, and Beyond.* Flushing, N.Y., 1999.

Queens Museum. *Remembering the Future: The New York World's Fair from 1939 to 1964.* New York, 1989.

Quintana, S. M. "A Model of Ethnic Perspective-Taking Ability Applied to Mexican-American Children." *Journal of Intercultural Relations* 18, no. 4 (1994).

Raju, Sharat, and Valarie Kaur, dirs. *Divided We Fall: Americans in the Aftermath.* New Moon Productions, 2008.

Rathbone, Susan W. "Social and Political Changes in Queens Chinese Immigrant Women From 1946 to 1989." Paper presented at the Fourth International Interdisciplinary Congress on Women, June 3–7, 1990.

Rahner, Karl. "Essays." *Theological Investigations* nos. 5, 12 (1966), no. 6 (1969), no. 14 (1976).

Richardson, Darby. "Illustrated Flushing and Vicinity." *Businessmen's Association of Flushing* (1917).

Reimers, David M. *Unwelcome Strangers: American Identity and the Turn Against Immigration.* New York: New York University Press, 1998.

Roozen, David A., William McInney, and Jackson W. Carroll, *Varieties of Religious Presence.* New York: Pilgrim Press, 1988.

Russo, David J. *Keepers of Our Past: Local Historical Writing in the United States, 1820s–1930s.* Westport, Conn.: Greenwood, 1988.

Rydell, Robert W. *All the World's a Fair: Visions of Empire at American International Expositions, 1876–1916.* Chicago: University of Chicago Press, 1984.

———. *World of Fairs: The Century-of-Progress Expositions.* Chicago: University of Chicago Press, 1993.

Sampson, Robert J. *Great American City: Chicago and the Enduring Neighborhood Effect.* Chicago: University of Chicago Press, 2014.

Sandercock, Leonie. *Cosmopolis II: Mongrel Cities of the Twenty-First Century.* London: Continuum, 2003.

————. *Towards Cosmopolis: Planning for Multicultural Cities.* Chichester: Academy Press, 1998.

Sanford, Charles B. *The Religious Life of Thomas Jefferson.* Charlottesville: University of Virginia Press, 1984.

Sanjek, Roger. *The Future of Us All: Race and Neighborhood Politics in New York City.* Ithaca, N.Y.: Cornell University Press, 1998.

Saveth, Edward N. *American Historians and European Immigrants, 1875–1925.* New York: Russell & Russell, 1948.

Schleiermacher, Friedrich. *On Religion: Speeches to Its Cultured Despisers.* [1799]. Cambridge: Cambridge University Press, 1996.

Schlereth, Thomas J. *The Cosmopolitan Ideal in Enlightenment Thought: Its Form and Function in the Ideas of Franklin, Hume, and Voltaire, 1694–1790.* Notre Dame, Ind.: University of Notre Dame Press, 1977.

Schlesinger, Arthur M. "The City in American History." *Mississippi Valley Historical Review* 27 (June 1940).

Schlesinger Jr., Arthur M. *The Disuniting of America: Reflections on a Multicultural Society.* New York: Norton, 1992.

Seyfried, Vincent F. *The Civil War Era in Flushing.* Garden City, N.Y.: Queens Community Series, 2002.

Seymann, Jerrold. *Colonial Charters, Patents, and Grants to the Communities Comprising the City of New York.* New York: New York City Board of Statutory Consolidation, 1939.

Shin, Eui Hang, and Hyung Park. "An Analysis of Causes and Schisms in Ethnic Churches: The Case of Korean–American Churches." *Sociological Analysis* 49 (Fall 1988).

Shorto, Russell. *The Island at the Center of the World: The Epic Story of Dutch Manhattan and the Forgotten Colony That Shaped America.* New York: Vintage, 2004.

Smelser, Neil J., and Jeffrey C. Alexander. eds. *Diversity and Its Discontents: Cultural Conflict and Common Ground in Contemporary American Society.* Princeton, N.J.: Princeton University Press, 1999.

Smith, Christopher J. "Asian New York: The Geography and Politics of Diversity." *International Migration Review* 29, no. 1 (Spring 1995).

Smith, Christopher J., and John R. Logan. "Flushing 2000." In *From Urban Enclave to Ethnic Suburb: New Asian Communities in Pacific Rim Countries,* ed. Wei Li. Honolulu: University of Hawai'i Press, 2006.

Smith, George L. *Religion and Trade in New Netherland: Dutch Origins and American Development.* Ithaca, N.Y.: Cornell University Press, 1973.

Smith, J. Carpenter. *History of Saint George's Parish, Flushing Long Island.* Flushing, N.Y., 1897.

Smith, M. G. "Ethnicity and Ethnic Groups in America: The View from Harvard." *Ethnic and Racial Studies* 5 (1982).

Smith, Timothy L. "Religion and Ethnicity in America." *American Historical Review* (December 1978).

Smith, Wilfred Cantwell. *The Faith of Other Men.* New York: Nabu, 1965.

Stanley, Edmund A. *Of Men and Dreams: The Story of the People of Bowne & Co. and the Fulfillment of Their Dreams in the Company's Two Hundred Years from 1775 to 1975.* New York: Bowne & Co., 1975.

Stephenson, George M. *The Religious Aspects of Swedish Immigration.* Minneapolis, Minn.: University of Minnesota Press, 1932.

Sternsher, Bernard. *Consensus, Conflict, and American Historians.* Bloomington: Indiana University Press, 1975.

Stocking, George W. *Race, Culture, and Evolution.* Chicago: University of Chicago Press, 1968.

Stout, Harry S. "Ethnicity: The Vital Center of Religion in America." *Ethnicity* 2, no. 2 (June 1975).

Suárez-Orozco, C. *Children of Immigration.* Cambridge, Mass.: Harvard University Press, 2001.

Suárez-Orozco, C., and M. M. Suárez-Orozco. *Transformations: Migration, Family Life, and Achievement Motivation Among Latino Adolescents.* Stanford, Calif.: Stanford University Press, 1995.

Sugrue, Thomas J. *The Origins of the Urban Crisis: Race and Inequality in Postwar Detroit.* Princeton, N.J., 1996.

Susman, Warren I., ed. *Culture and Commitment, 1929–1945.* New York: George Braziller, 1973.

———. "The People's Fair: Cultural Contradictions of a Consumer Society." In *Dawn of a New Day: The New York World's Fair, 1939/40,* ed. Helen A. Harrison. New York: New York University Press, 1980.

Sweet, William Warren. *The Story of Religions in America.* New York: Harper & Bros., 1930.

Takaki, Ronald. *A Different Mirror: A History of Multicultural America.* Boston: Back Bay, 1993.

———. *Strangers from a Different Shore: A History of Asian Americans.* New York: Little, Brown & Co., 1989.

Tchen, John Kuo Wei. *New York Before Chinatown: Orientalism and the Shaping of American Culture, 1776–1882.* Baltimore, Md.: Johns Hopkins University Press, 1999.

Thomas, William I., and Florian Znaniecki. *The Polish Peasant in Europe and America.* Urbana: University of Illinois Press, 1918–1920.

Thompson, Benjamin F. *History of Long Island from Its Discovery and Settlement to the Present Time* [1839]. New York: Gould, Banks & Co., 1918.

Thompson, Paul. *The Voice of the Past: Oral History* [1978]. New York: Oxford University Press, 1988.

Tillich, Paul. *Christianity and the Encounter of the World Religions.* New York: Fortress, 1963.

Todd, Jesse T. "Imagining the Future of American Religion at the New York World's Fair, 1939–40." Ph.D. diss., Department of Religion, Columbia University, 1996.

Toulmin, Stephen. *Cosmopolis: The Hidden Agenda of Modernity.* Chicago: University of Chicago Press, 1990.

Tracy, David. *Blessed Rage for Order: The New Pluralism in Theology.* Chicago: University of Chicago Press, 1975.

Trebor, Haynes. *The Flushing Remonstrance (The Origin of Religious Freedom in America).* Flushing, N.Y.: Bowne House Historical Society, 1957.

Trouillot, Michel-Rolph. *Silencing the Past: Power and the Production of History.* Boston: Beacon, 1995.

Tuan, Yi-Fu. *Place and Space: The Perspective of Experience.* Minneapolis: University of Minnesota Press, 1977.

Tweed, Thomas A. *The American Encounter with Buddhism, 1844–1912: Victorian Culture and the Limits of Dissent* [1992]. Chapel Hill, N.C.: University of North Carolina Press, 2000.

———. "Asian Religions in the United States: Reflections on an Emerging Sub-Field." In *Religious Diversity and American Religious History: Studies in Traditions and Cultures,* ed. Walter Conser and Sumner Twiss. Athens, Ga.: University of Georgia Press, 1997.

———, ed. *Retelling U.S. Religious History.* Berkeley, Calif.: University of California Press, 1997.

Tweed, Thomas A., and Stephen Prothero, eds. *Asian Religions in America: A Documentary History.* New York: Oxford University Press, 1999.

Valles, Madeline B. "A History of Flushing." MA thesis, Political Science, Columbia University, 1938.

Van Wyck, Frederick. *Select Patents of New York Towns.* Boston: A. A. Beauchamp, 1938.

Varzally, Allison J. *Making a Non-White America: Californians Coloring Outside Ethnic Lines, 1925–1955.* Berkeley: University of California Press, 2008.

Vaughan, Leslie J. *Randolph Bourne and the Politics of Cultural Radicalism.* Lawrence: University of Kansas Press, 1997.

Vecoli, Rudolph J. "*Contadini* in Chicago: A Critique of *The Uprooted.*" *Journal of American History* 51, no. 3 (December 1964).

———. "Ethnicity: A Neglected Dimension of American History." In *The State of American History,* ed. Herbert J. Bass. Chicago, 1970.

———. "From Pennsylvania Dutch to California Ethnic: The Odyssey of David Hollinger." *Reviews in American History* 24 (1996).

———. "The Resurgence of American Immigration History." *American Studies International* 17, no. 2 (Winter 1979).

———. *A Selected Bibliography on American Immigration and Ethnicity (Revised).* St. Paul, Minn., 1998.

Verba, Sidney, Kay Lehman Schlozman, and Henry E. Brady. *Voice and Equality: Civic Voluntarism in American Politics* (Cambridge, Mass.: Harvard University Press, 1995.

W. W. Munsell & Co. *History of Queens County, New York with Illustrations, Portraits, & Sketches of Prominent Families and Individuals.* New York: W. W. Munsell & Co., 1882.

Waldron, Jeremy. "Minority Cultures and the Cosmopolitan Alternative." *Michigan Journal of Law Reform* 25, nos. 3/4 (Spring/Summer 1992).

Waller, Henry D. *History of the Town of Flushing, Long Island, New York.* Flushing, N.Y.: J. H. Ridenour, 1899.

Walzer, Michael. *On Toleration.* New Haven, Conn.: Yale University Press, 1997.

———. "Pluralism: A Political Perspective." In *Harvard Encyclopedia of American Ethnic Groups,* ed. Stephan Thernstrom, Ann Orlov, and Oscar Handlin. Cambridge, Mass.: Harvard University Press, 1980.

———. *Spheres of Justice: A Defense of Pluralism and Equality.* New York: Basic Books, 1983.

Warner, R. Stephen. "Work in Progress Toward a New Paradigm for the Sociological Study of Religion in the United States." *American Journal of Sociology* 98, no. 5 (March 1993).

Warner, R. Stephen, and Judith G. Wittner, eds. *Gatherings in Diaspora: Religious Communities and the New Immigration.* Philadelphia: Temple University Press, 1998.

Waters, Ronald G. "Signs of the Times: Clifford Geertz and Historians." *Social Research* 47 (1980).

Weddle, Meredith Baldwin. *Walking in the Way of Peace: Quaker Pacifism in the Seventeenth Century.* New York: Oxford University Press, 2001.

Weintraub, Jeff, and Krishan Kumar, eds. *Public and Private in Thought and Practice: Perspectives on a Grand Dichotomy.* Chicago: University of Chicago Press, 1997.

White, Richard. *The Middle Ground: Indians, Empires, and Republics in the Great Lakes Region, 1650–1815.* Cambridge: Cambridge University Press, 1991.

Williams, Raymond Brady. *Christian Pluralism in the United States: The Indian Immigrant Experience.* Cambridge: Cambridge University Press, 1996.

———. *A New Face of Hinduism: The Swaminarayan Religion.* Cambridge: Cambridge University Press, 1984.

———. *Religions of Immigrants from India and Pakistan: New Threads in the American Tapestry.* Cambridge: Cambridge University Press, 1988.

———. "Training Religious Specialists for a Transnational Hinduism." *Journal of the American Academy of Religion* 66, no. 4 (Winter 1998).

Wilson, Edith King. *Bowne Family of Flushing, Long Island.* New York: Bowne & Co., 1987.

Winthrop, John. "A Model of Christian Charity." From the Old South Leaflets, Old South Association, Old South Meetinghouse, Boston, Massachusetts, no.

207, edited by Samuel Eliot Morison and published by the Massachusetts Historical Society in 1838.

Wirth, Louis. "Urbanism as a Way of Life." *American Journal of Sociology* 44, no. 1 (July 1938).

Works Progress Administration (WPA) Federal Writer's Project. Historic Records Survey, Church Records Series, 1936–1942. Published as *Inventory of Church Archives* and *Guide to Vital Statistics in the City of New York Churches.* New York, 1942.

Wuthnow, Robert. *America and the Challenges of Religious Diversity*. Princeton, N.J.: Princeton University Press, 2005.

———. "The Culture of Discontent: Democratic Liberalism and the Challenge of Diversity in Late-Twentieth-Century America." In *Diversity and Its Discontents: Cultural Conflict and Common Ground in Contemporary American Society, ed.* Neil J. Smelser and Jeffrey C. Alexander. Princeton, N.J.: Princeton University Press, 1999.

———. "Mobilizing Civic Engagement: The Changing Impact of Religious Involvement." In *Civic Engagement in American Democracy,* ed. Theda Skocpol and Morris P. Fiorina. Washington, D.C.: Brookings Institution Press, 1999.

———. *The Restructuring of American Religion*. Princeton, N.J.: Princeton University Press, 1988.

Yang, Fenggang. *Chinese Christians in America: Conversion, Assimilation, and Adhesive Identities.* University Park: Pennsylvania State University Press, 1999.

Yee, Shirley J. *An Immigrant Neighborhood: Interethnic and Interracial Encounters in New York Before 1930*. Philadelphia: Temple University Press, 2012.

Yoo, David K. ed., *New Spiritual Homes: Religion and Asian Americans.* Honolulu: University of Hawai'i Press, 1999.

Zunz, Olivier. "American History and the Changing Meaning of Assimilation." *Journal of American Ethnic History* 4 (1985).

Zwierlein, Frederick J. *Religion in New Netherland: A History of the Development of the Religious Conditions in the Province of New Netherland, 1623–1664.* Rochester, N.Y.: J. P. Smith, 1910.

Index

abolition, 56–57, 60–61

Ackerman, Gary, 129, 208

"Act Concerning Religion, An" (Maryland), 48

active intolerance, 202

active tolerance, 202

Act of Toleration (Maryland), 48

Adams, John, 55

Afghan Community in America, 123

Afghani, Al-Sayyid Mohammad Jamal al-Din, 258n74

Afghani Americans/immigrants: Hindu, 107–108, 126; Muslim, 122–124; response to September 11 terrorist attacks, 205, 206–207

Afghan Immigrants Center, 123

African Americans: early population and churches in Flushing, 55–56; housing problems and the civil rights movement in the 1960s, 92–93; Howard Beach incident of 1986, 188; jazz musicians, 84; population growth in the nineteenth century, 62; racial limits of religious pluralism in Flushing and, 166–169; relations with Korean immigrants, 190; Underground Railroad, 56, 57; world's fairs and, 84. *See also* black churches; Mace-

donia African Methodist Episcopal Church

African Methodist Episcopal Church, 55–56

African Methodist Society, 55–56

Afzali, Ahmad Wais, 123–124, 125–126, 205

Agama Sastras, 100

Ahlstrom, Sydney, 237n40, 246n54, 247n66, 248n85

Alagappan, Alagappa, 100, 101–104, 111, 112, 113

Aldegundé, José R., 147–149

Alexander, Jeffrey C., 239n47

Algonquin Indians, 35, *36*

Alien and Sedition Acts, 19

Allen, Richard, 55

Alley Pond park, 71

All in the Family (television show), 17

Al Qaeda, 124

American Boy Scouts, 132

American Party, 60

"American Religious History Canon, The" (Marty), 18–19

Ammerman, Nancy T., 266n44, 269n108, 270n124

Anand, Inderjit Singh, 119

Anbinder, Tyler, 248n84, 259n90

Anderson, Elijah, 25, 266n56, 273n27

Andhra Pradesh (India), 102

See www.empirestateeditions.com for a complete list.